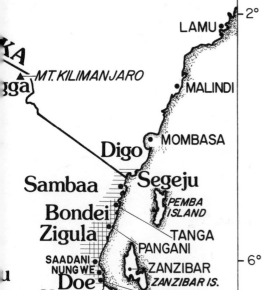

EQUATOR 0°

40°

2°

LAMU

MT. KILIMANJARO

MALINDI

6°

10°S

Digo

MOMBASA

Sambaa

Segeju

PEMBA ISLAND

Bondei

TANGA

Zigula

PANGANI

SAADANI
NUNGWE

ZANZIBAR
ZANZIBAR IS.

Doe

BAGAMOYO

Kwere

DAR ES

guru

Zaramo

SALAAM

R. RUVU

MAFIA ISLAND

R. RUFIJI

UTETE
MOHORO

KILWA
KIVINJE

LINDI

MASASI

Makua

Yao

NEWALA

MOZAMBIQUE

OLD BAGAMOYO
& HER
IMMEDIATE
WORLD

HERMENEUTICS
Studies in the History of Religions

GENERAL EDITOR
Kees W. Bolle
UCLA

Stephan Beyer, CULT OF TARA
Edward A. Armstrong, SAINT FRANCIS: NATURE MYSTIC
David R. Kinsley, THE SWORD AND THE FLUTE
Marija Gimbutas, THE GODS AND GODDESSES OF OLD EUROPE, 7000–3500 B.C.
Henry Duméry, PHENOMENOLOGY AND RELIGION
Wendy Doniger O'Flaherty, THE ORIGINS OF EVIL IN HINDU MYTHOLOGY
Åke Hultkrantz, THE RELIGIONS OF THE AMERICAN INDIANS
Kees W. Bolle, THE BHAGAVADGITA: A NEW TRANSLATION
Robert D. Pelton, THE TRICKSTER IN WEST AFRICA
Bruce Lincoln, PRIESTS, WARRIORS, AND CATTLE
Willard Johnson, POETRY AND SPECULATION OF THE ṚG VEDA
Mtoro bin Mwinyi Bakari, THE CUSTOMS OF THE SWAHILI PEOPLE

The Customs of the Swahili People

The interior of an eighteenth- or nineteenth-century mosque at Wassin
Island just north of the Kenya-Tanzania border.
[Photo by courtesy of J. de V. Allen]

The Customs of the Swahili People

The *Desturi za Waswahili* of Mtoro bin Mwinyi
Bakari
and Other Swahili Persons

Edited and Translated into English by J. W. T. Allen

Compiled in Memoriam with Notes and Studies by
Various Makerere Colleagues,
African, American, Asian, British, and European

University of California Press

Berkeley   Los Angeles   London

University of California Press
Berkeley and Los Angeles, California

University of California Press, Ltd.
London, England

Library of Congress Cataloging in Publication Data

Mtoro bin Mwinyi Bakari.
  The customs of the Swahili people.

  Bibliography: p. 313
  Includes index.
  1. Swahili-speaking peoples—Social life and
customs. I. Allen, J.W. T. II. Title.
DT433.542.M7813   305.8'963   81-3387
ISBN 0-520-04122-4   AACR2

Printed in the United States of America

1 2 3 4 5 6 7 8 9

Contents

Preface

The *Desturi za Waswahili* ("Customs of the Swahili People") ranks among the world's great but little-known literary achievements. It records something of the life and traditions of a numerically small people, of a culture that has grown up over centuries to give birth to its own literature, philosophy of life, and values. Too many such civilizations—each a unique and irreplaceable gem of human achievement—have disappeared without a trace. Some have left a few place names, a few genes and games, a fell disease or two, while others are brought to mind only by the descriptions of outsiders. Some have managed to survive to the present, be it by sheer refusal to die, by military prowess or nonviolent forms of resistance, or by the protection of the unhospitality of a xenophobic terrain. In the case of the Swahili we have a people few in number, inhabiting an open land that has no natural borders or defenses, who have gone serenely and happily on, while their invaders—various waves of outsider Africans, Arabs, Iranians, Portuguese, Germans, and British have disappeared, leaving behind their traces in ruins littering the countryside and in vestiges embedded in the Swahili language and culture.

The *Desturi* is an account of this Swahili civilization made when it was already centuries old and had achieved so much, at the very moment when it received the full impact of Western intrusion at its most ruthless and vigorous—the imposition of late-nineteenth-century German imperialism. That older Swahili civilization has left us in the late twentieth century much to excite our awe and wonderment: in the last few years we have come to know that over 180 sites of settlements dating from the ninth to the nineteenth centuries of the

Common Era exist on the east coast of Africa in an area stretching
from the mouth of the Zambesi northward for a thousand miles and
across to the Comoros and Zanzibar. Only two, Kilwa and Gedi, have
as yet been adequately described in print by archaeologists. Swahili
inland settlements of the earlier part of the nineteenth century spread
into the interior as far as Kisangani in eastern Zaïre, surviving more or
less intact. Premodern poetry equal in interest and volume to medieval French is becoming known to us. Of the *tenzi* or *tendi* (a kind of
short epic poem) alone, over seventy major pieces are now in print,
and more undoubtedly await discovery. The oldest we know at
present dates from the late seventeenth or early eighteenth century,
and we may reasonably suspect that other pieces were composed
earlier than the dates attached to them. There are also some material
relics, such as the great ivory *siwa* horn of Pate and the bronze horn of
Lamu, which go back three centuries, if not more, and bear silent
witness to a high level of cultural achievement. As we study the
history of the Indian Ocean, its trade networks and thalassocracies,
we detect vestiges of this civilization in the Arabic, Chinese, Portuguese, Dutch, French, American, German, and British sources of a
thousand-year period.

The European soldiers and administrators broke in, hardly able to
understand what they were taking over and what they were trying to
replace. Some Swahili rose in armed opposition, others tried to
interpret—"to give a hermeneutics"—of their civilization to the newcomers and thence to the world. The *Desturi* is the outstanding
example of this attempt at interpretation. Its prose, though from a
time when Swahili literature existed mainly as poetry, is of classic
beauty. (We may compare some of the finest Tudor prose, rare and
buried in various Bible translations, liturgies, and books of homilies
and obscured by the fame of Shakespeare's plays, which are, of
course, mainly verse.)

The Africans who wrote the *Desturi* were "pure Swahili persons"
around the town of Bagamoyo in Tanzania (directly opposite Zanzibar island). They were asked in the 1890s by Dr. Carl Velten, a
German linguist, to write down the traditions and customs of their
people.[1] This they did in Swahili, using the Arabic script. It is clear
from his introduction to the volumes he published in 1903 that Dr.
Velten was the compiler rather than the author. The internal evidence as well shows that a good part of the material was written by a
master of Swahili prose, who also worked over the whole and gave to
it homogeneity and distinction of style. This master was Bwana

Mtoro bin Mwinyi Bakari of Bagamoyo, who is recorded by Dr. Velten as being Lektor at the oriental seminar at Berlin and a collaborator. He appears in the body of the work in a number of autobiographical passages, without any sense of intrusion or self-consciousness.

In Bagamoyo he is still remembered. Bwana Idi Marijani of that town writes of him:[2]

Mtoro bin Mwinyi Bakari was a Zaramo. He attended the Qur'an school in Bagamoyo and then read *Ilimu* under Sheikh Abubakar bin Taha 'l Barawy. He became Sheikh Abu Bakar's senior pupil and was regularly sent by his Sheikh to preach the Friday sermon.

When the Germans introduced house tax he was made clerk in charge of its collection. As this was before the opening of European type schools in Bagamoyo, he used Arabic script.

Later on he was asked to go to Berlin and he agreed. There he taught Arabic and learnt German under Professor Dr. Velten. At the end of his tour of service, when he told his friends and pupils that he was about to return to Africa, some of them asked him why he was going. Would it not be better to remain and to open his own school, from which he might profit greatly? He agreed and left the service.

He married a wife in Germany; but all the same the Government required him to return to duty and he came out with his wife to the Secretariat in Dar-es-Salaam. The Germans were embarrassed by an African having a European wife and in those days they held the power. They complained bitterly to the Government than an African should not come out with a European wife. It would be better for his wife to return to Europe, leaving Mtoro here. He could visit her when he went on leave.

Mwalimu Mtoro refused. He said that she was his lawful wife and that he would not live apart from her, so he was told that he could not remain and must return to Europe. He consented and eventually he died in Europe.

Let us pause to consider briefly something of Bwana Mtoro's genius and achievement as he worked with his European colleague and his African collaborators. Mtoro did not give in to bitterness or hatred. He was one of those fascinating men who live in two worlds and work to interpret one to another. His writing shows him to be a person loyal to the past, one who has the poise and confidence to accept the verdicts of historical events and to retain faith in his people and their future. (While engaged in the very modern task of collecting government-imposed taxes for the improvement of education and roads, his life is saved—by his slave.) Every great writer has an ax to grind. He does not want to prove Swahili civilization is Arab, as some tried when the prestige of Arabness was high on the coast, nor that it is "purely" African, as some have tried in these days of authenticity. Like many people of the middle way, of the twilight/dawn, he knows where he stands and indicates it by what he says and even more by what he avoids. Mtoro is also a humane person, and his love for his people quickly becomes obvious. One sees his affection for the songs of children, women, and slaves at a time when some Victorian writers would have thought them too trivial to preserve. (He may have been influenced by the idea that prose is at bottom a form of storytelling.) He has a wonderful eye for detail and an insatiable curiosity to know such things as the calls of different birds and the properties of roots. He has a Rabelaisian sense of laughter and the ridiculous, and one suspects that the proverb he quotes as an illustration of the consequences of a too high ambition—that he who envies an elephant's dung will split his anus—may have been his own invention. Compare his "cure" for the young man who fears his penis is not long enough.

This love for his people and his deep nostalgia for the past cause him to depict the Swahili "warts and all." He is not ashamed to speak of what he sees as their deterioration. Out of respect for developing nations, one might be tempted to excise such passages, but this would be to underestimate Mtoro's own manliness and to belie his robust faith in the fundamental soundness of the Swahili. His deeply African understanding of the rhythm of human life, based in the kindly environment of the small town surrounded by fields and wilderness, river and sea, is coupled with a serenely Islamic knowledge that everything is for the best, in and through the will of God.[3]

Dr. Velten, the person who called together and suggested the task to Bwana Mtoro and his Swahili collaborators, was also a remarkable individual. Born in Germany in 1862, he was a careful scholar, highly qualified in Western learning and deeply respectful of and sympathetic to African civilization. He contributed greatly to putting "Africanistics" on the same level of academic respectability as "the classics" (that is, Greek and Latin) or Indology. He was, and has remained, loved and respected in Africa, though in recent years the not unjustifiable suspicion has arisen that he may have been the right-hand marker of rank upon rank of Western scholars who have published under their own names what was effectively the work of Swahili intellectuals. He arranged for the material to be put into Roman script, using the rules of orthography favored by the German authorities—the present orthography was standardized in 1925. After he edited and translated the work into German, it was published in two volumes at

Göttingen in 1903. (More detail of this is given below.) Dr. Velten states in his preface that his object in publishing his Swahili edition is to enrich Swahili literature and to provide pleasant and instructive reading for candidates for the overseas service, which will also help them to understand and treat properly the people they will seek to administer. Leaving aside the topsy-turviness of the colonial situation in which Dr. Velten wrote (wherein one finds the robber breaking in, taking over, and then claiming to have come to establish the rule of law), we can safely say that Dr. Velten succeeded well beyond his stated aims. Far more than being a mere listing and description of the customs and picturesque gyrations of a far-off people, the outcome of his and his collaborators' efforts is a piece of writing couched in Swahili of such excellence that it has become a model for the best in Swahili prose. It is a work that conveys an all-pervading sense of a truly human philosophy of life, a work with a universal message of its own.

The *Desturi* seems to have something to say about many of life's events—a well-brought-up girl "going off the rails," a quarrel between father and son, the death of a beloved one. As our lives become less human, this work serves to remind us of the spiritual achievement of the preindustrial, pretechnological way of life we have lost. It remains for the moment one of the few accounts of an African Traditional Religion and culture and its intertwining with an incoming world religion written by a person who is both an African and a Muslim.

The *Desturi*, being one of the earliest African works to become widely accessible in a European language, had a considerable influence in Africa, the Western world, and European empires in Asia and the Pacific.[4] Its profound respect for a civilization that the Europeans had overrun helped them get a glimmering of the fact that there were viable ways of life other than their own. Through it, the discerning undoubtedly realized that there were features in which the other culture excelled. The high achievements of Arab, Persian, and Indian civilization gained European admiration; the *Desturi* was one of the lone voices to tell them that African and other civilizations that did not depend on great buildings, artifacts, and writings had to be taken into account if historians were to capture something of the greatness and tragedy of the human race. In a way it did for the academic world what Africa through Picasso and others did for the world of art or what jazz did for the world of music.

The present work was begun by J. W. T. Allen as a new edition of

the Swahili text, using a modern orthography and developments of
Swahili philology since Velten's day.[5] He then made a translation
into English directly from his Swahili text and prepared some linguistic notes. The work that follows is a complete and unabridged translation except for the omission of a few chapters that constitute a
somewhat pedestrian summary of the law of Islam on certain matters.[6] (These have been dealt with more expertly and originally, in
both English and Swahili, in books readily accessible to specialists
and those interested in legal affairs.) Notes and other material, the
latter included mainly for the purpose of bringing out the intricate
interweaving of the African Traditional Religion and culture with
Islam, both components of Swahili civilization, were prepared by
Noel Q. King. To these he added much material, requested from
others or written by himself, meant to aid the general reader in
making use of what was originally a tome for specialists. He also read
the translation against the original Swahili to ensure consistency of
translation of technical words and reedited the whole compilation.
This edition and translation both remains a technical tool for African-
ists and Islamists and seeks to interpret and present an African classic
and to make it the heritage of readers from all over the world who
employ English as a means of communication.

It remains to thank the many persons who have helped with the
compilation of this edition, a project that has stretched now over a
ten-year period. In chronological order, these include Winifred Allen, Evelyn King, Clare and Alan Claydon, and an anonymous
scholar whose helpful critique we received through the Institute of
Swahili Studies at the University of Dar-es-Salaam (referred to in the
text as *Anon. DSM*). For the basic notes on the medical material we
thank Dr. Henry Foy, a distinguished malaria-research scholar who
has spent many years in East Africa. Dr. Thomas Hedley White
extensively revised and expanded these notes. Dr. Ernst Dammann
has throughout given encouragement. Before he died, J. W. T. Allen
asked that his thanks be extended to Vandenhöck and Ruprecht of
Göttingen for permission to make use of the two volumes published
by them in 1903, edited by Dr. Carl Velten, entitled *Desturi za
Wasuaheli* and *Sitten und Gebräuche der Suaheli*, giving a text and a
German translation, respectively. Our debt to Dr. Velten has been
great, but we have based our work on the original Swahili of Bwana
Mtoro and his colleagues so far as J. W. T. Allen could establish it
through his knowledge of Swahili use and custom and in consultation
with "native experts." The fruits of this labor were gathered by him in

an edition in Swahili with linguistic notes. This has been accepted by an East African publisher and awaits printing. Since it may be delayed, and for international reference, we give the page references to Dr. Velten's great edition in the margin of our translation and refer to it in the notes with a V. We also thank Dr. Freeman-Greenville for his advice, Sheikh Hamisi Kitumboy of Bagamoyo for checking out many details for us at Bagamoyo, and Sheikh Ahmed Sheikh Nabhany of Mombasa for supplying a most helpful series of remarks in Swahili on the Swahili text as well as the poem that concludes Appendix IV, "In Memoriam."

A draft was initially edited by Laurie Richardson King and typed by Susan Beach, Virginia Moore, Peggy Merrell, and Sheri Quistini. This was gone over by Kees Bolle, who has also been helpful in a large number of ways. He generously accepted the book for his Hermeneutics Series. Many suggestions for revisions came from Dr. James Brain of the State University of New York at New Paltz and Dr. Edward Alpers of UCLA. During the last years, a complete revision of the notes and appendices was made, and throughout this portion of the project J. de V. Allen of Lamu was most helpful. Additions and notes by him are explicitly indicated. He also provided two appendices, one giving a historical background and the other discussing musical instruments. He wrote a part of and enriched the Bibliography as a whole. Dr. Jan Knappert of the London School of Oriental and African Studies, despite prior calls on his time, went over the whole, and very many changes and additions made by him have been incorporated. Dr. Triloki Nath Pandev of the Board of Anthropology of the University of California, Santa Cruz, went through the book and made many valuable suggestions. Throughout the project, Winifred Allen at Oxford and her son Hubert at The Hague were indefatigable in helping to search out and provide any material requested. After the death of his father, the younger Bwana Hamisi Kitumboy assisted from Dar-es-Salaam and Bagamoyo.

The medical sections were recently read over by Drs. Felicitas and Maurice King, now at Nyeri in Kenya, and by Dr. Robert Parsons of the University of California, Berkeley, and their suggestions have been incorporated. The sections concerning girls' initiation and women's life and work were both carefully gone over again by Winifred Allen and Laurie Richardson King. If we judge Mtoro by the standards of modern-day California, we can only say his writings in a number of places show a certain asymmetry in dealing with the sexes. One has to add it is unscientific to fiddle with chron(e)-ology and standards, and remember that for the sake of his wife, Mtoro sacrificed his devotion to his motherland and went into exile to her fatherland. Since there is so much new work coming out on this very subject (see the Bibliography), the women directing this work considered it best to keep the notes to a minimum and reserve the matter for separate treatment at a later time.

A selection from this edition was used as a "guinea-pig text" for various classes at UCSC, including Humanities 6, History 106B and 106C, and numerous independent studies. We owe a debt to the young American students who joined in so cheerfully and gave us much feedback. Harry Charleson generously donated many hours of proofreading. So as not to plague the general reader and the non-specialist, names of books and authorities and suggestions for reading were moved from the notes to the Bibliography. A map was prepared by Noel Q. King with the help of Stanley Stevens and Janet Pumphrey. Douglas Slocum, Joan Vera Hodgson, David Martinez, and Cliff Anderson of the McHenry Library, as well as "the Reference Desk," as they call themselves, that is, Joe Michalak, Rex Beckham, Al Eickhoff, Alan Ritch, Margaret Robinson, and Judy Steen, were tireless in seeking out bibliographical material and producing farfetched books and articles. We are also indebted to our old colleagues of Makerere days, Professors Merrick Posnansky and Ali Mazrui, the former for giving encouragement and help last year when it had been decided to abandon the project, and the latter for his constant encouragement and his benevolence.

For typing of the final draft and for never-failing patience and encouragement, we thank Virginia Moore and Sheri Ginter. For help through the University of California Press we thank Stanley Holwitz, Nettie Lipton, and others.

This edition is offered as a kind of *labor monachorum amorisque*, in memoriam, for J. W. T. Allen, Hamisi Kitumboy, Mwana Amina Abukabar Sheikh, and all the other collaborators who made it possible and died in the last years of its completion, and to the Makerere University College of Sir Bernard de Bunsen's and Yusufu Lule's days, where so many of us served and which even now is rising from the ashes. It also serves as a memorial to the Board of Religious Studies (1974–1979), the South Pacific Center, and the college system (1965–1979) at the Santa Cruz campus of the University of California.

J. W. T. Allen died two years ago after an illness, and a major rewriting and replanning has taken place since then. Because only one person has made approaches and requests to the other collaborators, they have not met as a body, and there has not been time to put the finished work in their hands; responsibility for it in its present form must fall entirely on this one person. The name that follows is appended because someone has to answer for the offenses caused and the opportunities missed.

Merrill College   NOEL Q. KING
University of California, Santa Cruz

The Swahili Introduction

1   The customs of the Swahili, or people of the coast, are virtually the same from Lamu to Mombasa and across the German boundary from Tanga harbor to the country round Lindi; but there are some slight differences in local usage, such as in marriage, burial, and the care of children.[1] There may be some slight differences in custom; but on the whole they are the same, because from Lamu to Lindi all follow the same religion, while the usages of their neighbors show some variation. Their neighbors near Tanga are the Digo and Segeju, near Pangani the Zigua and Bondei, near Sadani the Doe, near Bagamoyo the Zaramo, near Kilwa the Ngindo, and near Lindi the Yao. The customs of all these peoples are similar; but there are some slight differences. Anyone who knows the customs of the Swahili will understand these customs as well as many of the customs of the people up country.

2   One who wishes to understand the customs of the Swahili should consult an old man or an old woman, because it is they who know them and follow the old customs more than do the young people of today. Many people have abandoned the old customs and follow few of them. The young people follow any new custom that is introduced and happens to please them. In the old days they followed Arab customs and used Arabic terms. Then they met Indian customs, and some adopted those that pleased them. Recently, since the introduction of European customs, they have abandoned those of the Arabs and Indians, preferring to follow the new customs. If they observe a European custom and like it, they follow it, and even in language, they introduce European words into their speech. But these young folk adopt these customs in their youth only. When they are mature, they revert to the customs of their ancestors, as they were taught by their elders.

1

Chapter 1 Swahili Customs before the Birth of a Child

Of the Treatment of a Barren Woman

If a Swahili has no child, he looks for a doctor to treat his wife so that she may bear a child.[1] The reason why a woman is barren is that there is something in her womb that prevents conception. So the husband goes to a doctor and tells him that he wants treatment for his wife. When they have agreed, he goes to the forest and digs for medicinal roots to take to the woman. He will require a chicken and sorghum flour and gram and beans and rice. The rice is cooked with various drugs, and when the medicine is ready the man and his wife come together to take it. When they have taken it, the woman steeps the medicine in water and drinks it during the following seven days. This is done at the time of her menstruation. Seven days after she has ceased to menstruate, the man goes to the woman, and, if God will, she conceives.[2]

Of the Diagnosis of Pregnancy

If a woman's period passes with no discharge of blood, she suspects that she is pregnant, and she goes to the teacher for inspection.[3] The teacher prepares for her a bowl of saffron or the rice ink of *araaita* or *inna aateinaka*, washing the cup on which these verses have been

written and giving her the water to drink.[4] She must drink this for
seven days, and if after seven days menstruation has not started,
another draft is prepared for her. Or she goes to old women or doctors
skilled in the reduction of spirits, who tell her if her pregnancy is
imaginary.[5] She is given roots to drink and herbs for cleansing, and it
is then known whether her pregnancy is real or imaginary.[6]

Of the Pains of Labor

On the night on which a woman is taken with the pains of labor, if
she is young and it is her first child, so that she has no experience of
childbirth, she is taken to her parents' house to be with her elder
relations, her mothers and grandmothers, as well as the *kungwi* to
assist at the birth.[7] This kungwi has with her another woman, called
the receiver or recipient, to receive the child when it is born. If labor is
prolonged, someone is sent for the husband, and when he arrives he is
told: "We have called you to pour rice," that is, to pray to God for a
speedy delivery.[8] The husband is given rice and says, "As I pour this
rice, if this child is mine may my wife be relieved of all waste
products, and if it is not, she can wait until the real father comes to
pour rice." Also the husband says, "If my wife and I have had a
quarrel, let us forget it. I am pouring rice with goodwill to her so that
she may be delivered." Then if God hears his prayer, the woman is
safely and completely delivered, that is, the child is born and the
blood of the birth is discharged.

Of Prolonged Labor

If the birth is delayed, the teacher is called for the woman to be
dosed to bring on the birth. For this dose they take a white plate and
rice ink. For rice ink rice is taken and roasted until it burns. Then it is
ground, and the charred rice is sifted. It is mixed with myrrh and a
little lime. Then it is put in the sun until it sets, and then it is put in a
bottle as ink.

With this ink the teacher writes verses of the Qur'an, *Al Kursi*, and
Wa qul jaa al-haqqu wa za haqa al-batilu inna al-batilu kana za huqa.
Finally he writes, *Wala haula wala quwwata illa billahi al-aliyi
al-adhim.*[9] On the plate he writes a figure like this:

6

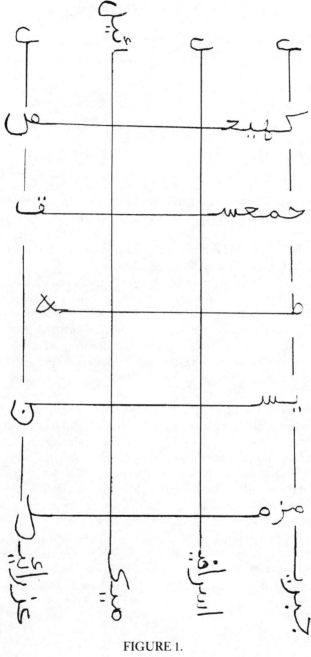

FIGURE 1.

These words are the names of prophets and of angels:

K h y ^c ṣ
Ḥ m ^c s q
Ṭaha
Yasin
Muzammil
Jibrīl
Israfīl
Mikaīl
^cIzrāīl

The first two are the covenant sworn by God; the next three are the names of prophets; and the four last are the archangels.[10] When this has been written on the cup, it is washed off with water and put in a bottle to be sent to the woman for her to drink. She drinks a little immediately when she receives it and the remainder later, whenever she is thirsty, until she is delivered.

7   If she is still not delivered, another bowl is prepared with a different verse and figure as is written in the books about childbirth such as *Majarabadi al-deribi*.[11]

Or the teacher writes for her some amulet, which is tied to her arm until she is delivered. Then it is removed, for its work is done; but if the woman likes to go on wearing it, she may do so. It does no harm, and it is for her to choose.

Or if complete delivery is delayed, that is, the discharge of the other things such as the afterbirth, she has an amulet written by the teacher with the *sura Tabaraka* from beginning to end, and this is tied to her belly.[12] If all is well and she is delivered, the amulet is removed. If she likes to continue to wear it, she may do so, but not on the belly. It will be tied in some other place of her choice.

Or if this amulet does not suffice, she is made a different one with another sura, such as *Wa al-mursalati urfan*, or the teacher writes an amulet with an *abjed* figure.[13]

Or if they have not gone to a teacher, the women call in other kungwi of great age, because the first have been defeated, to examine her and make medicine for her of wild plants. The roots are cooked with chicken and beans, and the woman in labor drinks the broth.

Chapter 2
The Birth of a Child and the Customs Following the Birth

8   Immediately after the mother is delivered, a message is sent to tell the father that his wife is delivered. He comes, and they let him in, and he asks, "Father or Mother?" meaning, "Is it a boy or a girl?" They tell him, and he says, "Let me see my child"; but the kungwi demand their fees before they give him his child. If it is a girl, he will give them two rupees and if it is a boy, four rupees, called the delivery fee. Then the husband goes to the shop and buys a bag of sorghum, a tin of sugar, and a *manni* of black pepper and ginger, if he has enough money.[1] If he has not, he will obtain credit at the shop. (Credit is a custom of ours. Even if he has cash, he will ask for credit.) When he has brought the things mentioned, the sorghum is pounded and the husked grain is cooked into strong invalid gruel with a lot of black

9   pepper and sugar every morning, and the cooked grain is made into a paste flavored with chicken or raw dried shark for seven days. The flour that makes the gruel for the child is cooked with sugar.

    To return to the old people: when the kungwi have received the child, they take from it the wrapping with which it emerged from its mother's womb. This is called the clothes or the cloth of birth. Then the cord is cut and tied with thread, which is fastened to the child's neck until the cord dries. After some seven days this piece of the cord drops off.

    When the cord drops off, a dry stalk of last year's sorghum is fetched and burned. Then it is ground, and the ash is put on the child's navel as medicine.

    The afterbirth and the bit of the cord they bury in the yard, and after seven days, when the child is shaved, its hair and nails are buried with these and on top is planted a coconut.[2] The palm is given to the child, and when he grows up he shows it to his companions, saying, "This is my navel." When they plant the coconut, they say, "As we plant this palm, may God bless our child to drink of its milk."

Of Calling the Child to Prayer

If the child is born at night, the teacher is called in the morning to call the child to prayer.[3] To do this he takes the child by the right ear and says:

> *Allahu akhbar* [four times].
> *Ashhadu an la ilaha illa 'llahu,*
> *Ashhadu anna Muhammadan rasulu 'llahi.*

10
> *Haiya al 'ssalati* [twice],
> *Haiya 'alā 'lfalahi* [twice],
> *Allahu akbaru* [twice],
> *La ilaha illa 'llahu.*

The reason for the child being called to prayer is for it to be known that this is a Muslim child and that it has adopted the usages of Islam.

Of Purifying the Mother

After forty days the teacher returns to purify the mother; that is, to cleanse her and make her clean with verses of the Qur'an and prayers.[4] The mother is shaved and puts on new clothes. The clothes that she wore at the time of birth are given to the kungwi. They do not allow the mother to walk outside the house of the birth until the forty days are complete.

Of Showing the Child Sun and Rain

On the eighth day, when they want to take the child out to show it the sun,[5] the senior kungwi says to the father, "Tomorrow have ready a cock and rice for us to cook the meal called 'Weariness.' " This is to make up for the lack of sleep suffered by the kungwi on the night of the birth. If the father has means, he slaughters a goat and rice is cooked and they eat. The parents are given their portion, and they eat by themselves.

For the sun to be shown on the eighth day, cloths are spread at the threshold, or someone takes the child on his lap and an old woman holding a pestle comes and says to the child, "God has brought you into the world; control yourself and do not covet other people's things. You have come into the world; close your ears to gossip. You have come into the world; if you are given something that is good, treasure it, but if it is bad, let it go. You have come into the world; do not be quarrelsome and irritate people, for the men of old have said:

> Speak that which is fitting,
> Swallow that which is unfitting.

You have come into the world; do not frequent the houses of other people's wives and lose your soul. God has brought you into the world; control yourself and be trustworthy. God has brought you to earth; treat others with respect, for the men of old have said:

> Civility, civility
> Is no slavery.

The reason for holding the pestle is for it to be placed over the child's chest as a symbol that its heart should be as weighty as the pestle with respect of property and the other things that we have mentioned above.

When this has been said to the child, it is taken out into the yard and tossed up seven times and told to see the sun. Then it is returned indoors.

Also, when they take the child out, one person takes it on his lap, and another puts water in a basket and sprinkles it with his hand, and they say, "Rain, rain, rain. He has seen the sun, and this is the rain."

Then the father asks permission to go, and they reply, "Take leave of your father-in-law." His father-in-law will answer, "Now I accept you as my son-in-law, and you have brought me a darling," if it is a girl. And he will tap her on the head with his knuckles as a sign of joy. If a boy has been born, he will address him as "my fellow husband," for they have the same relationship to one woman, whom they both call *bibi*.[6]

After showing the child sun and rain, the father returns home, and in the evening they bring him his wife, who was sent to her parents when her labor began.

There is another custom that should be mentioned. In some houses where a mother lives it is customary to extinguish the fire on the day that the birth is expected and to light it afresh.[7] No fire is taken out, nor is any brought in from outside, until on the eighth day the child goes out for the first time.

Of Husband and Wife after the Birth of a Child

Her mothers and her kungwi warn the mother to refuse if her husband wants to lie with her, because the child will be ill. For the child's welfare she must not know her husband for a year.[8] The reason for her being forbidden to lie with her husband is fear of harm to the child, which will take the form of rickets; it will be unable to stand up or to walk even at the age of two. It will be thin and its body mere skin and bones. And when people see it they will say that it is the fault of the parents, and everyone in the place will say that they have no self-control.

13   ## Of the Day of the Birth

If a child is born on a Friday, it is said that it has been born on a lucky day, because Friday is a sort of high day. A boy will be called *Juma* and a girl *Mwajuma* (*Mwana juma*), "Friday's child." If a child is born on a Tuesday, they say that he has been born on a bad day or a day of ill luck.[9]

Of Maulidi

After seven or fourteen days when he wants to shave the child, a man of means will shave it with a maulidi.[10] A poor man will shave it with no maulidi.

If he wants maulidi recited, he goes to the senior teacher of the place, who informs the other teachers, or the person holding the maulidi goes to tell them that he needs them. He calls his family, his friends, and his neighbors to attend the maulidi. When the teachers arrive they bring with them their pupils, their books of maulidi, and their tambourines for the accompaniment. The teachers sit in one room with the guests, the teachers on fine mats and cushions and the others on coarse mats, while the women and the child sit in another room, all silent to listen. In front of the teachers are placed trays on which are flasks of rose water and saucers of sugar, candy and granulated, and ginger and sticks of smoldering aloe and frankincense. The

14   sugar and ginger are for anyone who feels sleepy to take a little sugar and eat it with ginger.

The maulidi starts at 10 P.M. and goes on until dawn. Each teacher takes a quarter of an hour and then hands over to another. At the end of each section the pupils sing in chorus, beating the tambourines and singing, *He Allah, he Allah.*

At dawn the teachers say, "Now let us say the maulidi prayers; get ready." The child is brought in, and they prepare a bowl of sandalwood, rose water, and cloves. Then all stand, and the reception of the birth is recited:

> *Ya nabiyu salamun 'aleika,*
> *Ya rasulu salamun 'aleika*
> *Ya habibi salamun 'aleika,*
> *Salawatu 'llahi 'aleika.*[11]

All duly respond, and the child is taken in the hands of its father or of the teacher. The perfume is placed on the head and neck of the child, while the father and his family make gifts to the teacher of fifteen *pesa* to a rupee. Each takes a little of the remaining perfume and rubs it on his hands. The rose water is sprinkled for the people who are present, and the aloe is used to cleanse them.

When the ceremony is over they sit down, and the maulidi is concluded with the *fatiha.*[12] They go to the mosque for prayer while the women prepare food, rice, pilaf or with coconut. On their return from the mosque, food is put before them, they eat, and they take their leave of the holder of the maulidi with the prayer "May God bless your child and give you all prosperity." He says, "Amen," and they all go home.

15   Maulidi is recited annually from sunset on the eleventh of Rabi[c] al-awwal to dawn on the twelfth, because the Prophet Muhammad was born at dawn on Monday the twelfth; hence this practice. It is also recited on the day of the consummation of a marriage and when children come out of the circumcision camp, as a token of joy.

There are two sorts of maulidi. The Arabs favor that of Barzanji and the Swahili *Maulidi asharafi al Anami.*[13]

Of the First Haircutting

The origin of this ceremony is Arab; the Swahili used not to perform it, but now they do so. When the child is seven days old, the *akika* is performed for it. For this the teacher comes to recite the maulidi or other prayers. For a boy two goats are slaughtered. One is roasted and rice is prepared to go with it, and the other is cooked with spices and honey is brought to go with it, and people are invited to eat it. Its bones are not broken but buried in a hole dug for the purpose, for according to tradition it is written that on the Last Day the Lord God will of these bones fashion a camel for the child to ride to paradise.

For a girl, one goat is slaughtered, and a similar party is held.

16   The parents must prepare the akika for an infant; but a child of fifteen who can do so must manage it for himself.

If a child dies, the akika must be performed for him as described above, because the *khitima* is not recited for it.[14] Therefore akika is done for it.

Of Children's Food

A child is given sorghum ground into flour and placed in a jar to protect it from dust and sand. Every morning enough is taken out and cooked with sugar and given to the child. For feeding it, gruel is put into a little pot until it is cool enough, and then it is placed in a saucer. The mother takes the child on her lap. She puts some gruel in the palm of her hand and feeds it with her finger, and the child swallows it, and then she gives it water or the breast.[15] After this the child goes to sleep.

If the child will not sleep, she rocks it in a cradle or in a cloth on her back and sings it a lullaby. The mother sings:

Do not cry my dear.
Do not cry, my child,
My child, my baby,
Who eats warm pap
To take the pain from inside it.

Or she sings:

16   Oo aa, my child.
17   Be quiet, my little child,
My baby for whom I suffered
Alone with God
And the midwife.

Be quiet, my child,
Be quiet,
Oo aa, my child.

Or she sings:

The tide is rising slowly, slowly;
It reaches the rock with splashing and crashing.
How do you behave to her, my child, when you will not play with her?

Or she sings:

Do not cry, my dear, do not cry.
If you cry, you make me cry,
You remind me of my pain,
The pain of both parents.
They did well by me,
They married me to a fine man.
I went to him and I came
To prepare a little morsel.

Or she sings:

What's that, what's that across the river?
I called and he did not answer: he must give me pain.[16]

18   Or she sings:

I went for a walk
Toward Mangapwani.[17]
I met a fine sawfish
And asked, "Where are you going?"
"To take part in the mourning."
"But who is dead?"
"Hawk, our chief.
How can you chew betel nut
When the fruit is not ripe?"

Or she sings:

When you come, give my greetings, but do not say my name.
There are people at the entrance, and a sparrow cannot pass;
When you go, give him a hint to come to me in the evening.

When the child wakes up, it is washed and kohl is put on its eyes.
Muru is ground and given it to drink, and sometimes it is spread over
its whole body as medicine for worms. It is sold by Indians and
Hadhrami Arabs. And if the child is constipated, they cook it a
19   *mung'unye* gourd, the water without sugar or honey, or they put in
some coconut.[18] If it is still constipated, they lick its anus and it has a
motion. After a motion they wipe it with coconut fiber and then wash
it with water.

When it sleeps they put a knife under the head of the bed and tie
wild garlic[19] to its wrists against attack by a flying spirit, and in a
house where there is a baby a crab is hung up in the roof over the pole
between the rafters against flying spirits.[20] These spirits mean serious
illness for the child. It is a great bird that at night visits every house
where there is a baby. It spreads its wings and peers into the house,
and the baby hears the sound of the wings, even if it is asleep, and it
starts. Then in the morning it will have fever. Then a man must be
found who knows the old devil's medicine, and if he is not found, the
child will certainly die, or at the best, if it does not die, it will have a
long illness, after which it will have eyes that squint.

The man who comes with the medicine for the old devil agrees to
give the child protection, that is, to make medicine against the influence of fornicators and of the evil eye. He brings a brew of leaves,
which is put into a jar, and the child is bathed with it morning and
evening. If they do not do this and the child is picked up by a
fornicator, it will have rickets.

20   ## Of Children's Clothes

A small child wears around the loins a band of red, white, and black
beads, four fingers wide, called a *shegele*. It is joined to the *utunda*
beads and tied around the loins. When it reaches the age of two years,
they remove the shegele, and it does not wear it again. They dress it in
kanzu and *suruali* with a little cap on its head.[21] On ankles and wrists
they put little silver bangles and round the neck a string of beads.

A boy wears kanzu, suruali, and cap, but girls and boys are not
dressed the same. In a boy's ears are put rings of silver.

Children's Names

Small children have no names, only nicknames such as Mouse, Rat,
Cheeks, Cat, Twig, Ant, Sprat, Gap-tooth, Ichneumon, Rogue,
Grandfather.[22] Such names are applied to both boys and girls.

Some people give their children regular names after seven days, some after forty, and some after a year. Boys are named after their mother's family and girls after their father's. Many people make a vow
21 before conception that if a boy or a girl is born they will call it by such a name.[23] Then when a child is born, it must be called by the name vowed.

A great many children are called Runaway seven days after birth.[24] This means that the mother has had two children and they have died. Then the third is called Runaway. At its naming a string is tied from its neck to its loins. This is the sign that it is a runaway and that it must not run away as did its predecessors.

A child is called a runaway if he runs away from school, or a slave if he runs away is called a runaway too; but that does not mean that his name is Runaway.

The name given after seven or forty days or a year is retained until it goes to the circumcision camp. When it comes back from there, it is given another name, which it keeps until the end of its life. But one who is to be a chief takes the name under which its father ruled.

Some people change their own names. If a man has committed a crime at home and has moved, he takes another name; or a runaway slave who has gone to another place will change his name so that people do not recognize him. Some people change their names because they do not like the first.

Of Cutting Teeth

When a child is due to cut its teeth, they make the cutting medicine against cutting them wrong, the upper ones first. The old men and women make this medicine by digging the roots of nutgrass, and the child is made an amulet to wear on the neck until the teeth come through.
22 If the teeth are late, the child is treated by doctors, that is, medicine is prepared for it to use as lotion or ointment. *Hoza* medicine is prepared, made of wild plants, and is applied to the child.[25] After some days, the child's teeth come through.

If a child cuts its upper teeth first, in old times they did not bring it up, and even now some will not do so; but others say, "I cannot abandon my own blood; I will bring it up." And some do so; but they have no joy of the child. It is called *Kibi*, an old word for bad; but eventually it is given a name like other children. Some people fear to touch such a child for fear of death or illness.

If a child is born feet foremost, it too is called Kibi. They do not bring it up, but kill it or leave it in the mosque. People coming to the early prayers see it and know that it has been born wrong. Then somebody adopts it as his own. The reason for refusing to bring up such a child is fear of death. This custom some Swahili shared with the Zaramo.

Of Children's Illnesses and Their Treatment

If a child is ill the parents go to a teacher for examination. The teacher brings out his books and his divining board and says whether the child has been bewitched or is simply unwell. They ask the teacher what to do, and he says that they must treat it. "What is needed for the treatment?" He will answer, "Bread, coconut, a speckled fowl, seven shells, seven seeds of a single creeper, seven cubits of muslin or a length of calico." So they go to get these things.

Then they call the teacher, and he comes with his pupils, each with his copy of the Qur'an, and the teacher gives each a chapter to recite. Two people take a basket containing the things and carry it around. The shells are lit, that is, they are filled with sesame oil with a cotton wick. After the recitation by the teacher and his pupils, the shells are extinguished. On the ground is a pot of water, and the shells are taken and put into it until all seven are finished. Then they take a coconut, and, making a hole in it to let out the milk, they wash the child's head. Then they break the nut on the threshold. The man with the child leaves, and children find the pieces of coconut and take out the flesh and leave the shell. This they put into a pot of water and say, "Tomorrow take this to a fork in the road and leave it there." They give the teacher something as they feel inclined. The bread and the roast sorghum are given to the pupils to eat.

If an adult is ill, he is treated in the same way.

Of Identification Marks

After one year two cuts are made near the child's ears, a Swahili custom to indicate that he is freeborn. In the past when a child was to be scarred they used to have horns and pipes and drums as for a wedding; but this old practice has died out.

Of Albinos

There have always appeared on the coast some children who are quite white, although their parents are black. They believe such a child to be a changeling and the child of a devil, whose mother went outside to wash before it was a week old and left it alone without leaving a necklace or a knife under the pillow or tying wild garlic to its wrists. Then a devil found the child alone and changed it, leaving a devil child and taking the human child.

Others say that when she was pregnant the mother was covered by a devil so that the child was born white. That is why when the children are small the Swahili tie wild garlic to the wrists. It has a very foul smell, and the devil cannot bear it.

When the Swahili see such children, they are worried and they do not like them. Some would kill them, and if they do bring them up, people do not like to touch them any more than they like to touch people with leucodemia or leprosy.

Of the Care of Orphans

25   If a man is married and has a child and his wife has died while the child is small, the parents of either of them will take the child and look after it. If there are none and he has no near relations, he will agree with another woman to care for his child. The cost used was not great. The nurse who brought up a child until it could walk used to get three dollars; but it is now twelve dollars or whatever they may agree upon.

If the nurse has a daughter and her charge is a boy, they may not marry or have casual intercourse, for they always remain brother and sister; nor may the nurse marry him, for she is his mother, and it is an unlawful marriage. If children who were thus nurtured together in one town go to another and afterward unknowingly marry, when the relationship becomes known the marriage is dissolved, for they are relatives, they are called "milk brother" or "milk sister."

Of Kisukumi in Women

If a woman bears children but they do not survive, or if she is married and her husband dies young, men are afraid of this woman, and she is said to have kisukumi. If the kisukumi is the sort that "kills" her children, old wise women are sought, and the husband consults her parents about the treatment of his wife.[26] They give consent, and then the wise women take the wife out into the yard and undress her and pull her legs apart. The cause of her bearing children who do not survive is a growth on the tip of the clitoris, and it is this that kills the children. It is called the vaginal bean. The women look for this growth, and when they find it they cut if off. This is very painful, and some women are too frightened to allow it to be done. When it has been cut off, they put medicine on. There is no soreness and the pain goes immediately. The husband can lie with his wife the next day if he likes. After this growth has been cut off, if God blesses them with a child, it will survive.

Why the People of the Coast Have Few Children

The reason why the Swahili have few children is that they start intercourse too young, and by the time they come to be married their fertility is used up.[27] By the time a parent has one or two children, his strength is wasted to froth. In earlier times they were fertile because the parents would not allow them to marry or to have intercourse when they were too young.

There was a chief in the Kami country called Shenikambi, who had 200 children, not by one wife; he had many wives and concubines, and every one of them had 10 or more children.[28] Up country today may be found men with 5 or 6 children, but not in the coast towns.

There was a chief in the Kami country called Shenikambi, who had two hundred children, not by one wife; he had many wives and concubines, and every one of them had ten or more children.[28] Up country today may be found men with five or six children, but not in the coast towns.

Another reason for the infertility of the coast is the women themselves, who avoid childbirth by abortion when they are pregnant because they say that childbearing will age them and their husbands will leave them, so they had better have no children.

Chapter **3** Children's Games

27   Geli

The cat is a little piece of wood; they make a small hollow and place the piece of wood.[1] Then a stick is held in the hand, and the cat is made to leap into the air. It is struck with the stick, and it flies a long way to where children are waiting to catch it in their hands as it comes or to strike it with sticks. When the first player's turn is over, another plays. They are divided into teams, and if there are five of them there will be two on one side and three on the other. They appoint a captain, called the starter, who gives the children their turns. The others play first, and he comes last. When he fails, the other side comes in.

As they make the piece of wood fly, they say, "*Hiyo*," meaning, "It is coming," and the others say, "Let it come." They make a lot of fuss about scoring. They play up to ten; but they count differently—one, two, three, turn the albino's scrotum, eight, nine, ten. They insult those who are ready to go home:

We have played with dead people.
They have run, they have run for fear.

28   *Kites*

The kite is made of paper. First they tie raffia ribs with thread. Then they make starch and smear it on the raffia, and then they put it on the paper to dry. They fasten on a buzzer and a tail. Then they tie a

19

string to it and go to the seashore to fly it, and as it flies it makes a noise. If there are two, they compete with each other.[2]

Or they make a small kite called *kishada*. This is like a kite but has only a single cross strip of raffia. Or they make a "hawk," which is like a kishada but has no tail.

The Game of Guarding the Beast

For this game they make a rope of their clothes. Then they lay one child down, and another stands guard over him, holding the rope. Then he tells the children to hit the one lying down, while he tries to stop them hitting him. If he manages to hit one with the rope, the one who is hit is the next to lie down. If he cries, they chase him away.

The Game of Hide-and-seek

The children come together and say, "Who shall be the seeker?" One says, "I will." To make him the seeker, they lay their hands on his head and say:

29   Seeker, seeker,
Father of Mgaya,
Who has two chins
But an empty stomach.
The one with horns
Is naughty, is he not?

Then they say, "When you hear *kuru, kuru,* come."[3] They run to hide themselves and then call, "Kuru," and he comes to look for them. When he catches one he gives him a pinch, and that one becomes the seeker.

The Spider Game

The spider game is like hide-and-seek except that they take a child and cover his eyes with a cloth and ask him, "Spider?" He answers, "Yes?" "Where do you come from?" He says, "From Maskat." "What have you eaten?" He says, "Dates." "With what?" "Rotten coconuts."

Then they say to him, "Pinch the one that you can." The children run away, and he chases them. When he catches one, that one has his eyes bound up.

The Guessing Game

For the guessing game, they buy raw maize and roast it. One they eat, and with the other they play guessing. For this they strip off the grains, and one puts in his hand, say, two grains. He shuts his hand and says to his companion, "Guess." If the other says, "I guess two," and there are two, he hands them over. If there are more he will say, "Four," and the one who guessed two will pay two.

30

The Game of Lalalalalala

This too is played with maize. When they are together eating maize, one will say to his neighbor, "Say, 'lalalalala,' and I will say, 'gumgumgum.' " The one who says "lalalala" cannot chew his maize; but the one who says "gumgum" can.

Grown-ups play this game on a child when he is greedy. For example, when the child has taken some maize or something else that is chewed, his father may say, "Give me some." If the child does not, he may trick him, saying, "Let us play lalala."

The Game of Swings

For a swing the children tie a rope to the poles of the house. One sits on the rope, and another pushes, singing:

Swing, hurrah, swing,
Swing, hurrah, swing.
You, Maasati, swing,
Sit down on the swing,
When the millet is reaped, swing.
We will eat sorghum just ripe, swing,
Just ripe at home, swing,
Of pleasure, swing.

31

This song they sing for a swing of rope. Or boys and girls may come together standing up and holding hands. One sings, and the others reply. When a boy mentions the name of a girl, she squats down, or if the singer is a girl and she mentions a boy's name, he squats down with her. Or they sing:

Children, the tower, the tower on the road.
When father comes, I am going to tell him,

"Your bed is invaded."
It was talked about and talked about—I am sure of it;
Catch him on the rock.[4]

Or they play:

Mother told me to catch a hen,
And I cannot catch a hen.
I am lame and cannot walk,
Mother's grain is eaten by other birds.[5]
Ish ish.

When they say, "Ish ish," those who are not on the swing jump. Or
they sing:

I cry *ooyii*,
I cry for my baby;
My baby has been taken
By the people from the countryside.[6]
"How many children have you?"
"Oh, seven,
But Kitunguja
Has been taken
By people from the countryside.[11]

The Game of Trapping Birds

First they prepare euphorbia latex, cooking it with oil. When it is
ready, they smear it on twigs. Then they go to the fields and look for a
place where many birds settle, and they put down the prepared twigs.
The birds settle on the twigs and are caught, and the one who has
caught a bird shouts, "Birdie," and runs to collect his bird. Others
trap them with snares. They put a cricket under the snare, and it
sings. When the birds perceive the cricket, they come down into the
snare and are caught. Others trap them with bird cages. They put a
bird in a cage, and it sings *chiriku*.[7] They put millet in the cage and fix
the cage up a tree, leaving the trap open. The chiriku calls, and the
bird outside hears his fellow calling and comes down on to the trap,
which closes, catching the bird.

When the children have caught some birds, they kill them, roast
them with salt, and eat them. If they catch big birds they sell them.

But the chiriku are not eaten; they are kept in cages. That is the game of trapping birds.

The Game of Sailing Boats

They make their boats of the ribs of palm leaves, or they get down the sheath of the flower stem of the coconut. Of these they make masts and sails, and at low tide they go down to sail their boats, and they have competitions over whose boat goes fastest. They stay on the shore until the tide comes in. Then they take off their clothes and bathe and swim. In bathing they compete in duck diving, five against five. For this a person dives down and throws his legs in the air and kicks out his legs forward or backward.

They may play at diving. One says, "We will dive, and you look for us. Give a pinch to the one you catch, and then he can be the seeker."

When they have finished playing and come out, they sometimes find their clothes stolen, and they go home naked, crying for fear of their parents. When they reach home they are rebuked, because they are forbidden to play on the beach for fear of cramp. Sometimes the tide comes in when they are playing on a sandbank, and they do not notice that the tide is rising. When they think of coming back to the beach, the water is too deep, and anyone who cannot swim is drowned. That is why their parents forbid them to play on the beach.

The Kid Game

For the kid game the children stretch out their legs in one line. One, who is the starter, sings. "Little kid, little kid."

The others reply, "*Memeeme, memeeme.*"

He sings, "The kid farts."

The children reply, "So does the herdsman."

He sings:

The singer is proud.
Stretch out your hand
To go to Arabia
With your spear and sword.

They reply "*Kuku*" or "*Tutu.*"

He sings, "The lion is slack."

34

They reply:

The old one is slack,
The old thing of the old man.[8]

He sings:

Father has not slept;
He spent the night with his mistress,
With watermelons and cucumbers,
Twelve of them.[9]

35   Or when the children have stretched out their legs in this way, one
sings, "Whose is this?"[10]
          Another replies, "Father's."
          The first: "Whose is this?"
          The second: "Mother's."

The Crane Game

The children tie together long canes and put a kanzu on them.[11]
They add arms and a tail, and one gets inside and makes the crane
walk. It is called a crane because it is so tall. When someone sees it he
is frightened, especially a small child. When the crane passes,
naughty children are told, "The crane will take you if you do not
behave. All the children behind the crane are naughty, and the crane
has taken them."
          Their song while they are taking the crane around is:

The crane: here it is,
The crane.

And the others answer:

With its tail,
In your house,
Is there not
A very old crone?

36   ### The Game of Konya

          If children want to make a special friendship, they twist together
their little fingers. Then a third child comes as witness to tap their

fingers, and they say to him, "Be my witness that I am Konya, friend of so-and-so." The witness taps their fingers, and the Konya seals the friendship.[12]

When they have made this friendship, if one of them has anything, say, a new cap or something like that, if they meet in the road, the other may say, "Konya, your cap," and he has to take it off and give it to him. If he is a real friend, he gives him back his cap for fear that his parents will reprove him, but a trifle he will keep. If you see your friend coming you may say, "*Mbeembeembee*, my cap," and then he cannot take it.

The Game of Stretching

The children raise their hands and join their fingertips. Then they sing:

Stretch, stretch.
He had two coats
And a door with two panels
And an ornamental chest.
The higher one, jump.

At the end of the song, the child with the hand furthest up takes it away.[13]

37 The Game of the Little Chair

Two children stand holding each other's shoulders. Then a third child comes and sits on their arms, and they toss him up, singing:

The king's little chair.
Whose son? The chief's.
Let him sit on it if he can.
We will throw him up.
We will throw him up.

The Snake Game

For the snake they make a circle on the sand, and the children sit down inside it. One child stands outside the circle and says, "A snake, here he is, a snake." The children reply, "Let him go." Then he says,

"He is at Gongoni," and they repeat, "Let him go." "He is at
Mnyanjani," and they reply, "Let him go." ¹⁴Then he says, "He is
here at your feet." Then all the children jump up and run, and the last
to be up they jeer at and buffet:

> So-and-so has been eaten by the snake,
> So-and-so has been eaten by the snake.

Games of Grown-ups with Children

Grown-up people play many games with children, such as giving
them tongue twisters like *Kikuku kike, kaka, kwako kiko?*¹⁵ Nobody can
say these words quickly, as they get muddled up. Or:

> *Jana sili mananasi.*
> *Sivo nikopokagavyo.*

Or:

> *Wauao wawe wao.*
> *Waua wewe wauawa.*

Or: *Nanena nane ngapi?* The child will answer sixteen, but it is not
sixteen, but eight.

Chapter 4 School

Of the Child Going to School

When the teacher opens the school for teaching, somebody comes with his child and says to the teacher, "I want you to teach my child."[1] He asks how much he will charge and is told ten or fifteen dollars. When they have agreed, the teacher says, "Tomorrow bring roast millet and coconut and bring your child to school."

Next morning he sends him with two rupees, called *ufito* or *ubati*.[2] First of all the child has something written for him on his board, and when the child takes the board and thinks of tipcat and kites, all past for him, he cries, and when he sees the teacher before him, he thinks that he is in the presence of the Angel of Death.[3]

The first thing written for him is "A'udhu bi'llahi mina shsheitani rrajimi. Rabbi yassir wala tu'assir 'aunaka. Ya rabbi, ya mu'inu, ya latifu, ya Allah." When he has learned this by heart, he writes the 40 alphabet through, and he is given another sura to learn.[4] In the morning he comes before the teacher carrying his board and recites the sura set him by heart without looking. If he knows it the teacher gives him permission to go to the beach to wash his board. When he has washed it he puts gypsum on it. This is a sort of white, earthlike chalk, and it makes it easy to clean off the ink. The pupils are forbidden to clean the boards with their feet, for this is unlawful. If he does not clean his board properly, he is not allowed to go home.

When the children go to the beach to clean their boards, they strip and bathe and fight; and some fight with their boards. When they return to school, they have no boards because they are broken, and they run away for fear of being beaten.

When those who have unbroken boards reach school, the teacher dictates to them. For this the teacher takes his Qur'an and reads a verse to the pupil, who writes it down, and as the teacher says it aloud, so must the pupil. The children are much frightened of dictation. If there is a child who has qualified, he is allowed by the teacher to dictate to his fellows. The others have to give him his due, one or two pesa. If they do not, he will not dictate to them.

It is customary for the children to have to be in their places every morning by six. Anyone who is late is beaten. It is also customary for the children to greet the teacher on arrival by taking his hand and kissing it, and in the evening similarly when he lets them go. In the evening when they are released they pray for the teacher, one saying, "Let us remember God," and the others replying, "There is no god but God, and Muhammad is the Prophet of God. Our teacher, our teacher, may God bless him and grant him favor upon favor and finally bliss in paradise."[5] They take his hand and go home.

School Fees

Every Thursday until he qualifies each child brings two pesa to the teacher.[6] At the beginning of Ramadhan the teacher is given his present for the fast, eight, ten, or sixteen pesa. Every high day the teacher is given his present as at Ramadhan, and the pupils are given three days' holiday.

From time to time a pupil reaches a sura that demands a fee. First he reaches *Qul huwa 'llahu*, and he takes the teacher a chicken or money in lieu. The second sura is *Lam yakuni*, and he brings a load of firewood or money. The third is *Wa's-samai dhati 'l-buruji*. Here gruel and buns are made, and the teacher and his pupils come to drink it, or he brings money to give to the teacher. The fourth sura reached is *Juzuu ya'ama*, and bread is baked and brought with a dollar; because when he reaches this sura he is said to have started his pilgrimage, as he can read and write by himself. When he reaches *Ya sini* a rupee or half a rupee is sent, and the last fee is the two rupees, bread, coconut, and roast sorghum, with which he arrived on the first day.[7] When he qualifies, the teacher is given the fee as agreed.

The customs and fees that we have mentioned refer to pupils in the past. Nowadays teachers find it hard to get all these things. They are put off and told, "Tomorrow or the next day."

Rules of Behavior between Teacher and Pupil

Rule 1: Treat your teacher as though you were his slave. Anything that he gives you to do, you must do it.

Rule 2: The pupil must greet the teacher every morning and evening.

Rule 3: Treat your teacher's wife as though she were your mother, even if she is young.

Rule 4: If you find your teacher carrying anything, you must take it from him.

Rule 5: If you are in company with your teacher, you must not be in front and he behind.

Rule 6: If your teacher goes away, you must come and greet him immediately on his return.

Rule 7: If he is in conversation, you must not interrupt.

Rule 8: You must pay respect to any teacher, even if he is not yours.

Rule 9: Give to a friend of your teacher the same respect that you pay to him.

43   Rule 10: Do not sit in your teacher's seat, unless in his absence he has left you to take the class.

Rule 11: If your teacher passes by when you are in company and he greets you, reply civilly and stand up.

Rule 12: In class do not argue with your teacher.

The Cane and Other Punishments Given to the Children

The teacher plaits a cord of the fronds of the *doum* palm, plaiting two or three together; or the pupils are sent to the forest to cut sticks of wild jasmine, which sticks are pliant and as long as the cord; or the teacher buys a cane at the shop. With these the pupils are corrected.

If the teacher forgets his stick or cord and the pupils find it, they steal it and burn it. Next day when they are asked, everyone swears, "I have not seen it; I have not seen it."

If a child is naughty and comes late to school, the teacher keeps him in. He has his food brought to him at school by his parents, and on Fridays he stays at school and has no holiday.

If he persists in his naughtiness, he is beaten, or he is made to sit down with his legs out, and they and his hands are tied to the pole of the building; but when everyone has gone, he gets free with his teeth and runs away.

44   If he is very naughty he has a log chained to his foot. He stays at

school, and when the others go he takes his log and goes home. The log is kept on for two or three days, and then a friend of the teacher's pleads for him.

If the teacher is invited to a party in the country with his pupils, they are delighted, because on the way they play, knocking down the fruit of mangoes or guavas and cutting pineapples; and some of them fight. When they reach the plantation to which they are invited, the teacher receives complaints of what they have done, and they are punished.

It is customary for complaints to be made to the teacher when the pupils behave badly, and he corrects them by beating them.[8] If he does not, people abuse him behind his back, saying, "So-and-so's pupils have no manners. And why have they no manners? Because he has none. Naughty children fear nobody but their teacher."

If the teacher is very strict, they call him Redhot; if he is short, Hammer; if tall, Stork or Crane; and if he has a long beard, Billy-goat.

The pupils are often very naughty indeed if the teacher stays in class and will not go when they want to play. One pupil says to the teacher, "There is somebody inquiring for you and wants you to go to him." It is not true, but a lie; but the teacher goes and they can play.

That it is dangerous to play with schoolchildren is recorded in old stories.

45   *The Story of the Schoolchildren and the Devil*

A devil had seven children, of whom the seventh was called Confuser.[9] Their mother warned the children, saying, "If you want to please me do not play with schoolchildren, because they are very naughty." Six of the children listened to their mother; but the seventh paid no attention.

One day the devil called Confuser turned himself into a donkey and went to a fork in the road and lay down until the children were dismissed from school. They found the donkey in the road and were all so pleased that they did not go home for their food. Each one looked for a stick, and they beat the donkey; but it did not get up. So they looked for some chilies and ground them up and pushed them up its rectum. The heat made it get up and run, and they followed, beating it. It kicked them, and they tormented it all day until in the evening they left it.

When he came home the donkey told what had happened to it, and its mother said, "I told you, my son, not to play with schoolchildren, and today they have almost killed you."

Of Girls

A girl is called *kigori* when she is seven years old.[10] At fifteen she is called *mwari*. It is usual for such children to remain at home. First the ears are pierced with a thorn, and the day of piercing them is cele-
46 brated like a wedding. The child is taught how to behave in the house, to wash pots, plates, and basins. Then she is given the beginning of plaiting, and her daily occupation is to plait mats and to learn to cook.[11]

She may never go out except at night to visit near relations, but not alone. She is escorted by a slave girl or an old lady. If she strays all over the place, her elders beat her, and she finds it hard to get a good husband. People call her a gadabout who is familiar with every place.

In addition, if she is in the house and a stranger comes to the door, whether man or woman, but they do not know, she must hide in another room and not talk to the stranger. If her elders hear her they reprimand her severely, saying, "If you hear a call do you poke your face in so that anybody can see you?" When people hear that she does not hide her face, they say, "So-and-so's face is sunburned; she has no shame; she is not a girl to marry." She may get a husband, but not quickly. When a girl reaches the age of ten, a woman comes who is her kungwi and puts around her loins her utunda.[12] This is her most intimate friend, and the utunda means love, to attract a man to want her as his wife. If a woman has no utunda it is said her loins are paralyzed.

Of Students of Elimu

The age of these students is from twenty to twenty-five. After
47 learning the Qur'an, they go to a sheikh to read elimu, to learn the forms of worship, the rules of marriage and divorce, court procedure, about buying and selling and the whole law.[13] These students do not behave in a silly way like the small pupils, but treat their sheikh with great respect.

It is customary for people attending the class to greet the sheikh with *subalkhairi* or to take his hand and kiss it, if the sheikh has not begun the lecture.[14] But if he is teaching, it is not polite to greet him until the end. In a class of elimu the students and others listening should not talk much but should attend to the exposition given by the sheikh. Each one brings his book to the class, and these books are of different sorts. Some bring grammar, some *Min hajj*, some commentaries on the Qur'an; there are different books of elimu.[15] It is customary for the sheikh who is teaching to end with fatiha and for the people attending to answer, "Amen." Each person can make any prayer that he wishes; some pray, "God give me understanding so that I may learn elimu"; some pray, "God give me health and recovery from illness"; some pray, "God forgive our sins and hide our shame." Any person may pray as he wishes.

These classes are held in the morning and the evening; but some teach only in the morning. Some sheikhs teach in their houses and some in the mosques. The Swahili are by custom much attached to any person who knows the Qur'an and elimu. If a stranger arrives wishing to live in the place, he will immediately be given a wife if he likes. Every father is glad that a learned person should marry his daughter, even if he is poor.[16]

If a man comes from a long distance to live in a place as a teacher and says, "I am a teacher, I know the Qur'an and elimu," but the people do not know him, they set him questions; and if he answers them, he is accepted as a genuine teacher.

Chapter 5 Of the Qur'an Teacher

Concerning the Teacher

There is the teacher who has been taken by the head man of the place as was done in the past.[1] He receives a salary of twenty-five rupees a month and lives at the mosque to lead the prayers and to order the affairs of the mosque. He is paid from the alms that come into the mosque. A proclamation is made to all the people of the place that no person who wishes to get married may go to any teacher but this one. He receives a fee of two rupees from everyone who wishes to get married. The teacher is given a house to live in by the people of the place.

Then there is the teacher who is employed by people to teach their children in their homes. He agrees for a salary of ten to fifteen rupees a month. He comes to teach the children every morning and evening except on Fridays and high days, and he is given the prescribed fees such as for Ramadhan and high days; but he receives no additional fee when the children qualify, except that he is given a "turban." The agreement is not by the month or the year but until the children qualify, whether this takes one year or two. That is the agreement.

These teachers have much more work than teaching. On return from morning prayer at the mosque, he takes his Qur'an and reads it or tells his beads. The rosary is the names of God, all of which he repeats.[2] After he has recited the rosary, somebody comes and says, "I want you to perform two or three recitations for my parents"; or a man comes for an amulet for his child; or somebody wishes to build a house and wants Ya sini recited over the site. He takes up his Qur'an

33

manuscript and goes to the building plot. Or somebody wants to arrange a marriage. He tells the teacher and gives to him according to his means. Then, if he is *imam* of the mosque and it is blessed with land or house property from which revenue is derived, a great part of this is put aside for the mosque, for its repair and if necessary rebuilding, and part is divided between the teacher, the muezzin, and the man who draws the water.

Suppose a man comes from inland and wants to become a Muslim.[3] He goes to the teacher and says, "I want to be a Muslim." He tells him to go and wash his clothes, to shave, to wash himself, and to return. When he comes back the teacher teaches him, saying, "Say *ashhadu an la ilaha illa 'llahu wa ashhadu anna Muhammad an rasulu 'llahi*," meaning, "Ashhadu I accept with my heart and speak aloud with my tongue that there is no god but God. I accept with my heart and speak aloud with my tongue that Muhammad is the Prophet of God, and not his son."[4] When he has spoken these words and accepted them in his heart, he is a Muslim.[5]

51

He is taught about the Ramadhan fast, about worship and all its forms; to go to the mosque at the time of worship every day five times, to face the *qibla* at the time of worship.[6] He asks what is lawful and unlawful and is answered correctly. This man from inland comes of his own volition; there is no compulsion.[7] He asks and is taught how to slaughter meat, goats, and cattle, beginning with "In the name of God."[8]

Teaching children is hard work for little reward, because when children qualify, the teacher does not always get his money.[9] More are taught for nothing than those who pay, and when a child qualifies they cheat the teacher and give him nothing.

Chapter **6** Manners

52 *Children's Manners*

In bringing up children, manners are taught mainly about the age of six or seven.[1] Then he must attend carefully to the instructions of his parents. If they forbid something, he must pay attention. If he follows his own inclination, he has no manners.

They teach him to greet people, and particularly to greet any important person known to his parents. He is taught to approach grown-up people with respect and civility. If he is impolite and offends people, he is punished. If he begs from everyone who passes in the road, he is beaten. If he is with grown-up people, he may not sit down until they are seated. If he does so he is said to have no manners. If he is sitting in the presence of people, it is not the custom for him to talk at random. The people will say, "So-and-so's son has no manners."

53 If the boy has gone with his father to a wedding reception or a party and he is sitting with them as they talk, he must keep quiet and listen to what they tell him to do. It is not good manners to giggle with one after another. People will say, "That child has no manners, and he should not be brought to meetings." But if he is with his own companions, he may talk and laugh and make as much noise as he likes. He must learn not to show off before people.

If he is with his father, he must not go in front. Father goes first. Or if he is with his teacher, similarly, the teacher must go first. To do otherwise is rude to his father and his teacher and to himself, because

35

people will ask him, "Has your father taught you no manners, or your teacher, so that you do not know how to behave?"

A child must not draw attention to people's defects, as, "So-and-so's wife cannot cook," or "They had no dinner today and went to bed hungry for lack of food; their house is dark, they have no lamp." When a child talks like that, people know that he has no manners.

A child is often told by his parents, "If you are told a secret, you must keep it and not let it out to all and sundry. If you do people will say, 'This child has no manners; do not tell him secrets.' "

54   If guests come to a meal at the house, the child is told not to wash his hands before the grown-ups have done so; and if there is no one else in the house to wait, he takes the basin round for people to wash. If they go to somebody else's house where there are grown-up people, he will do the waiting. At the meal it is not polite for him to take a lot of meat; he should take meat only when they give him permission. And if at the meal he always picks out the best bit of meat, people will notice and say, "This child has no manners. Do not take him out another time, he disgraces you." Again it is not the custom at meals for him to gnaw food like a dog. He is absolutely forbidden by his parents to do so.

If a child does not obey his parents' teaching about manners and makes trouble in the neighborhood, like being rude to somebody or telling a grown-up person that he is a liar, the person insulted will come to his parents and insult them. If they find that he is persistently naughty, they will arrange for him to be sent to the circumcision camp, where he will be given a great deal of instruction in manners by the kungwi.

Every child must attend to the orders of three people if he wishes to please God: the king, his parents, and his teacher. These three he must obey: disregard of their orders is disobedience to God.

Of Yawning

If a child yawns, he is asked if he is hungry or sleepy. He is told not
55   to open his mouth wide when he yawns, and if he does not understand, his mother shuts his mouth for him when he yawns, for fear of flies going in.[2] If he can understand that it is not polite, she tells him when he yawns not to open his mouth in public and leave it open like a crocodile, for a crocodile waits on a riverbank when he is hungry with his mouth open, and flies go in. Then he shuts his mouth. That is why they tell him not to be like a crocodile.

Of Sneezing

A child is also taught that if his father or mother sneezes, he should give them the greeting *shikamuu*, and the parent will reply, *marahaba*.[3] Or he says, *mwinyi*, and his parent replies, *mwinyi wangu sayyidi*.
If the child is a girl, the parent replies, *mwana wangu sayyidi*.
If a child sneezes in front of its parents, they say:

Grow like grain
When the grain crop is tall.
Sit in a chair
Of ebony; and reach up
To heaven.

Then the parent says, "Give thanks; say, "Praise be to God.' "

56   ### Of Belching

If a child belches, some people tell it not to do so. They say, "Do not get into the habit of belching." Others do not stop a child belching. But if a child sneezes before a meal, they say, "Are you sneezing like a goat tied to a stake?" We are not ashamed to belch. It shows the host that his food is good and that we have had enough.

Customary Manners among Adults

When a man visits the house of another, he calls *hodi* and the people inside reply *hodi*. Then they say *karibu*, and he waits on the verandah until the owner of the house comes.[4] He says to his wife, "Bring the betel box," and if they are chewers, they chew betel nut and ask after each other, "How are the children and the grown-ups?" He answers, "They are well, the children send you shikamuu and the elders their greetings." If he has just come to call, he will then go away; but if he has come to stay, food and a place to sleep will be quickly made ready for him.

A second point: If a man goes to the house of a friend or relation, he calls "Hodi" and if nobody answers, he will wait a little while, and if there is still no reply, he goes away. Similarly, to enter a house without calling "Hodi," or to call "Hodi" and walk straight in, is rude. When you call "Hodi," wait at the door for a reply, for if there are people inside they may be busy and not properly dressed. That is why you must wait for an answer to your call.

When they answer they say, "Karibu, come inside," and he goes in. If he finds the man and his wife sitting together in the outer room, it does not matter, he will sit and talk with them, but if when you have come into the outer room you find that they are conversing in the inner room, it is very rude to enter the inner room.

If you go to the house of a friend and call "Hodi" and find the wife alone and the husband out, do not stop and make conversation, or your friend will be angry when he returns. Unless the lady has been told, "If so-and-so comes, ask him to wait for me." Or if you are with a friend, not arriving together but finding him on the doorstep of your mother's house or his, it is rude to go in and leave him outside.

Another thing: If one of your neighbors has a wife with a bad reputation, there is no need for you to visit that house. When people hear that you frequent that house, they will say that you are committing adultery with your neighbor's wife.

If you have gone to the house of a friend to call but his wife is alone, it is not good manners for her to ask you in nor for you to go in. Go away or wait on the verandah until your friend comes.

If a visitor finds a girl in the house and everyone else out, he calls "Hodi." The girl comes to the door, and the mans asks, "Is your father in?" She will answer by signs, but she will not speak to him in words. If he speaks and she answers him, her manners are bad and her mother will reprove her severely.

It is Swahili custom that if you come upon three or four persons sitting talking about their own business and when you pass by they do not ask you to join them, you should go on and not sit down to listen to their conversation. If you do, they will ask you, "What do you want here?" or "Who asked you to join in our talk?" And they will chase you away and say that you have no manners. If they are very civil, they will not chase you away; they will go themselves and look for another place to sit.

It is Swahili manners that if a man goes to a friend and they are brought food hidden by a cover, it is rude for the guest to uncover it. Even if he is invited to do so, he should not. Similarly, if they are brought the box for betel nut, the guest does not open it. It is rude for a guest to uncover anything that is covered. The owner of the house should do this, and if the guest does, according to Swahili custom it is bad manners.

Similarly, women do not uncover pots or anything that is covered. If a woman goes to a friend and finds a pot covered and uncovers it, there will be a quarrel: "Are you so stupid, or did your kungwi not give you any instruction under the tree?"[5] She is as angry as though she had removed her clothes and left her naked. So the Swahili do not uncover things.

The Swahili are always slandering one another, as was said long ago:

59   People are slanderers
        If they do not speak openly they speak slander.

If a man makes a profit and says, "I have done well this year," they complain, saying, "If that person brings off a little deal, he publishes it all over the place." Or if he fails and says, "This is a bad year, I do not know what to do," they say, "He is featherbrained; if he does not succeed, he publishes his disgrace everywhere."[6] It is not polite for a person to bemoan his condition in public.

Other customary manners: If a man invites a friend to a meal and his wife has undercooked the grain or the meat is raw, she will say to her husband, "Sir, the food is not good today; please do not ask anyone in." And the man answers, "Never mind; you did not do it on purpose." Then if the friend comes and they eat, he will ask him, "Did you have a good meal?" And he will answer, "Very good," although he did not enjoy it; but to say so would be rude. And when he goes out and meets other people, it is not polite to say, "I was asked in by so-and-so; there was too much salt, or the meat was raw." When people know that he is in the habit of disparaging other people's hospitality, they do not invite him if they give a party. Similarly, when he asks for a woman's hand, he may be successful but with difficulty unless he has a prominent person to speak on his behalf.

60   Again, if a friend is invited in, he will not immediately meet his host's wife. He will introduce his mother or his sister, but not if she is young. They will not come if they know that their brother is talking with a stranger, or people will say, "That girl's face is sunburned."

Then if a Swahili friend comes to visit another friend and stays for a month, the host friend feels the expense; but if on departure he gives him something, he will refuse it. Only after he has gone and when he reaches home may he send a present.

When one friend borrows from another, they make no formal agreement, except that the borrower promises repayment. This is all right if they are honest; but if not, there are lawsuits and insults and the end of the friendship. If he borrows from one who is not a friend, recovery is not easy, for they say:

> Borrowing is a wedding,
> Payment is a funeral.

Quarrels between a Child and Its Parents and Reconciliation

If a son quarrels with his parents and for days will not speak to them, the whole place says that he has no manners. If this becomes common gossip, he employs someone to whom he says, "Please, will you go and make peace between me and my parents?" So the man goes and tells them what the son has said. If they refuse, the go-between pleads with them, "Do not make too much of it and say that you had a good son and now have a bad one." Then he says, "You do not cut off a hand that has been fouled by a child; you wash it."

61 When the parents are agreeable, the go-between returns to the son and says, "Your parents are agreeable; but now behave well and do not be pert. Now take a peace offering to give them." So he takes a piece of cloth or a kanzu or something; and these things are called "the request for forgiveness" or "the falling at the feet." It is a Swahili custom that if a child quarrels with its parents and is reconciled, he takes them a present.[7]

To return to the go-between: When he receives these things, he takes them to the parents and says, "I bring you your son; forgive him for what he has done. Do not leave pots to bang against each other." Then the go-between says, "Greet your father and give him your hand." He greets him, and his father replies and prays for his son, "What is past is past; what is left is behind us." This is how the Swahili have quarrels and make them up.

Chapter 7 Of Swahili Greetings

62   In the past, when people met in the morning, they greeted each other.[1] If a young man met a chief or a person senior to himself, he said, *chelewa*, meaning, "Have you had a good night?" And he answered, *aaye*, meaning, "Thank you" or "Well." Then he said, "Mwinyi," and the answer was "Mwinyi wangu sayyidi." If the greeting was addressed to a *jumbe*, the person giving the greeting said these words and took off his cap and shoes, whether indoors or out. Or if a jumbe met a *waziri*, a *shaha*, or the *mwinyimkuu*, he would similarly take off his cap.[2] A freeman meeting a waziri or shaha did not take off his cap, but a slave did so. Young men greeted each other in the same way; but they did not take off their caps to each other.

   If people know each other, they ask the news of the house: "How have you slept at home?"

"All is well, thank God."

"The ladies and the children are well?"

"They are well, except that your father-in-law or your grand-daughter did not sleep well. She had fever; but she is all right today."

"May God take all trouble away from her."

63   "And how are you at home? Are all the ladies well?"

"They are well."

"When you go home give my humble duty to the ladies and greet the children from me and hold your son's ear for me," meaning that on his return home he is to take his baby son by the ear and say, "Uncle So-and-so holds your ear."

   If an old lady walking in the road passes some people sitting on a verandah or if she wants to go into a house where people are sitting, she takes off her veil and greets the people on the verandah: "Have you slept well, gentlemen?" And they reply, "Aaye, we have slept well, lady, honored lady, honored lady." And she replies, "Mwinyi wangu sayyidi, mwinyi wangu sayyidi." Or they say, "Our humble duty, lady"; and she replies, "Thank you, thank you, gentlemen."[3]

As she goes in, she says, "Are we at home?" and the women reply, "We are in," or she says, "The master, the master?" and they reply, "We are at home."

In the past if a man called "Hodi" at a house on the coast, he was reproved: "Hodi is not a coastal custom. Hodi houses belong to Arabs."

In the morning a child greets its father or mother or any elder with "Have you slept well" and is answered, "Well." Then it asks, "Is all well with you?" and the answer is "All is well." Then it greets its father with "Shikamuu," and the answer is "Marahaba"; or it says, "Mwinyi," and the answer is "Mwinyi wangu sayyidi." Children's greetings are still the same as in the past.

64   When a child greets its father or mother in the daytime, it says, "What of the day?" and is answered, "Good." Then it gives the greeting. If it is evening it says, "What of the evening?" The answer is "Good" and then the greeting.

Adults meeting for the second time in the daytime or the evening similarly say, "What of the day, or of the evening?"

If a child wants to go to bed, it first takes leave of its parents, saying, "I take my leave; my humble duty." They reply: "Sleep well, go to sleep in good health and wake in good health; sleep like a lion and wake like an elephant."

When small children greet one another, both in the past and now, they say, "Are you all right?" "I am all right." Then they ask, "Where are you going?" or "Let's go and play."

If a person sees a familiar friend, he says, "Are you all right?" and is answered, "I am all right." "Like a pearl?" Answer—"Like a pearl." "Like coral?" Answer—"Like coral." "Like red coral?" "Like red coral." This is to be used between familiar friends only or between children, because it is a sign of friendship; but these greetings are now rare.

If a man goes to visit a sick friend, he asks, "Are you all right?" and the answer is "I am all right." "How did you sleep with your illness?" "Today is not yesterday"—meaning that what he experienced today is not the same as yesterday. "God will relieve you." "Amen."

These are the old greetings of the coast, and they are still in use in

the houses of the older people; but young people prefer the Arabic greetings. For example, if they meet in the morning they say, "Good
65   morning," and the answer is "With the grace of God."[4] "How did you sleep?" "I am all right, praise be to God; and you, how did you sleep?" And the same answer. If they have not met for some days: "The past days?" The answer is "Well, and you the past days?" The same answer.

If they meet in the afternoon or at night, they say, "The afternoon?" and the answer is "With the grace of God."

If people are sitting on the verandah and someone passes by, he says to the people sitting down, "Peace be with you," and they reply, "And with you; come in." He says, "Do not move," or he says, "Please remain seated," whether he is coming in or going on.

Of Parting

In the past after talking one took his leave saying, "I take my leave," and the other replied, "Aaye." Then if he were an important person he would say, "Sir," but otherwise, "I am going home." Now they normally part with the words "Good luck," answered by "Good luck till we meet again," or there may be more words: "Go and come back"; "What has happened to those who went?" "Go and be hungry."[5] The other says, "Thank God, I am satisfied with the sight of you."

Greetings between Passersby

If a man is on the road, people say, "A blessing where you go, come back safe." He replies, "Amen"; or he is greeted, "A good omen, go and eat with the blind."[6] To this also he replies, "Amen."

A man returning from a journey is greeted with "Congratulations" or *hongea*, meaning, "Are you safely back?"[7] He answers, *tumeuya*, meaning, "We have returned safe."
66   If a man passes people at work of any kind, he says, "Skilled work?" and they say, "God first." After this they exchange the usual greetings. If a man comes upon a friend working in a field, he says, "It takes a magician to till a field on one rain."[8] When a fisherman returns from the sea, they say, "How is the fishing?" and he says, "Line and fish," meaning that the line has caught fish. Others on the coast say to a returning fisherman, "What is this?" and he replies:

Sink the turbot,
The angler has no rest.

When a hunter comes back from the country, people say, "Meat?" and he replies, "Of the country." Then they exchange news.

If people are passing by a man reaping, they say: "What crop?" and he replies, "Rice" or "Sorghum."

When a woman has had a baby, other women come to congratulate her, and they say, "Congratulations on the baby." She replies, "Praise be to God." Then they say, "This is an event; boy or girl?" And she says, "Girl."

Chapter **8**
Putting the Child
through the
Initiation Camp

Preparations

Some send their children at five years old, some at seven, and some at nine, after they have been to school.[1,2] When the father wants to send his child, first he calls his neighbors to dance the *nyago* before the circumcision.[3] In the afternoon the father and his neighbors go to sweep out the cemetery. There they sweep the graves and put on them *tibu* and *dalia*, saying, "We are come to you our ancestors; we are bringing to you your child and grandchild, may God bless him. You are dead, but your spirits are alive. May this child not be ill in the camp; when he is well, we will come and sweep again." So they sweep the grave and pull up any weeds and remove all rubbish. They bring incense in a censer, and after sweeping they place the censer under the head of the grave, because there is no point in censing a grave without incense in the censer. Whenever a man wants to pray to God he puts incense on the fire in the censer.[4]

At night the neighbors and others come together to dance the nyago. That is the name of the dance, and it is so called because in the early morning they make frightening things, tying up leaves or branches so that a man can get inside and dance. They may be like a camel or an elephant or another animal; so they are called nyago.

In the past they made beer, and people drank during the night of the nyago dance.[5] Now the elder relations of the person giving the nyago have food prepared for them. The *ngariba* or *mwinzi* attend the nyago and dance with the others, and the assistants are also invited to the nyago, and they come and dance too.[6] It is an honor for the assistants to be invited.

45

Of the Circumcision

When the nyago breaks up in the early morning, the ngariba goes inside the hut made in the night for the children who are to be circumcised, for they are not allowed to go out to the nyago. This hut is called the *kumbi* hut, that is, the "secret hut," and it is built in the forest.[7] No women are allowed nor uncircumcised men. The ngariba and the "maidens" go in, all being naked, and the ngariba has a little knife called *kirimbo*.[8] When he comes he calls one "maiden," called *kiranja*, who is a slave.[9] Kiranja is placed on the trap, a board large enough for a single person to sit on it, and he is held by someone. The person who holds him is called *shuwali*. The ngariba waggles his penis a little and then circumcises him with the little knife. Some people hold the penis with a wooden pincer before cutting. Some can bear it and some cannot; because when the inner skin is cut a person feels bitter pain, and some, seeing their companion crying, break through the hut if it is not well built and run away. If the ngariba has invited other ngariba, he does them honor by giving each two maidens to circumcise.

Of Treatment

After the operation the children have gruel cooked for them, or they are brought unripe coconut milk to do them good by making them pass water. Then medicine is applied. This is a powder made of wood. Some grind up *mkumbi* wood, which is applied to the wound and tied with cloth. Others do not do this but put on a bandage first and then pour kerosene over it.[10] This is now more usual than the old custom.

Every morning his kungwi, that is, the person who washes and tends him, comes and removes the bandage put on on the first day and washes the wound with warm water until it is clean. Then the medicine is put on again, that is, the powdered wood. Kerosene is not used again after the first day. Then the bandage is put on again, and this is done every morning for six days.

On the seventh day the parents are told, "The six days are over; tomorrow the children go to bathe." For this bath those who have been taken far into the country are sent to a river, but those nearby go to the seashore. They are taken to the shore very early, and as they go they are taught a song by their kungwi: "Come out, come out, let us go"; and they all reply likewise: "Come out, come out, let us go."

69

70

When they reach the shore, they wash their bodies all over. Then fresh medicine is applied, and they all return to the camp.

When the old people know that they have returned from the shore, in the evening they make a coconut paste and dip cotton into it and put it in a cup and take it to the camp. When the kungwi see the women, they take the cups from them as they have every morning taken the food brought by the old people for the children. As the food arrives and is received by the kungwi, he sings:

The chief's,
The chief's platter.

and they reply likewise:

The chief's,
The chief's platter.

When the kungwi has brought the cup of coconut paste, he and the shuwali apply it and bind it over with cloth, and while doing this they sing:

71   When I tap a tree for toddy
        My heart leaps.[11]
        When I tap a tree for toddy
        My heart leaps.

The "maidens" reply likewise:

When I tap a tree for toddy
My heart leaps.

Treatment with this paste and cotton cures the wounds of the "maidens." Every morning after they have washed, they are treated with medicine made of powdered tree bark and applied locally.

At the end of the second week they are again taken to the beach to bathe. On the way to the beach they have their faces smeared with gypsum that is dug from the earth. This whitewash indicates that they are maidens going to the beach.[12] On their return they are not again treated with coconut paste, because some of them are healed, but those who are not yet healed are treated daily with the same medicine as before.

If a child is a bad sleeper and restless, his wound does not heal, and for him mutton fat made from the inside of a sheep's tail is heated and applied with cotton fastened on a stick. Then he rapidly recovers. Most of the children recover in two weeks, but some take three weeks.

What the "Maidens" Are Taught in the Camp and the Songs That They Sing

When the "maidens" have been asleep, to waken them in the morning the kungwi sings to them:

72
> *Kwere kwerekweche,*
> *Kwere kwerekweche.*
> The *mramba* bird sings
> *Kwere kwerekweche.*[13]

or:

> "Maidens" awake
> In the house of the ancestral spirit.[14]

and they reply:

> "Maidens" awake
> In the devil house.

The kungwi and the shuwali stay continuously with the "maidens" in the camp, but the ngariba comes only once a day in the morning to inspect their wounds. He greets them, "Good morning, 'maidens.' " And they say, "Good morning, ngariba." Then the "maidens" parade naked before the ngariba for him to inspect their wounds.

The children in the camp are taught by the kungwi good behavior, as to be civil to their elders, to show respect to the magistrate, to fear their teacher, to pay respect to passersby, and how to treat the women of the household.[15] All good behavior is taught in the camp.[16] Also they are taught songs with a hidden meaning. After a song has been sung, the child is asked its meaning and is beaten if he does not know it. Then he is taught the meaning. The kungwi sings:

73
> 1. Shall I go with my brother-in-law
>   To till my plantation?

To till my plantation?
I say I shall stay at home.

2. I stayed at home
   And set a trap,
   And set a trap,
   And a dove entered it.

3. A dove entered it,
   But a beast from the wilderness,
   A beast from the wilderness, got her.
   A snake bit me.

4. A snake bit me,
   And I felt pain,
   And I felt pain,
   And went away crying.

5. I went away crying
   And on the way
   I met a woman
   With breasts full hanging.

6. Her breasts were fat,
   A forest great and a Hadhrami well.
   The wealth is used up,
   The wealth of the cattle.[17]

When they play in the camp and exchange insults and fight, the kungwi sings a song to annoy them:

74   With our hand
        Let us catch flies,
        With our hand.

Then he catches a fly in his hand and sings this song.
    If the kungwi finds them laughing, he sings a song to vex them, because he suspects that they are laughing at him. He sings:

Temper, temper, finger and ring,
Finger and ring, razor and hone,
Hone and razor, tongue and spittle,
Tongue and spittle; do you laugh at me?
And say that I do not know my job?

After sunset, the kungwi sings:

> The *shundi* bird sings at sunset,
> The little bird sings gently.
> The shundi bird sings at sunset.[18]

If the kungwi, the ngariba, or the shuwali wants something from their mothers, he sings:

> Have you no pity?
> Have you no pity?
> Give me a little
> When I sing a song.
> Father, give me a machete
> To cut raffia,
> To cut raffia,
> To plait mats,
> To plait mats,
> To go to the mkumbi tree,
> To buy *kwarara*,
> To appease the hunger of the rains.[19]

75

or:

> He put me, he put me,
> In a hole,
> Against my will.[20]

or:

> When the sun rises,
> Until it sets,
> I am like a grasshopper
> Until it is red again.

or:

> Father, give me a line
> To catch a *shemnungwi* fish
> To use for bait
> To catch a *kakaguu* fish.
> I cannot scale the kakaguu,
> I will cook it in its skin.[21]

76   or:

      The cuttlefish loves to dance,
      It dances wherever it is.
      It lives under a stone
      Where are mussels and sand.
      At first she was not silly
      But a cunning one deceived her.

or:

      The canoe Ngarumbwe is as fine as a coconut palm.
      Of two canoes, one drowned in the water.
      One is successful, laden with cotton
      And pepper wood, the mast of silver,
      The anchor of gold, coming into harbor
      With joy.[22]

or:

      The stump stands at the door,
      Give me a sickle to cut it away.[23]
      In the forest is a tree
      Four stems together.
      There are twelve boughs
      And the fruit is very sweet.[24]

77   or:

      A tree fell under a stone,
      The boughs stood up.
      I have no doubt
      That the planter was the owner.[25]

or:

      I saw a strange sight, a chicken in shoes,
      It stuck out its neck six cubits.
      It was called Maskat, after Rashidi the maneater.[26]

If the mothers of the children in the camp undercook the food, the kungwi sing:

The "maiden's" mother
Cooked watery food
And brought it,
Because while she was cooking
Her heart was on fire.

When the ngariba comes to inspect the "maidens," he sings:

My little mwari wood boat
Has floated here,
Rocked by the waves,
To the shore,
At low tide.
I have come to see it.

78   When the "maidens" are going to bed, they sing:

Ngariba, we are your children,
Let us go to rest.[27]

When the "maidens" are hungry and the food has arrived but they
have not yet been given permission to eat it, they sing:

Dish up, you, dish up,
Come and serve us our food.

After they have eaten, they are asked by the kungwi:

Birds, have you eaten?
Where will you go to drink?

They reply:

The frog croaks,
There is no water in the pond.

When they wish to say grace, they sing:

We have eaten,
Praise, praise, praise to God.

The "Maidens" Are Returned to Their Homes

When the days at the camp are accomplished, the ngariba reports to elders of the "maidens" that they have recovered. The elders have made ready by buying clothes for their children, because every child leaves the camp in new clothes, and the night before they come out the nyago is played all night near the camp as at the beginning. In the morning the children are shaved. Their fathers and brothers are present, but they do not speak to them. At the shaving, horns and pipes are played, and they sit on stools.[28] After the shaving they are sent to be washed, and on their return they are dressed in new clothes. Their old clothes and the mats on which they have slept are given to the kungwi as a present. When they are clothed they are shut into an *ukingo* so as not to be seen by people.[29] Then they are brought to the town, and as they come the ngariba sings them this song:

> I have not eaten your children,
> I have not eaten your children,
> I have *not* eaten your children,
> I have not eaten them.

The people respond to this song; the women ululate and pour rice to show that they are pleased with the children. When they reach home they give their hands to their mothers and aunts, and they give them presents—five to ten pesa. Until their mothers have so "unveiled" them, they are not allowed to speak to them. They are forbidden to do so by the kungwi, because this money is distributed among the kungwi, the ngariba, and the shuwali. After this, food is prepared for the children's party. If there are ten houses, in all ten food is prepared, and to all ten houses go the kungwi and their maidens to eat. Three days later they are taken around these and other neighboring houses, and at each house they are given a little money for the kungwi.

Of Swahili Young Men

If a young man has a small penis, he consults the doctor, saying, "My penis is so small that the young women laugh at me." The doctor replies, "Give me my rice to make medicine, and it shall be as big as you like." After haggling, they go into the country to look for *mwegea* trees just beginning to fruit.[30] This tree has long, thick, inedible fruit.

When they have found one, they both sit down under it, and the doctor takes a razor to scratch him, asking him how long he wants it, thumb to forefinger or thumb to little finger. He says, "To little finger." The doctor scratches him and then the *mwegea* fruit and mixes together the juice of the mwegea and the blood of his penis. He says to him, "Watch this mwegea carefully and after a week come and cut it. If you do not, your penis will grow too long." After a week he goes and cuts it off.

Chapter **9** The Customs of Girls

Of Puberty

From seven years old a girl is called kigori, until at thirteen people say, "This kigori has become mwari." She is called mwari when she loses blood for the first time.[1] When this blood first appears, the girl cries and does not wash or clean up for herself; but when her elders perceive that the blood has come, the kungwi is informed that her kigori has become a mwari.[2] The kungwi comes to the parents and carries the girl off to her own house to look after her. Every morning she takes her to the washroom to wash in very cold water and to teach her what to do next time the blood appears.

On the appearance of the blood they say that she is now grown-up, and one who does not have it they say is sick. It starts at the age of ten to fourteen, and if it is late, they make medicine for her. Her diet is changed, for whereas before she was not allowed to eat chicken, now she is allowed it; but another diet is prescribed for her.[3] They cook for her a medicine of roots and chicken cooked for seven days, and she drinks the broth. Then she must carry a doll.[4] Everywhere she goes, sleeping, cooking, pounding grain, in the washroom, the doll must be in her hands or on her back until the blood comes.

The kungwi gives her mwari a piece of cloth called *sodo* to absorb the blood when it comes, and this is fastened to her utunda.[5] A woman never allows anyone to see this cloth, not even her mother or her husband, only her kungwi while she is with her. She is also given a scent stone or rubbing stone to rub on herself. This stone is a piece of coral found on the shore on a tidal rock. It is worked by an expert until it is smooth and round. Women pay a rupee to a rupee and a half for one. In every town there is an expert who knows how to work these stones.

The use of this stone is that when a girl first menstruates, she is given it by her kungwi to impregnate it with scents such as tibu, dalia, *maua maulidi*, and so forth to rub on herself.[6] Secondly, it is used on the day of her marriage, when she rubs scent over herself in the way that we have described. If this stone is taken to a marriage or if a woman goes to an intimate friend to borrow one, it is not carried openly. She hides it in her clothes where it cannot be seen; but when it
83 is in the house after use, it is not hidden, and anyone may see it.

During the days of menstruation she wears *kaniki* to hide the blood if there is much of it.[7] She may not plait her hair until seven days are passed. This she does every time the blood comes.

The mwari is not seen by anyone but her kungwi and her family, and she stays with her kungwi for six months or a year. Some stay for a month only before returning to their parents. At her kungwi's house she is taught cooking and plaiting and how to behave respectfully to others and how to be a good wife when she is married.

Of the Wari in Their Camp

When the time of staying with her kungwi is over, her parents are told that now we must take this girl to the *muyombo* tree.[8] Her parents brew *pombe* and *togwa*, and at the muyombo tree there gather together a great number of women and girls.[9] Sometimes, if there is a house big enough in the country, they go into it, or they build a hut. The girls are taken at night so that they may not be seen, and they are carried by women, for each kungwi has her own girls who have already been through the ceremony, six or seven of them. She summons them to go to the muyombo and to carry their fellow. They have no choice, because no girl will disobey her kungwi, whose word she puts even before that of her own mother.
84 When the girl has been brought to the camp, a dance called *unyago* is played for her.[10] At the unyago dance some of the women vibrate their buttocks to show the girls so that they may do the same as the grown women. Those who do not know how to do it are taught. They sing:

When you hide with your loins,
Come and see mine, stranger.

or:

> You cry at the vibrating,
> Cry then.

or:

> When you grind, grind forward,
> Backward is silly.

or:

> Little grinder grinding,
> I will grind grain to flour
> With my girls.

or:

> Sweep the yard
> For the guest to come in.

or a puzzle song:

> The bucket grasped,
> And grasped,
> And grasped with its mouth.[11]

85   The girl has something put behind her back and picks it up with her
lips by arching her back, while she vibrates and they dance and sing
this song:

> Grind, grind,
> I will grind for my husband,
> Though I do not know who he is.

or:

> The spear pulses
> When it presses on me.

or:

> The month is built around,
> I sleep deeply.[12]

or:

> The great snake of Mlali
> Pokes in and out.[13]

When the kungwi have finished singing and the girl cannot interpret the song, or if she is set a puzzle and cannot solve it, she is beaten
and the meaning is explained to her. If she knows the puzzle all the
86   women shout, *chereko, chereko*, meaning, "Clever girl, clever girl."
Those who cannot grasp the puzzle have sung to them:

> Trouble today,
> Trouble today, and worry.

Then those who cannot see the puzzle are beaten and shown again.

Of the Girls Being Taken to the Muyombo Tree and Their Return

On the seventh day after entering the camp and when the dances
are over, the girls are taken to the muyombo, which is a tree. There all
the kungwi and the girls have further drumming and dancing, and if
there is any, they drink beer. They stay all day singing the songs
given above, and at sunset the girls are shaved, some only over the
back of the head. They are treated with kohl, and dalia is applied to
their shaven heads. Then they are dressed in new clothes and adorned
with silver ornaments. At sunset they are brought into the town with
no singing. Free girls have the unveiling done in their houses by their
families, who bring all sorts of things to the house.[14] Some give them
mats, other bangles or rings or cash. Slave girls are paraded round the
town by their kungwi, dressed up like the free girls. When they meet a
man whom they know, they hold out their hands to him, and he gives
them cash for the unveiling. If they meet a woman whom they know,
87   they kneel to greet her, and she gives them something. They are not
allowed to speak to anyone who has not given them an unveiling
present. They are paraded around for three days, and then the
ornaments are removed and they are given their ordinary clothes.

Of the Fall of a Young Woman

If a young unmarried woman strays away with a man who de-
flowers her, the whole town laughs at her, especially if she becomes

pregnant.[15] People say, "She has sold her virginity for lust." Her elders know of her pregnancy by her developing a great desire for something like limes or bananas, cane or sugar or sweet fruit. They know at once and ask her, "Why do you want this or that?" And she has nothing to say. If in the house there is a slave man or woman, he or she gets the blame.[16] Her breasts swell, her face shows light spots, and her menstruation ceases. Then the elders strip her and see that her navel is prominent, and they are sure that she is pregnant.

They ask her who is responsible, and she cannot refuse to tell them. They consider the matter, and if they think it best to proceed they send to the parents of the man, and if they can agree he marries her. When the child is born it is not legitimate, although the Swahili call it legitimizing the child.[17]

If the man in question is a slave and they do not want it known, they give her an aborting medicine. This is gunpowder drunk in water or medicine from the forest. After drinking this for seven days, she has an abortion.

Chapter **10** Of Amulets

88 *The Amulet in the Old Days*

In the old days when the Swahili did not know how to read, if they wanted an amulet for a child or an adult, they went to a doctor to obtain one.[1] The doctor dug certain roots for an adult and different ones for a child. For a child, after digging the root, he cut it into seven pieces; then he took a little gourd, a dried cucumber with castor oil and honey in it. He took a piece of paper and smeared it with the oil and added *usira*, which is the skin of a dead snake burned to ash; the burned skin is called usira. He mixed this with the roots and then put it in a black cloth and sewed it up. The cloth was sewn over with white thread until the cloth was completely hidden. This was hung around the child's neck against occasional illness.[2]

Alternatively a cord was prepared with seven knots, between which were placed the bits of root as described above for amulets.

89 Amulets for adults were made of different sorts of root. Thus a man might go to the doctor and say, "I want an amulet for a journey against attack by lions," or "I want a business amulet to speed up trade in my shop" or "a love amulet to attract the girls" or "a war amulet." The doctor knew which roots to dig for the required amulet. If it was against lions on a journey, he took a black cloth and usira of a lion's whisker, and with it he made an amulet, it and the roots being mixed with castor oil and honey and spread on the cloth in the proper way. If he wanted an amulet for some other purpose, the preparation was the same, but the woods were different.

Other doctors prefer to sew in the claws of a lion or a leopard; but such amulets are sold for a high price, and some cannot afford them. They cost from one to five rupees, according to their value.

Modern Amulets

Nowadays people use both wild-tree amulets and Qur'an amulets. Some country folk want Qur'an amulets and some townfolk wild-tree amulets.[3]

Qur'an amulets for a child a week old: A Ya sini cord is made of black thread plaited by the teacher after reciting Ya sini. Every time
90 he comes to the end he ties a knot, until he has recited Ya sini seven times and tied seven knots. Then it is given to the child to wear around his neck, and the cord protects him.

When he is six years old he is made an amulet for the evil eye. This amulet has written on it Ya sini or *Qul huwa 'llahu ahadu* or *Qul a'udhu bi rabbi 'lfalaqi* or *Qul a'udhu bi rabbi 'nnasi* or *Ayat al kursi*.[4] It is held over burning incense and sewn with black or white thread and worn around the neck. It is called an eye amulet because if enemies try to put the evil eye on him, he will not be harmed or made ill.

For adults, too, amulets are written with Ya sini or *Taha ma anzelna* or *Sura ala imran*,[5] the wishes of the person being consulted, whether for a journey or for trade or for war.

Among the greatest amulets of all are those called *Johari 'lqurani* or *Andhuruni* or *Seifu 'llahu'lqate'i*, these being prayers from the Qur'an.[6] These are the greatest of the amulets, because it is agreed that they have the greatest power. A person who carries one of them is confident that he will come to no harm, save by the will of God, which is not to be withstood.[7] These amulets are very expensive; if a rich man wants one of them, he has to pay twenty rupees or more. The poor can buy only those costing one to five rupees.
91 The writing of the amulets mentioned as Johari 'lqurani or Andhuruni or Seifu 'llahu 'lgate'i is governed by fixed rules. The writer must be ceremonially purified, and before starting he must perform two *rakaa*.[8] When it is finished the amulet is censed with frankincense, aloes, and aromatic gum.

If, for example, someone wants to go on a journey or to war wearing such an amulet, he will first cense it with frankincense, aloes, and aromatic gum, and then he will express his intention. Thus, if he is going on a trading mission, he will say, "May God open to me the gates of good fortune, to go quickly and to return quickly." Or if he is going to war, he will say, "I am going to war; may I go safely and return safely and may we vanquish our enemies."

The rules for wearing such amulets are that when a person goes to the lavatory, he takes it off, and if he lies with a woman, he takes it off. A menstruating woman may not touch any amulet.

Some people buy the Book of the People of Badr and sew it up in cloth and tie it around their necks so that the book hangs at their ribs.[9] This sort of amulet people wear on journeys or in time of war.

If a child has an amulet tied around its neck, it is firmly fastened, and the child is warned not to take it off or lose it or to allow a bad man to take it off and go and sell it somewhere or to take it to his own child; because people may not be able to buy amulets for their own children; but a thief can use the amulet, for its power is not lost.[10]

92   At the beginning or end of amulets like Ya sini is drawn a figure like this:

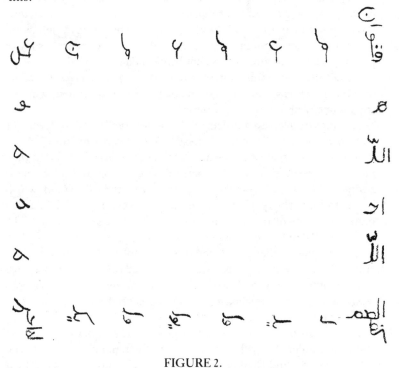

FIGURE 2.

That is, "Say, 'He is god, the One, God, the Eternal; he begets not, nor is he begotten, nor is any like to him.' "[11]

Chapter **11** Of Marriage

93   If a man wishes to marry a wife, first he must bring his suit, and that is why he is called a suitor.[1] For his suit he sends a relation of the woman to her father. This person is called the messenger.[2] When he hears and if he consents, he says, "Give me my shoe leather."

He says, "What is the charge for your shoe leather?" And they agree for a dollar to a dollar and a half; but some will do it for love. Some send the messenger to speak to the bride's father on their behalf, and some write a letter. When the suitor and the messenger have agreed, the messenger asks for his cloth. The suitor gives a cloth to the messenger, and the messenger writes, "To my elder relation ————, son of ————, I have to inform you that ————, son of ————, wishes to marry your daughter. This is a good match. A girl is perishable goods, like powder and fire or cotton and fire or onions. Please read this letter and let me have a favorable answer."

When the letter is finished, for its envelope is used the cloth as a sign of great respect. The messenger is given the letter to take to the bride's

94   house, and when the father has read it he calls the family, men and women, to discuss it, and some will be in favor and some against. Those who are against want to be given some small thing by the suitor, so when the suitor hears that there is disagreement, he sends something to the opposition, and now they will say, "There is no further argument; he can be her husband."

The father replies, "Your letter has arrived saying that ————, son of ————, wishes to marry my daughter. We consent." The messenger informs him of the answer given by the family into which he is marrying. Then he buys presents for his bride, such as fine cloths or good ripe fruit; but they do not meet from the day of sending money until the day of the wedding, whether this be a month or a year.

Immediately after the messenger has returned with a favorable answer, he sends him to ask the cost of "the turban" or "the things." The messenger goes back to ask the cost of the turban and the bride-price. The father replies, "My turban or our things are seventy dollars." Some will say sixty, some eighty, and some even a hundred. Then he adds, "And the bride-price of the woman is forty dollars." The price for a free woman is twenty dollars if she has been married before and divorced or widowed and forty for a virgin.

When the messenger has heard all, he returns and calls on the suitor and tells him what has transpired at the other house. If he agrees and has the money, he counts out to the messenger the price of the suit for him to take to the bride's father. If her father is dead, it is given to her brother or grandfather or, if they are not available, to another person selected from the male members of her family. If there is no such person, it is given to the woman herself.

95

To return to the father: when he has received the money, he calls all the members of the family to show it to them and divide it between them. The mother gets her *uweleko* for carrying the child—ten rupees—and a *kondavi* of five rupees.[3] If the father has a sister, she receives a little; if there is a grandmother, she receives a little; if the father has a brother, he receives a little. Every member of the family is given a little out of politeness, and the father retains the balance. They do not spend this money, but use it to buy presents for their child to give her on her wedding day.

If the suitor has not the whole sum, if, say, he has paid only ten out of seventy rupees, this payment is called closing the door or troth; because now the bride cannot receive the suit of another. If he has paid half, he is described as being betrothed, but having paid only half.

If they fall out and do not want him as a husband, they return him the money.

When the cost of the suit has been paid, there is no more to be said until he suggests a date for the wedding; but if he says, "I want to be married," they reply, "We hear you; but we want the woman's bride-price." The man says, "I have not got it now; but I will give it to you later. Let us agree on a period, say a year or more." Then they say, "We agree to the period that you wish; but write us a bond to keep." So the man writes a bond like this:

96

I, ———, son of ———, hereby agree that the bride-price for ———,
daughter of ———, is sixty dollars and that I will pay this in full within one
year.

Signed by me of my own free will.

Witness   1   ———.

Witness   2   ———.

A few days after this the man asks for his wife, saying to the
messenger, "I should like the wedding to be at the beginning of next
month." The messenger tells the bride's father, who answers, "Very
good, we are ready." He informs the relations, "On such day I shall
hold the coffee party." This is the duty of the bride's father; but the
groom gives it if he has the means and the father is poor.

Of the Coffee Party

No coffee is made, it is a name only. Buns are prepared and other
sorts of food. In the afternoon the tambourine is beaten.[4] The young
men wear their daggers and dance with their swords in their hands.
The women carry flowers and posies bought with their money.
Chiefly they buy frangipani of which they make a posy, and the
women give them to the dancing men, saying, "Dance, sir, dance," or
"Make the best of yourself, sir." The men respond to the drum:

> God is our help,
> There is no Lord but God.

or:

> God, God, our Lord,
> God, God, our requiter,
> God, God, our help.

They dance along slowly, so as to reach the wedding house about
six, although they started in the afternoon and it is only about quarter
of an hour's walk. On arrival the women trill, and one says, "Hi, sir,
hi, sir, hi, sir," and the others reply, "Hieee, sir." When they reach
the house, scent is poured out for all, both men and women. They are
given *betel* to chew, and some smoke cigarettes. The messenger has
been given a platter of mixed *tambuu*, which is betel nut with tobacco,
lime, cardamom, cinnamon, and nutmeg, all put together on the
platter. The messenger gives it to the assembled company to chew.

Then the people are told that they will be welcome on a certain day at nine o'clock, which is on the day of the feast, which is the day of the wedding. The invitation is given by a brother or friend of the bridegroom. When the day comes a servant carries a drum around the
98   houses to tell the people. To do this the servant carries a drum called *mrungura*, which he beats at each house, calling, "At nine the wedding reception."[5]

The people who were invited to the coffee party after beating the tambourine now at night play the *diriji*.[6] This is played like the portable tambourine, but in one place. The women sit on stools while the men dance in pairs with swords. The conductor holds a book and a tambourine in his hand and sings the verses, the people responding while he beats it.[7] The songs are the same as with the portable drum. Mainly they sing in Arabic; there is not much Swahili singing to the tambourine or the diriji drum. They sing:

> Lady, the child is crying too much.
> Lady, the child is crying too much.
> Give me my child to go, ah,
> Give me my child to go, ah,
> There where the water lilies are.[8]

or:

> Children joy, joy, ah.
> Oh God, children joy, joy, ah.

or:

> Do not trouble me, Wasiwasi,
> Go away from me, Iblis.[9]
> O, Lord, the rich Ruler,
> What the Lord wills will happen.

or:

99
> Lord, I am at the door, a poor slave,
> I stop at the door, a sinner I stand,
> With my hands, all ten fingers, I spread.
> I pray for mercy and forgiveness
> By thy grace, Ahmad, the precursor.[10]

or:

> O Creator of creatures,
> He is glorious, and praise be to him,
> God, the Lord of the worlds.

or:

> O God, O Lord.
> Ah God, ah God.
> God, O Lord God,
> Ah O God, ah.

or:

> Blessing and greeting
> To the intercessor,
> To the Prophet.
> God, God.

If the person giving the wedding can afford it, this dance is played for four or five days;[11] if he is poor, for one night only, because it is very expensive: morning and evening buns and other food, scent, tambuu, and cigarettes, for not ten or twenty people attend, but three hundred or more.

100

Of Inspecting the House

A few days before the wedding the bride's father tells the bridegroom to get a teacher to inspect the house. He goes to the teacher, who asks him his name and that of the bride. Then the teacher takes his board and calculates the two names to see if the house is good. Some teachers calculate the names from the *abjad* book; others need no book but take the board and calculate the values of the names without references.[12] First he takes a piece of ebony with the abjad written on it in letters separately, as, *alif* by itself, *be* by itself, *jim* by itself, *dal* by itself, each letter on a piece. Then he throws down the piece, and if he sees a letter from the name on the piece, he looks it up in the book of abjad under the letter that stands on the piece and so finds the value of that letter of the name.[13] To find the values of the other letters of the name, he throws again until all the letters are used. If at the first throw he does not see a letter of the name, he looks in the book under that letter for the value of its absence.

When all the values of the names are known, he adds them up. For example, if the man is called Muhammad and the woman Fatuma, the teacher will cast the letters of Mḥmd:

101   m   ḥ   m   d

            4   9   7   5

These total twenty-five. Of these twenty-five, thirteen have fallen, leaving twelve.

The name Fatuma is fṭwm:

            f   ṭ   w   m

            6   3   1   8

These total eighteen, of which nine have fallen, leaving nine. Thus, the name of the woman is less than that of the man, and he can marry her, for their stars agree. Their house is one, and there will be agreement in their house. But if the name of the woman exceeds that of the man, some men will refuse to marry her. Others change the name, the teacher saying, "Let us see whether with a different name this woman will suit you." For example, if Fatuma will not do, she may be called Lady Khadija. If that name is satisfactory, the bridegroom goes home and tells the father what has happened at the teacher's, that this name will not allow him to marry her. Nothing is said to the girl; but on the day of the wedding the father goes to the teacher with his two witnesses and the bridegroom. The bride does not go; she stays at home. Then the father tells the teacher to solemnize the marriage, and she is married under her new name; but the bride does not know that her name has been changed.

The reason for studying the names and for not marrying without this study is that it is bad if the house turns out to be wrong, as in the poem:

102   1. I begin in the name of God, Bismillah first, alone, without compare,
             the praised, the highest.

          2. To begin a little poem, with a variety of words, I am looking for inkwell, and
             paper too.

          3. Ink to write so that you may all hear. Have no doubt; my heart is
             pure.

4. Sheikhs and teachers have said for your understanding three things:

5. First, the majesty with the power and the message; common folk be not ill disposed; obey the Law.

6. Second, travel needs a man of understanding to observe the moon in the palace where he lives.

103   7. Third, marriage requires a man of tact to find comfort and to keep all well.

8. I will detail its qualities and make them clear so that everyone may know, because he clearly understands.

9. The house of the first sort, when I consider it, is dark with ill will, and there it is not well to marry.

10. The house of the second sort is where clothes are always good. It is a house of wealth and has people to care for them.

11. The house of the third sort has hard work and service; but the wife is not human; she flies into sudden rages.[14]

12. The house of the fourth sort, the brothers disagree and the parents are not at one. Here it is not well to marry.

13. The house of the fifth sort, the wife is fruitful; but one of them is not healthy and goes to an early grave.

104   14. The house of the sixth sort, the husband should not go to war. If he does, his bow turns back on him, and he returns sick.

15. The house of the seventh sort has blows and love. They never have enough to eat and are short of clothes.

16. The house of the eighth sort is bad, do not speak of it. The woman's clothes are ill made and the man's rucked up.

17. The house of the ninth sort is all coming and going; whatever they do, God takes it from them.

18. The house of the tenth sort, the wife has a tongue. When she is asked, she does not speak the truth, and she slanders all the neighbors.

19. The house of the eleventh sort is a house of longing for all that is far away, and the heart is far away.

20. The house of the twelfth sort, you all will be in sorrow. When there is a birth there is a shroud, and people mourn over them.

105   *Of the Cotton Ginning*

Four or five days after the coffee party, the men and women are again called by the messenger to the cotton ginning. The ginners are

women, and the men sit on the verandah playing *bao* or cards and
gossiping.[15] While they gin the cotton the women sing marriage
songs:

> I am so sleepy that my eyes prick.
> Make me a bed and a pillow
> Where I may play with a little jewel of turquoise.

or:

> A little steamer has come.
> Dress up ladies.
> Let us go to the consul,
> And he will raise the mast.[16]

or:

> I am not vexed; I am trying to love.
> Words are vain but not deeds,
> When a tooth is drawn there must be a gap.

When they have ginned all the cotton, they are given bananas to eat
with cassava, meat, and gruel, and then they go home.

106   Two or three days later the same people are again summoned by the
messenger, who goes to each house and says, "Ladies and Gentlemen,
you are called to the bride's father's house to sew the mattress and the
pillows." The mattress is sewn by craftsmen and the pillows, too, and
the people help to stuff them with cotton. The women sing their
songs, and the craftsmen are paid their wages when the work is done.
Then it is taken inside and placed in the bride's room. Over the
mattress are spread bedclothes. Then the pillows, three of them, are
arranged, and then they go home.

Of Other Arrangements for the Wedding Day

A few days after the ginning of the cotton and the sewing of the
mattress, the man is ready for the wedding. Those who live far off are
sent the messenger to tell them that on Friday the bridegroom will
enter the house. Those who live nearby already know and come to the
wedding of their own accord.

The bride's father buys rice, wheat flour, and butter and makes
buns, fritters, and pastries of all sorts for the wedding. He buys a goat

to garnish the feast. This is called the wedding platter, and the cakes are eaten during the seven days of *fungate* by the couple and by those who come to greet them.[17] The wedding celebration is usually held at the house of the bride's parents and lasts for seven days. On the morning of the wedding the house is decorated with crockery and seats and glass and scented with aloes and bottles of rose water.

107   *Of the Teacher Solemnizing the Marriage*

On the day when the bridegroom wishes the wedding, the bride's father, the groom, and two witnesses go to the teacher, or two witnesses are obtained there. When the father arrives, he says to the teacher, "I authorize you to marry my daughter to this man." Then they all sit down, and the teacher asks, "How much is the bride-price?" and they tell him what they have agreed. At this ceremony sweets are supplied for those present to eat when it is over.

The marriage ceremony starts with the teacher reciting the fatiha and the people responding. Then the groom turns to the teacher, who takes him by the hand and recites the marriage homily according to the verses of the Qur'an. When this is done, the teacher calls the groom by name, "Abdallah," and he replies, "I am ready, Sir."[18]

"Do you consent to marry Lady Asha, daughter of Faqihi, the bride-price being fifty dollars?"

"I do."

This is repeated three times, and the third time the father is asked, "Have you given your daughter in marriage to Abdallah for a bride-price of fifty dollars?"

"I have."

The teacher says, "I, too, give her in marriage." He recites the fatiha, and the people respond and pray for the married couple, saying, "May God bless your house and grant you good fortune, happiness, blessing, and mutual love. May you have children by the grace of God, the Lord of the worlds."[19]

The teacher's fees for the marriage—the groom gives two rupees if 108   the bride is a virgin. If she has been married before and divorced, his fee is one rupee. After paying these fees they go home.

Of the Wedding Day

In the afternoon her intimate friends and others come to scrub the bride. They take her to the bathroom and wash her and comb her hair

and rub her whole body with perfume and fumigate it with incense,
plait her hair and cut the little hairs on her face. After this she is given
other clothes to wear. They mark her eyes with kohl and a little on her
face, while they sing:

> Look as in a glass.
> Your husband is like a brother,
> Look as in a glass.[20]

or:

> When you deck the bride, the groom must deck himself.
> If you do not, people will call you a slave.
> He digs weeds. Ah, lady,
> He digs weeds at Silima's.[21]

or:

> She strays around into every hut,
> She is like a captain without a sailor,
> She is like a net, that lady,
> For every fish to come in.

109   When all this dressing up is done, after the evening prayer, the man
is brought to his wife's house by his friends with joy and celebration.
Some people drum him to the house. He is dressed in his best, kanzu,
joho, turban, sandals, perhaps his dagger and a sword or a walking
stick in his hand.[22] When the man reaches the wedding house and tries
to enter, the women oppose him at the door and demand their
entrance fee, saying, "We will have our fee to let you in." He produces
one to five rupees. If he tries to cheat the women, saying, "Let me in to
see my wife, and then I will pay you your fee," they will not agree.
        When he enters, the kungwi give him his wife, and he takes her
hand and greets her. This is the first occasion on which they meet.
The woman will not speak to her husband until he pays *kono, kipakasa,*
and *fichuo*. Kono is for taking her hand; he must pay to take the hand of
a new wife. Kipakasa is for her lap. Fichuo is for speaking with her,
because he has not seen her face or heard her voice. That is the
meaning of these fees, and he pays them. He may give her a ring as
kono or a bangle as kipakasa and a chain as fichuo. Or he may give
money according to his means, say, five rupees for kono, five for

kipakasa, and five for fichuo. Some will give more and some less.[23]
110   When he has paid these fees, the man goes into the outer room, and
the woman stays in her room. The groom drinks the wedding cup.
Then he puts cooked rice on a plate with meat, and it is carried for him
to the woman to eat. It is called the customary rice.

Meanwhile the young women are beating their tambourines and
cymbals and singing marriage songs. Thus a woman addresses a man:

> I have no use for a calico love.
> Buy a slave and put him in the house.
> I see plenty of sacks of maize
> But who is to pound it?

The man replies:

> You are to pound it; you are in the house.
> If you want a slave, go inland for one.
> Will you not pound sacks and sacks of maize?
> Are you too fine for that?[24]

or:

> Study the letter that I have sent you.
> If the Lord God is willing,
> I will come soon as your guest.[25]

or:

> I was in love, and my love betrayed me.
> I thought only of you and of no other.
> You, a sailor, run away from the surf?
> But it will catch you up.[26]

or:

111   Slave girl, Mwana Kombo, your mistress calls you in the house,
> Go and draw water until the cistern is full.
> There is plenty of water in the well and no need to wait.
> Who is guarded? A cultivated field is guarded
> Against birds. A pretty wife cannot be guarded.[27]

or:

> Refuse your husband? I did not ask him to come to me.
> I did not lay a trap, nor did I pull the string.
> He called one dark night
> And I let him in.[28]

or:

> My magic pouch is lost, and now it is in your house.
> Now I have no one to live with.
> If you cry with jealousy, you will grow very thin.[29]

or:

> Cut my throat, if you like, with a sharp knife,
> But do not lie to me with this and that.
> I am told that I am loved; but I see no sign of it.[30]

or:

> Poor me, my husband has gone on safari.
> He has returned where he was born.
> If I were a bird, I would go and join him!

or:

112

> I hear a rumor, what is it?
> Is it not mutual deception:
> Leave him to me, and I will show you the reason.[31]

or:

> I hear a story that the captain is raising his mast.
> If you go in, you will not find a mat;
> The silly frog watches the well
> Where the water is drawn.[32]

or:

> The bouquet of basil distresses me,
> When I enter the house I am bathed in tears.
> A good thing will not last: its life is short.[33]

or:

> Poisonous cake dough tastes ever so sweet.
> But when you eat it, do not munch too hard.
> Hold to the lee side, not into the wind.
> The water in the cistern is infested with rats,
> It is no good now and must be poured away.
> I have never seen poison being made into cake dough.[34]

or:

113

> The water of the pond is sweet, but no better than that of the well.
> If you wish to draw it, draw it honorably.
> A woman without love is like borrowed clothes.

When the people have finished eating the marriage platter, they recite the fatiha. Then men and women pray for the couple, saying, "May God grant you a good marriage, may there be good speaking and listening, may he increase your wealth, may he keep illness from your house, may he give you sons and daughters, may God preserve you from enviers, who have no god, by his grace, the Lord God."[35]

When they have eaten and recited the fatiha, the bridegroom takes off his clothes and puts on two cloths to have his feet washed. He wears one cloth below and covers himself with the other. He sits on a stool with his feet in a bowl or tray, and the bride's kungwi washes his feet while a slave girl holds the bowl of water. At the same time, the kungwi sings, and the women respond:

> We will wash the master's feet
> With water of Zamzam.
> We will wash the master's feet
> With water of Zamzam.[36]

or:

> In the helpers' tray
> Let them fall two by two.[37]
> In the helpers' tray
> Let them fall two by two.

or:

114

> Place rupees
> In the Swahili tray.

When the young people hear this song, they compete to contribute to the tray, one rupee or two or three, each according to his means, and he who has nothing is ashamed to approach the tray. When all have passed, the kungwi counts the collection. Then she calls the parents and they divide it into three parts, one for the kungwi, one for the parents, and one for the couple. The kungwi and the parents do not spend their shares; they use them for the necessaries for the fungate until it is ended.

After eating the marriage platter and the washing of the feet, the man goes to the bed. The kungwi brings a bit of muslin and spreads it under the bride. It is called *kisarawanda*. The man lies with his wife, and the blood of virginity soaks into the white cloth. Immediately after the man has finished his work, he goes away, and the kungwi comes and takes the cloth to show to her mother or grandmother or aunt that very night.

Further about the kungwi: They examine the girl before she is married to see if the hymen is intact. To do this they drop a chain into her vagina, and if it goes in the kungwi know at once that she has no hymen. When she is married the kungwi take a small chicken and cut its throat and put the blood on the kisarawanda, and that cloth is put under her.

When they want to go to sleep, a slave girl comes with scents, dalia, tibu, and boxes of aloe, and while the man lies on the bed, she anoints him all over, except his private parts, which she is not allowed to 115   touch. Then she is sent away, then the wife will take her husband to rub him.

To return to the kisarawanda: In the morning the kungwi shows the blood of virginity to the women of the bride's family, and the father is told by the mother. They are delighted and gather together to spread their joy abroad, singing the song of joy:

Guide, show the way.
The bride's father takes around the guard of maidenhead.

Because if they see no blood, they do not believe that the man's daughter has been found to be a virgin. If her father and mother have property, they give her her reward, a house or a farm or some silver object, a chain or a bangle. The groom too, if he can, gives her her reward, something that he owns. But if she was not a virgin, she gets nothing from her parents or from her husband.

If the man is impotent and cannot consummate the marriage, every
morning the kungwi ask the girl, "What do you think of this man?
What is going on? Time is passing." As the girl was asked, so, too, is
the man by his *watani*, who laugh at him and say, "Tell us, does she
kick you?"[38] Or they say, "He has turned into a girl." Some women
sing:

> This man can eat
> And sleep; but one thing defeats him.
> O, a little thing defeats him.

116   The man does his best to get treatment from the doctors, and if he is
lucky he finds one who can cure him. The medicine is a wild root
cooked with chicken. If the husband is useless, he will stay with his
wife for six months. If at the end he has not deflowered her, the law
sets her free. He pays half the bride-price, and the woman may be
married to another.

Of the Fungate

The six days following that of a wedding are called fungate. There
is no more feasting, only buns are made. Every morning men and
women come without invitation to call on the couple, men on the
groom and women on the bride; but her brothers may come inside to
call on their newlywed sister.

The greetings are—to the bridegroom: "Good morning, bridegroom," and to the bride: "How are you, bride?" She answers from
within, "I am well." Then they ask how she has slept. The woman is
not allowed to go out except for natural calls; but the man may go to
the outer room when people come to call.

In the afternoons the young men dance the *kiumbizi*, the dance with
sticks, and the groom may join in. At night they play the diriji, as we
have explained above when speaking of the *tari* drum.

Of the End of the Wedding

When the fungate is over, that is, the seven days inside the house,
117   the woman is sent to her husband's house. She is made a portable
cotton tent, a large curtain into which she goes with other women.[39]

Slave girls play on cymbals, and some of them have horns, and as they go they sing:

> Let the master come home.
> Let him go to his parents,
> His own parents, today.

or:

> Hurray, hurray, she is married.
> If you ask for toddy, you will be brought it.

They bring the woman to her husband's house, hiding her so that she cannot be seen.[40]

When they arrive, the husband calls adult women, relations of his or hers, for her to be shown over the kitchen. While she is being shown over, a great deal of food is prepared, and he invites any people he likes to eat this food, which is called "the showing of the kitchen." After this no further parties are given, and it is the end of the wedding.

Of Man and Wife at Home

When a man lives with his wife, she is allowed to do nothing whatever without her husband's consent. If he forbids something that he does not like, that is the end of it, and if the woman does it she is called recalcitrant, because she does not obey her husband. A free woman may not go out by day without excuse, except for natural calls. She must be veiled if she wants to go for a talk at a friend's house, and she must go at night between seven and nine, and she must be accompanied by a slave girl. If a woman disobeys her husband, it is for him to correct her; but for serious offenses he takes her to the magistrate for correction.[41]

118

Of Winning the Husband's Love

If a woman lacks the love of her husband or lover, she goes to a doctor and tells him that she wants a love potion.[42] The doctor brings out his pouch and a razor and makes a small cut over her face, into which he rubs castor oil from the pouch; or he gives her medicinal roots and says, "When you cook, put these roots into the food and give it to him; but do not let him see them." And the woman does so. Or he makes secret cuts, as in the groin, and says, "Persuade your husband to take you today, and you will win his love." Others have amulets made for them by the doctors, and if the husband asks what that is for, they say that it is only for illness.

The Customs of a Man with Two Wives

A man with two wives is in a difficulty.[43] He has to foreswear himself every day to keep the peace between them, for between cowives there is incessant jealousy. If he buys anything, he cannot come into the house to divide it. He must do so outside and then send each her portion. If he divides it indoors, there will be trouble. And food, too, he cannot eat a full meal at one house, because when he goes to the other and does not eat, there will be trouble. And sleep, he must share it equally, three nights here and three nights there, and whichever house he sleeps in, his wife must sleep with him. If he sleeps with one wife only, in the morning there is trouble. The other will complain to her parents that he does not sleep with her.

If he wants to marry a third wife, he must have the consent of the first two and must give them a present called "Reconciliation."

If he buys a concubine, he may not give her the same share of his sleep as his wives, but three nights with his wife and one with his concubine. If he buys clothes to give them, he must not give the concubine the same quality as the wives, or they will be vexed. But despite such fair dealing, there is no end to the troubles of a man with two wives. One wants this and the other that, and if they share a house, they disagree, particularly at night, if he goes to a wife when it is not her turn. The other will hear them talking and laughing, and in the morning there will be trouble.

When they quarrel it is most unpleasant. They bite each other and hit each other with sticks. Two wives should not be kept in one house. Some get along well, but not really. The customary treatment of two wives should be taught to a man thoroughly, or he should read about it in books. If he does not know it, there will be perpetual trouble.

Of Widows

On the death of her husband, a woman's *idda* is four months and ten days. On the completion of this period, if another man wishes to marry her, she will refuse, because she is still in mourning for her husband for a whole year. During her idda a woman stays indoors, wearing black or white clothes; but to do this the woman or her husband must be well off. Otherwise she cannot keep her idda, for four months involve necessities. So some keep their idda out of doors, saying, "I am a chicken; I have to find my food with my beak."

During her idda a widow may not do embroidery, use scent, or wear pretty clothes. The clothes that she wears during her idda may be washed when they are dirty, and she may wash her body; but she does not go to dances.

The reason for idda for a widow is to give time to ensure that she is not pregnant. That is why she may not be remarried during her idda. Idda is also a time of mourning for her husband.

During her idda a widow pays the customary dues. Every Thursday she sends oil to the mosque or she prepares food and invites people to recite the fatiha for her husband. Every year the khitima is recited at the grave or the house, and every *Dhu'l hijja* she buys scent, aloes, tibu, and dalia to take to the grave.[44]

If after a year a man proposes to her, she reports to her husband's brothers that she has received a proposal, and if they consent she may marry. If they do not, a brother of her dead husband will come forth and marry her and is called a husband of immediate entry. At this wedding there is not much celebration. The man marries her and goes in at once and gives her his hand. There are no dances in celebration.[45]

121   *Of Kissing*

It seems that in the old days our ancestors knew nothing of kissing; but now they have seen the Arabs kiss their wives and children and imitate them. If the Swahili are indoors with their wives, they kiss them on the lips, and to ask for it they say, "Kiss me, dear," or "Give me a kiss." They also kiss a small child; but after the age of seven it is not customary for his mother or aunt or sister or sister-in-law to kiss a boy. If his father likes to kiss him it does not matter. Her father or brother should not kiss a girl.

When his grandmother or his aunt or another woman comes, a child one or two years old is told to show his love for his aunt, and he goes to her. Then she tells him to kiss her, and he does so. Then he is told by his mother to show his aunt his tobacco, and he lifts his clothes and shows her his penis. She tweaks the penis and sniffs and sneezes and says: "O, very strong tobacco." Then she says, "Hide your tobacco." If there are four or five women, they all sniff and are pleased and laugh a lot.

There is another sort of kissing, when you meet a *sharifu* on the road or if a teacher is leading the prayers in the mosque or teaching in class.[46] When you come into the class you kiss him. But you kiss the hand, not the lips, of a sharifu or teacher.

Chapter 12 Of Dances for Enjoyment

122   *Of Ancient Dances*

From ancient times the greatest expression of joy at weddings or on other occasions is the dance.[1] If there is rivalry, they dance. All love the dance, the very old and the young. Even jumbes dance, for everybody loves it.[2]

The Great Dance (or The Big Drum)

It is originally the dance of chieftancy. For it two drums are placed on beds in the yard and beaten with two sticks. The drummer, unless he is a jumbe, bares his head and feet, and the piper, if he is a slave, has bare feet, and the horn player too; but a freeman retains his cap.[3]

After these drums the third great drum is set up on a log. It is called *mkuwiro*, and it is the most important of the great drums. When these drums are beaten, the people dance, two at a time. They must be

123   freemen: it is not the custom for slaves to dance the great dance. When the freemen dance, they bare their heads and feet. When jumbes dance, they do not bare their heads or feet. A shaha or waziri dancing with a jumbe takes off his turban but not his cap. The dancers hold swords in their hands and dance with them, and when a jumbe dances he has two attendant slave girls, who circle with him. This dance has no songs.

The Sendemre Dance

The most common competitive dance in the past was the sendemre.[4] For this a big drum is placed in the yard with two *chapuo*, a mrungura, a pipe, and a metal tray.[5] The big drum is set in the fork of a tree and beaten with two wooden sticks. The piper has a platform built for him in a tree. It is made of mats in the shape of a house. He has a bed made for him up there and a shade of betel branches. He plays and sings, and the people below respond with words such as:

We were together; now we are apart.
You eat from wooden platters; you have no plates at home.
Let us sew the Mtondoo people in a sack and throw it in the sea.

or:

The Sitirihali folk are slaves; let us use them as slaves.
No very sick person can meet with the Prophet.

or:

Do not incite me to sing,
124 Amri, or you will cry.
Your brother has built a house
And run off to Unyanyembe.[6]

In the dance the men hold swords, machetes, or walking sticks, and the women dance holding bunches of betel, and they dance round the yard. Then a man steps out of line and confronts a woman, and they dance together. This dance used to be danced on high days or wedding days or for fun or for competitions; but it is danced no more.

Of Competitions

In the old days there were on the coast many competitions. For this they said, "Let us form a society of one quarter of the town to challenge another."[7] They chose their leader, a vizier, a counselor, and a messenger. All affairs were referred to the leader—if a man died, or was going to be married, or was bereaved, the leader took charge. The vizier's business was that if any matter arose in the town, it was referred to the vizier, and he reported to the leader. The

125 counselor was consulted on every matter, and the messenger summoned the people, going to every house to tell them, "Tomorrow
there is a meeting at the leader's at nine o'clock, because somebody is
dead," or "We are going to a funeral," or "We are going to condole."
Then the society acted as one man. If anything happened to displease
the leader, all followed his instructions, and if at a party somebody
annoyed the leader, the party broke up.

In their dance competitions they danced all night for six or seven
nights of continuous dancing. They spent a great deal of money,
because if one society killed two goats, the other would kill four. On
the last night of the dance there was a party, and the visitors and the
local people were told. Every house made buns, and from every house
were sent three *pishi* of rice and one of wheat flour and butter and
sugar. If not, one house was in disgrace.

The song of the competitors is:

Mr. So-and-so, stop your gossip,
The wedding is tomorrow and the fungate next day.
You will be bankrupt; leave Gongoni alone.[8]

and the other society sings:

We ask for peace for the water to flow,
For the *kolekole* and the *kowana* to hide.
Do not pass where the enemy is.[9]

This is an account of the competitions; but now they do this less
than in the past, for "empty hands are not licked if they hold not a
single grain."

The Chando *Dance*

126 There are set up one chapuo, one *vumi*, a *mganda*, and a pipe. It is
performed in the yard by both men and women. They kneel down to
dance, and they sing:

Chando is indeed a dance [for adults],
How can you, a little girl, wander about at night?
Chando is indeed a dance.

or:

> We have come with the children to light a fire.
> We have come with the children to light a fire.
> The people of the house are asleep, not awake.
> Open the door for me to come in.

The Kigoma Dance

Originally this dance was held at weddings or just for fun. To it were invited men and women. When the women know that today there will be a kigoma, they get ready their best clothes and scent themselves. To perform the dance they use a house with a large outer room. The women stay on the roof with buffalo horns, and the men stay downstairs. One is the singer, called the *sogora*, two play the chapuo, one a vumi, and one a tray and one a pipe.

When the dance starts, the young men come out in their best clothes, with handkerchiefs in their hands. The sogora sings, "Here we are, here we are, you." Then two of the young men dance, and when they are tired two others relieve them. When the women see the men dancing, they trill on the roof, and they tie in a cloth chains or bracelets or rings to give to the dancers as their reward. Then the leader sings:

> So-and-so, son of so-and-so,
> Is dancing with his best friend.

and the men and women reply:

> Yoo yoo, sir, yoo yoo, sir,
> He is dancing with his brother.

or:

> Sleep, sir, sleep.
> Where you slept yesterday, sleep there today.

or:

> Like you, like you, like you, hee.
> Like you, like you, like you, hee.
> We shall get another as good as you.[10]

127

or:

> The way of the monitor lizard, the monitor lizard's way,
> Everywhere he goes, the monitor lizard's way,
> The way of the monitor lizard.

Finally at the end of the dance the rewards given by the women to the men are returned to the women. Those who have them ask, "Whose is this chain?" or "Whose is this ring?" The woman who owns it recognizes it and comes to take it. If the man likes the owner of the chain, he makes an arrangement with her and they become friends. But the flowers fastened to the clothes and called posies are taken by the men. They are made with cardamom and basil and treated with sweet oils. The kigoma is danced for three to seven days. There is no feasting, and the dancing starts in the afternoon or evening.

128

The Tinge *Dance*

This comes from inland. It is danced by men only and consists of buffeting each other without any drums. They arrange themselves in two rows, one on this side and one on that. They stamp with the right foot and then suddenly raise the right foot. If one raises and lowers it quickly and the other is too slow, he is captured and joins the other side. They sing:

> Who comes will be beaten—you,
> Who comes will be beaten.

or:

> The porpoise diving and coming up.

or:

> Friend, O friend,
> Move a leg, friend.

or:

> The tomato plant grows where you plant it.

or:

129   Who goes to Pemba, who goes to Pemba,
           Greet Mbaruk from Somanga.

or:

           Here is one, here is another,
           The tinge player is quiet.
           Here are two and another two,
           The tinge player is quiet.
           Here are three and another three,
           The tinge player is quiet.
           Here are four and another four,
           The tinge player is quiet.

and so on up to ten. Then they sing, "Here is none, and here is none."
    They cheer over the beaten side, saying, "You are tired, you are
tired." All respond, and they go on playing until they are tired.

The Kiumbizi Dance

This is in the form of a fight. They play the chapuo, the vumi, the
upatu, and the pipe. The dance starts at 4 P.M. and goes on until
midnight. It is danced under a tree that gives good shade, such as a
mango. The young men come dressed in their best kanzu, and the
piper plays:

           Come, devil, come, devil,
           We will whitewash him.[11]

130   The young men throw their sticks to each other, meaning that one
is inviting another to dance with him. They dance with the sticks, and
at first they dance properly with gestures, the sticks clashing together
with no ill will; but if one is dancing with one whom he dislikes, for
taking his wife or some long-standing disagreement, their enmity
comes out in the kiumbizi. When they wish to break off such a
kiumbizi at sundown, they play a *bondogea* roll, and they play with
thin sticks and dance with them.[12] Thin sticks are given to children to
learn the kiumbizi, and men use them for dancing with children.

The kiumbizi is now danced at weddings; but in old days it was danced at any time.

The Kidatu *or* Msoma *Dance*

This is danced by young women, *vigori*, *wari*, and married women.[13] It is danced at night, and it is danced in the yard, and the men come to watch. The women clap and sing.:

> Leave me, leave me,
> Ramadhani, leave me,
> Do not strip the whole tree,
> For a piece of jackfruit.[14]

or:

> Learning, you read learning,
> The Qur'an with jealousy is not Islam.[15]

or

131

> When a kigori is pregnant,
> She is partly a mwari—partly.[16]

or:

> She moaned, ah, she moaned,
> I am still but a mwari—and she moaned like a cow.

or:

> Leave off and take me again,
> Leave off and take me again.
> To be seduced is bitter.[17]

or:

> Not home, not home, Mkwaja is not home.
> You eat your grain, and I will eat my yeast.[18]

or:

    Bori's talk got him into trouble.
    First the flash, then the cannon.
    Bori's talk got him into trouble.[19]

or:

    He pounded the flour and licked it into his mouth.

or:

132   In the evening, in the evening, at the time of evening prayer,
    She was troubled because she did not please her kungwi.[20]

or:

    When Mwanakere refused the breast it was a disaster,
    And now Mparungo has set the whole coast on fire.[21]

This dance is performed by women in pairs, one pair taking over from another, coming out of the circle, and meeting in the middle while the others circle around. Sometimes they ask in a flute player, and they may pay him or he may play for nothing; but there are no drums.

The Mdurenge Dance

This requires two chapuo, a vumi, an upatu, and a piper. It is danced in pairs of one man and one woman, holding each others' shoulders and circling round the yard. The piper sings:

    My friend's lover loves me,
    Take a penny—he loves me.
    Take twopence—he loves me.

or:

    You search around and get
    A child, I have no doubt.

or:

> What will you do with two
> At Mwavi and Shangani?
> Let us set the coast on fire.[22]

133   *The Bondogea Dance*

Originally this is a dance of domestic slaves, and it is still performed in Zanzibar and on the coast. It requires one chapuo, a vumi, an upatu, and a pipe. The women take buffalo horns in their hands and the men machetes or sticks. They circle round, and suddenly one man comes into the middle to dance. When he stops, another takes his place. Women do not dance; some play the buffalo horn, and some merely look on. The piper sings:

> I am looking for Nasoro,
> He has robbed me of the money for my oil.[23]

or:

> Alas, she has broken her little bottle.[24]

The Sepoy Dance

The sepoy dance originates with the Indian police, who brought it to Zanzibar.[25] It requires two chapuo, a *dogori*, an upatu, and a piper. To perform it the men and some women have sticks. They raise their clothes high and look each other in the face, and in the dance they twist their necks. The song is:

> The sepoy slept out,
> The sepoy slept out,
> Because he had no wife.

or:

> You have taken my mate
> Today, Mazengo.

or:

134   I told you not to go
With Mtambalika.
What is wrong with you, you duck?
What is wrong with you, you duck?

or:

News of Zanzibar, there are mosquitoes and flies
The sepoys have been beaten, and the Nubians are dancing.[26]

or:

Are not yaws and scabies terrible diseases?
Even in the presence of your mother-in-law
Your hand is in front of you.

The Msanja *Dance*

This is performed in the yard or in the house with no pipe. It needs a dogori, an upatu, and a chapuo, and the women have horns. Men and women circle around the yard, and the singer stands in the middle singing, "Salim, you boast that you are the sultan's son," and the women reply, "Yes, by God," or "Eee nana." Then the singer sings:

I will sew my kanzu broad and long,
See how thin it is, like the sultan's tower.
Two clothes, sir, and begging for soap.

or:

135   The manner of Mr. Matthews all men desire,
When he puts on his coat to go down to the barracks.
When he takes betel nut to chew in his mouth,
When he wears silk clothes and thinks nothing of their value.[27]
A big gap between the teeth, not a cavity, makes a smile.

or:

Overseas, overseas, I trudge along to slavery,
When I go to wash, I must have a pot carried before and behind me.
I do not want you; I want a slave owner.

or:

> Clinging like the skin to the stone of a fruit.
> Who is skilled in love, tell me?
> He is skilled in love that has a loving heart.

or:

> I am very unlucky, and I know it.
> I am very quarrelsome, and there is no peace in my heart.
> Lord, I repent, I will not do so again.

or:

> Lord, if you love me, take me to Mecca,
> There will we perform the pilgrimage and speedily return.
> You are angry with me and I with you.

136   *The* Dandaro *Dance*

It is played in the yard, and its instruments are one dogori, one upatu, a chapuo, and a piper. It is danced by men and women. The women wear clappers on their legs, and the men carry sticks. They circle round stamping one foot after another, singing the refrains to each other. The leader sings, and anyone may join in. These are their songs:

> I go, I go from you; to return would be a shame.
> What course can I set to come to you again?
> I will not abandon my love, so well endowed.

or:

> Go away moonlight, so we may bring in the people of Brava.
> Come down into the valley, the flowers are in bloom.
> Do not think me too small; I can support you.

or:

> I rebelled at home to come to you.
> I do not want you; I want one better dressed.

or:

> Somangara, your friends say of you:
> "Somangara has taken gourds to tap palm toddy."
> May the day dawn; I find the *dandaro* a disgrace.

or:

> The master bought a bird that sang like a *kakatua*.[28]
> The slavery of Mr. Sefu endured till the sun went down.

137 ## *The* Kasangwa *Dance*

For this dance four drums are required, two chapuo, a *dogori*, and a mrungura, and also a pipe and an upatu. The people form themselves into a circle with the men on one side and the women on the other. It is a dance of confrontation. One comes out and preens himself before his partner and then returns. Then others do the same. Their song is:

> The girl's bed
> Has no mat.
> How vain you are.
> The girl's bed
> Has no mat.

The Mbenda *Dance*

This needs three dogori played by one man, a chapuo, an upatu, and a piper. It is danced by men only, dressed in women's clothes—*kitambi buraa*, *kaya za dismali*, and silver ornaments on their arms.[29] They dance with their necks, and they sing:

> Mlali, the great snake of Mlali.
> Shut the gate, beware of the girls.
> One of the Gobore has stolen an anklet.[30]

The Goma *Dance*

138 It requires two chapuo and a piper. It is a dance for men only. The women only look on. They dance with walking sticks. The piper gives the tune, and they respond together:

The *kisekeseke* bird
Was tied with a string,
The kisekeseke bird.[31]

or:

Stand up straight, Mbarangashi.
I have no child; whom shall I carry?

They circle around, and often they repeat together, "We are tired; we are tired," and the others reply, "Iyoo."

Modern Dances

For the banji they form two competing teams, one called *goboreni* and the other *seneda*. For the dance they build a hut for which is bought a bolt of calico sewn like a sail and called a canopy. It is raised on poles, and in the middle is set a flag. When the hut is ready they bring seats, and men and women are invited by the beating of the mrungura at each house to say that today there is a banji. They have their *mkuu*, one waziri, and a messenger. The mkuu and the waziri pay for their positions, and the banji is performed when the money is forthcoming. The candidates for office, all the members, and others collect the money. A man stands on one stool and the candidate on another. The first says, "May God appoint the mkuu." And the people answer, "Aaye." The man standing on the stool says, "So-and-so has come here wanting a dance and has brought so much money. Is he to be mkuu? Do you accept him?" All the people reply, "We do."[32]

On appointment he is given a name—"This is mkuu so-and-so." After appointment he is set on the stool, and the people raise the chair with him on it and carry him round the banji hut. The women trill, and the mrungura is beaten behind him. The money is divided among the members and the persons who have previously held offices. Then the banji is performed either all night or for three or four hours.

They go into the suburbs and make ready a party, to which are invited they themselves and all the people of the town. They often spend all day in the suburbs eating and dancing and then return with rejoicing to the town.

For the dance, some women sit on stools, and the *wakuu* and the waziri and the male wakuu and the members dance. For the dance, men and women are arranged, and they circle around singing:

139

140   Traveler, I pray for your safety.
        A drowning man does not cease to cry for help.

   or:

        Tell mother that I am in trouble,
        Tell mother that I am in trouble.
        We have outwitted the hounds,
        We have outwitted the hounds.

   or:

        The man who spends time choosing a hoe is no husbandman.
        I dance of my own free will; banji is no slavery.

   or:

        We have eaten 307 cattle,
        I do not want to lay eyes on Matende.

   or:

        Come, master, come;
        My master, ease my heart.

   or:

        Give me a pair, give me a pair and I will go,
        If you do not, I will give you no pleasure in rags.

   or:

        Binti Simba has teeth like a hippo,
        She is an adulteress and sleeps away from home.
        Maguru Kutimba can only catch flies.

   or:

        We will buy Noah's ark,
141   We will put the Seneda party in as crew,
        And they can haul the ropes and cook for us.

or:

> He did me wrong, he did me wrong,
> He stole my little piece from me,
> A rat did me wrong.

or:

> Desire is bad, desire is bad,
> Manga wore a dagger,
> But it came loose.

or:

> Do not speak, do not speak,
> I have outwitted the children.

or:

> You are called an adulteress who does not stay at home.
> I tell you the truth, my friend,
> Control yourself and stay at home.
> Must you say
> What is not sense?

or:

142
> I want to sing, my boy, but with whom shall I sing?
> I will sing with you, my girl, who are in the house.
> But you are half-blind and hunchbacked
> You have elephantiasis and syphilis,
> Let the man from Gobore go.

or:

> He roars like a lion, like mother,
> Aha, you are beaten.

or:

> Do not confuse me.
> If you do not want me—finished!
> Go away, go away,

Go and leave me alone.
A house full of crying
I do not want, get you gone.
Go away, go away,
Go and leave me alone.

It is the custom of the members, if anything happens in the town, or if somebody has done something disgraceful and he is a member, to sing his disgrace in the dance.

The Gobore and Seneda dance is now often danced, at weddings or for no reason, and the old dances are not performed much, except that occasionally they want a chando or a kiumbizi, or the women want a kidatu or a sepoy. Sometimes the young people at a wedding or just for fun want a goma dance performed in the old way. But the other old dances that we have mentioned are performed no more.

143   The Maniema nowadays dance their own dances frequently on the coast, and the Swahili go to watch.[33] For these dances they use a dogori played with no upatu or pipe. Both men and women dance, shaking their buttocks and singing, "Do not call Lubangula master."[34] The singing continues:

Response: "She cooked him vegetables."
Songora: "If you call him master, his head will swell."
Response: "She cooked him vegetables."

Chapter 13 Of Spirits

144   The Swahili, both men and women, hold polytheistic beliefs in male and female spirits.[1,2] If a woman has a three-day fever, she attributes to herself a spirit in need of reduction, especially if there is something wrong with her husband.[3] Her sickness becomes worse daily, and she does not leave her bed. When the parents see that their child is sick, they say, "Your wife has inherited her grandmother's spirit, and that is what is making her ill. When she was small we raised to her head the spirit of her grandmother, saying, 'Take care of this child until she grows up, and then we will give you your platter.'[4] Now her grandmother is dead, and her spirit demands its platter and has possessed its grandchild." If the husband does not attend to the words of his parents-in-law, people are offended with him and say that he is mean. They call him the one who has swallowed iron. But if he agrees with them that his wife has a *pepo* and that there must be a reduction, her parents are pleased and say that their daughter has a loving husband, and the woman agrees that he is a loving husband. He calls in a doctor to consult the omens, asking what is causing his wife's illness.

     "There is nothing more than a spirit."

145   "Will you treat her?"

     "First we must uncover the pot for her to see what is her condition."

There are two sorts of "pot"—stones and steam.

     For the pot of stones, "queen bread" is dug up. This is the fungus grown in white-ant hills. Seven lumps are dug out and set on fire, for this stuff is inflammable. A matting hut is built, and the sick person comes and sits on a stool. A hole is dug, and a pot of water is brought. Her face is covered, and the lumps are quenched in the water in the hole. She inhales the steam and breaks into a sweat. That is the stone pot.

The steam pot is made by plucking leaves that will steam and putting them to cook in a pot. The patient leans over the steam and breaks into a sweat, and with more of the steaming water she bathes her whole body. That is the steam pot.

Every day for seven days the pot is made ready from late afternoon to sunset, and she sits over it for an hour. She is glad when it is over, because she knows that she will soon be reduced. When the pot treatment is finished, they make ready for the reduction, saying to the doctor, "She is your patient; tell your other patients that we are going to hold a dance." The husband goes to the shop to buy the spirit clothes, red cloth, black calico, and white muslin. Trousers are made of the white and the red, and a hut is built either in the town or outside.[5] It is called a *kilinge*.

146   At sunset the woman is taken to the kilinge, and there a platter is made ready. In it are placed bananas, sugar, cane, raw eggs, bread, and all sorts of good food. At the time of evening prayer the possessed person has her face painted with black, white, and red spots, and then they start the sound to entice the spirit up to her head. They dance and sing the song of enticement:

> I pray thee, O Lord,
> Thou, O Lord,
> Undo my fetters,
> Thou, O Lord.

The people respond, singing for something like an hour. As the spirit rises, it shakes all her limbs. Then the doctor interrogates, that is, talks with the spirit; but what he says no one knows but the doctor and his patient.[6] The doctor orders the drum to be beaten hard, and the spirit rises to dance. The initiates dance, and the sound of the drum carries them away. Some of them fall down in the kilinge, and when they reach home they are themselves in need of reduction.

Whosoever takes part in such proceedings has to obey certain rules whether he is a doctor or not. A doctor or a person of importance in the town who comes to watch the dance should be given cooked rice in a cup to pour out in the kilinge as a sign of respectful greeting to the doctor. He takes off his cap and is given a stool to sit on.

This dance goes on day and night for seven days. If the spirit is a good dancer, it is given presents by the people; but these presents

147   belong not to it but to the doctor, the drummers, and the piper, for
        everyone who attends to watch the dance brings some money. This is
        not compulsory but voluntary. Every time the drum is beaten, the
        spirit dances and the people put money on its head.

           The sixth day is the day for the spirit to be named. This is the day of
        revelation on which it is disclosed whether it is or is not a spirit. It
        gives a demonic name that no ones knows, and when it does so all are
        much pleased.[7]

           The seventh day is the day of release. A goat is slaughtered on the
        shore, and all the spirits come together to drink the goat's blood. If
        anyone does not drink the blood, he is not possessed. When they see
        the others drinking the blood, the spirits rise into the heads of those
        into whose heads they have not yet risen. After drinking the blood,
        the spirit is carried home cured.[8]

           Swahili women and some men believe in the spirits and that if a
        person is possessed it must be reduced. If a woman is sick, she says to
        her husband, "Have me reduced." If he does not, there is endless
        trouble in the house, and she gets thinner and thinner. Men do their
        own reduction when they are possessed. Others say it is nonsense.

           I once had an illness of the back and limbs, and a doctor was called
        in to treat me. He brought me Dungumaro steam for seven days.[9]
        Then he said to my parents, "Mtoro has the Dungumaro; do not let
        him eat mutton or anything fried with onions." My parents believed
        him. One day he said, "He is all right now; but let us reduce him so
        that the spirit lets him rest." My parents agreed, but when my teacher

148   heard that I was to be reduced, he forbade me, saying, "Are you not
        ashamed to dance in the yard in the sight of everybody?" I was
        ashamed, and I told my parents that I would not be reduced. My
        mother was much frightened by my refusal, and when the doctor
        heard it, he said that I must not eat mutton and that if I did so I should
        die.

           One day my teacher was asked to a party and I with him. The Arab
        host had killed a sheep, and my teacher said to me, "This is mutton;
        are you going to eat it?" I said I did not know, and he said, "Put your
        trust in God; there is no spirit; it is nonsense." I ate the mutton, and
        when I went home I told my mother that I had done so. She was
        horrified and said, "Why did you do that? Do you not value your
        life?" I waited for five or six days and had no pain from head to foot,
        and now here I am in Berlin.[10]

Chapter **14** Of Spirit Dances

The Kinyamkera Spirit

There are many different sorts of spirit; but the first and most important of all is Kinyamkera, originally a pagan spirit.¹ They believe that it lives on the tops of hills. When a person goes there he falls ill in his head or eyes or belly. If other treatment fails, he is treated for Kinyamkera, that is, with Kinyamkera vapors. These are made of dry leaves. Each spirit has its own vapor; but all are made of leaves, which are heated on a potsherd to fumigate the patient, the vapor penetrating the patient's limbs. This is the fumigation, and if he or she recovers it is clear that he or she was affected by a Kinyamkera spirit.

When the person is well, the husband says to the doctor, "Hold your patient by the ear and keep up her strength, and next year we will hold the reduction." The doctor speaks with the spirit and asks it for respite for a year.²

The reduction of Kinyamkera: When the doctor is ready for the
reduction, he calls his female initiates and drummers—"On such a day I am holding a reduction, bring your drums."³

The initiates are women who have been possessed; but they have been treated, and the spirit has risen into their heads. When they went to the kilinge and the drums were beaten, the spirit rose into their heads. Or if she is at home and wants her spirit to come, she fumigates herself, and it rises into her head. If it has anything to say, the spirit speaks, and the people present hear. When the spirit leaves her, the

102   OF SPIRIT DANCES

people say, "Your spirit came today, and this is what it said," because
she herself does not know.

The man buys the necessaries for Kinyamkera—bananas, cane,
and eggs. At night the woman is taken into the country, where the
drummers are ready. The dogori drums for Kinyamkera are seven:
three *kirungura* placed together and played by one person with thin
sticks. The fourth is a big dogori, the fifth a metal tray, and the sixth
and seventh are chapuo. A chapuo is a double-ended drum. [4] When
the drummers are ready, the possessed person first has her head
shaved, then her face is daubed with red ocher, white gypsum, and
soot in spots all over.

At these dances a log is set on fire and kept burning day and night. It
is there by day also because its heat dries taut the drums. Every hour,
a single rhythm is given, and the drums are heated because they have
grown slack. The drummers bring them to the fire and tighten them
up. Then when they are beaten they can be heard a long way off.

The sick person dances with the others for the appointed period,
whether three or seven days, and the doctor sings:

> You, my girl,
> We will beat the tattoo for it.

They respond, and every hour the rhythm is changed and there is a
different song such as:

> Kinyamhunga,
> None like you,
> Kinyamhunga. [5]

When the dogori drumming is finished and the time has come to
break off, they make seven loaves of sorghum and six of ash with bits
of cane and egg and chicks and roast sorghum. The patient puts on her
head an empty flat basket and runs to her release under a baobab tree.
The others, the doctor and the rest, follow her, carrying the things.
When she reaches the tree, she falls down screaming. The doctor
takes his patient by the chest and sings the song of release—"Come
forth, Sengwa."
The people respond:

> Come forth, Sengwa, O come forth,
> O come forth, O.

152   The patient screams loudly as the spirit is about to come forth, and
        when the release is complete, the chicken is killed, and the little loaves
        of sorghum and ash are placed at a fork in the road. A little roast
        sorghum is scattered at the fork with the words "This is your food,
        Kinyamkera." Then they take the sick person home, and in the
        morning they wash her face and limbs. The doctor is given a fee of a
        dollar to a dollar and a half. The drummers have a dollar between
        them.

The Kilima Spirit

        The second spirit is called Kilima and is so called because they say
        that it comes from Kilimanjaro.[6] When it appears that a person is
        possessed, but they do not know by which spirit; they treat for all
        spirits, and the treatment that works they believe shows which spirit
        it was.[7]
        When it is known that someone has the Kilima, they agree with the
        doctor to release her. The doctor collects other doctors, the drum-
        mers, and a piper. A kilinge hut is built and its floor covered with
        matting. Beds are bought for the drummers to sit on, and the drums
        brought are two chapuo, one one-ended and one reversible, one *vumi*,
        and one metal tray put on a wooden platter to act as a sounding board.
        The piper stands on a box or a mortar.
        When they are ready, the patient is brought and fumigated, and the
        doctor sings the song to raise the spirit into the head:

153   Shivers and shakes,
            Trembling, ooya hee.
            When Kilimanjaro comes
            It comes with tremblings.

or:

            When Kiserere the powerful comes,
            The feeble one goes.
            It turns into a slow-moving snake
            And says, "Hee."[8]

or:

            I am tired of pounding for my sister,
            Give me some rice to pray to God.

The initiates take bells in their hands and respond to the doctor's song, and the piper follows the song on his pipe. When the sick person gets the spirit into her head, her chest is covered with a cloth and she dances, and as the other initiates do the same, they too are covered. As they dance, they have in their hands animals' tails or knobkerries. The head of the knobkerry is ornamented with metal studs, the decoration of the spirits as they dance. They have little bells fastened to their legs, and these ring as they dance.

The possessed persons dance like this for five days. The sixth is the day of the declaration of the name. The doctor says to the husband, "Today your wife will give the name of her spirit; we want our fee." He produces a dollar for the doctor. Sweets are made, and the platter is decorated with bananas and pieces of cane, egg, and sugar. When this is done, a turban of white and red is put on the spirit. It has two horns as a sign that it is a devil turban. On the payment of his dollar fee the doctor tells the messenger to tell the people that so-and-so has paid a dollar for his wife to disclose the name of her spirit. When the messenger has spoken, the people trill for joy, the drums are beaten, and all the initiates dance. They sit down on stools, and the spirit is asked its name and origin. In spirit language it says, "I am so-and-so, son of so-and-so," and it gives the name of the hill from which it comes. The people are glad when the name is given. If she does not tell the name, she is given *panjo*, that is, a small incision is made in the tongue, and she is given a medicine called panjo. Then she gives the name. If she still does not give the name, people say that she has not a spirit, because she has not given the name.

On this sixth day they drum day and night, and on the seventh they go to the shore to drink the goat. On their arrival, a goat is slaughtered, and a platter is brought to catch the blood. The spirits drink the blood; but the first to drink is the giver of the dance. When the goat's throat is cut, the spirit cannot wait for the blood to be caught in the platter; it falls on the neck of the goat to drink the blood, and when the people see this, they are pleased for so they are sure that she is possessed.[9]

After the blood drinking the doctor takes the goat and divides it among the drummers and pipers. The bread and the other things from the platter are divided among the doctor, the drummers, and the piper as their due. They stay in the kilinge all night, and in the morning the patient is taken home. Then the doctor is given the agreed fee.

154

155

The Dungumaro Spirit

If a person appears to have a Dungumaro spirit to be reduced, for the treatment a hut is built either inside or outside the town and is covered with matting above and below, and matting is spread on the floor. Stools are put in place and beds and a mortar. The beds are for the drummers to sit on and the mortar for the piper to stand on. The hut is protected with medicine for fear lest other doctors may come and put a spell on it and then the initiates within will fall sick. Then they begin the dance. It requires two chapuo, one dogori, and a metal tray. On the chapuo is played the catgut rhythm, and as they begin to dance the doctor summons the spirit to come into the head.[10] The summons is a song:

Leave, Lolo,
The time has come—to the town.
Leave, Lolo,
The time has come—to the town,
To possess her and make her sick.
O my pain, hee.
Leave, Lolo,
The time has come — to the town.

or:

156

Leave, Lolo, hee, Lolo.
Leave, Lolo, hee, Lolo.
Father Dungumalo,
Come and see
And be pleased with the water lilies.[11]

or:

Praise, praise, all of you,
Praise the doctors, hee.
Give me my cloth,
For me to carry my child in it.

or:

Yo hit me, Lelo, you hit me.
Simbamwene Mazi, you hit me.

We will give beans to Tatu.
Sholozi, you hit me.
We have at home a wonderful great goat,
Simbamwene Mazi, you hit me.
Father, in the town—wonderful.[12]

When the spirit has been conjured by these songs, it goes into the head. Then the drums and pipe are played and she dances. The other initiates help by dancing with her. Her chest is covered with a cloth, on her legs are bells, in the right hand a knobkerry and in the left a cow's tail, and her face is daubed with kohl. The dance goes on for the agreed number of days. If they are poor, they dance for only one day or two, without the mention of the name or going to the beach to drink the goat; but a promise is made to the spirit: "If you refrain from making your habitation ill, we will give you your due goat next year. As soon as the husband has made enough, it is he who will give you the goat." Then the spirit is reduced, and the doctor receives his fee.

157

If it is a spirit that requires the goat drinking, a *bene* is made on the fifth day; that is, a new mat is taken and sewn up with a little sorghum inside. It is put at the back of the patient as a cushion to support her until the day of declaring the name.

On the sixth day, when the spirit is ready to declare the name, into a pot are put water with medicine called *ushombwe* water, and this is placed before the doctor. Then the spirits come with their hands behind their backs and kneel down at the ushombwe pot and drink the liquid. The doctor receives a fee of one dollar, which he tells people is for the name. The people cheer, and there is a roll of drums for the turban. This is white, red, and black, and it too has two horns. On the seventh day they go to the shore to drink the goat.

The Galla Spirit

The Galla spirit is not very different from Dungumaro; but it is reduced with tambourines, without drums or pipes. The patient and the initiates have their chests covered with cloths, and the patient has in her hand an axe or a spear and a cow's tail. The axe is ornamented with brass studs and the spear with wirework. The spirit is conjured with the song

158

O God, O Lord of lords,
Smite him that smites thee.

or:

> O God, there is none but he.
> O God.
> If you are a doctor,
> Bend down and pick up the cow's horn.

or:

> Good, good, the daytime is good,
> Give me a board to sit on.
> Good, good, the daytime is good.[13]

On the sixth day, the name is declared in the same way, and on the seventh they go to the beach to drink the goat.

The Shamng'ombe Spirit

That a person has a Shamng'ombe spirit is known after she has had treatment for Shamng'ombe and recovered. It is then clear that this treatment cured her. The doctor tells her that she has a Shamng'ombe spirit and that she must not eat beef. If she goes out and beef has just been prepared but she will not eat it, people know that she has a Shamng'ombe. For the Dungumaro spirit mutton is forbidden and for the Kinyamkera spirit fresh food that has not been hung.

For the reduction of the Shamng'ombe spirit, the treatment is similar to that of the spirits already mentioned. First drums are beaten, two chapuo, one vumi, a metal tray, and a pipe as for Dungumaro. People say that Shamng'ombe and Dungumaro come of the same family. The patient is conjured by the song

> Lord Kisiki, Lord Manoru,
> I am tired of pounding grain for my sister.
> Give me rice and I will pray to God,
> I am tired of pounding grain for my sister.[14]

In five days, the name is pronounced, and on the seventh she is taken to the beach to drink the goat. The procedure is as described above.

The Dizzy Spirit

For the reduction of the dizzy spirit, a hut is built and matting is spread above and below. The hut is protected by censing all four corners of it. Similarly, when the dance is in a large house in which they have built a hut, it is censed. At every spirit dance the hut or house is first censed with vapor of the leaves of trees, and this is done for fear lest other doctors put a spell on the hut and then the initiates fall ill. Other doctors, seeing their rival doing the reduction, are envious because he will make money.

160   For the ceremony three drums are brought, one catgut chapuo, one reversible, one mrungura, and a piper. Its dance is performed with sticks. When the patient is approached, her clothes are tied around her loins to prevent them falling off. She is given a stick, and a man takes a stick, and they circle around. Then they crack the sticks together once and dance round again. The dance goes on like this. When one man is tired of dancing with the spirit, another man or a woman comes to dance with it. The song sung by the doctor is

> Allah, Allah, Mtelehi,
> This is a very fine goat.
> Allah, Allah, Mtelehi,
> When you come to slaughter it, call my son.
> Allah, Allah, Mtelehi.[15]
> Allah, Allah, Mtelehi,
> This is very fine bread.
> Allah, Allah, Mtelehi,
> When you come to cut it, call my son.
> Allah, Allah, Mtelehi.

or:

> I am hungry, I eat no beans.
> If I do eat beans, I only drink the juice.
> I am hungry, I eat no beans.

(This is a Zigua song.)
or:

> Majuma is married.[16]
> Let us chew the rice to reduce the dizzy spirit.

161   They dance for five or seven days. On the day of release the patient is taken under a tree for the release, and for this a bag of maize is boiled, coconut is broken, and all present eat it with the maize. Then the

patient is taken home. At this dance it is not customary for a goat to be slaughtered.

The Tambourine Spirit

To reduce this tambourines only are used. For conjuring it, maulidi responses are used, as in the treatment of the Galla spirit: "O God, the Lord of lords," or "O our Lord, none is like thee, O our Lord." When the patient dances she holds a sword in her hand and usually chews betel, for the juice of which she has prepared for her a cup with a white saucer. The cup is prepared with saffron and washed out with rose water. When she is approached, she shouts, "Peace be with you," and the people reply, "And with you be peace." Then the people give her their hands, and she stands up to dance. The turban is white with water lilies and pandanus fastened in it to give a pleasant smell.

They dance for the agreed number of days, and on her tray are placed good things such as bread, eggs, sweets, loaf sugar, bananas, cane, muscat nuts, cardamom, cinnamon, and betel. The patient continues to chew betel in which has been inserted things like muscat nut, cardamom, and cinnamon. She eats the sweets and the eggs, and the other things are eaten by those who are present in the kilinge.

When the agreed number of days is complete, she declares the name and is released. She has a pigeon killed for her; some people kill a goat; but the important part of the feast is the pigeon.

When she is taken to the shore to be released, she has made for her a dhow of the spathe of a coconut or of raffia. This dhow is fitted with mast and sail and loaded with food, bananas, a little cane, a little sugar, and a piece of bread. When the release is complete, the dhow is left in the sea to carry the spirit back to its home in the sea.

The Qitimiri Spirit

The Qitimiri spirit and the tambourine spirit come from Arabia. People believe that both these spirits are from the sea, while Swahili spirits they believe to come from inland, from the tops of hills or of big trees such as the baobab.

When a doctor undertakes to reduce a Qitimiri, he first takes his divining board to discover a suitable day for the reduction. For the divination he scores lines from the edge to the middle of the board. Then he draws little hooks to bring the divination to life. Inside the four hooks he writes a calculation, which tells which is a good or a bad day for the dance.[17]

163   The dance is held inside the house, which is protected with medicine. There are two drums, one reversible and a vumi, and there are a metal tray and a piper. The dance is different from those that we have described; it consists of running forward and backward, and when the patient is tired, she sits down. So the custom of Qitimiri is somewhat different from other dances; but on the seventh day they drink the goat in the same way.

The Pungwa Spirit

This is much danced in Kilwa and Zanzibar. It is performed in an open space with no pipe, but two chapuo, one vumi, and a can. In the space is set a mat, and the women sit on it. The doctor sings, and the women respond. The song is:

> Melons and gherkins
> Spread their tentacles,
> The coast is full of such.
> Going for wood and water
> Is a nuisance to the husband.[18]

or:

> You pass here and let me pass here,
> Where shall we stop? At Msagawi
> I saw a cat crouching
> Stalking mice in the roof.

or:

> Some medicine works,
> Other does not.
164 > The pox come out slowly,
> For the pox there is no cure.
> It is all the man's fault.

or:

> Where are they
> That roar on the rocks?

You, Bilali,
Will die of a dagger.

or:

War, war comes from Malimba,
Lady, can you deny it?
Of what have you eaten, Mashamanda?

or:

If I am quiet, do not say that I am silent.
You women trouble me,
Your slanders slander me.

When the patient is approached, she gets up and dances. For the dance men are on one side and women on the other. For the release they go on the seventh day to the shore and bathe with the patient. Then she is returned home.

The Paddle Spirit

165   The paddle dance is mainly performed in Zanzibar by the Hadimu and Tumbatu. For it a hole is dug in the yard and a pole is set up, supported by stones so that it may not fall down. To it are tied twelve cords. The dancers hold the cords and circle around. Then they kneel down, and the doctor sings:

Put in the paddle,
And the paddle.
When the sail is to the mast,
Put in the paddle.

or:

Shipwright,
Put in the pole.
And the paddles, you,
And the paddles, you, you.
Have you not said enough?
It is the rock of Kitame
That wrecks ships.
Paddles, you,

Paddles, you.
Have you not said enough?

I go carefully
to the rock of Kitame.
Paddles, you,
Paddles, you,
Since yesterday.

or:

Lady Makame, how did you fall in?
I fell at Malindi into the Singwaya River,
166   The river Singwaya, the river Singwaya.
I fell at Malindi into the Singwaya River.

or:

The guards, my dear,
Look out for the guards.
They were given a pole to guard,
Look out for the guards.

or:

Go to prayer.
Prayer is not prayer
If you only dip your clothes.
It is all nonsense,
Let my child go.
Paddle spirit, ho!

The paddle dance has no pipe or drums, but songs and responses. On the day of release there is no goat. They cook cobs of maize and eat them with coconut. This dance lasts only one day. The release is at 10 P.M., when the doctor takes the patient by the chest and squeezes 167 her right hand. Then the spirit leaves. This method of release is used for all the spirits that we have mentioned above; it is done after drinking the blood of the goat.

The European Spirit

The people believe that this spirit comes from the European sea. Its dance requires one chapuo, a vumi, a metal tray, and a pipe. When the doctor conjures the spirit, he sings:

I have white things.
I have white things.
If you men stay on the verandah
You slander the women.
You withhold your own, gentlemen,
And want us to give you ours.

The patient and the initiates dance for the agreed number of days.
To eat they have toast and biscuits, eggs, unripe coconut, mangoes,
oranges, and bananas.[19] The spirit enjoys eating these. On the day of
pronouncing the name, the patient is released. There is no drinking of
the blood of the goat; but the chest is held in the hand, the doctor
conjures, and the spirit leaves.

Chapter 15 Women's Work

Housework

Women do the cooking in the houses, and when the food is ready they dish it up for the man.[1] They wash the vessels of the house and the master's clothes and their own and sweep out the house and go to the well to draw water if they have no slave. At night she makes her husband's bed, massages him and oils his feet, and soothes him until he goes to sleep. By day, after eating she takes her hank of raffia and plaits a mat. Some make buns or cakes for her child to go and sell, or split wood into bundles for sale.[2] Some sell cassava or sorghum flour, and some buy raw fish and fry them in sesame oil with red pepper and sell them for one pesa or if they are short at two or three pesa. Others brew beer. When they intend to brew, they pound cassava and sieve the flour. Then they soak sorghum for seven days and then pound it. They boil the cassava flour for two days and then take the sorghum and mix it with the cassava flour, and this is boiled again for one day. Then they leave it to cool and strain it to remove the husks. Togwa is made in the same way as beer but with little cassava. It is often made of sorghum only, and then it is excellent.

When a Nyamwezi comes to the coast, he greatly likes to drink beer. Women make a profit out of it, because they sell a *kibaba* for a pesa. Some of the Swahili also drink beer.

Others sell toddy, strong and sweet, but the sweet is not much used.[3] The women make agreements with the Segeju, who tap the toddy from the coconut palms. Every day the woman goes to the tapper to fetch a vessel of toddy to bring to the town for sale. Others sell it in the country, where there are more drinkers than in the town, because in the country if they get drunk they make a lot of noise, singing and dancing, but this is not allowed in the town.

Drunkards have their own songs that they sing to the *kinanda*:

> Come down the Kizingo road.
> Find a corpse with a split,
> Cut it into little bits,
> Put it in a cracked pot.
> The brewer must have a hump,
> The user must be a cripple,
> There's a thing, Maua.[4]

or:

> The child Abdallah cries,
> His mother has given birth.
> She has tied a dagger to her loins
> Worth a hundred dollars,
> He remembers her beauty and cries.

170

or:

> He bangs and bangs, the sorcerer bangs,[5]
> The sorceror bangs, the sorcerer bangs.
> Tobacco is the cure.

To return to the tappers: When the Segeju wake up they climb a palm tree; but they cannot lift their eyelids for the toddy still in their heads. So the Segeju often fall drunk out of the palm tree, because they are so drunk.[6]

Plaiting Hair

When a woman's monthly period is over or she wants her hair plaited again, she takes it down and combs it with a wooden comb. Then she washes it in hot water until it is quite clean. Then she puts fragrant oil in a cup and goes to the hairdresser, saying, "I have come to you, dear, to plait my hair." The hairdresser asks her how she wants it, *mardufu*, *za kufundika*, or this, and she chooses the style that she wants.[7] The hairdresser sits on a stool and the client on the ground in front of her, and she plaits and gossips. They gossip about every-

171   thing that goes on in town, and this goes on until the hair is done. Or
        they sing:

> Do not be so jealous, Sitahamili,
> Is your man to be always on your back like a lizard?[8]

or:

> We two were in love
> And my heart was like the day.
> You will kill me, young man.

or:

> Sweet bananas are expensive,
> I have lost the egg where my jewel was.[9]

or:

> A letter came to us
> From Nur harbor.
> Mr. Salehe and Hamadi
> Are the best.

Of Cleaning the Teeth

        They clean their teeth with a toothbrush.[10] This is a stick or a root
        of a tree called *mswaki*. They chew the point of it into a brush, and the
        bristles poke into the teeth and clean them. If a person's teeth do not
        shine because they have been spoiled by betel or because they are not
172   shiny by nature, they burn betel husks and grind the ash and clean
        their teeth with this. Or they take charred wood and grind it and rub
        the teeth with it until they shine.

Cosmetics

        On the day when a woman wants to look her best, she asks her
        husband or her man for money, and he gives her a rupee or a rupee
        and a quarter.[11] She buys sweet oil and goes to the hairdresser to have
        her hair done and gives her twenty pesa or half a rupee. Then she buys
        aloes, rose water, tibu, and dalia and all sorts of scent and goes into her
        room and tells her companion to scent her all over. She lights a censer

and puts aloes on the fire. She puts on her best clothes and impreg-
nates them with the vapor. Then she sprinkles herself with rose
water, and if there is jasmine outside she buys it to spread on the bed,
and some she puts aside to go on her chain, and more she puts on her
string to wear around her loins.

Further, with the scents that she has bought, when they are ready
for bed at night she heats some water, and when her husband gets into
bed she washes the dust of the day off his feet with the hot water.
After washing him she oils him. When a woman takes a man's legs the
custom is for her to greet him first, saying, "I hold your feet," and for
the man to reply, "Thank you." She asks him if he wants her to
massage him, and if he says yes, she puts tibu in a cup and water in a
basin. Then she rubs the man until she has done the whole of his
body.

173   *Scents*

The most important of the scents is aloe. This is made of twigs
imported from Muscat boiled with water and fine oil. Coast people,
especially women, use its vapor. If a woman wants to go for a walk,
after washing her hair, she spreads the vapor around her and then puts
on fresh clothes. A man is pleased if she smells of aloe.

The second scent is benzoin, a powder from India and Arabia, and
it is cooked up with other scents. Its use is when a person has fever or
is chilly after being out in the rain. He inhales it, and the fever or the
chill leaves him.

The third scent is tibu, a mixture of many scents. First a stick of
wood called sandalwood is ground on a stone known as an Arab stone.
The sandalwood is ground fine and mixed with rosebuds and cloves
and put out in a cup to dry. This is used for rubbing in at night.

Other scents are musk and saffron, used together. The use of the
smell of basil is for nosegays made of basil and pandanus. Women tie
them on chains to sniff. Some people offer nosegays for the women to
buy.

The use of the smell of jasmine is for it to be put in the clothes or
spread on the bed or made it into posies to be sniffed as desired. Oil of
aloe is better than any of the scents that we have mentioned. An
elegant woman uses it in her clothes. Rose oil, jasmine oil, sandal-
174   wood oil, and Turkish oil are also used in clothes.

Rose water and sandalwood are also used for Hal Badiri.[12] If
somebody loses something, he goes to a teacher for a Hal Badiri to find

it. After the recitation, rose water is sprinkled and sandalwood is burned. These are also used at weddings and funerals. After a winding sheet has been made, it is impregnated with sandalwood and sprinkled with rose water. Finally, people sitting on the verandah are sprinkled with it.

Matting Work

For a mat people cut *ukindu* fronds of the phoenix palm in the bush.[13] This palm has leaves like those of a date. They are put out in the sun, and when they are dry they are brought into the town for sale at one pesa the bundle. Some is shipped to Zanzibar or to other parts of the coast. The women who get it tear it into thin strips and plait these into two sorts of *ukili*, black and white.[14] There are two sorts of mat, white and common. The white is used for winding sheets when somebody is dead, and the common sort is used to sleep on, to put on the floor, or to be sent to the mosque.

To make the common mat women take the ukindu and dye it. The dye comes from the *mdaa*, a wild tree with black roots. The country folk dig these and bring them to the town for sale, and the women buy them at one pesa the bundle. When the ukindu is boiled it turns black with the color of the mdaa.[15]

175   The second color is made by steeping the ukindu in water with alum. After four days it turns pale yellow.

The third color is madder, sold by Indians. It looks like little roots. The ukindu is boiled with the madder and takes its color.

The fourth dye is mkumbi yellow, made from the inner bark of the copal tree, boiled with albizzia.[16]

When a woman wants to start a mat, she first plaits thirty *pima* of white ukili and then thirty pima of black, and then she makes a common mat.[17] To start this she takes any of the ukindu that she has prepared, black, red, or yellow. She takes one handful and arranges the beginning as she likes. Then she decides the pattern, "moon," "stars" or *kanga*.[18] There are many names for the pattern of ukili. One is called "cloves" because its color is similar. One is called *gongo*; it is mixed red and yellow. There is a bird called gongo colored like this.[19] There is a pattern called "gem ring" because it looks like gems in a ring; or "bird," because it resembles a bird's feathers; "fly," because it looks like flies; "fish trap," because in the plaiting little holes are left as in a fish trap; "red spangle," like the ornaments on an Indian woman's dress; "coral necklace," because it has little raised balls. There are many patterns, "pipe," "roll," "love," "bracelet," "coral," "good work," "eyeball," "lizard."

176 Each piece of ukili is twenty pima, and she takes white and black and sews them together. She measures and sews until the mat is complete. Finally she cuts off the loose ends and folds them down, and the mat is finished.

A prayer mat is similarly made; but it has curved ends.

The *jamvi* is made of doum palm.[20] People cut the leaves and dry them, split them, and plait strips of fifty pima. They start the jamvi according to the measurement, hemming it when they reach the end. There is only one sort. It is used at weddings or at funerals. A big jamvi is spread, and mats are put on it, and the people sit on the mats.

Chapter 16 Men's Work

Of Swahili Petty Trading

Trade: Some people are unwilling to travel inland. If a merchant offers to supply the goods for him to go trading, he refuses. Such people hawk their goods around the town in small quantities. They buy coconuts, maize, sugar cane, groundnuts, sweet potatoes, cassava dried and fresh, oranges, bananas, jackfruit, and so forth and put them in little heaps that they sell for one to twenty pesa each. They make little profit, just enough for themselves and their wives. It just suffices for oil and betel nut; because if she is in the dark or has no betel in her casket, she is vexed and says, "Are we to sleep like bugs?" (The Swahili keep a light burning all night for fear of a snake coming in or of being stung by a centipede or a scorpion.) If somebody says, "Why do you not travel?" he replies, "I do not want to be rich. All I want is a pot on the fire. The rich man will die, and the poor man will die too. Why go inland and have a lot of trouble in the bush? Then all the risk is mine. If people's property is lost, I shall be in trouble or lose my life. I would rather eat roast cassava in peace."

Other petty traders wait for the Nyamwezi to come to the coast with their cattle and goats. They make it their business to buy cattle from the Nyamwezi and to sell to the Indians or Arabs. If they cannot get a good price for the cattle, they slaughter them and sell the meat. Some of them roast *mishikaki* and sell them for one pesa each.[1] Those who have not enough money to buy cattle make agreements with the Indians or Arabs. Such agreements are—"You go to the camp and buy for me, and I will give you two to four rupees' commission on each beast." To this they consent.

Of Fishing

Some are *ngalawa* fishermen.[2] They get up early and immediately take their sail, paddles, bailer, rudder, and lines. When they come to the beach, they launch the ngalawa, and when it is afloat they fix the tackle and raise the sail. They fish far out in the deep water where there are sharks and big fish. There they throw out the anchor, bait their lines, and cast them in.[3] When the wind comes up they raise sail and return. Some are lucky and some have empty boats. When those who have been unsuccessful are asked, "What luck?" they reply:

179

The water is dead,
Fisherman dead.

If there is a dead calm with no wind, they paddle or tow, singing:

Plunge in the paddles,
Plunge in the paddles.
If the sail is against the mast,
Plunge in the paddles.

Others trap fish in a trap made of wood. At low tide they take the *dema* out to a rock, sink it, and bait it. For bait they use a sort of seaweed or kingfish heads. When they have set the traps, they sleep until morning and then go to inspect the traps, haul them into canoes, and collect the fish.

Arabs and Digo fish with seine nets. When the Digo go to sea they beat a drum on return to let people know that the Digo are back. The Digo are great fishermen. They live in all the towns of the coast, and when the country folk hear, everyone comes with his money because fish is being sold cheaply. All sorts of fish come into the nets of the Digo. They sell the fish wholesale, as do also the ngalawa fishers and the trappers. Fish retailers buy the fish and put them on split sticks

180

and dry them over a fire to stop them going bad. If they do not do this, the fish rot rapidly. They sell one fish for three to ten pesa, and if sales are slow, they give the fish to children to put in baskets or on sticks and hawk them round. Fishing is poor at neap tides and good at springs.

Women also fish. As the tide ebbs they go to the sea to spread cloths for sprats or whitebait. For this they sew two or three pieces of cloth together to make one long piece. Then they take a large basket and go into the water up to their knees or chests. When they see the fry, either *madagaa* or *ushimba*,[4] they say, "Down with the cloths." Two of them hold the cloth, and one herds the fry into it. They gather both kind of fry together and put them in the basket. They catch a great many and even quite large fish; but there is some danger. This is the *nyenga*, a small ray that lives in the cracks of rocks.[5] When it hears the cries of the women, it comes out of the cracks, and there is danger that it may sting someone on the foot. But the women have a cure for this. If a woman is stung by a nyenga, another comes and spits on the place stung. When she gets home, she is given a medicine of roots. If she does not have this, the sore goes on and becomes chronic and never gets better. When they have caught fry of either kind, they sell it at one pesa a portion. Some they dry and send to the country to exchange it for cassava, because the country people have difficulty in getting anything tasty.

181   At night, when the moon is full, the women go down to the beach to look for whelks or cockles, which they take home and put to boil in pots. When they are done, they shell them. Others wait for low tide and go to poke out rays, cuttlefish, and mussels. This is dangerous because of eels. When the tide leaves the rocks, the eels come out. They are as long as snakes, and some eat them and others do not.

Fishermen's Songs

People who put to sea in ships and boats sing these songs:

Blow, north wind,
Blow the dew.
Let us tow the master's dhow,
Lest it go astern.

or:

Is it there? Is it on the rocks?
Is it there? Is it on the rocks?

or:

The vessel is rolling,
The vessel rolls, is rolling.
Keep to the weather side, captain,
The vessel is rolling.

or:

182   I want Zaina to play with her.
        The girl with the young breasts is here, hug her.

or:

        I love you, I love you,
        With my whole heart,
        From the day I was born
        Of my father and mother;
        I love you, I love you,
        With my whole heart.

or:

        I love her well. I love her well.
        A little lady, a pretty girl.

or:

        Give me two and I will go.
        If you do not
        There will be no ecstasy.[6]

or:

        Come, sir, come sir, come,
        Take my heart, my master.

or:

        What a disaster!
        Hamadi was no thief,
        Why was he jailed?

or:

        With my little ship I am off to Pemba.
        The big ship of the pilgrimage has sailed.
        Thank you, Sefu, for what you did for me, Sefu.
        Thank you, Sefu, for what you did for me, Sefu.

or:

183   I have my darling, slim and fair.
           I love her eyes and brows and lids.
           I love you, give me nothing.

Of Shipbuilding

First the builders go to the forest to split planks and to find a strong
keel and strakes and ribs. When they have these, they bring them to
the town, and ask their master craftsman and the teacher to cense
them as they begin their work, so that it goes well.[7]
First the keel and the ribs, the stem and stern posts and the guide
plank. They fix the planks with nails wound round with cotton and
coconut oil to make them firm. When the ship is finished, they deck it
fore and aft. Then they caulk it by filling any open holes with cotton
and oil. Then they proof it with shark oil and fill the ship with water
for seven days or fourteen to see whether it leaks or not. Then they fit
the tiller, and when that is in place they sew sails and select a mast, a
bowsprit, and a yard and an anchor. Then they spin ropes for hoisting
and for lowering the anchor, and the ship is launched.

Of Launching a Ship

When it is finished, the people are told, "Tomorrow the ship will be
launched. Meet at the shore in the morning." Nyamwezi and freemen
184   come together. The Nyamwezi haul the ship down for a fee and the
freemen for love. As they haul the ship down they sing:

           Hand over hand.
           Peace on high.

And they continue the song until the ship enters the water.
Three days later it goes out to try the mast and sails. People go on
board; but they pay no passage money. The ship goes out for the
whole day and returns in the evening. When the anchor is down, the
builders expect a present, and the owner pays them because it is their
due.

Carpenters building a ship sing:

Tell mother to pray,
and I will pray.
And he to whom we pray is the Lord.

or:

Split the planks and we will build,
Split the planks and we will build.
Carpenters, split the planks and we will build.

The song for raising the sail is:

Haul, by God! Haul, by God!

or:

We will raise the cow in the Nyamwezi style,
We will raise the cow in the Nyamwezi style.[8]

185   *Songs Sung at Work*

People like to sing at their work. They sing:

First today, first today.
In the morning and early
First we will pray to God.

or:

The slave girl has sharp teeth and bites.
I want her no more, send her to the country,
and let her dig.

or:

At Mother Yaya's
Today at Mother Yaya's
Are cassava and sweet toddy,
Let us eat at Mother Yaya's.[9]

or:

I will plant my own beanstalk.
I want a divorce.
The name "husband" is just a thing.

or:

Do not be so jealous, Sitahamili,
Is your man to be always on your back like a lizard?[10]

or:

A *suria* is still a slave,
Today the suria is still a slave.
Do not think about lying on a mattress,
A suria is still a slave.

or:

Clear the ground, clear the ground,
Hemedi's daughter
186   Hoed a clove tree.
Clear the ground, clear the ground.

or:

This, Magwangwara,
Is bitter cassava.
You will be sorry.
There is no god but God.
Feruzi was killed.

or:

Welcome the stranger, yoo yoo;
Welcome the stranger, yoo yoo.
On the first visit,
Welcome the stranger, yoo yoo.[11]

Chapter 17 Concerning Cultivation

Of Customs relating to Cultivation

When a man begins to clear bush for the purpose of cultivation, he prays to God, "O Lord, grant me to sleep with health and to rise with strength to clear my field, to plant, and then to eat; if not myself, then my children."[1] He then fells the trees, cuts up the trunks, and burns them. When the rains come, he plants first peas, maize, beans, and pumpkins, which grow easily and stave off hunger. On the second rains he plants cassava and other crops.

When he plants trees with edible fruits, such as banana plants or coconuts, he says, "As I plant this, may God give me health to eat of it, or if that is not to be granted to me, then may my children eat of it." When he is ready to plant, he has need of a mkumbi shrub.[2] This is a shrub kept by the Zaramo, and if it is near his planting, he goes to the Zaramo for mkumbi and mixes it with his seed. They believe that a field planted with mkumbi will flourish at the time of harvest. Mkumbi is a bark and is yellow in color. At the time of harvest the supplier of mkumbi is given as his due two or three pishi.

When the crop begins to get ripe, they build a *dungu* to keep away the birds. This is a tripod made of poles, on which are laid sufficient poles to support a man. The bird scarer uses a sling and mud pellets. He keeps watch to stop the birds alighting on the sorghum, and when they do so he keeps them off with his sling, shouting, "Aaah, haooo, birds" and casting a sling pellet. Bird scarers sing:

Birds, do not eat people's grain,
You will be killed.

or:

Kuikui is dead.
Our child has been made bird scarer.[3]

This song comes from the old tales told by our elders, and that is why
people like to sing it when scaring birds.

Of the Harvest

Men go out with billhooks to cut the sorghum stalks over the whole
field. They do not take them straight home but leave them for three
days before bringing baskets to carry them, and then they thresh
them. For threshing they spread out a jamvi, and each man takes a
long stick.[4] They beat the sorghum, and the grain falls out. Then they
sift it and put it in matting bags. If a friend comes to call, they break
for him a cob of maize and thresh it and put it on a saucer for him to
eat. When he leaves they break off for him three cobs as a present. At
189   the rice harvest, too, if a friend arrives an ear of rice is broken for him;
the woman fries it, and it is brought to the friend to eat. And,
similarly, when he leaves he is given three ears as a present. A man
who has a large crop of rice or sorghum puts some aside as alms for the
poor.[5]

They do not eat fresh grain without benzoin. Many of them suffer
from spirits, Kinyamkera, Dungumaro, Shamng'ombe, and so forth.
They inherit spirits as they inherit property, and if a man with a spirit
eats without benzoin he will have fever in the evening or some other
illness.[6]

The cassava crop: At six months if a man is in need he can lift a plant
of cassava and cook it and eat it; or he can leave it in the ground until it
is a year old and then lift it.[7] It is skinned and dried for three or four
days, and when it is dry it is put in sacks or bags. There are two sorts
of cassava, bitter and sweet. The bitter is called *nangwa*. It cannot be
eaten fresh, but when it is dried and cooked into a porridge, it can be
eaten. Cassava over which a snake has crept cannot be eaten as
porridge, but it can be used for beer.

The Swahili like a cassava field, because there are many different
ways of preparing it for food, which they like.

190   *Of the Cultivation and Use of the Coconut*

A coconut palm starts as a seed coconut with the husk on it. This is kept indoors until it is dry and then taken to the field to be planted. They sit on the ground if they do not want it to grow very tall; if they do, they squat on their haunches. It is planted on a rainy day, and the ground under it must be damp. It must be the fourteenth day of the month when the moon is full.[8] It takes six months to a year to shoot. After three years it produces leaves. In five years it has a trunk, and in the seventh year it begins to bear.

In bearing it first puts out the flower cover, which carries the *kidaka*.[9] In one such sheath there may be thirty, but after a month they all fall off and it produces a new lot of kidaka. Kidaka becomes *kitale*, of which a thirsty man can drink and the shell can be eaten, but there is little meat. Kitale becomes *dafu la ukomba*, which has no meat in it but is more like thick soup. Then comes the dafu with a fully developed shell. Then the *koroma*, half dafu, half coconut. It is not good to eat a lot of this; if you do and it does not suit you, you will have a stomachache. After the koroma comes the coconut, and that is the end of the development of it.

We will describe the uses of the coconut.[10] Women use it in cooking grain sauces and vegetables. Every sort of Swahili food must have 191   coconut with it. In cooking it is grated, and the grated flesh is used in cooking. Its second use is for the oil to be expressed, and the oil is good for scabies. The scabs are washed and treated with oil mixed with lime. The oil can also be used to fry fritters and to light lamps. The third use is copra. For copra the nut is broken open and the shell is removed. It is put in the sun until it is dry and then bagged and exported for sale in countries such as India and Muscat. The shell—if a woman has no money for firewood, she uses coconut shells for the purpose.

To return to the uses of the coconut palm. The trunk is used for the threshold of the door by people who cannot afford timber thresholds.

The tree also produces toddy. The tappers tap the tree by cutting the top of it and tying on a gourd.[11] The drops falling from the top are toddy. Another use is vinegar. Vinegar comes from strong toddy. When it is three days old it is too strong to be drunk, so it is put in a bottle and made into vinegar. Vinegar is good for rheumatism. It is put in something tasty to make it palatable, or it can be taken by itself. It is best if it is kept for a year. Another use is the shoot. When a tree

falls, people eat the shoot, the heart of the palm taken from the very
top. People eat it raw without cooking it.

192   A further use is the leaves, used for thatching houses, and they also
burn the leaves when making mishikaki of meat.[12]

The coir is used by women in making pots and by men to make
ropes. The use of it by women is as fuel to fire the pots. To make ropes
they strip the fiber, beat it soft, and twist it into rope. Such are the
qualities of the coconut palm.

A palm is worth a dollar, a dafu one pesa, and a coconut also one
pesa. Hucksters cut up the nuts and sell them at one pesa the piece, or,
if they are easy to get in the country, two for a pesa.

The collection of coconuts: The fee to the man who climbs it is one
nut for each palm.[13] The Swahili say, "He that was killed up a palm
tree was crushed by his own greed." And the women sing:

>   For the climber one,
>   As he sways about,
>   For the climber one.[14]

Chapter 18 Of Dissolving Marriage

The Cause of Divorce

Divorce starts when a man and his wife begin to quarrel. They quarrel because either the husband is straying or the wife. If the husband tells the wife to stay at home, she replies, "Do you want to keep me in the dark to ripen like a banana? If you want me, you must let me go out; if you do not, get yourself a stay-at-home wife." This reply annoys the husband. If he does not want to quarrel with her, he will go to the woman's parents and complain about the way she behaves. They call her and reprimand her severely and bring about a reconciliation; but a few days later the quarrel starts again. The real reason is that the husband does not love her and has another elsewhere.

A young woman does not understand such things; but she has a confidante who tells her about going astray. She says, "One man cannot fill a basket," or "If you till a field, you must have your own allotment." So she opens the young woman's ears. When he goes to bed she does not rub him down or wash his feet, and this is a great disgrace between husband and wife. If they cannot agree, the husband asks her whether she wants to live with him or not, and she
194 replies that she wants him to let her go. He asks if she will forgo the bride-price, and she consents. Then he writes a deed saying, "On condition that she foregoes the bride-price due from me, I give A, daughter of B, a triple divorce."

Then the wife packs up her pots and mats and everything that belongs to her and leaves and goes home. She tells her parents that her husband has divorced her. They ask if this is really true, and she says, "It is true, I have left him." The parents call her kungwi to come and wash her. This is the cleansing on divorce to cleanse her for marriage to someone else.[1]

She keeps her idda for three months and ten days, and until this is over she may not be married again. Then she will be married to another, and if she has quarreled badly with her former husband, she makes a great celebration of it so as to annoy him. That is the account of their parting.[2]

Chapter **19** Of Diseases and Their Cure

Fever

There are two sorts of fever, cold and hot.[1] Cold fever comes in the rains, when a man goes out and is caught in the rain. When he comes home, he feels cold and shivers. The cure for this is to have hot tea made to drink and the smoke of green benzoin passed through the limbs. Then he should wrap himself up until he sweats.

Hot fever is when the sun is fierce and a man has gone out in it and caught the sun and has fever. He shivers all over, sometimes sweating and sometimes cold, and his head throbs. The cure is to be rubbed all over with dalia water and to apply some to the forehead. When the dalia dries, his limbs grow cool and he feels better.

When a child has fever, seven sorts of smoke are prepared for him by the teacher in a paper on which are written the *ahtam fashadh*, and this is put in sesame oil.[2] Fire is brought, and the herbs are put in it, and the child is put in the smoke until he sweats. When an adult has fever, he is treated in the same way.

When a person has a high fever and shows signs of delirium, people say, "We will test his head." His head is shaved, and butter is applied with coconut paste spread on cotton and applied to the crown of the head. The butter is rubbed in until the skin oozes. Then it is fastened with a piece of black cloth. This treatment is continued for three days, and it is then known whether or not his mind is going.

199

133

Smallpox

There is no cure for smallpox except fire. After seven days the pocks mature and burst. Then a cloth is taken with hot sand and the smallpox patient is burned. If he cannot stand the heat, he is scarred all over, and if he is much affected on the face and is afraid of the fire, he goes blind. It takes two weeks, and every day fire is placed under the bed.

If he cannot open his eyes because of the number of the pocks, the urine of a child six or seven years old is applied to his eyes to prevent blindness.

200 A smallpox patient sees nobody except the person treating him. A person, man or woman, who has recently had sexual intercourse may not visit a person with smallpox, lest the patient be harmed. He is forbidden fish until he is well, and for two or three months after that he may not eat fish.

Smallpox begins with pains in the joints followed by fever. When old women notice that a person has fever and pains in the loins, they know that he is going down with smallpox, and he is given boiled maize to eat.

There are three kinds of smallpox: maize pox, sorghum pox, and sesame pox. If anyone is attacked by sesame pox, he is lucky if he recovers, for it is very severe.

The women like to sing this song:

I am leaving you, I am leaving,
Never shall I return.
I went down with pox,
Both the maize and the sorghum.
You thought that I would die,
And you would eat my flesh.
But now I have recovered
By the power of the Lord.

Yaws

Yaws is a very serious disease.[3] It attacks chiefly the nose or armpits or hands. It is like small coins. If a person goes down with yaws, he
201 must have people to look after him, and even if he has not, he must keep clean. The people take him to the shore to bathe him and to rub him with maize cobs until the pus comes away. Then he is treated with blue vitriol, which burns fiercely. If it is applied at high tide in

the morning, it works until the evening high tide. If a sufferer from yaws has nobody to treat him, his hands will be crippled, and he will be bent and lame. Also it stinks. Furthermore it causes sores on the anus, and when a man goes for treatment, it is clear that he has yaws.

Leprosy

This is a disease abhorred by people.[4] They will not eat with a leper nor live with him. There is no cure on the coast or inland for a leper. At first pustules and spots appear. These spread and make sores all over the body. When they are mature he loses his fingers or toes. People call him outcast, for they say, "You are no longer one of us; you are an animal and should go and live in the forest." When he hears this, he is very angry and says, "Outcast yourself, and your father and mother."

"Scabies," "Eczema" (Upele)

Of upele there are two varieties, scaly and pimply.[5] For the scaly the cure is to be washed daily in hot or cold water until the pus comes away. Then coconut oil is applied or coconut oil with lime; but washing in salt water is not good. For the pimply variety the treatment is the same; but it is a more serious disease. The pimples are the size of grains of sand, and the sufferer scratches all day long.

202

"Scrofula" (Maradhi ya mti)

First of all the limbs ache. Then it gets into all the joints. The treatment is hard rubbing with castor oil and kneading with the rough edge of an earthen pot. With luck the patient recovers; but if not, he is humpbacked, or his arms or legs are crippled, or his neck is awry. Its particular disfigurement is to destroy the nose.[6]

Hydrocele

Hydrocele is congenital.[7] If the father had it, so will the child; but some get it in later life from going with too many women. It is very shaming, and the Swahili laugh if a man has it. They say, "When is it going to rain?" and he answers, "Why? Have I got a hydrocele?" "Go to so-and-so; he can tell you about the rain; he has a scrotocele" (another form of the same thing). The embarrassing thing about this disease is that if a person is sitting with others on a verandah and outside there are clouds, his testicles will suddenly croak as though there were frogs in them. When people hear this, a modest man who knows that his testicles are beginning to croak goes away. A man with

203   a bad attack swells up like a pot. This is called warthog hydrocele. There is also cattle hydrocele; but it is not serious.

Children born with it may be treated at birth. It is treated with chicken and wild roots.[8]

The Nyamwezi and Sukuma like hydrocele when they are grown up. They call it *lung'ombe*, and a man who has it is respected for the size of his testicles; but they know how to treat it.

Syphilis and Gonorrhea

If a woman catches syphilis or gonorrhea, she should not be taken by a man, because he will catch it too.[9] If you take a woman with syphilis, you will be caught, as the song goes:

Keep a straight course,
Keep a straight course.
Syphilis makes me drip,
Syphilis makes me drip.[10]

The cure for syphilis is smoke. Leaves are collected and put into a pot. He sits on a stool, and the smoke goes into his private parts. If he is frightened and cannot stand the smoke, the whole of his private parts will drop off. Syphilis is a very serious disease; gonorrhea is not so bad.

The cure for gonorrhea is the root of a male papaw and white incense steeped in water and given to the patient to drink for seven days. If it is bleeding gonorrhea, he will get relief. That is the account of syphilis and gonorrhea.

204   ### Asthma and Consumption (Pumu na kifua kikuu)

Asthma causes the victim to cough.[11] His breathing is light, and he cannot raise his voice. He has no strength, cannot run, has a body as parched as a dried fish, and pants like a cat. The disease is worst in the rains. The trouble is that if he drinks water, it runs straight through him, as does everything that he puts in his mouth. There is no cure for this disease.

Consumption is similar. It too starts with a cough. If he eats anything he is sick, and as he digests it, he coughs until he farts, and his lungs sound like a drum. If he is indoors a passerby knows that in that house there is a sufferer from consumption. He coughs up blood, and it is dangerous to step in his spittle, as anyone who does so catches the disease; and no one should eat the same thing that he eats.

If these two diseases afflict a man, the only cure is the hoe and *kiunza*, that is, the grave.[12] It is wise to keep away from sufferers.

Whitlows

First a finger swells under the nail for no reason.[13] If a person finds his finger painful, he suspects a whitlow. The treatment is to soak the whole finger in shark oil or to cut open a sodom apple and wrap it around the finger. After five or six days the finger is so swollen and painful that he cannot sleep. When it is ripe, it bursts of itself in the night, and a lot of pus comes out. He treats it again with shark oil to make sure that no pus is left, and then he takes off the fruit.

205

Rheumatism (Dry Cold)

When this starts, the sufferer grows thin; his complexion is dull; he has not the strength to move fast; and his heart thumps and flutters.[14] He is constipated, and if he does have a movement it is as hard as goats' dung and very painful. To cure it he is told to eat rich food like fat meat or curdled milk. He is not allowed skim milk or anything dry like lean meat or rice without butter. Or he is told to eat cleaned raisins and in particular boiled sorghum and vegetables every day. He recovers in about a month.

Dropsy (Wet Cold)

The man's legs swell, and his cheeks.[15] If he is dark, his face goes yellow. His hands swell and become thick. He too cannot move fast. He is forbidden to eat fat meat or butter. If he is treated, he is for seven days given boiled sorghum flavored with young shark cooked with coconut vinegar. Not much salt is put in his food, or he will continue to swell. He is not allowed to sit still for long, but advised to walk about. He must eat nothing fat such as ripe mangoes, ripe bananas, or rice with a lot of butter.

206   Tambazi

This disease starts in the belly before it emerges.[16] When people know that a person has tambazi, they buy charcoal and grind it on a plate and give it to him to drink.[17] It is very bitter. After three days the disease shows itself as eruptions or swellings. The sufferer continues to be ill until it bursts of itself. Where it has burst they rub in something like household soot, or they grind dalia and apply that. They observe which medicine is effective. If they do not grind charcoal for him to drink at an early stage of the disease, it remains inside and the man dies.

Elephantiasis (Tende)

At first the legs swell to the size of mortars. There is no cure for this disease; the swelling never comes to a head or bursts. A person with elephantiasis cannot move fast. Some have it in one leg only and some in both. The Swahili believe that its origin is a spell (tenzo), something prepared for him and left in his way. When he stepped on it his leg swelled. It is called elephantiasis (tende) because he has had some action (kitendo) done (tendewa) to him.[18]

Safura

At first the patient has swellings all over, even on the eyes, and he turns yellow, because his limbs are full of pus instead of blood.[19] If you touch him you sink right in. The treatment is to take iron filings, pound them, and cook them with sugar syrup. He is given a little of this to lick every morning for seven days. His diet should be boiled sorghum with spinach, young shark, or vinegar for seven days.

207

Jongo

First a muscle is knotted in one position. If this is above the knee, it is rubbed with castor oil. Jongo spreads over the whole body, and if it reaches the back, they still rub in castor oil, and something heavy is put on the back or chest until he gets well.[20]

Herpes (Choa)

This causes little pustules on the limbs, and they become blisters. The treatment is to grind copper coins and apply the water to the sores. If he does not get better and the disease develops, it turns to leprosy.[21]

Prickly Heat

This is common in the hot season because of the amount of sweat on the limbs. The symptoms are outbreaks all over. The treatment is to rub in dalia water all over. This cools the limbs as it dries, and the patient gets better.[22]

Fits

The cause of this is that something is passed in front of a person at night, and when he sees it he starts.[23] After this he has fever, and after the fever, when the disease comes on, he falls down. He falls every month, and when he falls, he froths at the mouth like a horse. There is no cure for this disease. Another person should not share anything that he eats or drinks. If he does so he is infected.

Warts

A pimple with a hard top grows. Its cure is to be cut with a razor. Then body dirt is applied where it has been cut, and it quickly dries up.[24]

Disfigurements

If a person has a squint, when his mother was advanced in pregnancy, if she looked much at the moon or if she saw a person with a squint, that accounts for the child being born with a squint.[25] There is no cure.

Having only one eye is caused by a disease of the eyes or a blow on the eye in a quarrel so that it was blinded. The patient is told to wash his eyes with dew every morning; or he collects pea water and squeezes it into his eye; or saffron is ground and the juice is put on clean cotton and bound over the eye; or leaves of *mwingajini* are collected and the water similarly squeezed into the eye; or leaves of *mkablishemsi* are treated in the same way. The treatment is applied first to the good eye and then to the other.[26]

Deafness is caused by an insect entering the ear and dying without emerging. If a man has trouble with his ear, medicine is made for him.

208

209

It is poured into the ear, and then he bends down and the liquid runs out, bringing the insect with it.[27] If it does not, the treatment is repeated.

Dumbness: A person may be born dumb, or tongue-tied, or with a stammer. There is no cure for this.[28]

Madness may be caused by loss of property or the death of a dear wife. At first he talks to himself, and people who hear him laugh at him and he gets angry. He is treated by being put in a dark room so that he does not know where he is or that he is under treatment. After a month inside he is brought out to see how his mind is. Another cure is to kill a dog, and the patient is given it with his food, not knowing that it is dog meat. When he has been given this once, it becomes clear whether his mind has recovered or not.[29]

Locusts

The year in which locusts descended on the coast was a disaster, and there was much sickness. First there was the stomach sickness. If anyone said to his family, "I have a stomachache," they went straight to the Indian to buy a winding sheet, and by morning he was dead.

210

Then came smallpox. A man said that he was unwell and had a fever. He went to bed, and by morning the pocks were all over him. It lasted for six days, and on the seventh he was dead. There were so many funerals that eventually even women were carrying out the corpses to bury them.

After this there was a great famine. Nothing that was planted came up because of the locusts coming down in swarms. There was nothing in the fields, no cassava, no potatoes, no rice, nothing to eat. Even the leaves of the coconut palms were all gone, because the locusts settled on the coconuts or mangoes to eat the leaves. If a man wanted to walk outside, he had to keep his mouth shut so as not to swallow a locust.

The Nyamwezi and Sukuma who were on the coast at the time would go to the fields to catch locusts. They bagged them and brought them to town to sell to the Baluchi and the Arabs, who fried them, salted them, put them out to dry, and packed them up to go to Arabia and Baluchistan as presents. They like locusts to eat as much as do the Nyamwezi. Some of the Swahili eat locusts; but others will not.

Another sort of locust is the little one called a hopper. They come into fields of sugar, bananas, or rice and eat all night until in the morning there is nothing. Their droppings are bad.[30] What they do leave of sugar, cassava, or potatoes is not good for a person who eats it. The sugar is rotten, the cassava bitter, and the rice bad.

211 To drive them away when they descended, they heated cans or made flails to beat them; but they did not go. It was best when it rained. Many of them died, and their eggs did not hatch.

The same year, after the locusts had gone there came a plague of drought worse than the locusts. Everything in the fields dried up. The sun was fierce, and there was much sickness in the town. They said, "God is vexed with us, for we have sinned." They said, "We must repent." In repentance, every time they went to the mosque they prayed to God for forgiveness and that he would take away the plague that descended upon them. They said, "O God, who seest all things that we do but art not seen, receive our prayers and take from us the sickness and want that thou has brought upon us, of thy kindness."

Jiggers

To the coast have come creatures called jiggers,[31] which are very bad. They are the size of grains of sand, and they come originally from the Cape, brought in by porters in their loads, and they have spread all over the coast. The trouble that they cause is that they get into a man's foot without his noticing. He is only aware of an irritation in his foot where one has gone in. Three days later it is the size of a grain of sorghum or maize. It may enter anywhere, the hand or the foot or somewhere else.

It can be removed with a needle; but the person who takes it out must know how to do it. One who does not makes a sore where he digs it out, as he must get it out whole. Because of people removing them 212 badly, many persons have lost fingers or toes, because their juice is very bad and makes pus. If a man's feet are dirty, they settle there and do not go away. He must wash his feet in hot water morning and evening, and when the creature is extracted he must be washed with hot water even if there are not many of them. They are like small fleas. The worst is when they get into the feet of small children. If care is not taken their feet are badly damaged.

Chapter **20** Of Burial

When someone dies, if it is at night, a man goes to inform his brothers. When they arrive, they give orders for a pit to be dug, and this is done under the bed on which is the dead person. For there are four things to be done for a dead person: he must be washed, wrapped in a winding sheet, given the observances of his religion, and buried in a grave.[1]

There are three persons to wash the body. The ladle holder pours water on the corpse, and this runs into the pit under the bed. The presser squeezes out the excreta, and the supporter holds up the body. With us the washing is done with water containing the leaves of the jujube tree. Finally cloves are arranged around the body, and they cover it over with a new sheet. They do not go to sleep again that night, and men and women wail.

In the morning they send around news of where they have placed the body, whether in the town or the country, and people come, each carrying money or muslin for the winding sheet. The visitors are taken to the room where the body is, and each one pours on it three ladles of water from head to feet.

Then someone is sent for the teacher and the chiefs, and if the dead person is a citizen of the place, the person in charge will consult the chiefs about the burial. They will answer, "Is the grave dug?" If it is not, the chiefs will ask, "Where will you bury him, Kingani or Nunge or Pangapanga?" for on the coast everyone has his place of burial. The people of Pangapanga must go there. If they do not there will be an argument, or half the people will not attend the funeral. The reason why everyone has his place of burial is that coastal descent regards the

tribe. A certain tribe should be buried at Pangapanga and a different
tribe at Nunge; but strangers, people from Zanzibar, are not buried in
these cemeteries, nor are slaves.[2] That is why the burial places are
distinct. Every town of the coast has its cemeteries in the manner that
we have mentioned, giving the names of those at Bagamoyo.

When this is settled, they go to dig the grave in the place indicated.
The chiefs give the order for the winding sheet to be sewn and the
dead man's announcement. The town piper is called, and he stands at
the door with a shaha, who says, "Gentlemen, understand that so-
and-so has left this world." Then the piper plays, and in the yard is
beaten the great drum. The women weep indoors, and the men sew
the winding sheet.

The winding sheet for a man is three pieces of cloth and a kanzu and
a turban, and for a woman seven pieces, five jamvi, a cover over all,
and a long piece of dark muslin for the head. When they have sewn it,
the watani demand their fee, they put in dalia and rose water and
215   scent it with incense.[3]

If the dead person is a man, three men go in and clothe him in the
winding sheet and cover the body with a mat. Then they place it on a
bier, and at the threshold they bless it. They give the bier threefold
protection.[4] Then four men, two in front and two behind, lift it,
saying, "There is no god but God. There is no god but God. There is
no god but God, Muhammad is the Prophet of God." The people
following the bier respond until they reach the mosque, where they
place the bier inside and go in with others for the religious ceremonies
to be performed for the dead man. Then they go to the grave for the
burial.

For the burial, the grave is covered over with a cloth, and three
persons wait in it to receive the body, and when it comes one of them
gives the call to prayer. Then they lay the body in the niche and place
the kiunza board over it, and then they fill in the grave.

The three persons who dug the grave do not leave it until it is quite
filled in; but they do not do this work alone; everybody helps. If they
are watani and have not received their utani fee, they will not allow the
body to be buried until they have their due.

After this they bring a pot of water, and the teacher sits at the head
of the grave and digs a hole. He recites the burial prayers and pours
the water of evidence that this is a Muslim. Then he plants castor-oil
plants at the four corners, and when they grow they show that this is a
grave. Then the people recite the fatiha and go away, and the bereaved spouse must cry loudly.[5]

216   *Of Condolences*

The people leaving the grave go to the house to comfort the bereaved. They say, "It is sad," and the answer is "It is still with us" or "It is finished." Or they say, "May God bring good out of your sorrow," and they reply, *Allahu al baqa*, "God will remain with us."

Of Mourning

After giving their condolences, the people ask whether there is to be a mourning or no. He answers, "There is." They ask when he will hold it, and he replies, "At nine in the evening." At this time each man brings his mat and pillow to spend the time at the mourning, and the women too. At night they tell stories, and the men do the same, and some play cards. At dawn the piper comes; the women and some of the men weep, and some go to the mosque. At nine in the morning the men and women meet together again to arrange the *mashambizo* washing.[6] The women fill in the pit under the bed and then take the cloths used in washing the body. These are the mashambizo. They are put on a large tray, and they make a canopy, that is, a long cloth like an awning fastened up with three to seven women inside it.[7] Three women carry the mashambizo on their heads down to the beach to wash them, and the piper follows, singing:

217   Sing sadly today,
       O sing sadly today.

When they reach the shore, they go into the water to bathe, and any who do not are asked by the others why they do not bathe. They exchange riddles such as "Some people have pea leaves and do not want them to be seen."[8] When they have washed the mashambizo, they return to the town as they came, inside the awning. When they reach the mourning they divide the mashambizo, but not at random, among the persons closest to the deceased. It is their right as a memento of the person who is dead.

Every attendant at a funeral brings something according to his means, a dollar, a rupee, some pesa, or something else, and after some seven days this is used as alms in the house for the deceased, for the *hitima* is recited, they hold a party, and people are invited to come and eat.[9] The widow is very sad and cries and wails, "So-and-so, you have abandoned me. People will stick their fingers in my eyes, and there will be none to prevent them." Then somebody stops her, saying, "Hush, do not cry, this is the way of the world, to be born and to die. You are not alone, it is the common lot."

If the widow is poor, the hitima is recited the following year; she waits until she has enough money. After forty days alms called "the dead man's forty" are given.

218 At the mourning the old women tie up their heads in cloths. In the past they were in danger, because when they went out, sorcerers came and performed all night.[10]

Once upon a time a woman died in Bagamoyo and was buried. At night the people were sleeping at the mourning when there came a sorcerer called Mother of Ibrahim and put a spell on the mourning.[11] Sorcerers go naked, and Mother of Ibrahim tied a cuttlefish over her private parts, for that is how sorcerers dress. At dawn she went home and met her husband, Bwana Mzee, whom she seized, saying, "Cover my nakedness, and I will give you anything you like." Bwana Mzee said, "I will not let you go; you are a very wicked woman, and you have troubled the spirits of many people." He took her to the mourning, and everyone saw her nakedness. When the sun came up, they covered her all over with *pakacha* basketwork and paraded her around the town. Everybody saw her and asked her, "Are you going on with your sorcery?" She promised to do it no more, and they said, "We will bind you with an oath so that if you do it again you will die." She consented and took the oath; but a few months later she took it up again in secret. God sent her mad, and she wandered about the town naked and insulting people, and in the rain she put mud on her head. She died young.

To catch a sorcerer requires a grown man; a boy cannot do it because he will be afraid of being harmed or falling sick. If you see a sorcerer at a distance putting a spell on you, the remedy is to throw a lime at her. If she says, "Do it again," do not do so; go straight in and catch her. That is the end of the account of condolences and spells.

219 *Of Letters of Condolence*

If a man dies away from home, the news is brought to his brothers in the town in a letter:[12] "After compliments, we have to inform you that your brother so-and-so has left this world. *Inna lillahi wa inna ileihi raji'una hadha sabili'ddunya wa tariqu 'l akhera.*"[13] Or, "We have suffered the loss of so-and-so, who is dead. This world is a road, and this is the end of it. He had maize smallpox for five days, and on the sixth he died." When the brothers understand the letter, they weep, and the drum is ordered to be put in the yard if he is a person "born on the drum," that is, if his father and mother were of drum rank.

Of the Death of Jumbe

If the dead person is a jumbe, on the morning that they hear the news that jumbe so-and-so is dead the people gather together for the funeral.[14] The *tanzia* announcement is made, "We have to inform you that jumbe so-and-so has left this world." Everyone takes off his cap, kanzu, and sandals and is left with one garment only. If the dead person is a shaha or waziri, the townspeople do not take off the kanzu but bare only the head and feet, and jumbes remove their turbans.[15] If a man of the coast refused to remove his clothes, in the old days he would be beaten; but now people are only vexed with him, because of government prohibition.

220   At the funeral of a jumbe no one but a shaha is allowed to wash the body, or, if no shaha is available, the son of a shaha. After the burial all the jumbes meet at the mourning, and some women dance in the yard while others wail. This dance is called *mwanamama*. In the yard are sounded the great drum, the *siwa* and the pipe, playing the *kibagaja*. Two jumbes go out and dance, each carrying his contribution to the winding sheet for the burial and those of others. The *watani* members are given their dues, and so are the gravediggers, the diggers of the pit, and the teachers who are present.

When the winding sheet has been arranged, the shaha goes inside and wraps the body in the sheet. It is then placed on the bier to be taken to the grave for burial.

The mourning is for two weeks or, if they are poor, for one week. Every afternoon people come to the mourning to play cards and the great drum, and the women dance the mwanamama.[16] On the last day of the mourning they buy an ox. It is slaughtered and shared according to a complicated ritual. The jumbes are given the hump, the shahas and waziris the foreleg, the quarters go to the teachers, and the remainder of the meat is cooked for the party.

In the past, if a man gave a party and killed an ox for it but did not give the jumbes the hump and the shahas their shares, nobody would come to the party, because they said that so-and-so has no manners and what he has done is all wasted, for the jumbes are angry. He has to go and apologize and give money.

When jumbes eat, they do not have their food on the verandah with others.[17] It is laid for them in the room, and no one goes in except the waiter, and if they want anything they tell him. While they are eating, the siwa and pipe are played. If there is only one jumbe present alone but on the verandah there is a sharifu or a teacher, he will tell one of them to be called in; but no one else eats with him, except in his own house when there is no party. A teacher removes his cap; but a sharifu does not. Or a teacher may be given permission by the jumbe not to uncover while eating with him.

221

Of the Pebble Ceremony

When a person dies and has been buried for three or seven days, the people in charge look for pebbles.[18] These are small, very hard stones, which they wash in water until they are perfectly clean. Then they go and collect five or seven teachers, and when they come they have mats spread for them. The pebbles are placed in front of the teachers, who perform with them the *hallil*. This means that each teacher takes one pebble and says, "There is no god but God." If the number of the pebbles is a thousand, every teacher says a thousand times, "There is no god but God," and they speak to no one until the end. When they have finished, the pebbles are wrapped in a cloth and taken to the grave and left there. The teachers are given a meal; they recite the fatiha for the repose of the deceased; they are given their fee for the ceremony as agreed, five to fifteen dollars.

Chapter **21** Of the *Jumbe*

222

Of the Installation of a Jumbe

A person who is born to the *jumbeate*, whose father was a jumbe and is dead, and who can raise the cost informs the jumbes appointed before him that he wishes to be a jumbe.[1] They reply, agreeing, provided that they receive their dues. He gives them their dues in cloth or money sent by the hand of the shahas. Then he gives their dues to the shahas, the waziris, and the townsmen; because if they do not receive these, he will not be recognized by them, but only by his own family and slaves.

As the time approaches, seven days before he wants to be installed, the jumbes come together, and one of them says, "We wish to announce that on such a date, Mwenyi so-and-so is to be installed under the name of jumbe such-and-such." Then the crier is called, and he goes around the whole town with the buffalo horn, saying, "The horn of announcement, not of peril; the horn of the chief (*shomvi*)

223 and his forty, of high and low, of townsfolk and their children, of domestic slaves and of bondslaves, of Makame of Shani, of the freemen of Winde, of Uqasimu and the freemen of Shanga, the horn of chiefdom, to inform you that on Monday the *kishina* and mwanamama will be played; on Thursday Mwenyi so-and-so will be installed under the name of Jumbe Mkomatembo."[2]

At night men and women gather together to dance all night until morning. They sing:

What is hidden, let it be hidden.
Take a cloth to catch a shrimp,
A man and his mother-in-law.[3]

148

or:

Gadding about does not bring up a child.

In the morning the great drum is beaten, and in the dance each jumbe has two slaves dressed up and each with a fan to fan the jumbe. The new jumbe is inside being invested with his turban, and when this is done, he is placed on a palanquin, and with him is a slave woman with an umbrella in her hand. The people carry the bed on their shoulders around the town, and when they return the new jumbe dances too. Then he sits on the verandah with his fellow jumbes on a heap of mats. They dance all sorts of dances of joy for six or seven days, according to their means.

224   It is not customary for a jumbe to go out of doors bareheaded, not to sit bareheaded indoors; but if there is no one to see, he sits bareheaded. Nor is it the custom to put any other cloth over the turban that he wears. If he does so and the shahas see him, they find him guilty of breach of custom. He does not argue; he produces what they demand and pays them.

The Story of Jumbe Simbambili

Some four years ago Jumbe Korandi died and people came to bury him. Now Jumbe Simbambili turned up and called a barber to shave his hair, which he did. Then he went to the mourning, and when the jumbes saw him they asked why he came shaved to a mourning. He replied, "Do you give judgment on my head?" They told him that he had broken the custom of the coast; but he said, "I have only shaved; any hairy person may shave." They were vexed with him, and the jumbes held a meeting and instructed the townsfolk not to pay respect to Simbambili. Wherever he went, they were to say of him, "This is the jumbe who laid a spell on Jumbe Korandi by making himself smart when he attended the mourning."

One morning he went out without his turban, and people asked why a jumbe had no turban. He replied, "I am not a jumbe; I do not want the position if none of the people of the town pay me respect." His relations remonstrated with him, saying, "It is a bad thing for a

225   jumbe to resign; it is a great disgrace." He resumed his cap and turban; but the experienced people of the town prophesized that he would not live long.

Three months later he went to Khutu, where he lived, and stayed

there for two months. Then he went down with hydrocele, and they
brought him back to the coast. When he reached his country house, he
stayed there for seven days, and on the eighth he called his relations to
bid them farewell, and that night he died. They brought him to the
town for burial; but the jumbes and the townsfolk refused to bury
him. He was buried privately as not being worthy of a jumbe's
funeral.

The Customs of the Jumbe in the Past

In the past a jumbe had under him shahas, a waziri, a mwinyimkuu, and an *amir*. The amir was the head of the common folk. If there
was a problem in the town, the jumbe told the amir, and he informed
the commoners.[4] If, for example, a letter reached the town from
another town to say that somebody was dead and they should give
condolences, the amir told the commoners to "go home and say
goodbye. Tomorrow we go to such a place to give our condolences."
For this went both men and women, and the jumbe was supported by
two or three female attendants of his household. In the morning came
two tribesmen, a piper, and a horn player. The jumbe went in front
with the shaha and the waziri to talk to. The horn and the pipe played
until they were outside a town, when the horn was silenced. When
they came near another town, the horn started again. The jumbes of
that town came to meet them on the way, and there they would spend
the day, or they would sleep there for the night and go on in the
morning to another town. When they approached the town to which
they were going, a person was sent to announce the arrival of jumbe
so-and-so. That town had houses ready to receive the visitors, and the
local jumbes came out to welcome their fellow jumbe and to escort
him into the town. So they entered with horn and pipe, and the other
jumbes came with horn and pipe. If the dead person was a jumbe, the
visiting jumbe and his people uncovered. Then they entered the town
and were shown to their lodgings. In the afternoon they went to the
mourning, and on their arrival the great drum was beaten. The local
and visiting jumbes danced, and they stayed until the end of the
mourning.

If the dead jumbe had means, it was not customary for the visitors
to pay for board or lodging so long as they stayed. Such was the
practice of giving condolences in the past.

But today the custom is for the jumbe to consult with neither the
commoners nor the shaha; nor do the waziri consult with the com-

moners. They are divided into cliques headed by men or women. If something occurs such as we have described, the jumbe is sent a formal letter, and the commoners have a formal letter written to their leader. When he has read the letter, he calls a messenger to beat the mrungura drum at each house. When people hear this, they ask what it is about, and the messenger says, "You are summoned to the leader." When they come, they are told the news that has reached him.

The Authority Vested in the Jumbe in the Past

In the past they had authority over land and fields. The fields were bush without mango or coconut trees. If a stranger arrived, an Indian, an Arab, or a Swahili, and wanted a field to cultivate, the jumbe asked him whether he wanted to purchase or to rent.[5] The applicant said which he wanted, and if it was to rent, he would say, "Give me as *ubani* five or six rupees."[6] When they had agreed, he showed him the field selected. If the agreement was to purchase, he wrote him a deed of sale.

227

Inside the town there were plots, and if someone wanted to build a house, he went to the jumbe and made an agreement with him for rent or purchase. Secondly, authority over traders: If foreigners came into the town with merchandise, they must go to the jumbes' houses, for they must not sell without the permission of the jumbes. Then there were the Nyamwezi caravans carrying ivory; in this and in the matter of cattle Indians and Shihiri and other traders could not buy freely. Everyone buying a goat paid an eighth of a dollar and on an ox a dollar. If an Indian bought ivory, after the transaction he had to come to an agreement with the jumbe, but these powers have now gone from them, for there are no more fields for them to lease nor plots to sell, and from trade they get nothing.

Fees Due to the Jumbes

1. Any person who slaughtered an ox in the town, whether for sale or for a party, had to send his due, the hump, to the chief. If he was not given this he was angry, and if he was angry he was given something to pacify him.

2. If a fisherman caught a shark or a dugong or any large creature, the jumbe was sent a bit, called *mboni*.

If anything was found in the sea or if a ship was wrecked with valuables on board, the salvage was taken to the jumbe. If the ship-owner heard of it, he went to the jumbe to ask for his property. The jumbe received salvage money, also called mboni.

228

If someone's slave ran away and fell into the hands of the jumbe, he was held until the owner should come. If no owner appeared, he was a mboni slave and the jumbe retained him. If the owner did appear, the slave was sold, the jumbe received his mboni, and the owner took the balance.

3. At Bagamoyo there is a place called Nunge near Kingani. It is on a salt flat surrounded by mangroves behind the ancient graves. Here annually there springs up a mound of crystallized salt.[7] In the past, when the fisherwomen saw this mound, they came to the town and told the jumbes and the shahas that the Kingani mound had appeared. When the jumbes heard this, they met to arrange for its disposal. After this they held the "ceremony of experience," some of them performing the propitiatory rite all night, for it was not the custom to go without this ceremony.[8] According to ancient custom, those who approached without protection had trouble on the way when they approached the mound, large snakes or bees to chase them back to the town or lions or leopards roaring in the forest. The morning after the ceremony they went to sweep the graves, and the third day after this the jumbes went with their sons and daughters and their domestic slaves to the place where the salt was to break it up. They went with

229 horn and pipe, and at the mound they were told to break it up and the salt to be taken. The dues from this salt were as usual, the hump to the jumbes and half of the mound was their share and that of the shahas and waziris. On the sixth day after this, the townsfolk were allowed to go and take the salt, and they went with the natives to take it.

Nowadays, when the mound grows up they go to take the salt with no ceremony; except that they give advance information to the government so that it may know that people are going to Nunge for salt, because there is a lot of disorder.

Chapter **22** Of Taxes and
Tolls

Of Taxation in the Past

In the past there were taxes on the coast levied by the jumbes. For example, if strangers such as Nyamwezi arrived with ivory for trade in the coastal districts, they went to one of the jumbes and the ivory was stamped by order of the government. On being stamped, each *farasila* paid eight dollars to the sayyid, and a lodging fee of one dollar, making nine in all, was paid to the jumbe, in charge of the stranger.[1] This was the custom.

Then before the Nyamwezi entered the town, the jumbe had to send him something as a present, because this was the practice. It was called the "covering," and the leader of the caravan, his women, and his followers had each to be given a piece of cloth. Those who came ahead of the caravan had also to be given cloth.

On entering the town the leader of the caravan contracted for rent and had to pay "land ivory" to the chief of the place, that is, to the jumbe to whom he had gone. Then he was allowed to trade.

When the trading was completed, the jumbe had to give the Nyamwezi a parting present on his departure before he left. When he had left, the jumbe took three dollars for each farasila, which he had to be given by order of the sayyid. If there were a hundred farasila, the jumbe was given three hundred dollars out of the ivory of his guest.

Hindus and Indians, too, who came into the town with goods for trade or set up shops went first to the jumbe as head of the town. He found them houses and arranged leases for them, and when they were settled, they were told all the customs of the country. After this a merchant had to pay on each house twelve dollars a year. This had to be paid to the jumbe as head of the town because it was ancient custom. In addition he was given cloth and other things according to the merchant's means.

The jumbes used to levy other dues. If a caravan came into the town with cattle, goats, and sheep, the jumbes levied dues on these animals. The rate was that if a man bought one head of cattle he must take one dollar to the jumbe, and if he bought a goat he must take an eighth of a dollar to the jumbe.

If an Indian or an Arab wanted porters, the person who supplied them to the Indian or the Arab was given a rupee for each porter as the jumbe's due. This levy was not all sent to one jumbe, but to the jumbe to whom the caravan had come.

The inland jumbes levied a rate called *hongo*.[2] If a man arrived in the town from the coast, he had to pay such number of kitambi as they might agree; and if he came from inland he paid in inland goods.[3]

Of Taxation in the Present

232   Now the German government has made a custom of taxing houses and the establishment of shops by people such as Indians, Hindus, Arabs, or anyone else who starts a shop. Thus a Swahili rectangular house must pay twelve rupees a year, a house with a ridged roof but no gables six rupees, and a one-story stone house seven and a half rupees. A shopkeeper is assessed on the value of his shop; if it is big he pays a lot, and if it is small a little.

Many of the Swahili think that the government keeps this money; but the government does not use it except for the benefit of the townspeople as in maintaining the town and its roads. In the old days there were only little paths running inland from the town; but now there are broad roads, and these improvements have cost money. Secondly, people sleep in their houses at night under the protection of the police. While shopkeepers sleep the police go their rounds inspecting the shops. The police need salaries, and salaries cost money, and the government pays. Thirdly, if somebody is attacked and robbed or if his brother is killed, he takes his complaint to the government, and the government takes his side to obtain justice for him. Fourthly, the wells on the coast: In the past the wells were very bad; but now the government has built fine, clean wells and paid for them out of the taxes. Then it has built bridges over the small rivers, and over the big river it has established a ferry, and travelers can cross without danger.

In the old days the canoe used to capsize, and the people or their goods
233   would go to the bottom. Then again, in the past people had no
employment; but now the government has given them employment;
and they do not serve the government for nothing, they are paid by
the government. That is why government levies taxes; but the money
derived from these taxes is not enough for the government. The
government in Europe sends a lot of money annually to the coast to
supplement the local revenue, to organize the country, and to help the
people.[4]

Of Tax Gatherers on the Coast

Every African house on the coast has written on it a number and the
name of the householder; but it is customary for the Swahili to be
difficult, and their behavior is deceitful. When a government servant
comes to inquire and write up the houses, frequently they do not tell
him the truth, because some of them are afraid of having their names
written down in his register. They often ask what is the object of
having their houses and names recorded. Many of them do not
understand what taxes are nor why government needs them. Many of
them think that the government will keep the people's money, and
some say, "No doubt the king has sent to ask the names of the people
of the coast." Others say, "They are writing because of taxes; but then
perhaps they will want to come." Everyone gives his opinion, and
when the old women see the government clerk coming to record their
houses, they run away, saying, "I want to be safe; if they want my
house, they can have it."

Today if a European asks whose is a house when the owner is
234   absent, but another person is present who answers saying whose
house it is, and if later the owner hears that there was a European here
with so-and-so and he asked whose house it was and he told him—
then when they meet there will be a quarrel, and he will say, "So-and-
so is a troublemaker." Similarly, if they meet a European who asks
their names, or if he asks one of two his name and the other immediately tells him, there is a quarrel on the way home.

Collecting tax on the coast is a troublesome business. Some pay,
and others will not. They collect the tax for the current three months
and owe the first. When the government sees that a lot of people have
not paid, it calls them in, and when they reach the office each one is
asked where is his tax. He answers, "I paid it to so-and-so," thinking
of the last tax, but forgetting the first. The officer says, "That is in

hand, but there are still three rupees to come." He says, "I understand, sir, I will go and look for them." Then he goes away saying, "The tax collectors are cheating us," because he does not understand the dates of the months nor the arrangements of the tax.

I used to be sent by government to collect tax on all the houses, and I was accompanied by two policemen, because some people made a lot of trouble over paying. The rule is that for houses in the country one rupee is payable every four months. For collecting tax in the country I used to receive a fee of five pesa; but for collecting tax in the town I received nothing over my salary. Everybody hated me.

235
One day I went into the country to demand tax, and I found at home a man who was always dodging me and not paying. On that day I seized him and demanded the government tax, and he said, "I have not got it, go away." I was annoyed by what he said, and he was annoyed. He took an axe in his hand and tried to hit me; but I had with me my slave, Serenge, and he gripped the hand with the axe. On that day I had no police with me. I wanted to take him to Bagamoyo, but the people came and pleaded with me to let him go. I did so, and he went in and gave me the money.

Chapter **23** Swahili Journeys

Their Customs before Traveling

There is a Swahili custom that if a man intends to go on a journey or to borrow something and if on the way he meets somebody coming the other way, he returns saying, "My journey is bad."[1] He will not enjoy it if he persists in going, or he will change his plans and return home and start again next day. If he is in a hurry, he will wait half an hour before starting again. On the other hand, if a man starts a journey and on the way he meets two people, he says that it is a good omen, especially if they are women and if they are carrying things in their hands.[2] Then he is even more pleased and says that it is a very good omen. If he is about to go on a journey or to go into the country or to an Indian to borrow from him and he meets a man with one eye, he says, "This journey is bad; I have seen an evil omen," and he returns home. If he is going inland or into the country and comes on snakes fighting, he says, "I shall find trouble where I am going, or we shall be involved in a fight." If it is a big journey, they start with a sense of anxiety about what is going to happen to them on the way. If he meets an old woman by herself, he says, "This is an evil portent. If I call on someone he will not be at home, or if I try to borrow I shall be unsuccessful"; so he returns home.

If a hunter leaves his house and meets an old woman or any one person, he abandons his hunt for fear that he will be wounded by an animal or will have a fruitless expedition and spend his powder for nothing.

If you are on the way and you meet a Sykes monkey, go back; do not continue that journey. It is no use, and you will have trouble. If you are on the way and you meet a snake with two spots, a cobra that we call a *pito* and which is very poisonous, if you see that serpent, you will receive very bad news. If on your journey you meet a pot being carried and in it is grain or something of that sort, you say, "This is a good journey"; but if when you meet them it is empty, you say that it is bad.

If a man leaves his house to go somewhere and trips over a stump and bruises his right foot, he says, "I am going wrong; I shall get into a quarrel or meet somebody who will do me wrong, because the omens are against the way that I am going." In Lindi, when a man trips on a stump and hurts himself, he says that his wife is unfaithful.[3] If a man trips with the left foot without bruising himself, he calls it a good omen. It is a good omen if a bird on top of a tree sings, "Kwapee, 238   kwapee." If it is raining hard and this bird calls, travelers say that the rain is over.

Let us say a bit more about Swahili beliefs. If a wood owl settles on a tree and calls persistently, somebody in the town is going to die. In Mgau there is a bird called *matonohi* with a queer call—"Hum hum."[4] If it calls near a town, some important person is going to die. If a *shorwe* calls from a tree near a house, a visitor is coming.[5] In Mgau they say that if a dog drags its hindquarters on the ground, a visitor is coming to the town. If a child sweeps the yard, they say that a visitor is coming, or if the chickens cackle, they say that a visitor is coming.

It is a Nyamwezi custom that if a man is going along a road and in the middle of the road there is a man with a walking stick, a Nyamwezi will not go along that road. He will take another road and will abuse you in the belief that you have cast a spell to prevent his reaching his destination, and that is why he will not pass.

Agreements between Merchant and Traveler

When a Swahili plans a journey, he goes to talk to his Indian merchant, saying, "I have come to you, *Mukki*, to borrow trade goods for a journey."[6] The merchant answers, "I will not refuse; but bring a 239   reputable person to guarantee you, before I give you the goods." He says, "I have no one to guarantee me but myself; but trust me, and you can supply me without hesitation or anxiety. God will accomplish all, and if he will, you will be pleased when I return." The merchant says, "Good, I hear what you say, and I will think it over." As they part, he says, "When shall I come back for your answer?" and he says, "Come back after a week."

At the end of the week, he goes to the merchant and says to the merchant, "I have come to hear your decision." He asks him what capital he has in fields or houses, and he says, "I have none, but I assure you before God on my honor that if I live and God will, I will repay you." The merchant says, "I understand you; but I require a legal agreement," and he says, "I agree to sign an agreement." The merchant says, "How much merchandise do you want?" And he says 1,000 dollars.

"For how many months?"

"Two years."

"Too long; make it one year."

So he agrees to one year.

When they have agreed on this, they go to the government to write a bond for 1,000 dollars, and this is officially stamped. They go to the shop, and he asks him what goods he wants, and he tells him— "Twenty bolts of Bombay, thirty bolts of *sun*, fifteen bolts of *majigam*, and ten bolts of *gamti*." All these are varieties of white cloth. Then, "Cloth for turbans."

"What sort?"

"*Kareati, buraa, rehani, sturbadi, barawaji, kikoi mzinga, pasua moyo*.[7] And one barrel of beads, and four sacks of cowries, seven boxes of sugar, six coils of brass wire, and a tent."

When he has reckoned all this up, he wants the cost of porters, and he agrees with sufficient porters for his loads. To each he gives his pay, half of it in advance. When the porters have been paid, they have to make up their loads, and when they have done up their loads, he goes to the merchant to take leave of him. The merchant says, "Go with good fortune in safety," and the traveler goes home.

Then he goes to his parents to take leave of them and to pray to God for them. On departure he gives them a present, and if he is married he gives his wife her upkeep; but some do not do this because they know that once the husbands are away they will waste it.

If his parents are dead, he takes incense to the grave and there says the same words as if they were alive—"My parents, I have come to take leave of you. I have borrowed goods, and I am going on a journey. You are dead, but your shades are alive.[8] May God take me safely with the goods and bring me back safely to pay for them. If I make a profit, I will remember you with alms and a hitima." Then he

sweeps the grave and weeds it and removes any rubbish and sprinkles
tibu if he has brought any. Thus do the Swahili take their leave before
a journey.

When a man starts on a journey, the women sing:

Beloved, my beloved, go far.
My husband is absent, go far;
He has gone to the country, go far,
To watch over slaves, go far,
And he was a slave, go far.

241   When he has taken leave of his parents and his wife, he gives a
farewell party for his brothers. His wife makes him bread, and he
entertains people. After food, he tells his leader to take the caravan to
the country. He will sleep in the town and follow his caravan in the
morning.

It is customary for a caravan to have a guide, followed by a
drummer and then a conch player. Every caravan must have a guide,
who is so called because he knows the way. If he goes ahead, followed
by people who do not know the way, he must leave at every fork a
mark so that those who follow may know which way to go. The mark
is this: if the road goes to the left, he puts fresh or dry leaves or digs a
furrow on the other side. Then those who are behind see the dry or
fresh leaves in the road and know that where these leaves are is not the
way.

When the guide comes to a place where there is plenty of water or a
good camping site, he beats the drum. When those who are behind
hear the guide's drum, those who are tired have fresh strength, and
when a thirsty man hears the drum he cheers up. If one has sat down
he resumes his load and hurries to the water or the camp. In the wild
in sunny weather, water is a great trouble.

When the caravan leaves, the guide must beat the drum again, for
some are asleep and some are away in other towns. When they hear
the drum, they hurry back. If the drum does not sound, they will
leave them in the place, and this is not the custom of the caravan. The
242   leader of the caravan must keep careful watch on his porters, or they
will steal people's goods without the owners' permission.

The *kome* is a stick that the Nyamwezi require when traveling.[9] It
takes the place of an amulet to protect them from the dangers of the
road.

When the caravan reaches Nyanyembe, the guide fires a gun, and
men and women come to welcome their brothers and to relieve them

of their loads. They go to the camp, where they rest. This is how they leave the coast to go inland.

Of Trade

When they reach Nyanyembe, the porters hand their loads over to him, and he is left alone with the loads.[10] He looks for friendly Nyamwezi to help his trade. They publish among their neighbors that a Swahili has arrived with good wares, and they come with ivory, small tusks, and cattle. He trades with them, and if his goods are not exhausted, he climbs the hills in search of ivory. There is no end to haggling about the price until he pays the "handshake." If the ivory is good, he pays a kitambi as handshake, and the headmen must be witnesses.[11] If he does not give this, there will be trouble over the price and all will go wrong. It is their custom at all buying and selling to shake hands at the end and say, "It is a deal, brother," or, as a joke, "It is dead."

If the leader of the caravan does a lot of business, he writes to his merchant and sends a reputable person with the letter and the purchases, whether ivory or rubber or other things. In the letter he writes, "To my dear merchant, greeting.[12] After greeting I have to inform you that so-and-so comes with my letter. I have entrusted to him to take to you three farasila of ivory. Take them over from him. I need more goods as before. Do not send anything different, for these are satisfactory. Send them soon, for the Makua have gone hunting for ivory and will be back before long. I want the goods to be in hand when they return, for God's sake, my merchant. Give the bearer of this letter a good kitambi as reward, because he is a good fellow. *Wasalaam*."

243

Goods Brought Down to the Coast

After buying ivory and other things, he comes back to the coast. For the return journey he pounds the "cotton for the road," sorghum and maize flour put up in a goatskin, which the porters use as bags. On the journey the porters have to do everything, putting up the master's tent and finding water to bring him if he has not his own people, until they reach the coast.

As they approach the coast he sends a messenger to his merchant and to his own house to say that Mr. so-and-so has reached Mpwapwa.[13] He has had a good journey and has done well. He is

sending to you for clothes and some other things. When the merchant
hears this, especially if he is a Hindu, his loincloth flaps with glee. He
packs up for the messenger the things wanted, and at his house they
make good things to take to him when he reaches the river.

At the crossing he sends a second messenger to say that he is at the
crossing and is coming over with his caravan. His friends go out into
the country to wait for him with a group of women to welcome him.
Everyone has a cup of rice, and when they meet him they pour the rice
on his head. His parents say, "Welcome, dear; you have gone safely
244   and returned safely. That is the point. Go abroad for experience; if
you do not go abroad, you see nothing." In the past people fired
salutes all the way to the customs house. In the next two or three days
the ivory was stamped for tax, and then the leader of the caravan took
it to his merchant for the reckoning. This is the account of the return
to the coast.

Of Accounts with the Merchant

After taking over the ivory, the merchant reckons up everything
that he has taken, beginning with the goods and the porters. When he
has done this sum, he says, "You took so many dollars, and you have
brought back so many. Your profit or loss is so much." If he and the
merchant agree, there is no argument; but often they quarrel, because
the merchant wants to take the whole of the profit. He charges a high
price for his goods, and if he gets his money back he wants to make a
large profit on the ivory.

If he wants to make another journey, he writes a bond for goods to
go again in the hope that this time he will make a bigger profit. Such
were in the past the trading journeys of the Swahili inland.

Modern Swahili Journeys

In the past people did not travel; they tilled the soil, and those who
had no land wandered about like untended cattle, because they would
not travel. It is the young people today who are the travelers, and their
journeys are not so much to Nyanyembe or Maniema, because this is
not profitable.[14] The inland pagan tribes have grown wary, and prices
245   inland and on the coast are the same. So they travel to Nguu to buy
rubber or tobacco, or to Uhehe, taking merchandise to make money.[15]
The Nguu and the Hehe also have become wary; but they think it
better to work for nothing than to travel for nothing, as people used to

say, "The foot that travels always gets its bit." Some people like travel but are not trustworthy, and the merchants will not give them anything. Nor do the travelers of today receive a great welcome on their return, for "an empty hand is not licked; if it is licked there is something in it." That is the proverb, and that is the end of that.

Nyamwezi Journeys in the Past

When the Nyamwezi came down to the coast, they brought cattle, goats, ivory, hippo teeth, and ostrich feathers. None came to the coast unless he had a contact in the town, a jumbe or a citizen whom he could inform of his arrival at Usako and ask for a house to be put ready for him and plenty of beer. His friend would rent a house for him and for his caravan leader and his overseers. In the morning the local man would say to his women, "Tomorrow we will welcome our friend in the country." To welcome him they would say, "Food, food, to please our guest."

When he reached the town he went into his house, and the ivory was sent to the customs. For the next six or seven days he would be drunk. The Indians came and went, asking his caravan leader when he would do business over his ivory; but when the porters arrived they had already sold everything that they were carrying, goats, rhino horn young and old, and spears, because their leader allowed them to 246 sell immediately, and they bought trinkets to pack up ready to take them to their families inland.

When the ivory has been stamped, the day comes when the Nyamwezi owner of the ivory wants to do business. He goes with his friend to the Indian shop, and there they lay it out. Their idea of business is that for each tusk they should receive the whole contents of the shop; but the Indians understand the business. They start in the morning, and by noon they have not agreed over a single tusk. First he wants this color and then that, and all the time they must be brought dates and coconut, and then they are pleased and think that the Indian is a good fellow. The Indian says, "I will give it you for nothing; we need no account of our dealings." But the Indian has everything written down in his book.

Then they talk more business until they fall out and say, "We are hungry. Let us drop business and come again tomorrow." Next day they go, and if they do not come to an agreement, the business is not completed. Perhaps on the third day the Indian will make an agreement with the Swahili sponsor: "Talk your friend into finishing the

business." Then he gives good advice to the Nyamwezi, and he
finishes the business. This is done by his abusing both the Nyamwezi
and the Indian, saying, "You are too stupid to understand business."
He asks the Nyamwezi, "What is it that you want and the Indian will
not give you?" He says, "I want these colors." Then he asks the
Indian, "Will not you lose by it?" and he says that he will. He says,
"Never mind; give him what he wants because you will get a lot of
ivory from him." He gives it to him; but even then the business is not
finished. The parties want their complimentary cloth or something of
that sort. Then he takes their hands and reconciles them, and the
business is finished. Such are the business methods of the Nyamwezi.

247   *The Work of Porters*

When they reach the town, they go to sleep. In the morning each
man takes an axe and goes into the bush to cut wood. Some cut laths,
some rafters, some props, and some strip-binding bark, everything
for building a house. They bring these to the town for sale at ten to
sixteen pesa a load. This gets them their livelihood, enough to eat, but
they are not satisfied. Others work in the town. They go around
asking for work, and people ask them what work. They say, "Any
work, carrying water or plastering the house"; but if you suggest
digging a latrine, they refuse, saying, "Digging a latrine is a lot of
trouble." Others work in the fields by agreement with men or women
who send them to help in the fields on daily rates. They receive the
agreed amount on return in the evening. Others arrange with them to
go to the river to carry loads of cane. They like this work best because
they get free cane to chew. Such is the work that Nyamwezi porters
do in the town.

Of the Return Inland of the Nyamwezi

When the business is done, the Nyamwezi go into the bush to cut
rods. Their rods are sticks for fastening up their bundles.[16] Then they
are given their return wages, and they buy what they want and tie up
their bundles. One bundle will contain ten bolts of cloth and some
kitambi, and these they carry on their backs. Both men and women
248   carry loads, and if he has bought a lot he has to carry another's load
and tie his own to his loins.

To please the porters on departure from the town, they are all given
red cloth to wear, and some of them have bells on their legs which

tinkle as they walk. The guide is similar; but he wears a *ngara*.[17] This is made of all sorts of birds' feathers, and he wears it on his head. When the caravan is made up, they go to the country and arrange their loads in the tent. Then they return to the town, because some of them have things that they have forgotten to buy. They bring a bolt to sell; but they get a poor price for it, because if you buy something in an Indian shop for ten rupees, the Indian will give you five. They are barbers and shave people dry. When they have bought their things, they go to the country, and the caravan departs.

In the old days on the night before starting, the Nyamwezi used to dance the tinge or celebrate *mapasa*. For this ceremony they plastered their faces with flour, and men and women exchanged insults, with no ill will but because it was the custom. Then they took flour and a new pot to a fork in the road.[18] This was their ceremony, and in the morning they started.

Marching Songs

On their journeys they sang:

Is not this a caravan? Is not this a caravan?
The Mwera from inland have come,
Is not this a caravan?[19]

or:

249   My mother, my mother, listen.
The rich coastal people are swindling us.

or:

Take, take, my son,
My spear, haa,
Take my spear, my son.

or:

All is gone in dues and taxes,
O father, all is gone.
Go away, you coastal people. Be my mother,
We have come to see you with our friends.
O mother of cowards, be my mother,
We have come to see you.

or:

> The little claw of a dove,
> The little claw of a dove,
> Is the fighting of the Gogo, O father.
> The little claw of a dove.

250 After this song they shout, "Are you there? Are you there?" Others reply, "Here we are, here we are," or "The coastal people are no men; they have beaten Katate with chains." At the end of a song they often say, "This place is not well cooked." Or they sing, "We will leave the men at home, to be idle with the women."

Chapter 24
Of Blood Brotherhood among the Swahili

The Origin of Blood Brotherhood

In the past the inland people and the people of the coast feared and robbed each other. If an inland person came to the coast with goods, he was robbed, and if the coast people went inland, they were robbed of their goods and murdered. So they wanted blood brotherhood to remove the fear from their hearts.[1] Once they had made it, they were no longer robbed but became brothers.

Of Blood Brotherhood

If a man wanted to make the friendship, first a chicken or a goat was slaughtered according to their means. Then the liver was taken and thoroughly cooked, and after this there came a man with a razor and a hone. He was called the maker of the friendship, because that is what he did. He addressed one of the two by name, "Mwenyi Kombo, do you wish to have Mwenyi Khamisi as your friend and for his brothers to come into your house and take what they want of yours without angering you? Mwenyi Khamisi's brother is your brother, and if you are angry you will die." They replied to the witnesses, "Aye" or "Yes."

The operator continues, "If you know of an attack to be made on Mwenyi Khamisi and you know of it and do not speak, you shall die." Again they reply, "Aye."

"Or if in council you speak against your brother Mwenyi Khamisi, you shall die." "Aye."

While he is saying this, the operator sharpens the razor on the hone over his head, or if he has no razor he sharpens a machete, a sword, or a knife. This is to put fear into them so that the man and his friend may live in amity and not break the brotherhood.

When this is over a different man comes to Mwenyi Khamisi with the same words that we have said above. The parties sit on a new mat covered with a new cloth, and when the words are done, the liver is brought. Each of them is scratched, their blood is rubbed into the liver, and both eat it. Then it is taken away, and each returns to his own place.

Then come the watani and ask for their friendship fees, and the witnesses ask for their friendship fee.[2] Those present ask for "the stripping," that is, for the mat on the floor to be taken away and the removal of the covering cloth. One operator takes the mat and the other the cloth.

Others do not go through the ceremony, but trust each other without it. They cook food and invite people and eat and recite the fatiha to ask God to bless their friendship. The inland people are not satisfied with anything but blood brotherhood before accepting any-one as their brother.

Chapter **25** Of Slavery

The Origin of Slaves

The origin is that a man is struck by some disaster such as war between one country and another. Those who are taken prisoner in war are not killed, but roped and taken to the town and told to remain as slaves.[1] They do so, and they marry among themselves, and their offspring are slaves too. Or slavery may arise from a debt of blood money. If somebody has killed another and his family is poor and he has no money, he is liable for blood money; but if he cannot pay, he is taken and sold, or he goes as a slave to the creditor. If he has killed a freeman, the blood money is a large sum, and if he has a brother or an uncle, he also may accompany him into slavery. Or if a sorcerer has killed somebody and is known to be a sorcerer, he is killed, or he may go as a slave to the place where the killing took place. Or if an adulterer has lain with another's wife, he has to pay compensation. If he cannot, he becomes a slave. Compensation for adultery used to be paid inland and on the coast, even among the Swahili. Or in time of famine people would sell themselves to each other. Or a person may pledge a child or a brother-in-law, and when he has not the money to redeem him, he becomes a slave. A man cannot pledge or sell his wife, even in a severe famine. If he cannot support her he will divorce her.

To return to consideration of the inland country: prisoners of war, pawns, and persons taken in adultery whose families cannot redeem them become slaves. Arab and other slave traders go inland and buy them and bring them to the coast and sell them to others. This is the origin of slavery. The purchaser of those brought to the coast must keep a close watch on them or they will run away, and some on arrival on the coast claim to be freemen.

In the time of Sayyid Barghash there was a famine, and the Zaramo sold and pawned each other. When the Zanzibar Arabs heard that slaves were easily obtained on the coast, they came to buy Zaramo slaves; but when they went to sleep at night, the Zaramo ran away and by morning was back at home. Once he was there it was hard to recover him. Those who were shipped to Zanzibar stayed for a month and then claimed not to be slaves but freemen and the courts were full of complaints. When Sayyid Barghash found out that the Arabs were going to the coast to buy Zaramo, he rebuked them, saying, "Anybody who goes to the coast to buy Zaramo is throwing his money into the sea, and in addition I shall give him six months in fetters." The reason for this was that they were not being bought; when people were going out of the town into the country and they saw Zaramo women and children, they would seize them, gagging them so that they could not cry out, and bring them into the town to sell to the traders.

255   Many of the Arabs traveled inland to make war on the pagan tribes and to enslave those whom they made prisoner. Or a pagan would go to an Arab and offer his services. The Arab would agree, and if he had any family, they would come too. Then he made them slaves. That is why some of the inland or Maniema slaves give a lot of trouble on the coast, saying, "This Arab did not buy me. I took service with him, and now he wants to make a slave of me."

Types of Slaves

Mzalia is one whose mother came from inland. On arrival she was married to another slave and had a child. He is called mzalia. There are two sorts of mzalia, first-generation mzalia, second-generation mzalia, et cetera, until the seventh generation. The meaning of the seventh generation is that his mother was born in the town and his father likewise. Such a person's status is that of a freeman, he is simply said to be of slave origin.[2]

Then there are raw slaves. Raw means that he has just arrived on the coast and does not know the language or customs, nor how to wash clothes, nor how to cook.[3] He is called a raw slave, and if he is sold his price is smaller than that of a trained slave.

The mzalia was not often sold in the past, unless he had bad manners and was rude to freemen. A freeman would marry a mzalia, for they became part of the family. Children born to a mzalia by a freeman are not slaves.[4]

The Work of Raw Slaves

256 On purchase they were given new clothes and bought a hoe and sent to the fields. There there were an overseer and a headman. When the master came to the field, he called the overseer and the headman and said to them, "I have brought you a recruit." They said, "Good, we see him."

In the morning the overseer and the headman showed him where to dig, and his plot was marked out for him. He was given a task, that is, a section in which he must dig cassava and plant vegetables and beans. The master did not have to give him the yield of this plot unless he wished to do so. If he grew rice or sorghum, he gave him a little rice as *pepeta* or sorghum as *msima* out of kindness.[5]

Some slaves have three days and some two. They work in the fields from early morning until eleven o'clock, when they return to the houses. They go out again in the afternoon until five, when they knock off.

If a slave is unwell, he does not go to work. He tells the master that such a slave is unwell. If the illness is serious, the master treats him until he recovers. If he dies, he provides the winding sheet and tells the others to bury him.

Songs of Slaves after Work

They sing:

Overseer, your work is done,
Give us something to straighten our backs.

or:

257
If you go to Malindi, kanzu and vest,
If you get any money, let it roll,
Or Msengesi will ruin you.[6]

or:

> Sir, I am not well, send me to the field
> To dig wild jasmine and pomegranate.
> This is not smallpox but chicken pox.

or:

> The silver dollar never tells a lie.[7]
> Though you put it in the mud
> Your heart rejoices and you have no bitterness.

The Work of Mzalia

The work of the mzalia is to serve in the house, to wash vessels and plates or clothes or to be taught to cook, to plait mats, to sweep the house, to go to the well to draw water, to go to the shop to buy rice or meat; when food is ready, to dish it up for the master, to hold the basin for him to wash his hands, sometimes to wash his feet, and to oil him; but only if his wife approves. If the wife wants to go into the country or to a mourning or a wedding, she accompanies her, and if she has an umbrella, she carries it for her.

258   A male mzalia travels with his master to tend him if he is unwell, to wash his clothes when they are dirty, to shop for him, and to do any other service that he wants. He may be sent into the yard to learn to sew a kanzu or to embroider clothes or caps, or to be taught carpentry, to make carved doors, or to build stone or timber houses. When he knows these things he retains his own profits, and if he is a good mzalia he remembers his master and gives part to him.

How Slave and Master Should Behave

A slave should obey his master; if he is told to do something, he should do it. If he is called, he should come at once to hear his orders. He should not answer his master back. If he sees his master carrying something, he should take it from him. If he goes into his master's room, he should take off his cap. When he is with his master, he should not go in front, and if they go where there are stools, he should not take one. Every morning and evening he should wait on his master to do anything required. When a slave greets his master, he does not offer his hand, even when they are traveling, nor does he ever enter his master's room without speaking. A slave must eat any food that the gentry are eating; but he does not eat with them. A mzalia eats with his master.

Of Slaves in the Past

In the past slaves were given no consideration by freemen on the coast. A slave was known by his dress, for never in his life did he wear a cap, whether a jumbe lived or died. He never wore sandals nor a kanzu long enough to cover his legs. Nor did a gentleman address him by name; he said, "You." He did not protect himself from the rain with an umbrella; although they did cover themselves in the rain with umbrellas made of doum palm. Nor did he ever in the house wear clogs. At parties they sat separately, not with the gentry, as the town crier said:

259

> The news horn,
> Its sound means that all is well.
> The horn of the jumbe and of the forty,
> Of the officers and the locally born slaves,
> Of gentlemen and their sons,
> Of the mzalia and of slaves.

After this introduction the required announcement was made. Female slaves accompanying free women do not wear a veil or a headcloth.

Nor does a slave sit on a cane chair nor have one in his house. If he does so, people say, "This slave thinks himself as good as us. He has cane chairs in his house."

Slaves began to give themselves airs some fifteen years ago. There was a jumbe who had many slaves. One day he went to the shop and bought kangas and *kayas* for his slave girls to wear.[8] They were astonished, and the other jumbes heard that jumbe Kisoka had given kayas to his slaves. They went to ask him about it, and he said, "I want to please myself and my slaves, as anyone may do if he likes." All the jumbes were angry, and they wanted to oppose him; but others said, "That will not do; he has a lot of supporters, he is well born, and he has many relations in the town," but the jumbes hated him.

260

A year later there was in the quarter of Gongoni a jumbe called Gungurugwa, who said, "I am going to give my slaves kayas and umbrellas." The young citizens made no objection, and he put his domestic slaves into kayas, and they went around the town carrying umbrellas. The other jumbes were angry and said, "These jumbes are breaking the traditions and doing things that our ancestors never did. There will be trouble in the town. There will be a revolution if slaves are treated differently every month. Next time a jumbe dies, half the place will uncover in respect, and half will keep their caps on." There was a lot of disagreement, and to this day they do not uncover on the death of a jumbe. Very few do so because they do not think it necessary. And the slaves no longer do the work that they used to do. They do as they like, and if they do not like it they do not do it. If one is disobedient, his master cannot correct him. He takes him to court and says, "This slave is disobedient and will not work in the house." The government punishes him. That is the difference between slaves now and in the past.

Marriage of Slaves

261   In the past, if a slave wanted a wife, he asked his master's permission to marry her. The master asked if they were agreed, and he said that they were. Then he told the slave to give him a dollar for his turban. A raw slave paid a dollar for the turban, which he gave to his master, and the bride-price was five dollars. After paying for the turban in accordance with old custom, they did not go to the teacher for the marriage, but the master said, "I marry you to your fellow slave so-and-so," and he went at once into his wife's house.

Now they go to the teacher to be married in accordance with custom. There are no wedding feast, no celebration, no invitations, and no sewing mattresses and pillows. These customs are not followed.

A freed slave does not inform his master of his proposal to a fellow slave. He finds the woman that he wants, and when they have agreed, he goes to his master to tell him that he wishes to get married, because to do so is respectful. The master says, "Very well, it is for you to decide."

On the day of the wedding the master comes to preside over the feast, for he is the father. If the freed slave can afford it, he has a celebration like a freeman with dancing and many invitations. The bride-price is ten to twenty dollars, and a turban of five dollars is given to the bride's father or brother or, if she has neither, to her owner. A freed slave, or, as the Swahili say, a slave of God, marries another slave of God. A freed domestic slave can marry a free woman, but a raw slave cannot.

262   Children both of whose parents are slaves are slaves. If a freeman marries a slave woman, their child is a slave; but if a free woman marries a slave man, their child is not a slave, because free birth is matrilineal.[9]

Of Suria

A suria is when a man buys a slave girl and introduces her into his house, and she learns cooking and all domestic customs. When she is of age, her master says to her, "You are my suria, and you may not go outside. If you want anything, tell others to buy it for you." When her fellows realize that the master has spoken so, they give her respect. She is bought a bed and a mat and pillows and is given her own room like a wife. If the master is married, he spends three nights with his wife and one with his suria. If he is not married, the suria is his wife. Some people prefer a suria to a wife, because they say that a suria is a piece of luggage, meaning that if you travel you take your suria with you; but a wife, first you have to persuade her, and then you have to consult her parents before you take her on a journey. That is why they prefer a suria. Others prefer a wife, because when they have a child, he can say, "My father is so-and-so and my grandfather so-and-so, and my mother is so-and-so and her father so-and-so," because he has good blood on both sides. That is the reason for preferring a wife. But the son of a suria is a freeman and may not be sold nor called a slave, although he has no rank through his mother.

263   ## Of Runaway Slaves

If a slave runs away, if you bought him in the town, you go to the vendor and say, "My slave has run away, please bring him to me if you see him." Or you go to the river or the seashore and say to the ferrymen, "My slave has run away; his description is like this—he is wearing such clothes, his tribe is Ganda or Sukuma, he is a raw slave, short and dark. If you find him trying to cross, stop him, catch him, and bring him to me. I live at Bagamoyo near so-and-so, and my name is . . ." Then he goes back to the town.

If the slave comes to the river and the ferrymen see him, they ask him what he wants, and he does not know what to say, so they catch him and take him to the man's house in the town, and he must pay a recovery fee of one dollar. In the old days the slave would be locked up in the house in a room by himself for two or three days. Then he was promised on oath that if he ran away again he should die.

Of Charms to Recover Slaves

If a man ran away, a coil rope was bought and Ya sini was recited over seven knots in it by the teacher.[10] It was given to the owner of the runaway to take home. There he stood in the doorway and called his slave by name seven times. Then the rope was hung over the door, and if he was lucky the slave came back or was caught and brought back by others.

264   ### Of Giving a Slave as Security

Any debtor can send his slave as security, whether the slave likes it or not, if security is required of the master. Such a slave is allowed one day to go and visit his master and to return on the next day. A married slave can be used as security and his wife too, and they have to do the same work as they did for their master. If they are idle, he can send them back and demand his money.

Of Borrowing by Slaves

A slave cannot incur a debt without his master's authority. If a merchant advances money to a slave, he knows that if the slave takes the money and goes inland or dies or runs away and does not return to the coast, his money has fallen into the sea. He cannot go to the master to claim it. If it is a written agreement and he wants to borrow, he may do so by himself if he is in need of money; because if he loses it, he alone, and not his master, is liable.

Of Manumission

If a man has many slaves, he may see one under his authority and call him, saying, "Mabruk" or "Majuma, you shall have a deed of manumission and be no longer a slave." Or if he has but one slave who has been with him for many years, he may manumit him. If he has a

265   little field, he gives it to him and makes him his brother or his son. Such deeds are usually written when a man is growing old and wants to do a good action, whether he has children or not. He says, "I wish to make slave so-and-so a slave of God, and when I die, let her be as your sister. Do not cast her off." Then a deed is written and given to her, and she is free. One with such a deed cannot be sold or used as security.

The Deed of Manumission

If a man wants to give his slave a deed of manumission, he writes, "I, A, son of B, hereby declare that I set so-and-so free before God, a free person. None may dispute this while I am alive or after my death. Any person altering what I have written in this deed is answerable to God for altering it. I have made him free. Any person making him a slave contrary to this deed must answer to God."

Such was the bond; but nowadays they go to the court, and the deed is drawn there and stamped with the seal of the central government.

Chapter 26 Of Generosity

Anyone able to do so likes to invite his friends or visitors to the town to a meal at his house, and anyone who makes a little money or some other form of profit buys a goat and cooks it and invites people to come and eat it. Even a porter gives a little party for his fellows when he is paid.[1]

Another form of generosity is to come on one who has no clothes and to give him sufficient money for them and to invite him to a meal; but it is not proper for the host to say, "I have given such-and-such to so-and-so."

Another is to find someone who has nowhere to sleep and, if there is room in the house, to invite him in and show him to a bedroom without charge and give him food.

Another is to meet half a dozen poor people in the road and to take them home and to give to each one pesa or more or some rice or sorghum.

If a man is leaving the market after buying maize or mangoes and meets a friend, he says, "Please, take a mango or a little maize." And if they are at the market together and he is going to buy fruit, he buys two portions, one for himself and one for his friend.

If a man is smoking a cigarette and meets a friend in the road, he says to him, "Finish this for me." Then he smokes a little and returns it, or he asks, "Do you want it back, or shall I keep it?"

Of Guests

Similarly, if a stranger comes to the town and has no house to go to, he goes to the mosque, where someone will see him and ask him where he is from. He replies, "I have nowhere to go and nothing to eat."

Then the man takes him to his house and shows him to a room and says, "Stay as long as you like." He charges nothing for lodging, and when there is food they eat together. If the host can do so he gives him clothes, and if he is not a passing visitor and is a good man, he looks for a wife for him. They give her to him, and he becomes one of them. If he has no work, they introduce him to the business of the town, and if he is a cultivator they take him out and show him a plot to till, and so he becomes a citizen.[2]

But if he is idle and will not work but just eats and sleeps, he says, "Enough is enough," meaning that a guest who outstays his welcome is disliked, as is described in "The Song of the Guest":

1. The guest on the first day,
   Give him rice and coconut heart
   Served in the shell,
   To welcome the guest.[3]

268

2. The guest on the second day,
   Give him milk and butter.
   As affection grows,
   Show more to the guest.

3. The guest on the third day,
   There is nothing in the house
   But three kibaba,[4]
   Cook them and eat with the guest.

4. The guest on the fourth day,
   Give him a hoe to use,
   On his return, take leave of him,
   And let him go home.[5]

5. The guest of the fifth day
   Pricks like a needle.
   The house if full of whispering,
   All against the guest.

6. The guest on the sixth day—
   Go into the corners
   To hide when you eat,
   From that guest.[6]

269

7. The guest on the seventh day
   Is no guest but a pest.
   If the thatch catches fire
   Blame it on the guest.

8. The guest on the eighth day—
   "Come in, let us part."
   When he goes outside—
   "Goodbye, go along, guest."

9. The guest on the ninth day—
   "Go, man, go,
   Do not come back,
   Do not return, guest."

10. The guest on the tenth day—
    With blows and kicks,
    Get rid of no one
    So long as you are rid of the guest.

The Reception of a Distinguished Visitor

When a new governor visits the coast, the people hear that the governor is going to pay them a visit that day, and they gather on the beach to see him and welcome him, and they take drums and pipes, if the government allows. When he comes ashore, the drums and pipes are played with great joy.

The song of those who carry the visitor is:

Yoo yoo, our visitor,
Author of luck and joy.
Yoo yoo, our visitor,
God has brought him to us.
Yoo yoo, our visitor,
270   Give him a good place to stay
Yoo yoo, our visitor
Until his return home.
Yoo yoo, our visitor.

They take him with honor until they have brought him to his own place, and then they return. If they have permission they dance for two or three days.

The custom of celebrating the arrival of a visitor: In the old days, when a notable man of the town returned after several years' absence, his arrival was celebrated, and he used to give presents. Or when a Nyamwezi came to the coast with a lot of property, his arrival was celebrated, and he produced presents for the people. But today the custom of celebrating the arrival of Nyamwezi is no more. That is the account of the welcome given to a visitor.

Chapter 27 Of Vows

Vows

Suppose a person is at sea, and the wind rises, and the ship is likely to sink because of it: one of those on board comes forward and says, "If God preserves us, we vow to take so much money to sharif so-and-so."[1] If then the wind drops, they have to pay this money to the sharifu mentioned, for a vow is like incurring a debt, and payment must be made.[2]

Or if someone is sick and says, "If I recover, I will recite Hal Badiri," if he recovers, he must do so.[3]

Again, a childless person may say, "If God grant me to get a child, I will take an earthen basin of rice to the grave of sharif so-and-so." If he gets a child, he must do so.

If a man has lost a slave, he may make a vow, "If I find my slave, I vow to draw water and take it to the mosque."

If a person is sick, he may vow, "If I get well, I will take oil to the Friday mosque." If he recovers, he must take it to the Friday mosque; but it must be to the mosque where the Friday service is held. If he has said, "If I get well I will take oil to the mosque," but he has not mentioned whether it is or is not the Friday mosque, then he may take it to any mosque.

Chapter 28 Of Oaths and Ordeals

The Ordeal of the Billhook or Axe

If a man has stolen something and not been seen but people suspect him, or a magician (*mwanga*) has been caught or someone is suspected of being a magician (mganga), the suspects ask for an ordeal.[1] A doctor (mganga) is called in, and he is given the ordeal of the billhook.[2] This is of iron, and a verse of the Qur'an is written on it—*Wa qul jaa 'lhaqqu wa za haqa 'lbatilu inna 'lbatilu kana za huqa*.[3] Then it is made red-hot on a fire of ebony. Or an axe is taken and made red-hot. It is then given to the person undergoing the ordeal to lick, in the morning before he has had any food. The person who licks says, "I have been accused of sorcery (*uchawi*); I know nothing of it, white or black, and now I take the ordeal. If I go out at night to cast spells (*kwanga*), or if I prepare food for a neighbor's child to cause its death, may the truth of the ordeal fall upon me. No, neither I nor my father or mother know anything of this art. I am being slandered, and may the ordeal clear me." Then he licks the billhook with his tongue, and after this the doctor (mganga) tells him to open his mouth, and he shows him. If his tongue is not blistered, the ordeal has cleared him; if it is, he is convicted. If the ordeal has convicted him, everybody speaks openly of him as a criminal who brings evil to the neighborhood. They say, "Now we will put you on oath to abandon these practices," and he consents to be sworn.

If the ordeal acquits him, there is much trouble for the complainant, for the defendant on acquittal will complain that he has been falsely accused of sorcery. Old custom makes this a ground of quarrel

and fighting, for sorcery is a grave matter to the Swahili. He may pay
compensation in cash, and the quarrel will be ended. This is the
account of the magician (mwanga) and the ordeal of the billhook.

The Ordeal of Rice

If somebody is a thief and denies it, but someone else accuses him,
he says, "Tomorrow we will go to the teacher to settle our minds and
be sure who is and who is not a thief."[4] When they are agreed, they go
to the teacher to tell him that they will come on the following day. He
tells them to bring husked rice, and they buy a little and take it to the
teacher. He says, "Come tomorrow; but do not sleep with a man"—
or, to men, "Do not sleep with women." Then the teacher recites over
the rice; that is, he takes it in his hand and recites a verse of the Qur'an.
Some teachers leave the rice in the mosque overnight and bring it
home in the morning. Others keep it at home.

275   In the morning, both parties come, and one of them says, "I want to
be the first to take the ordeal." The teacher takes a handful of rice,
again recites a verse of the Qur'an, and gives it to the person taking the
ordeal, who says, "An ordeal of truth: If I am a thief or the accomplice
of a thief, may the ordeal convict me. If I am not a thief and am being
slandered, may the ordeal clear me." Then he puts the handful of rice
into his mouth to chew it—dry, uncooked rice—and the teacher
recites Ya sini from beginning to end.[5] If he is a thief, before the end of
Ya sini the rice has filled his mouth with flour and he cannot chew it,
and the teacher says, "The ordeal has convicted him." If he is not a
thief, he chews the rice, his mouth is empty, and he is acquitted.

If he is acquitted, there are quarrels, recriminations, and even
fights. "Why did you call me a thief, and the ordeal has acquitted
me?" They will be brought by others to an agreement; if he is to be
paid compensation, he will be paid, and if he does not want it, he will
say, "I forgive him; I do not want anything." this is the ordeal of rice.

The Ordeal of Acacia

If a person is a sorcerer or a thief, hot gruel is cooked, and into it is
put medicine made of acacia. When it is ready, those who are to take
the ordeal come before the doctor, who puts the gruel into a little pot,
and this is given to the person to be tested. The gruel is very hot, and
he must drink it without hesitation. If he is a thief, his lips and tongue
will be blistered; but if not, he will be no more burned than if it were

276   water. This form of ordeal is much used by inland people; but some of
the Swahili use it. This is the account of the ordeal of acacia.

The Ordeal of the Needle

This ordeal a teacher administers. For it the persons who are to take
it come to him, and he asks which is to be first. One of them says that
he is. The teacher takes a needle and recites over it a verse of the
Qur'an. The person to be tested says, "This is a true ordeal. If I am a
thief, may it not pierce me; if I am not, may it go through like needle
and thread." Then the teacher takes his ear and pricks it with the
needle. If he is a thief, the needle will not go in, and he feels pain. If he
is not, the needle goes straight through, and he is acquitted.

The Ordeal of Sanga

This ordeal comes from the inland people, and it too is a needle.[6]
There used to be a man in Bagamoyo called Dogori who administered
it by taking a needle and inserting it in the person's eye, singing:

Come out for me, needle,
My son.

If he was a thief, the needle did not come easily out of his eye,
unless the people sang the song vigorously, and then it would come
out. If he was not a thief, the needle did not stick in his eye. In the eye
of the needle there was a thread, which he pulled if the needle stuck.
Then both eyes of the thief would be bloodshot. If he was not a thief,
his eyes would not be bloodshot, and he would say, "The ordeal has
277   acquitted him; give me my fee"; because he was a professional and
people placed much faith in his ordeal. This is the account of the
ordeal of the sanga.

Ancient Swahili Oaths

If somebody had not done something but another suspected that he
had, he would deny it, and the other would say, "Will you swear?" If
the person were a man, he would say, "By my mother, I did not do
this," or "By my sister, Maatumu, I did not do it," or "By my aunt,
Mwana Fatuma." If the person were a woman, she would swear, "By
my father, Mwenyi Amiri" or "By my brother, Mwenyi Khamisi, I

did not do this." Both sexes, but chiefly women, would swear on the place "where my parents lie" or "where my parents sleep." Or they would say, "May Lady Makuka cut my throat if I did it." Or they would swear, "When the sun goes down, may I go down with it." Or "May Dungumaro destroy me" or "May the Punda spirit destroy me."[7] To this day women and some country folk swear like this; but men do not; they swear by the name of God, *Wallahi.*[8]

Chapter **29** Examples of
Swahili Beliefs
about God's
Creation

Of the Sun

We do not know about the beginning and end of the earth; but we see the days come and go, and we see the sun rise and set.[1] We believe that, as our ancestors said, when the sun sets there is a great bang like a cannon near the place where it goes down as it falls into the water; but no one can hear it but children and animals.

We see the sun rise daily, but we do not know what happens. We do not understand the hand of a clock, because in the past we had no clocks. If you ask anyone the time, he will reply, "Look at the sun" or he will look at his shadow and measure its length with his feet. If the sun is overhead, he knows the time, and if his shadow is nine feet long, he says it is nine o'clock. At night they do not know eleven or twelve. On rainy days they know when the cock crows that it is five or six. If they do not crow, they do not know the time. That is what the Swahili believe about the sun.

Of the Moon

We do not know whether it is made of glass or what. We see its light, and God created it. When it is eclipsed, we say that it has been caught by a snake, because when it crosses the path where the snake is established and the snake sees the moon, it says, "Why have you come to my place?" The moon says, "I have lost my way today." The snake swallows the moon, and the world becomes dark. It is then our custom to beat drums with all our might because we are frightened.

Then the snake says to the moon, "People on earth love you very much." So the snake vomits up the moon. Then the snake says to the moon, "When the sun goes down, people do not pray for it; everyone goes on with his own business." Such are the beliefs of the Swahili. Some still hold them; others do not.

When there is an eclipse of the moon, those who are awake tell those who are asleep, "There is an eclipse of the moon; do not stay asleep." Then they take cans to beat, and those who are still asleep hear them until all are awake. Everyone who goes outside has a can or a hoe, and they beat them all around the town. The government does not object on such a night, because it knows that there is an eclipse. They sing:

> Let us pray, let us pray,
> Slaves, let us pray.

or:

> I climb my beanstalk
> Above the mosque,
> I did not eat the beans
> For God has taken it.[2]

280

Or one sings:

> In the name of God, repent.
> In the name of God, repent.

and the others respond:

> In the name of God, repent.
> In the name of God, repent.

But when the teachers know that there is an eclipse, they go to the mosque, and the others follow them. They formally wash themselves, and then the teacher stands before the gibla and leads them in prayer, the people following him. After this he preaches a sermon. The service at an eclipse of the moon is very long, and the teacher taking it must know a long sura by heart. When the service is over, they recite the fatiha to ask God to take sickness from the town. When there is an eclipse of the sun, the teachers hold a similar service; but the people do not pray for the sun.

Of the World

The Swahili are ignorant of this; they do not know the nature of the earth, whether it be vegetable or mineral; but they do know the meaning of *ulimwengu*. It is *ule mawingu*, and they believe that the world is supported on the horns of a cow.[3]

281 ## Of Earthquakes

Every year the coast is affected by an earthquake. The whole town shakes, pots and plates are broken, and people are giddy. The Swahili say that the cow supporting the earth has moved its horns. This is what they believe about earthquakes.

Of the Sea

They do now know the origin or nature of the sea. They believe that it entirely surrounds the land so that people live on an island, and that there are other lands surrounded by the same sea. In the sea there are jinns shaped like cattle but larger than those of the land. They sink passing ships; they do not eat people, but they suck their blood. If a man dies at sea and is washed up, they say that his blood has been sucked by the jinns.[4]

Of Thunder and Lightning

When they hear the thunder, the Swahili have always said that God is speaking with his angels. When the lightning flashes, they say, "God is pleased. He is laughing, and this year there will be much rain and food." If there is no thunder or lightning, they say, "This year God is angry, and we shall be short of food." When there is thunder and lightning, they do not allow their children to wear red lest the lightning kill them.

282   The Swahili make use of lightning. They take seven metal pots and cover the last with white and red cloth. Underneath is a pit with mud in it. When the lightning strikes, it goes through all the pots into the last, and they know that it has been caught. It does not melt, but is left for seven days. Then it is taken up, and they find that it is metal of a very rare type called *suwesi*. It is much used for knives and swords; but it is very expensive.[5]

Of the Stars

They believe that the stars are like small stones, which God has placed in the sky to shine over the world. When they shoot, they say that the devils are trying to climb up to heaven to hear what God is doing. When the angels hear the devils climbing up, they take fiery brands and beat them back. Some fall and some climb, and that is why they go in all directions.[6] In form the devils have one leg, one eye, and one arm and are as tall as a palm tree. They go out mostly at sunset. The Swahili will not allow their children to walk about at sunset nor to eat in the open road, because the devils are abroad by day and at sunset.

If a star falls and someone finds it and later has a child, he works it into the child's necklace, and the child wears it. In this necklace are the seeds of all sorts of fruits. When the child goes to sleep, it is put under his pillow, and when he wakes it is put around his neck all day to protect him from harm. It is like a child's amulet.

283

Of Clouds and the Rainbow

The Swahili know nothing whatever about the clouds. When the clouds gather, we say that it will rain, and when we see the rainbow, we say, "The bow is bent; there will be good rains this year"; but of the origin of the rainbow we know nothing. When the moon has a halo, we say, "This year the rains will be heavy."

Of Prayers for Rain

If for a long time there has been no rain and the fields are parched, the Swahili pray to God. For this they go first to their ancestors' graves and sweep them. At the graves they take off their sandals, cap, and kanzu, and then they sweep, saying, "We have come to you, our ancestors; this year the sun is hard upon us, and there is nothing in the fields. We have come to sweep, so that by your grace, our ancestors, God may be merciful to us."[7]

If there is no rain, they consult the teacher. "This year God is vexed with us; there is no rain; what should we do?" The teachers say, "Let us arrange to buy an ox as a sacrifice for the town, for the sun is fierce and there is much sickness." They buy a black or red ox or a speckled one, for such is a sacrificial ox.[8] When it has been obtained, all the

284   teachers of the town are called with their pupils. They burn incense in
       a censer. They give the ox to a man who goes in front, and the teachers
       follow, reciting Ya sini for every ten persons and then *burdai* for every
       person.[9] The pupils recite the shorter suras known to them. With the
       ox they go around the whole town to the end, and at the graves they
       recite the fatiha. Then they slaughter the ox, and the meat is distri-
       buted to the poor. At every service in the mosque, they pray for rain:
       "O Lord, send rain on us thy servants; take from us the evil of disease
       in our town and bless us, God of the worlds." If God hears the prayers
       of his servants, it is not many days before rain falls. Everyone rejoices
       in town and country. That is how the Swahili pray for rain.

Chapter **30** Of High Days

Of the New Year Wash

When, except for the last two days before the new year, the Swahili year is over, the first of these two days is called Corncob Day and the second Go-bare Day.[1] On Corncob Day they roast sorghum in ashes and scatter it with the ashes in the corners of the house. This is a very old custom, because they believe that on Corncob Day and Go-bare Day devils are at large, and the roast grain is put down to keep them away.

On Go-bare Day everyone able to do so cooks a pot of mixed maize and beans, and when it is done they put it out on the verandah for any passerby to eat. It is not customary to eat it indoors. Like the Ramadhan breakfast, no one is rejected; it is for anyone who likes.

Schoolchildren too have three days' holiday, Corncob, Go-bare, and New Year's Day. On New Year's Day they color their boards all colors and go out with them, singing:

> Not ours, not ours, our teacher's.
> Ours are the weapon, the board and the pen,
> Give us a little to go away.[2]
> If you are men, come out to us
> And we will pound and grind.
> Officer Abdallah is a womanizer.[3]

Then they sing:

> Magubeda, Magubeda,
> The belly of the *chafi* fish swells with fatness.[4]

They sing this song at every house, and at every house they stop and are given money. In the past there used to be fights between one school and another when they met.

Everywhere on New Year's Day people wake up early, men and women, young and old, to go to dip in the sea—the New Year wash. They take mats and beds to wash them, that is, to remove from them and from themselves their impurities and to see the New Year in.

When a man dips himself, he says, "God, take from me sickness and give me health. Let me be clean this year and the year to come." Then he dips himself.

Of Ramadhan

In the month of Ramadhan, the Swahili custom is to fast for the whole thirty days. That is, they do not eat in the daytime or drink, nor smoke from four in the morning until six in the evening, when they eat the meal called *futari*. Their food is gruel and buns and rice flour or cooked cassava, bananas, and meat, or fish roasted with coconut. From the third hour to the fourth they eat the *daku* meal of rice and meat; and this is their custom until the end of Ramadhan.[5]

At the end of the month they hold a feast called the minor feast. Rich people invite many others to come and eat. Some cook platters of rice and go to their neighbors to eat it. A married man buys new clothes for his wife and for his child, too. They call on important people to give them the festal handshake. And they give them presents and cook a great feast and invite people in. They sprinkle rose water and cense them with aloes. On the twenty-seventh of Ramadhan, the women cook food and take it to their friends. This food is called *bembe* and is very expensive, because they make buns and fried meat and every sort of dainty.[6] Some take it to their parents and lovers, and those who are brought it eat it and then buy things such as nice clothes to recompense those who have brought it.

In the month of Ramadhan, all must fast who are at home and fit. A sick person need not fast, nor a traveler; but they must make up the fast, a sick person when he recovers and a traveler on return to the coast.

288   The rule for women is that a woman in childbirth or a nursing mother may eat in the daytime. A pregnant woman may eat by day if she cannot fast. These days must be made up when the child is able to walk.

Old people may eat by day if they cannot fast; but their fast is made up by others, and they pay in money.

Children are told to fast from the age of seven; but they do not all do so. It is not absolutely compulsory until the age of fifteen.

A man who is fasting breaks his fast if he lies with a woman, and for this one day he must pay sixty days or pay a penalty. The penalty is to free a slave or to give sixty kibaba of sorghum to the poor.[7]

Of the Major Feast

Two feasts are celebrated on the coast, one on breaking the fast and the other on the tenth of the third month after this. It is called the major feast. On this day the slave girls buy a long cane of sugar or bamboo and decorate it with cups and little bowls and scraps of red cloth. They carry it around the town for three days, singing:

> How shall we arrange the flowers?
> Flowers have no needles,
> Flowers have no needles,
> How shall we arrange the flowers?

The boys sing their own song:

> Kindu, Kindu, has no teeth
> On the shore, on the wharf.

(Kindu being a person who had lost all his teeth).

All the children have their pitch, for there are two or three canes and every quarter of the town has one cane and its supporters.

At night the women dance the msoma dance, and in the afternoon the men put on their kanzus and go to a shady mango tree and dance the kiumbizi until they are tired.

Chapter **31** Double Meanings

The reason why the Swahili use double meanings is that if someone does something improper, people speak with double meaning so that he may not understand. If he knows the meaning, he can interpret it, and if he does not, he cannot. So when they do not want a person to understand, they use a double meaning, saying, for example, "If you pass elephant's dung you will split your anus," meaning, if you see someone build a fine house, and you want one like it but have not the money to build it, and you try to build it, you will steal and get into trouble. That is what it means.[1]

He that has two does not wear one.
He that is blessed with content will die content.

He that is in front does not stay behind.
He that is ahead does not fall back.

290   A plank does not grow without an adz.
Nothing can be obtained without expenditure.

He that climbs a ladder falls: do not be foolish.
A man was king of a country and despised the people. Then he was
    deposed.

When the cat is away, the rats are the rulers.
If the teacher or the king leaves the city, the citizens do as they like.

The bad thatcher, give him more grass.
Your enemy—be ever more generous to him.

He that goes slowly does not hurt his foot.
A patient person has no misfortune.

A child is not told ancient history.
It is not good to explain everything to a child.

Repentance comes behind.
If a man does something wrong, in the end he will be sorry.

As you bring up a child, so will he be.
Another man or woman will do that to which you accustom him.

If the tapper is praised, he waters the toddy.
If a singer sings a lot and people admire him, he will sing songs that are not
    fitting.

This hand does not cut off that.
A man and his brother or a man and his child—he does not put evil in his
    way.

If a child cries for a razor, give it to him.
If a man will not listen, leave him alone.

A ringless finger is dressed.
A slave who works well for his master has a reward.

291 From Pembamnazi to Mwenyi Shabani's log.
     From one end of the coast or the town to the other.

If you want what is under the bed, you must bend down.
A suppliant must abase himself.

He that has eaten does not notice the hungry.
A rich man does not know a poor man.

The coast is rapacious. If you are not eaten by a baboon, you are eaten by a
    monkey.
The coast is a big country. If you are not eaten by the townsfolk, you will be
    robbed by the slaves in the country.

Kendwa is no place to go. If you go ten, you return nine.
Kendwa is the coast. If you take a hundred, you will return with ninety and
    your money will be taken. If a hundred men go, ten will die of hunger.

The love of a child is in its mother's womb.
A child gives no pleasure unless its mother is loved by her husband.

The pain of childbirth is known to the mother.
He who is hurt feels the pain. Another does not feel it.

The punishment of the grave is known to the dead.
He who feels the pain is the sick person in bed.

It is better to be underdone than burned.
It is better to get half than to lose all.

He that invites you in does not tell you to go. He does things to irritate you.
A person who wants to be rid of you does not say, "Go away." He does things
    that do not please you.

If you pay attention to what the chicken eats, you will not eat the chicken.
If you examine a woman too closely, you will not stay with her.

292   What you eat is yours. What is left belongs to the gravedigger.
A man's portion is what he uses while he is alive. If he dies, his heirs have it.

If a poor man makes a profit, his buttocks go "pop-pop."
If a poor man makes anything, he is too much pleased.

A liar's road is short.
A liar is soon found out.

You do not know what goes into your eye.
If there are thirty people, you do not know who is on your side and who is
    your enemy.

Water is earth and drink. If you drink it alone, it makes the heart sick.
A man cannot drink only water for breakfast. If you do, it will give you a
    stomachache.

Words are silver. The answer is gold.
It is easy to talk. To reply is difficult.

The heart is bile and turns into mud.
The heart of man changes this way and that.

A freeman without shame is like a cow without horns.
A shameless person is worse than a beast.

If you see that your own is on fire, your neighbor's is blazing.[2]
If you say, "I have not got three rupees," your companion will not have three
    pesa.

You are a stone; I am a coconut.
You are the king and I a subject. Or you are the knife and I the shaft.

Charcoal will not boil meat.
It is my loss that I was not there.

293   To have long nails is an illness self-induced.
He who will, can bear up; he who will not, can give up.

The lime snake neither cultivates nor eats the fruit; but he catches those that
  do.[3]
It is enmity or intrigue that prevents people having things.

The featherless arrow does not go far.
A king without soldiers has no strength.

The poor man's boat will not sail close to the wind; if it does, it sinks.
Nobody listens to a poor man. If he is heard and answered, he is in trouble.

The poor man's business does not prosper, or if it does it is shaky.
The poor man's business does not prosper; if he makes a profit it is only luck.

It is arthritis that cripples.
It is enmity or intrigue that leads to quarrels.

My friend was bereaved, and I comforted him; now my friend is dead, where
  shall I take my comfort?
When my friend was bereaved I comforted him; now he is dead, to whom
  shall I go? No one knows me.

Quarreling is for pigs; for man ill feelings.
When you are angry, you have the ill feeling; but when I am angry, you do not
  feel it as much as your own.

294   Teeth are like tusks; they are not forbidden to one who laughs.
       I may laugh; but I am angry.

The tree is affected.
A great man is sick.

The elephant has fallen.
The king is dead.

His house is on his back.
When a woman is always quarreling with her husband and they cannot agree
  together, he always tends to move from one house to another.

Nine is nearly ten.
Persevere.

If you give the scraps to the cat, what will you eat yourself?
Said of a mean and miserly person.

If a man wants two things, one will escape him.
Said of a covetous person.

Be thankful for what is in your pocket.
What is useful to a person is what is actually in his pocket.

The chicken's prayer does not reach the hawk.
When someone curses another without reason, it has no effect. The accusation does not affect him.

It is also customary among the Swahili for one who does not get on
well with his neighbors or others, when he buys a slave, to give him a
riddling name so as to puzzle his neighbors and others, as to call him
"What do you want?," meaning, "What do you people all want of
me?" "Things are from God," meaning that everything comes from
God, not from man, and your enmity is unimportant.

Chapter **32** Our Restraints in the Past

Of the Kongwa

In the past we had neither prisons nor chains. People were tied to a wooden log called a kongwa. This was fixed to one leg, one log to each person. If he wanted to move, he could do so a little; but he had to take the rope in his hands to lift the log so as to be able to walk. When people were asleep, he could untie himself and go off; but it was not customary to do so, for fear of getting his family into trouble; because the old custom was that if a prisoner escaped, they went to the town of the fugitive to arrest his *kole*, that is, persons related to him. If they were caught, they were held until the fugitive returned, so he could not run away. But people who did not belong to the town were closely guarded lest they break the kongwa and disappear. To break it they inserted a stick and broke the bolt and then extracted the foot and ran away. That is the account of custody in olden days on the coast and inland.

Of the Mbano

If a man was a sorcerer charged with casting a spell but pleading not guilty, he was fixed into a mbano.[1] This was a piece of wood split in two, fastened over the head, and tied with rope. If he found it painful and had in fact cast a spell, he would admit bewitching the person named. They would remove the mbano and ask who else, and he would tell them the names. Then they would sentence him for sorcery, to burning, drowning, or taking an oath to do no more sorcery.[2] That is the account of the mbano.

If anyone had stolen a child and taken him away for sale and was charged and pleaded not guilty, he would be sentenced to the mbano on his head in the same way to persuade him to confess.

Of the Gandalo

When the Liwalis were established on the coast, they introduced the *mqatale*, or gandalo.[3] This is a log of wood four or five pima long with some ten to twenty holes in it. If a person did anything seditious, he was put in the gandalo. This means that he sat down, the upper part of the gandalo was raised, he inserted his foot, and it was closed. People so confined did not all sit on one side, but two on this and two on that until the number of holes in the gandalo was complete. They had guards in case they wanted to defecate; but for urination they had a bottle or a gourd. In the morning they all went to the beach to pour away their urine. The gandalo was fastened by a wooden bolt at the end called *kikwamizo*. When the people had all inserted their feet, the guard brought down the upper part and drove home this bolt.

299

Then in the old days there were no prisons; but people were put into dark rooms in their own houses, and that was their prison.

At one time, thirty years ago, there was on the coast an officer called Saburi whom Sayyid Majid had brought to the coast to be governor of the Swahili.[4] When he settled on the coast, he had no prison. He would put people in the gandalo and leave them out in a hut that he had built. One day when people were asleep, two leopards came there where they were tied and tried to take them; but they could not be taken, because they were tied. The leopards leaped hither and thither and wounded many of them, and one was so badly torn that he died. The prisoners cried out when they saw the leopards, and the officer's Baluchi troops woke up. One of them had a flintlock and tried to shoot a leopard; but he missed and hit a fellow Baluchi. Another Baluchi with a flintlock hit a leopard and killed it; but the bullet unfortunately killed another man.

300

To return to Sayyid Majid: When he heard what had happened on the coast, he called the officer and asked him why he left his prisoners outside. He replied that it was because he had no prison. Then the sultan sent people to build a prison on the coast. It was the first prison on the coast, and it is near the present district office of Bagamoyo.

Of Prisons and Fetters

After the building of the prison on the coast, the Arab governors of the sultan of Zanzibar introduced restraint by fetters and chains and made rooms for criminals and debtors.

A person charged with debt or assault with a stick or any other offense of minor importance was sentenced to imprisonment in the debtors' room, but there was no need for him to be chained. We say this because to be chained is a serious punishment, and to be sentenced to it, the universal Arab and Swahili custom is that a man must be guilty of a serious offense. If a debtor confined in this room had a child or a brother or a friend or anyone known to him who asked permission to visit him, he was given permission to do so, because it might be that among these people was one who would arrange to bring him money to pay the debt. But no one was put into the criminal section without a magistrate's order on a charge of homicide or of assaulting a magistrate or of subverting the magistrate's authority. Such a person was put into the criminal prison and fettered. He was not allowed to have the door opened except to be brought food. Nor were people allowed to visit him except on Friday, when he was given permission for people to visit him. The door was opened, and while it was open on a Friday, he was not fettered but only handcuffed. Thus in the past the prisons were not all alike because offenses are not all alike. For a petty offense, the prison was suitable and the sentence light. It was sufficient punishment for him to be locked up.

If the offender was a slave, he had to be chained, because a slave is a person who serves and in chains he will still serve; but a freeman should not be so treated unless his offense is very grave. It is not feasible for a murderer to be chained and for a thief to be chained and for one who has insulted another to be chained and for one who has broken a court order to be chained. These offenses are all of different gravity; they are not all the same—some are serious, and some are petty, so the sentences should not be all the same. It is not feasible for the punishment for homicide to be the same as that for debt, nor for that for stealing to be the same as that for debt; it is not reasonable.

301

Chapter **33** Of the Law of Stealing

What follows is written in the books of the law; but our ancestors did not know them. They may have been in use for two centuries or more in our country.[1]

If a man is a thief and the owner adequately identifies the stolen property as his and that the accused is the thief, according to ancient custom his hand was cut off and the hand taken was the right; but for this it was essential that the thief be an adult, not a juvenile, that he be *compos mentis*, not insane, in which case his hand was not cut off because an idiot has no sense. The third condition is that the thing stolen must have value. A hand is cut off for that but not for the theft of two or eight or ten pesa or the contents of an amulet. It is theft; but the sentence is made compatible.

For a second offense after his hand has been cut off, he has the left foot cut off; for the third offense, the left hand; for the fourth offense, the right foot. If he steals yet again, he is judged differently and is killed; but not without deep consideration, for it is a very serious matter to take a person's life and may be a grave sin.

On the other hand, according to our Swahili custom, if a thief was caught in possession of the thing stolen, it was taken from him, he was beaten and warned not to offend again.[2] Then the Arabs introduced to the coast the practice of imprisonment after beating. On release he was warned not to offend again.

Another old custom: If a thief came by night and dug through the wall of a house and entered with intent to steal, and if the owner half woke up and killed the thief, he was not liable; because when a thief entered a house and saw the owner, he usually wounded or killed the owner, so if the owner woke up and struck first and killed the thief, this was the old custom.

The sentence for stealing on the Swahili mainland was that, for example, if a thief stole from a field where there was much property, not by day but by night, and happened to be killed, there was no

304   offense under old custom; but if he was apprehended by day, he must not be harmed or killed, but must be arrested and taken before the magistrate.

Then highway robbery: If a man lay in wait to attack travelers and killed them but did not take their property, his sentence was death by the same method that he had used to kill others. If one shot another, he was shot. If he killed with a sword, he was killed with a sword; if with a knife, he was killed with a knife; if a spear or an arrow, he was killed in the same way. If he lay in wait on the road and killed those whom he met and took their property, he was killed and exposed on a gallow for all to see. If he lay in wait on the road and robbed people but did not kill them, he had his hands and feet cut off. If he threatened travelers and they were frightened, but he neither robbed nor killed them and they ran away, throwing down the things that they were carrying, but he did not take those things, his sentence was imprisonment, but he was not killed or beaten, only admonished. When he repented of what he had done, that is, when he showed clear signs of repentance, he was released at the magistrate's discretion.

If a man formed the intention of robbing you of your property and you knew that he was coming to take your property or your life, or if

305   you had a child that he intended to take from you on the road, kill him if you are sure that he is intending to kill or rob you; kill him first. If you do kill him, you are not liable for homicide before the magistrate because he was going to kill or rob you and you felt that it was better to kill him first. Then you are not liable. But there must be witnesses to the fact that he was going to kill you.

Again, a person riding a horse or donkey who damages the property of another is liable for damaging the other's property just as if he had robbed him of it.

Chapter 34 Of Assault and Homicide

Our ancestors used to say, "On the coast, the only place to finish an argument is in the bush." In the past, if there was an argument and someone was killed, the two sides came before the jumbe, the head of the place. The jumbe used to take the matter to the *pazi* and say to him, "I have a dispute before me, which I shall hand over to you to take. Find out the rights and wrongs and reconcile the parties."[1] The pazi consented and fixed a day for a meeting in a certain open place. On the day on which they had arranged to appear, each of the parties collected his followers, each coming with his followers armed, and the pazi came also with his followers armed. When they reached the open space, they sat down in three groups, two of the opposing litigants and one of the pazi, or magistrate, with his followers. When they were met, the magistrate asked for a copy of the Qur'an and swore, "Before God, as you speak I will not favor either side, but will speak what is right. If I speak ill, may this oath kill me; if I speak right, may this oath that I take be my protection."

After swearing, he told them to produce their arguments, and he laid his dagger in front of him while he listened. The hearing continued from nine until four, each disputing the other's story so as to defeat him. By four o'clock the pazi had understood the case and silenced them to give judgment, saying, "Let every man have his weapons ready, while I give judgment according to the law." Then each took his weapons and stood ready while he gave judgment, and they listened. If the case involved blood and they did not see the blood avenged, they fought there and then, their own battle and their own quarrel. Such was the old custom.

307   After this, if one killed another, the magistrate had to arrest and detain him. He was not killed nor sentenced unless charged by those whose member was killed. First the father of the deceased was consulted or, failing him, the whole, or uterine, brother, or if they were not available, the most suitable person to represent the deceased. The court asked, "Your brother has been killed, and the accused killed him, and now I have him in custody. What do you propose? Do you wish him to be killed as your brother was killed, or do you wish us to take compensation from him and you be paid in cash?" The choice then lay with the family; if they said that they wanted him killed as their brother was killed, the magistrate would plead with them, but not insist, that they accept compensation and pardon him of their own free will. If they would not listen to the court's pleading and insisted on vengeance, the court had to allow the vengeance of the family of the deceased, and they killed him. If they did accept compensation, he had to agree to give them twenty to thirty dollars, and he was then released. The money paid in compensation was divided into four parts, one for the court and three for the family. Of the three parts two went to the father and one to the mother, and if he had no father or mother the families of the parents shared the three parts. Such was our old custom.

       If a man killed another's slave, the magistrate had to call him and detain him to be awarded a punishment by the magistrate. Then the magistrate would summon the master of the slave to say what com-
308   pensation he claimed for the slave. If the person had been killed deliberately, the compensation would be penal; but if it was not intentional, the compensation would be small. This was the old custom.

       Again, if people quarreled and fought but no blood was spilled, the magistrate would sentence them to two or three days' imprisonment at his discretion; but if the blow had caused harm, the jumbe would detain the person giving it and summon the family and consult them, whether they wanted blood for blood or would accept compensation. If they accepted compensation, he would say to those present, "What do you consider the value of the damage?" Three or four sensible persons would say how much it was worth. If he had lost his nose or the whole of an ear, or an eye so that it was quite blind, or a hand so that it hung down or was useless, or a foot so that he went on one leg, or a tooth, or if he had been castrated—for each of these seven things the price was twenty-five to thirty rupees; but not the same for a freeman and a slave. According to our tradition, people say that one

who puts out another's eye should have his own put out, and that one
who cuts off another's ear should have his own cut off, and that one
who knocks out another's tooth should have his own knocked out, the
same damage for each; but if a man does one of these things and they
go to the magistrate and say, "That must be done to him that he did, as
he has knocked out a man's eye and must have his own put out, for this
is God's justice," the magistrate will plead with the speakers present,
the man who has lost an eye and his family, until he persuades them to
309   agree to accept compensation.[2] If the person who has lost an eye is a
slave, compensation is based on his value, half of which is paid to his
master and divided into three parts, two for the master and one for the
slave. That is the old custom. If someone has struck another with a
knife or spear, the magistrate detains him while he inspects the
wound. If he recovers he must pay the value of the wound; but if he
dies he must pay full compensation. If he struck him with a stick and
he dies, compensation must be paid, but the compensation will be
small, because a stick is not used with intent to kill. It is iron that is
used with intent to kill.

Chapter **35** The Customary Law of Debt

In the past, if a man was owed money and the debtor would not pay, the creditor went to other people and said, "He will not give me my rights; I want you please to come and help me." He gave them something between two and ten rupees, and they girded themselves and went to the debtor to demand payment. If he did not pay and had a slave or something else, they would take that. If the debtor had relations and friends who thought him ill used, they would assist him with words or deeds until people appeared to reconcile them.

Another old custom: If a man owed a debt to an Indian or a Hindu[1] and the debt arose from a business loss, as, for example, if he had advanced him goods for a trading expedition inland and there had been fighting and the goods had been lost, or the goods had been stolen by thieves or been destroyed by fire when the goods were in a house that caught fire; in the event of any of these three disasters happening to the man who had borrowed the goods, he had to pay, and the payment fell on him. If he had enough, that was all right; but if he had not, he would be given a further advance to go on a second expedition. All the profit that he made would go to pay the debt; but he was not imprisoned or bankrupted in the event of these three disasters.

The fourth case is when a man takes goods on credit and goes to trade in ivory, rubber, or gum when the price in the town is high. He goes inland knowing the prices of these things, and he buys them inland; but on his return he finds that the price has dropped. He has bought, and because he has already bought he does not know what to do. He goes with it to his merchant and sells to him at the low price and makes a loss on the goods. Then he must advance him more goods to trade with to make up the loss. But he will give him time to look for the balance—he should not take him to court. If he insists on taking him to court and the court interrogates him and he replies giving this sort of account of his loss, the magistrate will tell him to come to an agreement, to give him time to make it up or to give him more goods to continue trading, so that he may pay out of the profit on them; but the magistrate should not imprison him nor be in a hurry to bankrupt him for such a debt before he has been given time to make it up.

312

If two persons are in debt to each other and one says that he owes nothing while the other says that he does, the magistrate must call for evidence of the debt. The plaintiff will say that he has it, and he will be told to produce it. He will do so if he has a bond or witnesses who can give evidence that the debt is owed. Then the magistrate says to the defendant, "Here is your evidence." If the defendant denies the debt or the plaintiff has no evidence, the defendant must swear that he owes nothing, and the case fails. Alternatively, the defendant may refuse to swear and agree to pay if the plaintiff swears to the debt. Then the plaintiff must swear to the transaction and take his money. He is stopped from refusing to accept the plaintiff's oath.

A debtor is not imprisoned for debt unless he has property and refuses to pay; if he has already a judgment against him and has asked for time and a second time he has asked for more time, the third time the magistrate will commit him to prison. If he has property, he will be compelled to pay. If he has not enough, he will be bankrupted so that his creditors may be paid something.

313

The reason for imprisonment is that he has property and persistently misleads the court. Firstly, it is wrong to mislead the court, and secondly, it is dishonest to have the means and refuse to pay, so he is imprisoned. If he has no property, he is imprisoned to teach him how to behave and to make sure that he really has nothing. Once it is known that he has nothing, he is released.

Chapter **36** Of Treasure
Trove

The Old Custom

If a man found something in the road, it was his duty, if the thing was of value, to take it to the court, and the magistrate ordered it to be taken around everywhere where there was a fork in the road and to the market until the owner was found and given it in the magistrate's presence. Or the magistrate would hold the thing until the owner appeared looking for it. Then the magistrate would interrogate him, asking what sort of thing it was and when and where he lost it. If it was money, he would ask him how many dollars, and if the man had genuinely lost it he would say, "So many dollars, in a cloth, and the cloth was white, or black, or red." If he was speaking the truth, he had to be given his property. If he was not speaking the truth, as, for example, if he said sixty dollars and the money found was forty dollars or less, he would investigate further in case the finder had hidden some part of it and this accounted for the difference. So he too was interrogated, and if there was evidence or proof that the person who lost it was speaking the truth, he had to be given his property. If the finder was a reputable person and the proof was not forthcoming, the discrepancy was not resolved, and he did not get his property. If the owner did not appear and the thing was valuable, the magistrate retained it; but if it had no great value, the magistrate gave it to the finder.

If a man found a trifle, he advertised it by going to the mosque, probably the Friday mosque, because many people come there. He asked if anyone had lost anything, and if somebody had he would say what it was that he had lost. If it was correct, he gave it to the owner, and if not, he did not give it to him but looked for somebody else.

Then if something was found in the sea or on land and was brought to the chief (*mkubwa*) of the area, such as the jumbe, the chief would order it to be divided into two parts, one for the chief and one to be given to the viziers and people of the area, who divided it between them. It was the custom that a person who found anything of value was not allowed to keep it, but must take it to the chief.

If a man found something and kept it, he was fined on conviction if he had property. If he had not, he lost his "presence." If there was a party or something like a wedding, the sort of thing that was attended by the chief, the man who had kept public property did not go until he had paid up in accordance with Swahili tradition. Then he could go to people's parties. An obstinate man was expelled from councils and not allowed to be present. Also, a letter was written and sent around the towns to let people be informed that he was not welcome at councils or parties. So you will understand that wherever he went, whether to a party or a wedding or a funeral, if you saw him on the verandah, he was chased away. If then the offender went to the chief and begged his pardon, the chief received him and took him to the jumbe, saying, "He has come to beg pardon for his offense." He received him, and all was as before.

The Custom of Finding a Slave

The man took him to the jumbe, and the jumbe detained the slave. When the owner came and said that he had lost a slave, he was asked what tribe, and he answered. Then he produced the slave and asked him if this was his master, and he agreed. Then he gave him to him, and he paid a finding fee of two rupees, and these two rupees were given to the finder. If the slave denied that this was his master, the jumbe retained him and told the master to bring witnesses to give evidence that he was really his slave. If the slave had no master, he became the jumbe's slave and was asked if he were willing to return to his master. If he refused, the jumbe retained him to work for him.

The Swahili World of Mtoro bin Mwinyi Bakari

J. de V. Allen

The concept of the "Swahili world" was much clearer in the 1890s, when the *Desturi* was being compiled, than it is today; and only one example of the confusion that grew up during (and to a large extent as a consequence of) the colonial era is Bwana Idi Marijani's recent identification of Mtoro as a Zaramo, whereas to Velten, and presumably also to Mtoro himself, he was a "pure Swahili person" from the area of Bagamoyo.[1] I do not propose to deal here at any length with the tangled problem of Swahili identity, about which a considerable academic literature has grown up;[2] but some picture must be provided, first, of the social boundaries of the Swahili community at the time Mtoro lived, and, second, of how far what was true of Bagamoyo was equally true further up and down the coast and in the settlements that were already springing up in the interior.

Swahili Identity

The Swahili world was, and saw itself as, a cultural unit, not a racial or tribal one. Swahili was the language spoken as a first language by virtually all the inhabitants of the coastal settlements between Barawa in the north and Lindi and Mikindani (near what is now the Mozambique-Tanzania border) in the south. All these people likewise shared, to a remarkable degree, a single, homogeneous culture that gave them a sense of community stronger than that created by any ties of origin or ethnicity which they may have had in common with smaller groups or with outsiders. With only relatively minor variations they observed the same customs regarding birth, initiation, marriage, and death; aspired to the same sort of education; subscribed to the same religion (Islam with a not-inconsiderable admixture of African Traditional Religion); dressed in the same way; ate the same foods; used the same household items; appreciated the same literature and the same sorts of stories and jokes; and, above all, held the same values. Preeminent among these values was a certainty that they, as townspeople and Muslims (usually in that order), were superior to the rural dwellers who lived outside their settlements and further away in the interior. This superiority was based, not on race or tribe, but on culture, which to them—as to so many societies in history—was an urban prerogative, something that country dwellers altogether lacked. Those few who had had experience of urban settlements in Asia or elsewhere might acknowledge that other cultures existed, but to the majority who knew only Africa, theirs was the only culture, their way of life the only possible one for a civilized being. Accordingly, possession of this culture, which could be acquired only by prolonged residence in a Swahili settlement, was far more important, and so more effective as a unifying factor, than such factors as tribal origins or shared racial characteristics.

There were, of course, some cultural differences within the Swahili world. Of these, those associated with social class were probably the most important. Some of the settlements—though probably not very many of them at any given time—were relatively large, with populations of eight, twelve, or even twenty to twenty-five thousand people. In such places, distinctions between rich and poor, between property owners, merchants, and laborers inevitably developed. Such distinctions were reflected in outward cultural manifestations and also to some extent in values. Economic distinctions were, however, as far as possible translated into cultural gradations. The elite of each settlement generally consisted of certain long-established lineages, who were held to have acquired more "culture" by virtue of their longer residence and so to merit more respect and greater rights than relative newcomers. A general term for such people was *wa-ungwana*, and they enjoyed certain privileges, including, in most parts of the coast, the exclusive right to build and live in stone houses.[3] Tensions naturally existed between these long-established groups and wealthy or prestigious newcomers, including many from Arabia and (no doubt) India who were not necessarily acculturated at all but who sought a share of the political and economic power. (Such tensions, however, need not concern us for the moment; we shall return to their nineteenth-century manifestations below.) Between the wa-ungwana and other, more humble town dwellers there was something of a cultural gap, but it was nowhere near as important as that which existed between all town dwellers on the one hand and the country dwellers on the other. Its significance also varied considerably in practice according to the size and economy of the settlement. In large settlements and in those heavily dependent on trade, it was much greater than in the medium-sized and small ones, where agriculture was more important.[4] The traditional pattern well into the nineteenth century was for the vast majority of able-bodied males in all but the most trade-oriented settlements to go together into the countryside to grow crops for several months out of the year. Such a practice was an effective leveler, especially in comparison to the arrangement that replaced it in some areas—a system whereby all agricultural work was carried out by plantation slaves, who seldom, if ever, saw their largely absentee landlords.[5] Excessive class differentiation was also more difficult in the smaller settlements, where everybody not only knew everyone else but was well informed about neighbors' origins, financial circumstances, and personal frailties as well.

Alongside other differences based on social class or status and those arising from the size and economy of the settlements, there also existed certain regional variations in Swahili culture. One of the most important Swahili subcultures of this regional type was the Shirazi one. Since Mtoro's Bagamoyo was in many ways a typical Shirazi-Swahili society—a fact that gives his account special interest, since relatively little has been published on Shirazi-Swahilis[6]—it is important to establish precisely what this designation means.

The Shirazi-Swahili Subgroup

Shirazi is a word that substantially changed its meaning during the colonial era, when it came to refer to a pre-Omani substratum in coastal society and culture which was presumed to have existed all along the Swahili coast and was said, often on the basis of evidence that was Social Darwinist or frankly racist in flavor, to have come from southern Persia.[7] It was one of the achievements of J. S. Kirkman, as the first professional archaeologist to work on the East African coast, to discredit these theories of a Shirazi "civilization" that had existed before a later, Arab-oriented one and that was held responsible for most of the older ruined settlements. There is, as he pointed out, no evidence for more than one civilization in the architecture and archaeological finds of the regions, and he deprecated discussion of Persian influence "until there [should be] some evidence of the Persian speech and Persian customs which have not been adopted by the Arabs."[8] In spite of this, some scholars have persisted in seeking to trace some migration or series of migrations from the province of Fars, after whose capital, Shiraz, the colonists might have come to be known, basing their arguments chiefly on a widespread oral tradition among Swahili speakers which concerns a certain sultan of Shiraz and his seven sons who sailed in seven ships and founded seven towns on the East African coast. Two "origin" interpretations of this myth have been considered: one, that migrants sailed direct from Fars to their disembarkation points (variously listed, but including many towns between Mogadishu in the north and Kilwa in the south, as well as, in most cases, somewhere in the Comoros); and the other, currently more fashionable, that they went first to the Benadir Coast in southern Somalia and moved steadily south from there at some later date.[9] The myth itself is of considerable antiquity as well as being widespread, for it first occurs in the *Kilwa Chronicle* recorded by the Portuguese in the sixteenth century. There are, however, several ways of interpreting its significance and *raison d'être* from the viewpoint of the societies in whose traditions it is enshrined. The most plausible of these interpretations suggests that it is not in fact an origin myth at all and that it tells us not anything about the geographical source of the East African Shirazis,[10] but, rather, something about their "mode of dominance"; we shall return to this below. Nor can other, less formal oral traditions concerning a Persian origin which are occasionally collected nowadays be taken very seriously, since we are dealing with a time span of some thousand years, and anyway, as we shall see, there are excellent historical reasons for twentieth-century Swahilis to claim non-African origins, as only by doing so could they avoid compulsory labor and become entitled to various educational, political, and other privileges during the colonial period.[11]

Modern scholars who still think of Shirazis as originally Persian immigrants who spread up and down the coast are also ignoring two important facts: One is that there are large areas—notably the region north of Mombasa, and especially the whole Lamu-Pate district— where Shirazis are only very seldom, if ever, mentioned in modern oral traditions, in contrast to other areas where they are frequently referred to; and the other is that there still survives today, living astride the Kenya-Tanzania border, a clearly identified group or society—what colonialists would normally have called a tribe—who

call themselves, and are called by everybody else, wa-Shirazi. There
is even a ruined site near Fundi Island in southern Kenya known as
both Kifundi and Shirazi. Today it contains only the *mihrabs* of two
ruined mosques, but at the turn of the present century it was reported
to include the ruins of houses, tombs, and town walls, and according
to some sources it was the last capital of the wa-Shirazi before they
were dispersed in the seventeenth century.[12] Not surprisingly, it is in
the neighborhood of these modern Shirazis, specifically from
Kifundi/Shirazi in the north down to Tanga, and to a slightly lesser
extent as far as Bagamoyo in the south, that oral traditions about the
Shirazis are most common. Indeed, we may reasonably affirm that
outside this central region and the islands of Pemba and, to a lesser
degree, Zanzibar opposite it,[13] the only Shirazi oral traditions that can
be regarded as completely uncontaminated by colonialist myths are
those that refer to Shirazi dynasties of other Swahili settlements, not
those that speak of them as a people as such. Thus, unless we are to
disregard totally the contemporary oral tradition, the Shirazis as a
historical people or community can with reasonable certainty be
narrowed down to a homeland (or, since the possibility of an immigration in the remote past cannot yet be completely ruled out, perhaps
we should say "heartland") between Bagamoyo or, more precisely,
Tanga and Fundi Island.

The historical traditions regarding the "heartland" Shirazi are
unambiguous and plausible enough. They are said to have lived
between Tanga and Kifundi in eight towns or settlements (*miji
minane*, although the number eight may have a symbolic rather than a
practical significance, for it seems likely that, at times at least, there
may have been more than eight).[14] Between about A.D. 1600 and 1630,
these settlements were attacked and one by one subdued by a small
immigrant group, probably originating in Kau or Ozi (on the Ozi
River, which has since become the lower Tana) and associated with
Pate,[15] who made their capital in Vumba Kuu, almost exactly on the
present Kenya-Tanzania border, and became known as the wa-
Vumba. The wa-Vumba were assisted by a much larger group of
newcomers, the wa-Segeju, who were not at that time Muslims and
who claimed to have originated in Shungwaya north of the Tana,
although some modern scholars have expressed doubts about this.[16]
The wa-Vumba, who included two lineages of *sherifs* (that is, lineages
who claimed descent from the Prophet Muhammad), would appear to
have represented a non-Shirazi type of Swahili, but in the centuries
that followed they adopted many typically Shirazi institutions and

probably also a southern Swahili dialect. Nevertheless, after defeating the Shirazis, they imposed upon them a number of conditions, which included forbidding them to wear sandals and turbans and insisting that they humble themselves before their Vumba overlords at least once annually. Many Shirazis, we are told, found such culturally humiliating terms unacceptable and went to live outside the orbit of the Vumba rulers. A few migrated to Mombasa, Pemba, and elsewhere, but the majority seem to have moved south of Tanga to occupy the stretch of coast between Tanga and Bagamoyo which we shall call the "extended Shirazi heartland." Here they appear to have set up three or possibly four Shirazi confederations, that is, loose unions of petty settlements: one at Tanga, with fifteen settlements (five of which, however, are sometimes described as forming their own confederation centered on Mtangata), one at Pangani, with five settlements, and one at Bagamoyo, with ten. Once again, the numbers may have a symbolic rather than a real significance.[17]

What distinguished these Shirazis from other Swahilis such as the wa-Vumba, wa-Pemba, and wa-Hadimu? There is a Swahili dialect in the area, known as Chi-Chifundi or Ki-Shirazi, which modern Shirazis speak, but in view of evidence regarding the volatile nature of Swahili dialects which could be adopted and more or less lost again within four or five generations,[18] dialect alone does not seem to be a satisfactory method of identification over a long period. A more reliable criterion would appear to be the recognition of a whole hierarchy of rank and title holders, including jumbe, waziri, amiri, *sheha* or shaha,[19] mwinyimkuu, and possibly *akida, tajiri*, and others as well.[20] Such titles are only relatively rarely recorded among other Swahili groups and, where reported, do not all seem to have coexisted at the same time—or else the titles imply different things from what they imply among the Shirazis. (The term *jumbe* or *yumbe*, for instance, refers in the northern Swahili world to a council of elders or to the council chamber, not to an individual ruler;[21] and the mwinyimkuu in Zanzibar was the supreme ruler in the pre-Omani period, whereas in the Shirazi settlements it is only a relatively minor title.[22] Elsewhere, too, the wa-ungwana tended to be the dominant group, even if there was a sultan or sheikh above them (which was not always the case); whereas among the Shirazi-Swahili we hear relatively little of the wa-ungwana,[23] and their elite role would appear to have been largely taken over by the title holders as a group. While the wa-ungwana were distinguished by their exclusive right to live in stone houses, and a number of rituals centered around these houses,[24] it is far from clear that the post-1600 Shirazis built stone houses (though they built stone mosques and tombs),[25] and Shirazi title holders appear to have laid more stress on (and evolved more rituals concerning) the clothes they wore to distinguish them from the "commoners." Finally, the Shirazi title holders had to be installed according to customary procedures (almost all of them, incidentally, very characteristically African) which, while in many ways reminiscent of Swahili rituals generally, do not seem to be echoed in detail in any other part of the Swahili world.[26]

It remains to suggest how the Shirazi exiles of the seventeenth century (and possibly also some of their predecessors) might have secured and maintained their dominance outside the original miji minane, or eight towns. Much research remains to be done on this topic, but several points made by Mtoro are interesting in this connection. First, it is necessary to distinguish between the extended Shirazi heartland, that is, the area from Tanga (or wherever Vumba's control ceased) south to Bagamoyo, and other areas to which they migrated, such as Pemba and Mombasa. In the former they not only established dominance but also perpetuated their sociopolitical institutions. In the latter they may have succeeded in inserting themselves at the tip of the social pyramid, that is, as rulers, sultans, or sheikhs, above the wa-ungwana or parochial aristocracy, but they did not succeed in ousting this aristocracy and replacing it with their own system of title holders. Rather, they gradually became absorbed into it and were treated as little more than first among equals. This explains the distinction between Shirazis in the Kifundi-Bagamoyo region, who really are a people, albeit part of a larger Swahili community, and Shirazis elsewhere, who were merely ruling families. Mtoro was, of course, writing about the former, but some of their customs may also be supposed to have assisted the latter in the business of establishing their dominance in other areas.

What we are speaking about—and it is necessary to be clear about this—is not a "ruling race" of non-African origin sailing in and "founding" settlements,[27] but small, probably very small groups of people moving about and getting themselves accepted as rulers or (in the extended Shirazi heartland) as a sort of upper class by existing local populations. The difference between the extended Shirazi heartland and elsewhere may have lain in the fact that a much larger population of Shirazis infiltrated into the area immediately south of Tanga (which was, after all, adjacent to their original heartland), but it may equally well have been that the area immediately south of

Tanga did not, in the seventeenth century, contain many (or many surviving)[28] long-established non-Shirazi Swahili settlements, whereas Pemba and Zanzibar did, and so did the coastline from Mombasa north and from Bagamoyo south. In this case, the incoming Shirazis would have found it much easier to perpetuate their own political systems over a Zaramo substratum south of Tanga—although, as the Swahili *Chronicle of Bagamoyo* suggests,[29] they did not manage this without some opposition and, finally, considerable concessions to the Zaramo ruler living inland.

The methods they employed are not very different from those modes of dominance employed by many groups elsewhere in Africa. First of all, they had the confidence typical of all Swahili townspeople that they were more "civilized" than, and so superior to, the people among whom they moved. Next, they commanded and continued to control very strictly all overseas-originated trade in certain sorts of items, mostly prestige items. It appears that independent local markets selling perishable foodstuffs and no doubt some locally made artifacts survived their arrival and continued well into the present century, but such goods as cloth, imported beads, and glazed porcelain were bought and sold solely by and through the Shirazis (as they were through the wa-ungwana elsewhere in the Swahili world), and they presently managed to secure a monopoly of, or anyway the right to tax, certain valuable commodities such as ivory as well.[30] Their existence as a small group in virtually every settlement allowed them to form a network, reinforced, no doubt, by lineage and marriage ties, over a relatively large area, and as they created a taste within this area, first for the exotic goods that they alone controlled (and that they represented as indispensable to a "civilized" life), and then for Swahili culture itself, their power grew correspondingly. It was almost certainly bolstered by claims to certain magical or semimagical powers. At least the *Diwans* of Vumba, who, as we have seen, were not themselves of Shirazi origin but adopted many Shirazi institutions and ideas to consolidate their power, were well known as practitioners of all types of magic, including rain control, divining, and healing, and it is likely that their Shirazi predecessors utilized similar methods to persuade the non-Shirazis to accept them.[31] They also laid great emphasis on ritual as a part of everyday life, in time coming more or less to control it, and by virtue of this and of their magical powers they came to be accepted as arbitrators in disputes as well.

All these aspects of Shirazi life and behavior can be clearly detected in Mtoro's description of the jumbes and their fellow title holders:

their insistence on controlling any long-term commerce within their settlements (V 227); the rites with which they surrounded such events as the dividing up of the salt that appeared naturally each year at Nunge near Kingani, no doubt designed to ensure that they received their share by threatening with magic anyone who partook of the salt before the rites were performed (V 228–229); their insistence on formal dressing (the jumbes' turban, for instance, discussed in V 224–225, was no doubt made of some imported cloth to which only jumbes had access—hence their demand that the turban always be worn in public and never covered by any other cloth); and the endless ritual with which they sacralized themselves, with music, formal letters, and the like (V 225–226).[32] If a jumbe did not receive the hump of any ox that was slaughtered in his settlement, he was, we are told, angry, "and if he was angry he was given something to pacify him" (V 227). Likewise, runaway slaves would go to him or be taken to him. This is another practice that recalls the Diwans of Vumba, who, it is said, kept a special drum at the door of their house: if any slave could reach it and beat it, he became the property of the Diwan and no longer belonged to his former owner.[33] There are many more examples of the same sort of thing, although it is also clear that by the time Mtoro was writing, things were changing fast, and not to the jumbes' advantage. This is a point to which we shall return below.

Two other points may be made here about the Shirazi title holders and their capacity for establishing their dominance elsewhere. The first is that there is some confusion about how new title holders, and in particular new jumbes, were created. It is generally accepted, and Mtoro confirms (V 222), that any son of a jumbe might become a jumbe after his father's death, provided he was wealthy enough to pay for his own installation. Most writers have assumed, however, that it was not sufficient simply to be the son of a jumbe and to be adequately wealthy: one must undergo some selection process, or perhaps have a vacant jumbeate (usually conceived as a territorial unit) as well— otherwise the number of jumbes might rise, in a prosperous period, to constitute an intolerable proportion of the society. It is noteworthy, though, that Mtoro says nothing of this, nor of a limited number of jumbeates (whether conceived territorially or otherwise); and this suggests that—in his period, at least—the number of jumbes may have been limited only by the number of sufficiently wealthy people of jumbe descent. In this case, we have here another mechanism (strictly, a mechanism at a different level) for the extension of Shirazi dominance, first within the extended Shirazi heartland, then outside it: for Shirazi society would have been one of those societies that, in a time of prosperity, produces too many aristocrats for its own economic good and therefore has to—so to speak—export them to other societies where there is room for them at (or somewhere near) the top. Another society that "overproduces" aristocrats is, of course, Hadhramawt, where any son of a sharif or descendant of the Prophet is automatically a sharif and is entitled to reverence as such. The Hadhramawt has exported an aristocracy of this kind to almost every shore of the Indian Ocean. The Shirazi aristocratic surplus, which would have occurred only in times of prosperity, would have been much smaller, but it might well have "colonized" the Swahili coast with varying degrees of success, both in the era before and, later, in competition with Hadhrami sharifs.

The other point to be noted is that trade with the interior, as described by Mtoro, involves a strange division of function between the Swahilis and the Indo-Pakistani merchants. The latter financed caravans to the interior, but it was almost invariably highborn Swahilis who led them. Virtually no Indians ventured into the interior of the continent before the so-called Pax Britannica. This suggests that although there was obviously a difference of scale between purely coastal commerce and commerce based on caravans to the interior, the social mechanism may have been much the same in each case: or, in other words, wa-ungwana or, among the Shirazi-Swahilis, title holders may have used substantially the same techniques when pioneering routes to the interior and setting up trade points along the way as they had previously employed when "colonizing" the coast. Just as their dominance in the coastal regions depended largely upon excluding Indians or anyone else who might breach their monopoly of prestigious imported items, at least until their own positions were secured, so they took care to keep Indians from themselves penetrating the interior for as long as possible. Many of the techniques they employed are noted by Mtoro: blood-brotherhood pacts and joking relationships (Swahili *utani*) with societies living along the routes; extensive use of "magical" formulas—flags, for instance, written by Swahilis for a prescribed sum, which had to lead the caravan; reading of the omens before setting off; and a number of superstitions to be observed while on the march.[34] No doubt all these formulas could be manipulated in such a way as to make it virtually impossible for anyone but a highborn Swahili to lead a caravan. No doubt, too, these or similar techniques had been in use for many centuries to establish the Shirazi title holders (or, elsewhere in the Swahili world, the wa-ungwana) as dominant groups in territory where they had not previously lived up and down the coast.

There was, of course, one significant difference between Swahili "colonization" of the coastal regions and Swahili penetration of the interior: namely, the fact that many trade centers of the interior fell (or already were) under the control of non-Swahili chiefs or rulers who, for whatever reason, did not yield political power to the new-comers. This was to be almost invariably the case along the caravan routes that opened up to the north of what became the Kenya-Tanzania border. South of this line, however, only some trade centers were under local control. Elsewhere, in places like Tabora and Ujiji, there grew up in the late nineteenth century typical Swahili settle-ments, very much under the control of Muslims, mostly Zanzibari, Swahili, or "Arab." (It is worth noting that Mtoro speaks, at V 232, of "inland jumbes," who drew their wealth from a tax called hongo levied from passing travelers or traders.) Where no non-Swahili monarch or elite forestalled the process, these settlements developed very much along traditional Swahili lines and ended up not so different from Bagamoyo as described by Mtoro, or other comparable coastal settlements. Ujiji, on the shores of Lake Tanganyika, which (like Lamu in northern Kenya) was relatively little disrupted by colonialism, remains in many ways an absolutely typical Swahili settlement today.[35]

Arabizing and the Swahili Decline

The Shirazi-Swahilis, as we have noted, were only one subgroup within the wider Swahili community, although one that was rather more distinctive than most. Other subgroups included the Bajunis, the Swahilis of the Lamu Archipelago, the wa-Mvita of Mombasa, the wa-Pemba, the wa-Hadimu and perhaps also the wa-Tumbatu of Zanzibar, and the Swahilis of the southern Tanzania coast. By the time that Mtoro wrote, however, the whole idea of a Swahili com-munity, depending for its sense of identity as it did upon a certainty of the superiority of Swahili "civilization" over the rural-based cultures adjacent to it, was threatened. Probably the main underlying cause was the change of scale which overtook east-coast commerce in the nineteenth century. For reasons that need not concern us here, but that included technological progress (for instance, the development of steamships, which in turn led to increased, large-scale immigration from Asia and to the growth of a few large ports at the expense of the many smaller settlements that had previously existed), the advent of European imperialism to the western shores of the Indian Ocean, and the development of a plantation economy that was largely in the hands of new immigrants from Oman rather than the former Swahili elite, the Swahilis' confidence in themselves and their culture faltered. And by the 1890s, when Mtoro was living in Bagamoyo, it was under heavy pressure from a number of sources—pressure to which it eventually, if only temporarily, succumbed.

The most important of these pressures was the arabizing tendency that invaded Swahili culture starting from Zanzibar in the second half of the century. It is worth pausing to consider what the term *arabizing* in this context means. It was not, for instance, comparable with another more or less contemporary cultural trend that may be described as "indianizing." Upper-class Swahili tastes became increasingly indianized from about 1830 onward (but most notably after the accession to the throne of Zanzibar, in 1870, of Sultan Barghash). This meant that they increasingly tended to jettison or despise their own products and prefer imported furniture, fabric, jewelry, even house plans and wood-carving styles;[36] but they did not at any point call themselves Indians. Arabizing, however, was a different phenomenon. People who had hitherto felt that the most important thing, regardless of their racial origins, was to be a member of the Swahili cultural group now began to feel it was more important to claim—whether justifiably or not—to belong to the Arab racial group; and so they called themselves, not Swahilis, but Arabs. Arabizing in this sense was not, of course, unique to the Swahili world. It is fairly endemic in the Muslim world and had probably also occurred, on a smaller scale, more than once in Swahili history. It had a number of traditional rationales: the idea that the Arabs, as the original Muslims, were in some sense "better" Muslims than anyone else (an idea reinforced by the tradition of sharifian *baraka* in areas like the East African coast, where new waves of sharifs often arrived from Arabia); the idea that Arab civilization was a superior one, superior even to Swahili (expressed in the appearance, about the end of the nineteenth century, of the Swahili word *usta-arabu*, meaning, roughly, "being like an Arab," as the usual word for culture, where previously *u-ungwana* or perhaps *utamaduni* had been more prevalent);[37] and—thirdly, and arguably separate from both of these—what Trimingham calls simply the "Arab racial myth."[38]

In the past, arabizing trends arising out of these ideas had been more or less effectively offset by Swahili acceptance of u-ungwana, that is, of the idea that those who had resided longest in the settlements were the most acculturated and hence supreme. During the nineteenth century, however, other new forces favoring arabization were added to these traditional rationales, forces that were destined to upset the traditional equilibrium. First, in the period after around 1780, the Omanis, by what can perhaps be best described as a series of coups d'etat up and down the coast, seized political power in most of the settlement.[39] Then, since they were Ibadis and not orthodox Sunni Muslims of the Shafi school (as the Swahilis were), political leadership split from religious leadership, and the latter became the almost exclusive preserve of Hadhrami sharifs.[40] Such people had, of course, been coming to the Swahili coast for many centuries, but as a rule they had been obliged by Swahili rulers and ruling groups to acculturate to the Swahili way of life before they were able to occupy positions of leadership. Now, after about 1840, they embarked on a steady campaign of "cleaning up" Swahili Islam (which in many cases meant making it approximate more closely the Hadhrami type), undermining in the process many of the beliefs and rituals upon which the dominance of the wa-ungwana (and, in the Shirazi heartland, the title holders) had previously rested. It was under this double attack from Omani or Hadhrami immigrants on one hand and from the economic and technological forces cited above on the other that Swahili self-confidence began to reel; although arguably the coup de grace was not administered much before the beginning of the twentieth century, when European imperialism, based as it was on a rough Social Darwinist philosophy, started to insist that all credit for the coastal civilization of the past must belong, not to any African people (and the very word *Swahili*, while it was separated as widely as possible from the term *African*, could not, in the last resort, be divorced from it), but to Asian immigrants: to "Shirazis" from Persia and to mythical "Arab empires," of which the Omani regime in Zanzibar (which just happened to be Britain's strongest ally in the region for most of the time) was only the last in a series. Under colonialism, especially British colonialism, all who called themselves Swahili were systematically discriminated against in terms of education, participation in the political process, labor laws, wages in government service, food rationing in wartime, and so on; even in Fort Jesus jail in Mombasa so-called Arabs received better treatment than those who insisted on retaining their Swahili identity. Not surprisingly, Kirkman was able to note, by the 1950s and 1960s, that hardly anybody on the East African coast willingly described him- or herself as a Swahili at all.[41]

When Mtoro wrote, however, all this was still in the future, and the battle between the arabizers and those who clung to Swahili identity was only just beginning. Broadly speaking, what appears to have happened is that arabizing began in Zanzibar, the capital of the Omani Busaidi dynasty, spread from there by about 1900 to Pemba and the mainland opposite, and gradually extended northward in the two following decades until it covered the whole Swahili coast, although it was always rather weak in the extreme north and south.[42] Baumann, writing in what was then German East Africa in the 1890s, asserted that already by that time nobody was willing to be called a Swahili any longer, but Werner indignantly refuted this, at least with regard to Mombasa and points north, in a work published as late as 1919 (though she was referring to the period before 1910).[43] Subsequently, arabizing continued to spread, penetrating more and more deeply into the poorer sections (and also the more indisputably African ones) of Swahili society; and Ingrams, writing of Zanzibar and Pemba in 1931, noted that many people who could not by any stretch of imagination be called Arabs now claimed Arab identity.[44] In effect, it took the Zanzibar Revolution of 1964 to reverse the trend, and one way of looking at this revolution, coming as it did so immediately after independence, is as a violent reaction to the massive cultural distortions for which British colonial policies had been largely (if not initially) responsible.

Mtoro's work is therefore an important piece of documentary evidence for the early stages of this cultural struggle within the Swahili world. Indeed, it can usefully be interpreted as a credo or charter, although pitched at an unemotional and, on the whole, academic level, on behalf of the antiarabizers. Its very title, *Desturi za Waswahili* [The customs of the Swahili people], unequivocally asserts the existence of the Swahili community, and the author's preface deserves, in this context, to be read very carefully. Anyone wishing to know the customs of the Swahili, he writes, "should consult an old man or an old woman, because it is they who know them and follow the old customs more than do the young people of today. Many people have abandoned the old customs and follow few of them. The young people follow any new custom that is introduced and happens to please them. . . . Recently, since the introduction of European customs, they have abandoned those of the Arabs and Indians, preferring to follow the new customs. If they observe a European custom and like it, they follow it, and, even in language, they introduce European words into their speech. But these young folk adopt these customs in their youth only. When they are mature, they revert to the customs of their ancestors, as they were taught by their elders" (V 1–2). By dismissing arabizing as a transient cultural fashion no more significant than indianizing or westernizing and lumping all three together as mere infantile disorders, Mtoro is aiming a shrewd blow at the arabizers who were undoubtedly already prominent in Bagamoyo (with its close proximity to Zanzibar) in his period. It can hardly be accidental that he only very occasionally even mentions the term *Arab*—and then with a fairly clear implication that it implies something alien—throughout the rest of his work.[45]

Mtoro's book may be contrasted, in this context, with another, almost contemporary prose work in the Swahili language (also recorded and compiled by a German):[46] the autobiography of Tippu Tip.[47] The latter was an energetic arabizer, and his concept of coastal culture is, in many respects, diametrically opposed to that of Mtoro. Although all sources agree that his facial features were remarkably negroid,[48] he always insisted on being called an Arab (in Swahili, *mu-Arabu*), and throughout his book he systematically distinguishes between "Arabs" like himself and wa-ungwana or *wangwana* (a term circumspectly rendered, in the most recent translation, "freeman, as distinct from both slaves and Arabs,"[49] but usually left untranslated), making it perfectly clear that the latter were a separate and, in his view, inferior group. He scarcely uses the term *Swahili* at all and favors Arabic over Swahili vocabulary in his text whenever possible: numerals, for instance, are commonly given in Arabic, and his editor thought it necessary to give a glossary of about seventy-five words that the average modern Swahili reader would find difficult to understand. The vast majority of these are introductions from Arabic, a few of them commercial terms from Indian languages.[50] Tippu Tip's autobiography, in short, is almost a paradigm, in the literary field, of the sort of cultural arabizing of which Mtoro's *Desturi* is implicitly so critical; and Tippu Tip himself was a typical Zanzibar arabizer. No doubt he had Arab blood, and possibly (though this is less certain) he was in spite of his features "pure" Arab on both sides; in any case, since his father called himself an Arab, he was, by Arab custom,

entitled to call himself one as well. The significant point is that had he
been born a few decades earlier, or perhaps in Mombasa or even
Bagamoyo instead of Busaidi-ruled Zanzibar, he would probably not
have done so, but would have been proud of his Swahili cultural
heritage. He was the precursor of many who took advantage of new
political conditions and at least a proportion of Arab blood to assert a
form of *racial* superiority, which was at variance with the traditional
Swahili idea of *cultural* superiority. The latter was based on generations of residence in Swahili settlements and so—in principle at
least—open to people of unmixed African ancestry, such as Mtoro
most probably was.

Indeed, the fact that arabizing was appreciably easier for people of
mixed ancestry may well have colored the emotions of Mtoro and his
fellow Africans when they contemplated it as an increasingly successful cultural trend. Although in later decades pure Africans were not
above claiming that they were Arabs (for, let it be said, entirely
comprehensible reasons), at this comparatively early stage of the
controversy most Swahilis who lacked any claim to Arab ancestry
would almost certainly have sided against the arabizers. They would,
in other words, have been cultural conservatives, although they
would have had to take care, as does Mtoro throughout this work, not
to appear to be defending un-Islamic practices in Swahili Islam too
enthusiastically, for the Hadhrami-sharifian religious leadership was
ultimately on the arabizers' side. As the colonial era wore on, the
arabizers—thanks, no doubt, to the unexpected support of the British
colonial regimes—seemed to be having things all their own way.
"Arabs" were favored, while the very name "Swahili" nearly disappeared from official documents (and also, to some extent at least,
from common parlance),[51] and Mtoro's work, no doubt significantly,
remained unrepublished and untranslated, while the autobiography
of Tippu Tip received a good deal of attention (insofar, that is, as
Swahili texts received any attention in the colonial period after about
1914). Ironically enough, however, the longest-resident Swahili-
speaking town dwellers of Tippu Tip's east Zaïrean empire,
especially those living in its capital at Kisangani (formerly Stanley-
ville), called themselves, even in the colonial period, wa-ungwana,
and they claimed their right to do so by virtue of the fact that they
were descended from Tippu Tip himself.[52] And in modern times the
term *Swahili* has been rehabilitated once more and is applied—though
somewhat haphazardly, and apparently according to different rules in

Kenya from those recognized in Tanzania—to large numbers of people, including many with no sort of claim to Arab forebears even in the remotest past.[53]

To resume: Mtoro was writing at a time and in a place where there already existed the threat that the arabizing trend in Swahili culture, for long only one among several, would swamp all the others and revolutionize the whole nature of Swahili culture itself. Although he clearly recognized this threat, he probably saw it as only temporary and reversible. Nevertheless, it colored much of what he wrote, and may even have been his reason for writing. This has to be borne in mind when one is considering, for instance, his discussion of the jumbes and other title holders, who under the former, traditional dispensation would have been more or less independent Swahili rulers, uniting political and religious leadership and commercial dominance in their own persons (although no doubt often enough dependent upon the Zaramo and other mainland African chiefs for military support). Even though he says at the end of chapter 21 that they are no longer so powerful as they were, it may well be that he still in fact exaggerates their authority as of the 1890s in order to avoid having to discuss the parvenu arabizing outsiders, like Tippu Tip from Zanzibar, who had to a large extent taken over Bagamoyo by 1900. (By the same token, it seems very likely that Tippu Tip himself understates the residual power and influence of the traditional Swahili rulers, except where he appropriates it to "Arabs" like himself.) Again, Mtoro had to tread cautiously when discussing the residual traces of African Traditional Religion in the traditional Swahili form of Islam, for he could not afford to give offenses to the Hadhrami sharifs and bring their wrath down upon his head and the heads of the "conservative" Swahili school of thought. (It is probably for this reason that Mtoro seems to have omitted a certain amount of information about Swahili rituals and religious practices—although he has managed to include an impressive amount nonetheless.) Finally, we should remember that things have in a sense turned full circle since the victory of Tippu Tip and his arabizers, so that although Bwana Idi of Bagamoyo, who would have lived most of his life under the colonial regime and would be inclined to accept its categories, called Mtoro a Zaramo, there are today good grounds for remembering him, as he would no doubt have wished to be remembered, as—at least in the cultural sense (which is the only possible one)—a "pure Swahili person."

Conclusion

By way of conclusion, let us take another look at Mtoro's Bagamoyo in the light of what has been established about it. By comparison with towns like Mombasa and Zanzibar, it was a medium-small or even small settlement, though growing fast; but it was less dependent upon agriculture, and correspondingly more so on trade (and especially the caravan trade to the interior), than other settlements of similar size, on account of its special economic and geographical relationship with Zanzibar town, whose gateway to the interior it had become. In some respects it was changing very fast during the 1890s, but in others it was absolutely typical of traditional Swahili settlements everywhere (including a few such as Tabora and Ujiji, growing up in places along trade routes to the interior where no local, non-Muslim potentate was particularly dominant); and some of the customs and traditions observed by Mtoro are still very much alive. His account of the rituals and customs concerning young children and their training in manners and early religious education, for instance, still holds true for many Swahili families in Mombasa, Lamu, and parts of Zanzibar and Pemba today. At a slightly different level, many of the values and attitudes he recounts can be identified, even in modern times, not only along the eastern coast but among Swahili or Swahilized peoples throughout East Africa and some eastern parts of Zaïre, in spite of the colonial experience and the radical transformation of the economies of many of people concerned.

The areas where most changes have taken place are, generally speaking, religion and politics. The element of African Traditional Religion in Swahili Islam was much more overt in the past, although it can be argued that it is not so much eliminated as simply disguised at the present time. In at least some Swahili societies, for example, belief in spirits (pepo) and the practice of spirit dances are still widespread, although such activities are usually conducted in secret on account of the attitude of the religious leadership. A certain, perhaps superficial, Hadhramization of Swahili Islam may also have occurred. Some important changes, though, are indisputable. Certainly initiation rites for both sexes have now disappeared in most regions,[54] and males are usually circumcised in hospitals during infancy. Improved communications within the Islamic world have also played their part, and during the present century, most Islamic intellectuals in the Swahili world have found it increasingly easy to obtain publications from all parts of the Islamic world.

Politically, Mtoro's Bagamoyo was always rather exceptional in being a typically Shirazi-Swahili settlement. The jumbes and other title holders he describes were never found far outside the Shirazi heartland, that is, between Funzi Island and Bagamoyo itself, and today they survive, with very attenuated authority, only on the northern Tanzania coast. The role they played and the mechanisms by which they were able to play it, however, were very similar to those of upper-class Swahili groups, the wa-ungwana, in the wider Swahili world. Control of imports and, later perhaps, of certain vital, mostly long-distance trade items such as ivory; a widespread network of trade links reinforced by kin and marriage ties; the use of certain quasi-magical powers—divination, mediation, rainmaking perhaps, possibly also curing and protection—to assist them in asserting and later maintaining political dominance: in all these ways the Shirazi-Swahili title holders and the wa-ungwana elsewhere in the Swahili world were much alike. Only in certain forms, such as the importance they attached to dress, their type of installation ceremony, and the style of some of their rituals, can they be distinguished. It seems likely, however, that the significance of the term *Shirazi* in the past would have lain in the fact that it indicated a particular mode of dominance, distinguishable by such forms from the ungwana or the sharifian or any other mode, rather than in any real or imaginary historical or descent links with Persia. "Shirazi" dynasties outside the Shirazi heartland should also be understood in the light of this observation.

Bagamoyo's distinctive Shirazi-type political institutions, which were probably less than three centuries old, were already under severe strain when Mtoro wrote. The circumstance that Bagamoyo was, in a sense, an economic extension of Zanzibar town affected their position, since the new-style Omani and Indian merchant princes of that place were much too powerful to treat mere jumbes as even notional equals—and in any case had not been acculturated to understand the rules by which the Swahilis played the game. Cultural and social arabizing and the take-over of the religious leadership by Hadhrami sharifs and their associates also undermined them; and, finally, the German administration superimposed yet another layer of de facto authority over them, which reduced them to little more than village headmen and ciphers of the colonial regime. Mtoro's picture of the jumbes and other title holders is likely to have been even more outdated than he admits, but of course it is nonetheless valuable to historians for that.

Surely the greatest value of Mtoro's writing to historians, however, is as a corrective to the arabizing bias that affected not only every aspect of Swahili society but, almost more significantly, virtually every interpretation of it during this century. His simple, straight-forward analysis of coastal life, written with a disapproving eye on his arabizing contemporaries, it is true, but written perceptively and without guile or deliberate distortion, should be read by every non-Swahili student of the East African coast, and no doubt many Swahili ones as well. It should put an end once and for all to the enduring colonialist myth that the Swahilis, as an identifiable and self-aware community, did not exist. It should modify, too, the views of those (often modern East African) historians and sociologists who like to see Swahili culture and civilization as something fundamentally alien to the continent, non-African, perhaps even in some sense repre-hensible. It should enable us to revise what I venture to suggest is still a general idea of Swahili culture as a sort of two-dimensional spectrum extending from town to country, from "civilization" to a simple peasant existence, from the shores of the Middle East to those of Africa, and, behind but implicit in each of these antitheses, from "Arabs" to "Africans,"[55] and to replace it with something much more sophisticated and accurate. In the new schema, arabizing is no more than one of several cultural forces that are constantly ebbing and flowing, interacting with one another to produce something new, syncretistic perhaps, yet quite original and autonomous: Swahili culture, within an urban or semi- or quasi-urban African context. If the publication of this new translation of *Desturi za Waswahili* can achieve at least some of these objectives, it will be a major landmark in modern Swahili studies.

Appendix II

Weights and Measures

Money

It must be remembered that for many years before and for a few years after the date of publication of the *Desturi*, currency was so stable that a fixed rate of exchange could be used with little or no fluctuation. The chief coins were the Maria Theresa dollar (*riale*) and the Indian rupee (*rupia*) worth half a riale. The rupee was divided into 64 pesa. The other divisions of the rupee used in India were not known in Africa. It is not always immediately clear whether fractions refer to the riale or the rupia; but in fact there seems to be only one passage (V 95) where there is room for genuine doubt, and the distinction has elsewhere been made clear in the translation. Thus if the word *nusu* (half) is used alone, it usually, but not invariably, means half a riale. For half a rupee Mtoro usually uses the term *nusu rupia*.

Later the rupee was divided into 100 *heller* in German East Africa. In British East Africa the shilling, valued at half a rupee, was divided into 100 cents. Neither of these words is used in this book; but the older words are still in use today. *Hella* (two cents) is common in Tanzania, and so also are *pesa* (two and a half cents), *thumuni* or *sumli* (one-eighth of a riale, or twenty-five cents), and occasionally *robo* (one-quarter of a riale, or one shilling). [Note also *pesa nane*, one-eighth of a rupee, which was two shillings, hence twenty-five cents; and *saba na nusu*, seven and a half heller of a German East African rupee, hence fifteen cents of a British East African shilling.—J. de V.A.]

It is to be noted further that Mtoro and others habitually use a word such as *kilemba* ("turban") when in fact the payment for the turban has been commuted into cash.

Length, Weight, and Volume

Swahili units of length, weight, and volume and their equivalents are listed in table 1.

TABLE 1
SWAHILI UNITS OF MEASURE

	Swahili Unit	Equivalent
Length	*Dhiraa*	Cubit—about eighteen inches
	Pima	Four dhiraa or four meters
	Kitambi	Five to six dhiraa
	Jora	A bolt of cloth, usually thirty yards
Weight	*Manni*	Three ratili (pounds)
	Farasila	Thirty-six ratili (pounds) = sixteen kilograms
Volume	*Gao*	Handful
	Kibaba	More than a pint, about a liter
	Pishi	Four kibaba
	Fungu	A small heap, no fixed amount
	Kicha	A small bundle
	Debe	Hindustani *diba*, a large tin can, four imperial, five American gallons

Time

Mtoro sometimes counts the hours in the Swahili style, in which *saa sita* (the "sixth hour") means twelve o'clock (noon), and sometimes in the European style, in which it means six o'clock. There is no passage in which there is room for doubt, and this has been clarified in the translation without comment.

Appendix III

Ngoma: Music and Dance

J. de V. Allen

It is impossible to find a satisfactory English equivalent for the term *ngoma*. The translator must in each context choose between the words *dance* and *drum*. *Ngoma* means either, but more often both simultaneously. The English reader must bear this in mind, noting that in every place where either English word is used, he or she is at liberty to substitute the other if the context allows. Occasionally only one meaning is possible, as in V 157, where we have a *ngoma* ("dance") in which no *ngoma* ("drum") is used.

A similar difficulty arises in translating in a musical context the verbs *-cheza* ("to play, to play an instrument, to dance") and *-piga* ("to hit or strike," also "to play an instrument, to take"—e.g., a photograph). As playing and dancing are more or less inseparable, it is often convenient to translate *-cheza* "dance." Thus V 123.1 may be translated in two ways: "Those who perform it must be freemen; it is not proper for slaves to perform the great dance," or "Those who perform on it must be freemen; it is not proper for slaves to play the great drum." The reader must bear in mind that it is not necessary to choose which is the more correct translation; both may be correct simultaneously. Again, where we have references to *-piga mbiu* or *-piga siwa*, they might mean "to play" (blow) or "to play" (hit, beat). Since the siwa is too fragile and valuable an instrument to beat, we must assume *-piga siwa* means to blow the siwa (although there is also a special ritual word for blowing a siwa, namely, *-vumiza*). On the other hand, the mbiu is normally just a cow or buffalo horn, usually with a hole near its tip, which can equally well be blown or struck, and so it is better to adhere to the general term *play*. As we shall see,

233

however, in the Bagamoyo area there is a type of mbiu that is in fact a drum, and there the English verb *beat* is accordingly applicable.

Musical Instruments

By far the largest group of instruments, almost all of them indigenous, is the percussion group, especially the drums.[1] Unfortunately, with drums, as with many Swahili musical instruments, there are considerable problems of nomenclature. Not only are there occasional regional differences and differences of period (the same name referring to different instruments in different regions or at different periods in history), but there may even be differences within a single region at a given time according to the use to which an instrument is being put. Thus the same side-blown horn may be given one name if it is being employed to summon the people to war and quite another if it is being used merely to make a public pronouncement.[2] The same is sometimes true of drums, and here the fact that virtually every drum has a dance named after it (or vice versa) is relevant, for the dance may go out of fashion and be forgotten, leaving the drum, as it were, suspended, until different communities take it up for different dances, attaching to it quite different names.

Bearing all this in mind, let us take a look at such information as is available from a number of sources regarding the six or seven different sorts of drum and the other musical instruments named by Mtoro. (To prevent confusion, instruments actually mentioned in the text will be written in capital letters.) Clearly the most important drums in Mtoro's Bagamoyo were the state drums, or NGOMA KUU. He reports that there were three of these (presumably per settlement, but possibly per confederation), one of them larger than the other two and called the *mkwiro*, and that they were used only by chiefs on important occasions. They are described as long, tapering drums, that apparently came to a point, since they were played either resting on a bed or in the fork of a tree. Sacleux and the other lexicographers give *mkwiro* as meaning a drumstick, not a drum, but possibly the largest of the three was played with this sort of drumstick while the other two were beaten with another type—possibly the *pirigo*, made of palm. In any case these drums sound as if they were closed at the base. No drum north of Mombasa is known as the ngoma kuu: indeed, insofar as *ngoma* is not used as a generic term for all drums and dances, it tends to mean a medium-sized drum, generally one-ended, played with a stick and closed at the base; while a large drum, as Krapf points out, should strictly be referred to by the augmentative form *goma*. A goma drum is known elsewhere, and, as we shall see, more than one dance (including one in Mtoro's Bagamoyo) is also known as a goma. Other drums with state or secret-society functions to the north of Bagamoyo are the *tutu* or *chuchu* (among the Bajuni, and also reported in the Comoros), the *ngaji* (among the Pokomo), and the *mwanza* (among the Mijikenda). Of these the ngajis are split tree trunks closed up with skin, laid on their side, and filled with water so that they roar when a stick inserted through a hole in the skin is rotated. The tutu is sometimes similarly described, but Ingrams illustrates a tutu in the Zanzibar Museum, along with a number of other drums, all presumably from the Zanzibar-Pemba region,[3] as a small, tapering drum with a closed base—looking, in fact, not unlike a miniature ngoma kuu as described above. Other tall drums used for ceremonial purposes on the Kenya coast are the MSONDO or *chondo* with one leg (also illustrated by Ingrams and associated by him with a women's dance that may be the one mentioned by Mtoro in chapter 9, V84–87, and the VUMI, known also to Mtoro. The vumi usually has three legs and is open at the base, although the one illustrated by Ingrams appears to be double-ended. Prins also lists a *mshindo* as a three-legged, open-based drum (the name is not mentioned in the dictionaries, and it is probably largely restricted to Pemba and its environs), but the illustration in Ingrams shows that this is a squat, fairly shallow drum on legs as high as its body. Ingrams, incidentally, suggests that different drums must be covered with different skins and gives a duiker skin for the mshindo; but, nowadays at least, no Swahilis seem to make this distinction, and goatskins are almost invariably used.

Along with the vumi, Mtoro mentions the CHAPUO and CHAPUO CHA VUMI. The chapuo is one of the most widely and regularly used drums in the Swahili world. It is double-ended, is large enough to have to be strung around the neck, held between the knees, or possibly placed on some sort of a stool in front of the player, and is played both with the fingers and with the palms of the hands. The chapuo cha vumi (Sacleux gives *chapuo ya vumi*) is of a similar size but upright with three feet and an open base like the vumi. Another drum named by Mtoro is the DOGORI, which is said to be very large, as much as thirty inches high and eighteen inches in diameter, and sits on four legs. Sacleux gives the term as a Zaramo borrowing, and certainly the writer has not encountered such a drum north of Bagamoyo. It is not clear whether the base is open or closed. The MRUN-

GURA is doubtless another southern drum; at least the name derives from a southern dialect, and Prins links it with Pemba. One informant describes it as a long drum with a wide base, about six inches in diameter. This does not altogether fit with Ingrams' description of the Pemba mrungura as a "small drum standing on three or four legs, which are all on a stand." He adds that the legs and stand are often beautifully carved and made from a single piece of wood. Sacleux says that it is customarily used to summon laborers to and from work on the plantations. Mtoro also mentions a smaller version, the KIRUN-GURA, usually played in sets of three by a single person. This is reminiscent of the three ngoma kuu, and it is possible that playing drums in sets of three is a feature of Pemba-Mrima music.

We may here note a number of other drums reported from this region and illustrated (although not very clearly, unfortunately) by Ingrams. He mentions the *kindimba* (for which the skin of a monitor lizard was used), formerly featured for the *marinda* dance in Zanzibar, and shows a very small one-legged drum described as the *kiminingo*. He also mentions the *rewa*, which he says "is used as a gong as well as a dance" and which he describes as a larger edition of the tutu. His tutu (which he says is covered with a gazelle skin and which is, according to him, the only drum beaten with a drumstick) is used to announce a ngoma, or public dance. As we have seen, it is not unlike the ngoma kuu in shape, but smaller, so a larger version of it (topped with oxhide) might well be very similar to the ngoma kuu. Once again, though, the lexicographers do not recognize the rewa as a drum, only as a type of pepo, and hence as the term for the dance required to exorcise it; so the rewa may very well be a case where the name of the dance is extended to the drum used for it, and the same drum may be known under another name in other circumstances.

Apart from drums, indigenous percussion instruments include UPATU or *utasa*, diminutive *kitasa*, a metal tray beaten with a switch, and later (and perhaps for louder dances) the DEBE, a four-gallon tin (itself, of course, imported, but its use as a musical instrument indigenous) that has largely but not entirely replaced it. Not mentioned here are the *marimba*, or xylophone, which may or may not have been imported many centuries ago from Indonesia,[4] and the various bells worn on legs (*njuga* if made of metal, usually iron; *misewe* or possibly *manganja*[5] if made of seeds). There are also rattles (*sanji ya cherewa*, *kidebe*, and others that consist of a tin containing seeds or pebbles; *kayamba*, made of reeds or occasionally porcupine quills in a frame, with seeds inside them); and Ingrams mentions the *miwale*, flat pieces of the midrib of the *mwale*, or raffia, palm which are clashed together as cymbals. To this should be added at least one drum from the interior, the GANDA, mentioned by Mtoro as used in the chando dance. It comes from Uganda, but its use was already widespread in western Tanzania by Mtoro's time. Unlike most coastal drums, whose skins were tautened by pegs or by a ring of some flexible fiber stretched over the end of a frame and so often had to be tightened by exposure to fire, the ganda skins were fastened by loops down the side of the frame. We should also add several instruments from Asia, notably the MATUWAZI, or cymbals, possibly Indian in origin (although a pair of them were part of the Vumba royal regalia,)[6] and the TARI (also known north of Bagamoyo as *mtari* or *mtwari*, and also referred to by Mtoro as MATUNGA). This is a tambourine, sometimes with bells attached, found all over the Muslim world.[7] The VIKUKU, bells worn on the ankles for some dances, are possibly of Indian origin (they certainly exist in India) but are the sort of thing that might well have evolved spontaneously in many places.

Turning to wind instruments, we should first note the large family of side-blown horns that are an exclusively African genre.[8] Undoubtedly the largest and finest of these was the SIWA, mentioned by Mtoro only in connection with funerals. The siwa was a typical regalia item, and the bronze siwa of Lamu and ivory one of Pate, on the northern Swahili coast, have often been cited as masterpieces of African art.[9] A small ivory siwa is known to exist as close to Bagamoyo as Vumba, on the Kenya-Tanzania border, but this is said to have come from the north, from Ozi, which was associated with Pate. Most siwas in modern Tanzania are made of wood, including the two in the Zanzibar Museum, the one associated with the Kimbu people in the Dar-es-Salaam Museum, and the one reported still in use relatively recently at Mweni.[10] Of these, at least the two associated with the mwinyimkuu of Zanzibar comprised several hinged sections, like their northern counterparts. Siwas were blown on all solemn state occasions and at all family rituals of the leading families of any Swahili settlement. They had important symbolic and sociopolitical functions. The *Pate Chronicle* contains a story about a wicked uncle who tried to deny his young nephew the right to inherit the sultanate by denying him the siwa for his circumcision ceremony (or, rather, by insisting that he should share the ceremony and the siwa with his, the wicked uncle's, own children, thereby acknowledging that they had equal right to the throne). And there is a story that a claimant to the throne of Kilwa threw the Kilwa siwa into the sea, thereby, in his own view, "drowning" the sultanate itself.[11]

Less grand than the siwa were a number of other sideblown horns, the MBIU, *baragumu*, *zumbe*, and *gunda*, and below these there exist—at least among the Bajuns—a whole hierarchy of conch shells that are also, strictly speaking, side-blown horns, including the *iduvi*, *chondothi*, chondo, and chondo *dodi*. (The chondo, confusingly enough, is also used among the Swahilis who speak the Ki-Ungwana dialect, that is, those who live around Kisangani in Eastern Zaire, as a dialect form of the msondo drum.) The gunda, in central and southern dialects, is an antelope horn, but among the Bajunis it is the largest of the conches.[12] The zumbe and, usually, baragumu are also as a rule antelope horns. Scholars have spent a good deal of time trying to establish which name is appropriate to the spiraling koodoo horn and which to the more common, straight oryx horn, but, as already indicated, this is probably a waste of time, because they often change their names according to the way they are being used. Thus a zumbe (evidently a northern-dialect word) is usually used for a summons to war or for a similar emergency, while a baragumu (in the Comoros said to be made of buffalo horn, presumably because there are no gazelles there) is generally associated with summoning people to a major assembly or with the announcement of the arrival or departure of a caravan to the interior.[13] The mbiu, which is the only one mentioned in Mtoro's work, is usually employed for less important occasions. (The Swahili proverb in the text, *Mbiu ya mgambo akilia haina jambo*, may equally well be translated as "If the horn sounds for a meeting, there is something up" or ". . . there is nothing very serious afoot.")[14] Mtoro, however, distinguishes between a specific MBIU YA MGAMBO, which a local informant describes, not as a horn at all, but as a small drum carried on the shoulder by a town crier and used for fairly important announcements, and a MBIU YA PEMBE, consisting of a cow or buffalo horn (which is what is normally understood by *mbiu*) either struck or blown. The translator who wishes to stress the difference should perhaps speak of "beating" the former and merely "playing" the latter. (It has been suggested, however, that when a Swahili wishes to emphasize that he or she is striking, not blowing, a mbiu, yet another verb, *-gonga*, is appropriate. Mtoro's use of *mbiu ya mgambo* to refer to a drum must be regarded as an extreme example of an instrument changing its name according to its function, or rather of the name being applied to a completely different instrument, since the word *mbiu*, elsewhere applied only to a horn, is here applied to a sort of drum used for the function a horn normally fulfills. A final word on the cow horn: A cow horn *without* a hole bored near its tip, which can therefore only be struck, not blown, is a common musical instrument among women[15] and when so used is simply known as a pembe or, on the north coast, a *vugo*. Strictly speaking, this is a different instrument from the town crier's (mbiu ya) pembe, which is designed to be either beaten or blown and is still used in both ways today.

From side-blown, or transverse, horns we turn to end-blown ones. The Portuguese speak of encountering *anafils* on the Swahili coast, and this term seems likely to be connected with the Arabic *nafir*, meaning a brass bugle or trumpet, but no trace of such an instrument has been found or otherwise recorded. A *parati*, an end-blown horn made of wood and hide with a slight bell at the base, is still known, and Sacleux says the term is an archaic borrowing from the Zaramo. There is also a *panda*, or wood instrument, also end-blown and also, apparently, archaic. Both the parati and the panda are probably indigenous, and the nafir may have been. (The fact that the Portuguese used an Arabic term for it does not, of course, prove that the Swahili did, nor—even if they did—was it necessarily imported.)[16] Nowadays almost the only end-blown wind instrument used is the *tarambeta*, the Western-type cornet or trumpet, which is of course imported. In Allen's translation, however, *mbiu* is sometimes translated "trumpet" (V 133).

The most important wind instrument, in the sense of being the most frequently played, is the ZUMARI (*zomari, mzomari*), which is here translated, neatly but incorrectly, "pipe" or, occasionally, "flute." It is in fact a sort of oboe or shawm, a double-reeded instrument, whose use is very widespread throughout the Muslim world (and so it is almost certainly not indigenous to East Africa, though it was probably played there for a long time). Those who play it spend many years learning to distend their cheeks to a considerable size and to breathe in through their noses at the same time as they blow out through their mouths, a technique that enables them to play continuously for quite long periods.[17] An interesting aspect of the zumari is that it is considered, from an Islamic viewpoint, an unclean instrument and so is not played in mosque functions (where it is replaced by the *nai*, a type of flute probably of Indian or Persian origins). This regulation is nowhere made very explicit in the *Desturi*, and it is possible that it was only rigidly enforced by the Hadhrami sharifs, who had evidently not yet imposed their entire code upon the Bagamoyo population of the day: the presence of a zumari player at a funeral, for instance, as described in chapter 20, V 214, would certainly raise eyebrows among orthodox Swahili Muslims today.

Lastly we turn to stringed instruments. The Swahilis have a very simple single-stringed instrument, usually played with a bow, known as the *uta*, and two two-stringed instruments, the *zeze*, played with a stick, and the *mdube*, which is plucked. The *pango*, a five-stringed instrument on a calabash base, seems to have disappeared, as does the *gambusi* or *gabusi*, an elegant mandolin that is imported from Arabia and may ultimately derive from the Turkish *qubusz*. By far the finest of the Swahili stringed instruments is the KINANDA, described[18] as a long-necked lute with a wooden body, skin belly, and a hollow neck. This is quite different from the *udi*, which has a far bigger body and is the Swahili version of the Arabic or Persian instrument from which the European lute is derived. Nowadays, however, the real kinanda is virtually unknown, and the name is used for a number of other instruments, including, in some contexts, a harmonium, a mouth organ, and even a gramophone.

A word should perhaps be said about the time depth and nature of the music produced by such instruments. When Ibn Battuta reached Mogadishu, at that time almost certainly a Swahili town, in the first half of the fourteenth century, the ruler went about accompanied by drummers and players of "oboes and trumpets": the former were doubtless a type of zumari, and the latter were probably siwas (by analogy with the instruments that attended later rulers further south) but possibly some sort of nafir. When Vasco da Gama reached Malindi, its monarch was accompanied by men playing "two trumpets of ivory, richly carved and the size of a man, which were blown from a hole in the side, and made sweet music with the *anafils*." The surviving Pate siwa fits this description almost perfectly. Moreover, there are numerous other Portuguese references to siwas, made both of "copper" (perhaps bronze) and ivory, and to royal drums and bands of musicians celebrating royal occasions.[19] The antiquity of the Swahili musical tradition, combined with the fact that so many of the instruments it employs are indigenous, strongly suggests that traditional Swahili music is unlikely to have been more than casually influenced by Arabic or other non-African music; and while, of course, this cannot be regarded as proved—at least until more research on musicological material is carried out than has yet been done[20]—the impression gained by listening to it is that it is essentially sui generis, although, of course, influenced by Arab and Indian music in certain spheres, especially over the last century or so. The common assumption that this music is substantially Arabic should certainly be treated with serious reservations until it is better supported than is so far the case. Only too often it is grounded, as are so many statements about Arab bases for other elements of Swahili culture, in a mixture of ignorance and latent racism of one sort or another.

Dances and Songs

A full-dress academic study of Swahili dances is long overdue. As can be seen from the most casual reading of the *Desturi*, they (or rather ngomas, musical occasions of some sort or other) mark every important moment in the traditional Swahili life: every rite of passage, every occasion for happiness or sorrow, even such events—which must have been common enough in a place like Bagamoyo—as the departure of a caravan. They are a part of the process of healing people who are seized by a pepo, and songs are even commonly sung in the presence of victims of smallpox (though since, as Mtoro acknowledges, recovery from smallpox is unlikely, it is probable that such songs are designed more to comfort the sufferer, and possibly his or her family, than to cure). Children sing in their games; porters sing on the road; and so on. No song is too trivial to attract Mtoro's attention (here he records some 250 of them, though most are very short), and there are countless occasions when, as he shows, it is conventional to summon a zumari player or to beat a drum without necessarily singing. Even political, social, and other tensions are resolved, at least to some extent, by music: speaking of the kiumbizi (in northern dialects, *kirumbizi*) dance (V 130), Mtoro observes that it may be performed between young men who are enemies because one has taken the wife of the other, and this writer has personally witnessed such an occasion (the rightful husband won his wife back, to the evident delight of most of the spectators), while the banji dance, better known as *beni*, seems to be designed largely to polarize many naturally fissiparous groups or sections into two main ones, and then, by providing an approved, nonviolent method by which they may catharsize their antipathies, bring about an overall unity at the settlement level. Doubt has been cast, however, on whether beni dances, or more precisely *lelemama*, their female equivalent, are as effective at promoting social unity as has been supposed.[21]

Given their importance on so many occasions, it is not surprising to learn that ngomas are manifold. Not only are dozens listed under different names (one or two of which might turn out, on closer inspection, to be the same dance), but several that are listed under the same name are in fact quite different dances. (The goma dance is one such case: at least the goma described by Mtoro bears some resemblance to only one of the two gomas that are still danced, at the time of writing, in the northern Swahili world, that is, to the goma *la Ndau* danced by the people of Ndau. It bears little resemblance to the goma *la hazuwa*, however, which is danced by the people of the northern mainland around Kiunga.) Nevertheless, it is quite informative to assume for the moment that dances that share names are the same dances and to compare four separate lists of dances which have been published at various times and which have special reference to various parts of the Swahili coast. These four are as follows: (1) Mtoro, referring to the Bagamoyo area in the 1890s; (2) Skene, referring to the Kenya coast in 1910–1915;[22] (3) Ingrams, referring to Zanzibar and Pemba in the 1920s;[23] and (4) Wiesauer, referring to the northern Kenya coast in the 1970s.[24] Taking Mtoro's list, we find that apart from the various pepo dances, only seven of the twenty or so that he cites are mentioned in any of the other lists (see table 2). (This should possibly be increased to eight if we assume that his nyago and *unyago* initiation dances are more or less the same as those that appear in the other three lists as *kinyago*, *vinyago*, and *manyago*.) As regards the pepo dances, we find the following pepo names are shared: tari, Qitimiri, Dungumaro, and ki-Galla (shared with Ingrams) and possibly also Shamn'gombe (shared with Skene). This leaves the names of six pepo dances (plus the two later ones mentioned by Bwana Idi, the Bwana

TABLE 2
SWAHILI DANCES MENTIONED IN FOUR MAJOR LISTS

	Mtoro	Skene	Ingrams	Wiesauer
Kiumbizi	1	1		1
Chama ("competition")	1	0		1
Banji (*beni*)	0	0		1
Mdurenge	0	0		1
Bondogea	0	1		0
Bandaro	1	0		0
Goma	0	0		1

Mkubwa and the Ngwindi)[25] appearing only in Mtoro's list. If we take Skene's list and exclude the four dances that he specifically says are Arabian, not Swahili, we find that seven out of thirteen dances appear on other lists, but only two out of his twelve pepo names. In Wiesauer's list, which does not include pepo dances, ten out of seventeen names are also known from elsewhere. If we take Ingrams's enormous list of forty-six dance names, however, out of which thirteen and possible more seem to refer to pepo dances, we find that only about seven dances and four pepo dances are recorded from elsewhere at other periods.

Even allowing a wide margin of error (to cover the possibility of reduplicated dances, incomplete lists, and so on), these figures suggest that Swahili dances changed at a fairly fast rate and also varied, in many cases, from region to region, and this is indeed pretty much what we should expect in an urban-oriented society in which considerable value was always attached to "the latest," whether in dances, clothes, or any other area in which fashions reigned. Even over the last fifteen years, some dances have more or less disappeared, while others have come on the scene to enjoy an immediate but often short-lived vogue. The instruments selected to accompany each type of dance were simply the most appropriate available, and the fact that one or more such instruments might be nonindigenous tells us nothing about the origins of the dance itself except in a very few cases where the newly arrived instrument gave to the dance its special flavor of novelty. We can also be reasonably certain that dances that retained the same name over a long period (say, from Mtoro's 1890s to Wiesauer's 1970s) in fact evolved and changed considerably during that time, especially over different regions of the coast.

Given all this fluidity and multiplicity, studies of dance perhaps make sense only if their authors take one or two dances (as Ranger took the beni) and follow their fortunes through space and time. Some interesting points can, however, be made at the more general level. Of Mtoro's nonpepo dances, only five are specifically mentioned as being performed solely by men (and of these, the mbenda is performed by men in women's dress, which may mean it was the preserve of transsexuals, while women are specially mentioned as having an important role in the kigoma) and one, the kidatu or msoma, is exclusively for women, leaving ten in which both sexes explicitly take part. This is a much higher proportion of male-and-female dances than would be found in any list of Swahili dances drawn up today and certainly reflects the freer status of women in the Swahili world in the era before the Zanzibar- and Lamu-based Hadhrami sharifs tightened up the rules of sexual segregation. (As a matter of fact, they may already have been in the process of being tightened up by the time Mtoro wrote, for he observes somewhat wistfully that many of these dances are already out of date.) In some dances mentioned by Mtoro which still survive or have only recently disappeared, such as the banji/beni and the mdurenge, women no longer figure at all, at least in the larger towns. The small-town status of Bagamoyo, in which many if not most males would have been closely related to the wives of others, may also have contributed to a freer atmosphere in this respect.

Another aspect of these dances to which it is worth drawing attention is the proportion of them that are said to have originated as the dances of slaves or of other low-status persons. Mtoro himself specially mentions the bondogea as a dance of domestic slaves in origin, and Skene adds that the *dandaro* is "rarely if ever danced by free men," although Mtoro has nothing to say about this. The tinge is also said by Mtoro to have originated "inland," which would mean among low-status people, since they would not have been Muslims; but Anon. DSM affirms that the tinge in fact derived from the Swahilis of Kilwa. It is now reasonably clear that the whole nyago family of dances also originated in Malawi and was brought to the coast by slaves from there, although very few Swahilis recognized (or yet recognize) this fact, and there may well have been others that came from the same source. Finally, the sepoy dance was, of course, introduced by outsiders, but once again Mtoro does not specifically say that is is not danced by everybody.

We have a potential contradiction here. On the one hand there are some dances, like the great dance, or ngoma kuu, which may be danced only by the social elite and in which each rank had its special role and distinctive form of dress. On the other we have dances introduced by slaves and outsiders in which at least most people, later probably all of them, participate. Such a contradiction in fact runs right through Swahili society and is part of the dynamic of Swahili culture. The elite, the old, established families, were constantly seeking to entrench themselves, to make themselves almost a caste apart, distinguished from other groups by any number of cultural and sociocultural indications; and almost as invariably they failed, because of insufficient economic differentiation, perhaps, or simply because they were too few in number or the resources on which their wealth depended were too vulnerable to ecological and other forces.

At the other end of the social spectrum, new groups were constantly being absorbed, sometimes almost wholesale, who brought with them certain cultural traits and values that they did not discard (though they often modified them to make them more acceptable to an urban and Islamic society), and these frequently became so important in the cultural scheme of things that the elite had to accept them along with everyone else. Ranger has pointed out that in some towns beni dances were performed only by low-status groups but were extensively subsidized by the rich, who could not afford (and no doubt could not bear) to stand aside from something with such important consequences within the community. In other towns high-status groups paticipated along with everyone else. One of the minor Shirazi-Swahili title holders, the *akida*, is said to have originated as an officer in charge of the dance bands (and when sexual segregation became more prevalent, it became necessary also to have a female akida for female dance groups).[26] The impression of a rigidly hierarchical society conveyed by such things as the regulations for the ngoma kuu was, in fact, misleading, except perhaps in a few large towns at very wealthy periods in their history. Cultural initiatives often came from below, of which the elite was obliged to take cognizance. Arguably, indeed, Swahili culture was at its best, in terms of creativity and originality of output, when pressures from above and those from below were more or less in equilibrium.

It remains only to add a few remarks about dances generally and about those described by Mtoro in particular. Of the goma, it is reported by Bwana Idi that a dance of this name is still popular in Tanga and Pangani: the men carry candles and sticks, and each has a woman behind him. (Neither the candles nor the women appear in modern northern versions.) Of the banji/beni (whose name derives, of course, from the English term *band*), he writes that the women form a circle with the men in the middle, but it is not clear from this whether the women are participants or spectators. The instruments used are said to be three drums, a debe, and a zumari, but it is hard to believe that the number and even the names of each instrument are as rigidly prescribed as statements of this sort imply: provided that the basic instrument or instruments are available, dancers nowadays generally make do with whatever else is available. The widespread appearance of the ki-Galla among spirit, or pepo, dances is notable. Even at the peak of their power the Galla did not reach much further south than Mombasa (although one Vumba ruler is remembered, perhaps incorrectly, as having been "carried off" by them); and after their final defeat in the late 1860s they virtually disappeared except as a small group near the Tana. And yet we find ki-Galla spirits still threatening the inhabitants of Bagamoyo in the 1890s and Zanzibar-Pemba in the 1930s, and they are still not unknown today. No other racial or tribal invaders, not even the Europeans (*ki-Zungu*) nor the Arabs (*ki-Arabu*), seems to have such an impression on the spirit world. It is conceivable that this has something to do with the fact that a victim of a ki-Galla pepo might wear the muslin (*bafta*) robes and turban that were generally the mark of a high-class Muslim, although the Galla were only very seldom Muslims before the middle of the present century. (The fact that the tambourine is used also indicates that the ki-Galla pepo is visualized as a Muslim one.) It is generally and on the whole plausibly assumed that sufferers from pepo, who were in the vast majority of cases women, were suffering from intense social frustration arising out of their suppressed conditions, and the opportunity to wear, for some time, high-status male clothes and to behave as such a person was supposed to behave, with complete impunity, was no doubt extremely salutary. As noted in the Bibliography, however, much research remains to be done on the vast and fascinating topic of Swahili pepo dances before we can really say we understand them properly.

The same can be said of Swahili dances generally. They are more than a leisure activity, more than a form of artistic self-expression, more even than a palimpsest of the society from which they evolved. To a very large extent they actually encapsulate that society and its culture: they form its paradigm, its skeleton, and a good deal of its flesh as well. It is to be hoped that some scholar who is equal to the task will shortly fill the gaps in our knowledge which Ranger and Strobel, in their all-important pioneering works, have left.

In Memoriam

Iohn Willoughby Tarleton Allen, Lowlli Wichie
Hamisi-Kitumboy, and our other collaborators
who died during this project, 1969—1979

"From God we come, and unto God we return."[1] Forty days ago there died at Oxford, England, aged seventy-four, the man whose *Introduction to Swahili Language* and translation of Mtoro bin Mwinyi Bakari's *Desturi za Waswahili* you have used in typescript, whose opinions on so many things African and on the African achievement of independence have been given to you. He came of an old family of British servicemen and clergy. The "Tarleton" in his name goes back to maternal ancestors who included Dick Tarleton, Queen Elizabeth's court jester (perhaps the model for Hamlet's Yorick), and the dashing young cavalry colonel of a Loyalist regiment who took the American Revolution seriously from the beginning. His father, Roland Allen, was one of the best missionary theologians the Western world has produced, who, when he saw the Chinese burning the Peking legations, gave a prophetic warning to Christianity to escape from her associations with imperialist powers. Largely at his own expense (that is, his and his family's) he visited many of the infant churches in Africa, Canada, and India advising on the indigenization of Christianity. He was of course unheeded in his own day. Here in California, thirty years after his death, the father is something of a cult figure among Christians who face the accusation that the church is always the friend of oppressors. On Iohn's mother's side he was descended from an old line of British navy men who had, among other things, served in the great patrols that ended the slave trade.

At Oxford University Iohn Allen read the old classical school
Litterae Humaniores, "The more humane letters." He rowed for his
college, he debated, he asked the ultimate questions. He went out to
the great cotton-growing scheme on the Gezira in the Sudan. His
married life was singularly happy: his wife, Winifred, was an Oxford
graduate who had lived in Mexico and France, learned languages
easily, and loved God and people. They formed a unique and most
effective team, as we shall see.

Iohn was not a believer in anyone's God-given right to rule another;
he was convinced that as the peoples of the old British Empire moved
toward freedom, they would need the services of educationalists who
knew both them and the Western world. He went to Tanganyika in
1929, where he served as superintendent of education and his wife
opened a school for girls which would not contradict either modern
educational principles or their Africanness or their Islamicity. They
both carried further their study of Swahili, he especially as a trained
classical philologist, she as someone who could enter deeply into the
lives of the womenfolk who are the guardians of some of the greatest
achievements of Swahili civilization and refinement of culture. They
also served for some years in Arabia, where they were able to deepen
their knowledge of Islam and Arabic, but returned to various forms of
service in Tanganyika—Tabora, Lindi, Newala, Tanga, Arusha,
Pangani, and Mwanza—especially the congenial task of preparing for
independence. On handing over his work in Tanganyika Iohn came to
University Hall, Makerere University, Kampala, Uganda, as warden.
After some years he again made way for a local successor.

Since the mid-thirties Iohn gave time to service on various East
African committees connected with the Swahili language and publi-
cations such as *Mamba Leo* and *Swahili*. His editions of classical
Swahili poems appeared at intervals in *Tanganyika Notes and Records*, of
which he was the founder-editor, or as booklets published by the East
African Literature Bureau. On retiring from Makerere in 1965, he
began a three-year task of seeking out and photographically copying
Swahili manuscripts. He and his wife traveled to the north beyond
Lamu and south to the Comoro Islands. Mrs. Allen was now a
grandmother and able to share that most honorable status with Swahili ladies who are also often the best experts on the language and the
poetry. Swahili people tell of the Allens' exquisite manners, their
honesty, their scrupulous keeping of promises. Alas, not many field-
workers either earn or obtain such accolades. The originals of the
manuscripts were returned to their owners or purchased, if the owner

wished, at a price he or she named. Manuscripts and the film copies were lodged in the Swahili Institute at Dar-es-Salaam. A set of copies, made by permission, were brought to Oxford by Iohn and deposited with the School of Oriental and African Studies at London, where he had studied in 1932. (At that time he had also visited Swahili experts in Germany, with whom he maintained contact so far as the European wars permitted.)

He and his wife returned to East Africa for a few years more to teach the Danish volunteers and to complete certain Swahili work that needed constant reference to a living Swahili milieu. Some idea of the publications and studies completed in these years may be assessed from the partial list of his publications tabled before you. Harder to assess, because one keeps coming upon it in out-of-the-way places, is his encouragement to others to persevere in academic studies in this field. Thus you all have benefited through his regular letters discussing abstruse themes both African and Islamic. He wrote equally meticulously to an old Tanzanian traditional scholar, ill and half blind on a small island in the great lake. There are an amazing number of Catholic priests who have given a large part of their lives to Africa who in their retirement have been assisted by him to gather together and write up their academic, especially philological and mythological, recollections.

It is hard for a friend to pick out which of his qualities we can least afford to lose: the total hospitality to a stranger who appeared on his doorstep without any resources; the prophetic insight by which he saw the way politics would go in Africa until the times of a new security and true freedom were reached (we are still to reach them, but he was serenely confident); his imagination as a teacher, for instance in approaching New Testament Greek through Bantu languages when teaching Luganda-speaking students; perhaps most, his insights into theology—the recognition over thirty years ago that African Traditional Religion had a profound metaphysic that could contribute to worldwide understanding, for instance of the relation of good and evil and death within the divine dispensation. But of such things he would not write nor speak in public. He is mourned by us all, by his widow, three children, and eleven grandchildren, for whom today we pray.

Iohn was a man who took an intense interest in other people and made very deep friendships. One of our mutual friends and collaborators died a few months ago while we were working to finish this task. In recent years he was our main field correspondent in Bagamoyo. It is good to set before you a brief outline of his life also not only *in piam memoriam* but because so few accounts of the lives of East Africans who survived from German times to the present are readily available in the West.

Bwana Lowlli Wichie Hamisi-Kitumboy was born on September 18, 1910, near Ujiji, Lake Tanganyika. He was the only son of a famous mganga (traditional practitioner). He learned Qur'an from the local teachers and behind his father's back got some of the rudiments of Western education at a mission school. He had to return home to look after his father's "guests" (patients) and help tend the gardens. He longed to enter the new world that was emerging and as soon as possible left home "to take employment," first as a tax clerk and then as a railway clerk. The railways sent him to Dar-es-Salaam, and he took courses in typing and accounting.

By 1932 he was with the Tanganyika police, and when he left them in 1958 he was one of the three African senior inspectors and had worked in most parts of the land. For three years (1959–1962) he was organizing security policies for a bank in Burundi, and then, in 1964–1971, he was court clerk at the district magistrate's court at Bagamoyo.

Bwana Kitumboy since he was a boy spent all available spare time studying "to improve himself and to serve better," as he used to put it. He made friends with European officials and Indian merchants of scholarly inclination. He made a study visit to India and longed to see Europe and America. He helped part-time with Swahili translation and vocabulary work conducted by the University College at Dar-es-Salaam in 1971–1972 and then went to Arusha until 1974 to teach at the center training Danish volunteers and concentrate on researching word lists in technology. He then became camp manager for Mowlem Construction Company at their camp near Bagamoyo.

In 1976, Mr. Kitumboy, who had always been a faithful practicing Muslim, became convinced that the Bilal Mission of Tanzania, which was teaching the Shia[c] approach to Islam, was proclaiming the truth and that its message would lead to a quickening and propagation of Islamic life throughout Africa and thence the world. He therefore joined the Shia[c] in 1976 as a missionary (*tabligh*) and especially devoted himself wholeheartedly to the greater service the Swahili language could do to Islam, for it could be used as an instrument of teaching right across Africa. Accordingly he traveled to Bujumbura and other places in and beyond the western boundaries of his land.

On one such journey, on October 11, 1978, after he had performed the ablutions and the morning prayers, he succumbed to a heart attack. He is mourned by a widow, twelve children, and six grand-children, as well as a host of friends at home and abroad.

We may conclude this memorial by quoting in full a poem com-posed by Ahmed Sheikh Nabhany of Mombasa, with whose family at Lamu Iohn Allen studied poetry. Sheikh Ahmed Sheikh Nabhany tells of how he took him to meet his "grandmother, whose full name was Amina Abubakar Sheikh, who is a *Shaha*, Queen of Poetry. Her mother, Khadija, was also a Queen of Poetry and her sister, Kupona Abubakr Sheikh, was also a poet. 'M'maa' [a term of the greatest respect but also of close relationship and affection] was born in 1861 and died in 1975." We think then too of all these who have gone before us, in the web of whose poetic and scholarly kinship and love and service of God we have had the privilege of being involved. Tabled you will find a list of J. W. T. Allen's publications. Here is the poem Sheikh Nabhany composed in memoriam.

Twamlilia Allen

1. Asubuhi nichamka, kakimbiliya kazini,
   Saa nee ikifika, kikaa pangu mezani,
   Nikaletewa waraka, utokao Ingilani,
   Kumbe ni bwana Alleni, amefariki duniya.

2. Machozi yalidondoka, yakangiya baruwani,
   Rafiki kimkumbuka, wa tangu na wa zamani,
   Duniyani metutoka, metuepuka mwendani,
   Imenijaa huzuni, na moyo nimetosheya.

3. Maisha tamkumbuka, kwa wema na ihisani,
   Mbele zake kuniweka, kama mwana wa nyumbani,
   Kwa kusema na kuteka, hana kinyongo moyoni,
   Kinioneya imani, mazuri kinivutiya.

4. Nakuombeya, Rabuka, Winifred mjani,
   Subira atakuvika, ya Ilahi Rahamani,
   Mume wasokuondoka, mzee wetu Alleni,
   Takuliwaza Manani, mtima ukituliya.

5. Pole kwenu twatamka, kwa dhati ya ulimini,
   Mno tukisikitika, na kutindika maini,
   Hili M'ngu ametaka, viumbe tufanye nini?
   Mimi wenu Nabahani, mke wangu na dhuriya.

Tears for Allen

1. On hurrying to work early in the morning,
   At the office on the stroke of ten,
   I found on the table a letter from England bearing
      ill tidings,
   Dear Allen had parted from this mortal world.

2. Tears rolled down from my eyes, smearing the letter,
   On remembering my friend of since long,
   Who had deserted us from this earth.
   I was filled with great sorrow and intense grief.

3. I shall always remember him for his warmth and kindness,
   He used to have me in his presence like a member of the
      family,
   He used to enlighten me with talk and laughter and
      openheartedness,
   He used to feel sympathy for me and always wished well
      of me.

4. O God I beg you: Winifred the widow,
   Fortify her heart with patience, O Compassionate One,
   Patience for the departure of her husband, our dear Allen,
   May she be consoled and her heart be at peace.

5. Heartfelt condolences we extend with great sincerity,
   We are deeply saddened and heartbroken,
   What has passed is God's wish; what can we mortals do?
   This is from me Nabahani, my wife and children.

The following is a partial list of publications in which J. W. T.
Allen participated (he detested proprietary claims in literature or
learning) as author, editor, translator, or collaborator:[2]
   Maandiko ya Kizungu (London, 1934).
   "Arabic Script for Students of Swahili," *Tanganyika Notes and
Records* (1944).
   "World Literacy," *Tanganyika Notes and Records* (1944).
   "Utenzi wa Kiyama," *Tanganyika Notes and Records* (1945).
   "Rhapta," *Tanganyika Notes and Records* (1949).
   "Utenzi wa Wadachi," *East African Swahili Committee* (1955).
   "Utenzi wa Kutawafu Nabii," *East African Swahili Committee*
(1956).
   Nikahi of Ali Hemedi (Dar-es-Salaam, 1959). Translator.

Sheria za Serikali Kuu of Muhammad Kombo (Dar-es-Salaam, 1958). Collaborator.

"The Collection of Swahili Literature and Its Relation to Oral Tradition and History," *Tanganyika Notes and Records* (1959).

"The East African Swahili Committee," *Recorded Sound* (1961).

Utenzi wa Abdirrahmani na Sufiyani, East African Literature Bureau (1961).

Habari za Wakilindi, East African Literature Bureau (1962).

"The Bible in Swahili," *Swahili* (1963).

"The Complete Works of the Late Shabaan Robert," *Swahili* (1963).

The Kilindi, East African Literature Bureau (1963).

Diwani ya Shaaban (London, 1964).

"A Note on Dr. Nyerere's Translation of Julius Caesar," *Makerere Journal* (1964).

Utenzi wa Seyyidna Huseni bin Ali, East African Literature Bureau (1965).

"Muslims in East Africa," *African Ecclesiastical Review* (1965).

"Documents in the Files of the Institute of Swahili Research," *Swahili* (1965).

Review of L. Harries's *Swahili Prose Texts* (Nairobi, 1965), in *Swahili* (1965).

Greek for African Learners through the Medium of a Bantu Language, (Kampala, 1967).

"Swahili Prosody," *Swahili* (1967).

"Utenzi za Hiawatha," *Swahili* (1968).

Review of van Spaandonck's *Practical and Systematic Swahili Bibliography* (Leiden, 1965) and Mioni's *Cahiers d' Etudes Africaines*, no. 27 (1967), in *Swahili* (1968).

Review of Alfons Loogman's *Swahili Readings, Notes, and Exercises* (Pittsburgh, 1967), in *Swahili* (1968).

"The Collection and Preservation of Manuscripts of the Swahili World,", *Swahili* (1968).

Review of A. H. J. Prins's *The Swahili-speaking Peoples* (London, 1967), in *Swahili* (1968).

Additional note preparatory to new edition of "Arabic Script for Students of Swahili," *Tanganyika Notes and Records* (1968).

Review of Whiteley's *Swahili: The Rise of a National Language* (London, 1969), in *Azania* 4 (1969).

"Muhammad bin Abubakr bin Omar Kidjumwa Masihii," *Afrika und Übersee* 52 (1969). With Ernst Dammann.

"Utenzi wa Qarneni," *Swahili* (1970).
"Mbwe, Mbwa, and Mbawawa," *Swahili (1970)*.
"Shakespeare in Swahili," *Afrika und Übersee* 54 (1970).
The Swahili and Arabic Manuscripts and Tapes in the Library of the University College, Dar-es-Salaam (Leiden, 1970).
Tendi (London, 1971).

Notes

Preface

1. See the German prefaces to Dr. Velten's Swahili text *Desturi za wasuaheli na khabari za desturi za sheri^c a za wasuaheli* and *Sitten und Gebräuche der Suaheli*, Vandenhöck and Ruprecht, Göttingen, 1903. Parts of the material were published in periodicals as early as 1898. The text and German translation have long been out of print. Dr. Lyndon Harries published parts with a translation in *Swahili Prose Texts* (Nairobi, 1965). On the identity of the Swahili, see Appendix I.

2. Bwana Idi Marijani was still alive in 1978. He was born at Bagamoyo circa 1887. He and other people of his generation were consulted over many details in the work. Another important collaborator was Sheikh Hamisi-Kitumboy, born in 1910. See Appendix IV, "In Memoriam."

3. See the section on Bagamoyo in the Bibliography.

4. Mwalimu Mtoro's clear delineation of life's stages anticipated Van Gennep's famous *Rites of Passage* (1907) by several years and could have influenced that scholar.

5. For details concerning the late J. W. T. Allen, see "In Memoriam," Appendix IV. The system of transliteration of Swahili followed here is that used in his edition of the Swahili text, that is, an adapted form of the Inter-Territorial Standard System, which he helped to formulate. A number of his idiosyncrasies, such as preference for the form *mwinyi* (as a title) over the spelling *mwenye*, have been retained. Arabic material given here is based on the same text, that is, it is Arabic as incorporated in a standardized Swahili text in Roman script without diacriticals. For us to have gone back to the original Arabic, of the Qur'an, for instance, would not indicate how far the Arabic has become indigenous.

6. These are chaps. 32–48, Velten's (hereafter abbreviated V) pp. 297–364. They were written by Mwalimu Baraka bin Shomari of Konduchi and

255

others who collaborated with Velten on legal material. Most of this material is easily available in more authoritative statements in both English and Swahili (see the Bibliography); where material is original and not duplicated elsewhere, we have included it in full.

For those who would like to pursue the topic in Velten, the headings of the chapters we have not reproduced are as follows: chap. 36, "The Customary Law of Guarantee" (V 314); chap. 37, "The Customary Law of Sales" (V 315–317); chap. 38, "Of Making Pledges" (V 318–320); chap. 40, "The Customary Law of Deposit" (V 324–325); chap. 41, "Of Partnership" (V 326); chap. 42, "The Customary Law of Evidence and of Oaths" (V 327–330); chap. 43, "The Customary Law of Marriage" (V 331–334); chap. 44, "The Customary Law of Divorce" (V 335–336); chap. 45, "The Customary Law of Adultery" (V 339–342); chap. 46, "Of Orphans" (343–344); chap. 47, "Of Testamentary Depositions" (V 344–353); and chap. 48, "Of Inheritance" (V 354–364). Chap. 39, "Of Treasure Trove," has been included here in full but has been renumbered as chap. 36.

The Swahili Introduction

1. The numbers in the outside margins refer to the pages of Velten's text. Where they are referred to in our text they are prefaced with a V. On the meaning of "the Swahili," see the detailed discussion given in Appendix I. Internal evidence leads one to suppose that this introduction was composed by Mtoro bin Mwinyi Bakari himself and placed at the beginning of the collection of traditions that he culled from other "pure Swahili persons."

1. Swahili Customs before the Birth of a Child

1. The word translated "doctor" is *mganga*. This is from a widely used Bantu root that seems to signify the idea of wholeness, healing, or putting together. Dr. Livingstone showed respect for such practitioners, but in later days they were often classed as "witch doctors" or quacks. See the section of the Bibliography devoted to the topic.

It appears to have been customary to use this doctor's services simultaneously with (and without contradiction to) those of the Qur'an teacher. The Swahili word used for this gentleman is *mwalimu*. In common parlance today, this just means "teacher," and it can be used of a good Catholic like President Nyerere (who, incidentally, has a graduate qualification in teaching from Edinburgh). It is naturally of Arabic derivation, from the triliteral root ʿlm, referring to knowledge. The mwalimu is one who has or imparts knowledge. In the Islamic context of Mtoro's day, knowledge was essentially of Islamic lore and law. (We may similarly compare the medieval Christian usage *Deus, dominus scientiarum omnium*, "God, the Lord of all the sciences," with the more limited present use of the word *science*.) The mwalimu in Swahili custom not only taught in his Qur'an school (Chap. 4) and exercised the art of healing; he furthermore fulfilled some of the functions of English parsons or Scots dominies and ministers (chap. 5).

2. The word for God used here and regularly is *Mungu*, a word of Bantu derivation which is used by followers of the African Traditional Religion, Muslims, and Christians. It will be noticed that in the *Desturi* it is used interchangeably with *Allah*. If we may judge by the cases of 'Nyame, Olorun, and Katonda (Akan, Yoruba, and Ganda, respectively), it may have been a traditional term associated with the Supreme Being or a demiurge, who did not necessarily have any too great prominence in the old local cultus. The term was taken over by the Muslim pioneers and in due course by the Christians. The plural, *miungu*, means "idols." It is difficult, however, to ascertain how much of the original African context was brought into the immigrant religions along with the terminology.

3. The word translated "teacher" is *mwalimu*. See n. 1 above.

4. Qur'an sura 107 *ayat* 1, and 108:1.

5. "Reduction of spirits"—see the note on V 144 where pepo, or spirits, are dealt with in detail and it is explained why *reduction* is the right term to use, rather than *exorcism*.

6. "Real or imaginary"—the Swahili is *ana pepo au ni mimba*, literally "whether it is a spirit or she is pregnant." The implication is that the blood of menstruation may be held up by pregnancy or by a pepo.

7. The *kungwi* ("tutrix") is the older woman who sponsors a girl through initiation camp and, as we shall see, plays a role in her marriage, motherhood, and divorce. *Godmother* in English is hardly strong enough; the role of the *madrina* in a Spanish-speaking Catholic community is somewhat closer. See the relevant section of the Bibliography.

In the matter of childbirth, one must bear in mind that pre-Victorian women were relatively accepting of and comfortable with the natural functions, and also that before the male-dominated medical profession in the West made a monopoly of such knowledge and skill, experienced older women (the "mothers" mentioned would include all the elder female members of the extended family) and the midwives had the empirical knowledge to be able to cope with most of the possible emergencies.

8. The pouring of rice and acceptance of paternity under the aegis of the kungwi and the grandmothers is paralleled by ceremonies using verses of the Qur'an. Stricter Muslim doctors admit that the latter have come down in practice among various Muslim peoples but point out that to the learned they smack of the superstitious.

9. *Al Kursi*—2:256.

   Wa qul jaa . . . —17:83.

   Wala haula . . . —"there is neither power nor strength save in God."

10. A slight correction should be made here: The first five (horizontal)

words are the letters beginning some suras, and of these the last two are·
treated as epithets of the Prophet. *Muzammil* is a Qur'anic name for him. The
last four words are the names of the archangels.

11. *Majarabadi al-deribi*—Sheikh Hamisi-Kitumboy of Bagamoyo says this
may refer to a book containing selections from various authors on childbirth.

12. *Tabaraka*—sura 25 or 67.

13. *Wa al-mursalati urfan*—sura 77.

"An *abjed* figure" (properly speaking *abjad*)—a numerological arrangement
of the Arabic alphabet which goes back to Jewish and possibly Babylonian
sources. Hence the term comes to be used of various forms of magic on
numbers.

2. The Birth of a Child and the Customs following the Birth

1. The reader of our Preface will recall that since Allen's edition of the
Swahili is awaiting printing, we give the page references of Velten's Swahili
edition in our outside margins and refer to these in notes with a V. The
Swahili text at V 8 is very precise: the father asks permission to enter the
house where his baby has been born, and it is the kungwi who gives permission and demands a customary gift. "A *manni* of black pepper"—about three
pounds.

2. No detail is given of any ceremony in connection with the collection and
disposal of the afterbirth, umbilical cord, nails, and hair, but it is clear that
they are treated with care. This and the planting of a sapling with an
invocation, by analogy with, for instance, Ganda custom, indicate that the
afterbirth elements are considered a kind of twin or double of the living
person. An ill wisher could manipulate them to the person's detriment.

3. Typically of the *Desturi*, an African traditional custom is followed or
paralleled by a Muslim "usage." (The Swahili uses the word *mila*, which is
related to the Arabic *millat*. Mtoro is throughout highly precise in his use of
desturi, *mila*, and *adat*.)

One of the first things a child hears and learns to say is the call to prayer. Its
marvelously beautiful rolling alliteration and assonance flow through the
child's ears and around his or her tongue and into the deepest consciousness. It
is on the person's lips as he or she sinks into death. (We may compare the
shema[c] of Judaism and the Our Father of Christianity.) With it, a Muslim is at
all times strengthened, protected, and in touch with the source of being.

4. The purification of a person after contact with the life principle in the
form of blood is most ancient in many religions. The basic concern is not
sanitation, but, rather, contact with the life principle in an elemental, numinous, and hence potentially dangerous state, in the face of which ordinary life
has to be safeguarded. Certainly the rejoicing and marking of a new and
enhanced status as a woman returns to normal life is more prominent in the
practice than any other idea.

5. In Ghanaian English this ceremony is appropriately called "The Out-dooring." In Ghana the custom seems to have been indigenous to the Ga people, but it is fast becoming a nationwide birth custom. The Swahili custom is remarkably similar in nearly every detail. The ceremony celebrates the coming of a new person; he or she is introduced to the sun and sky and rain and to the ancestors and is exhorted to imitate their virtues. The hope-prayer that he or she will see rain and never drought is expressed. The whole serves to remind us all of our place in the cosmos and in society.

6. *Bibi*: The word is used by both grandfather and grandson toward the woman who is wife and grandmother.

7. The ancient and nearly universal symbolism in the dousing and kindling of flame should be instantly apparent. As a means of bringing in new life and ushering out the old, it is expressed in forms ranging from the birthday-cake candle to the funeral pyre.

8. Actually it is not for a chronological period like a year, but rather for a "kairological" (seasonal) and legal (*fiqh*) time that the husband must not have sexual intercourse with his wife; that is, until the child is independent of breast-feeding. Among many peoples the period can extend to eighteen months or two years. If the husband has no other wives, there is nothing against the customary solace of intrafemoral intercourse. Where the food for the mother is not plentiful, another baby on the way during breast-feeding may well mean deficiency diseases such as rickets or *kwashiorkor* for the first child. It is said that the word *kwashiorkor* is from the Ga of Ghana and signifies the envy the fetus has for the child at the breast.

9. *Juma* being, of course, the day of general congregation at the mosque. Compare the British nursery rhyme "Sunday's child is fair of face" and the Akan-Ghanaian use of day names, where *Kwame* ("Sunday born," the day of 'Nyame, the Supreme Being) is most auspicious.

10. *Maulidi*—a Qur'anic recitation and ceremony of rejoicing associated primarily with the birth of the Prophet.

11. These words calling for "peace, the peace of God, upon the Prophet, the messenger, the beloved" easily lend themselves to antiphonal recitation and are greatly beloved by maulidi congregations, who join in with gusto.

12. The opening sura of the Qur'an.

13. Dr. Jan Knappert, in correspondence, points out that these words mean "the birth of the best of mankind." It is the title of Jaafar Barzanji's book. Mtoro or his editor may be running together name and title.

14. *Khitima*—a Qur'an recitation.

15. It is to be hoped that Mtoro is ill informed about the feeding of babies. If a baby was really being fed on flour, sugar, and water, with mother's milk as an optional extra, there would be little wonder if his overly pessimistic view of the physical deterioration of his people had some justification. Recently, because of advertising encouraging mothers to take their babies off the breast in countries as far apart as Zambia and Papua New Guinea, big manufac-

turers of processed baby formulas were prosecuted for causing death by malnutrition.

16. This is an old theme, with a woman or man longing for someone on the other bank of a river. He or she calls and is not heard.

17. *Mangapwani*—literally "the shore or landing place of the Manga." Here, according to Bwana Idi, *manga* does not mean Arabs but refers to a place in Zigua country. [There is a site on Zanzibar island with this name. It is now abandoned but was associated with Segeju.—J. de V. A.]

18. "*Mung'unye* gourd"—a gourd whose mush can be used for cooking and eating while its skin can be dried for use as a cup.

19. The belief that asafetida or garlic is a prophylactic against devils appears to be held by virtually the whole human race.

20. "Flying spirits"—*ndege*, literally "the bird." [This may refer to a fear of the stork, usually the European bird on its winter migration.—J. de V. A.]

21. *Shegele* or *segele*—a child's belt of beads. *Utanda*: the beads worn by a woman around her loins. *Kanzu*—a long-sleeved shirt down to the ankles. *Suruali*—from the Persian for "trousers." Note the color symbolism—it recurs in the chapter on spirits.

22. Names are dangerous, for the knowledge of them can give power to those who hate you.

23. "Make a vow"—the *naziri* is a person vowed (cf. Jesus, who is probably originally a nazir rather than a person from Nazareth). Mtoro himself was a naziri. The Prophet Muhammad was a "warner" (Arabic *Nādhir*, Swahili *Nadhiri*—a different word).

24. "Runaway"—Swahili *Mtoro*, the author's own name, a reminder of the infant death rate until recently prevalent throughout the world. For other reasons it was a name fairly common among gentlemen who were slaves by status.

25. "*Hoza* medicine" is a vegetable concoction given to teething children. Infanticide for "deformity" is common among traditional peoples, and one even hears modern medical experts praise the resultant fitness and genetical purity that resulted. Islam has fought and tried to ameliorate such things from the beginning. We hear of one of the first caliphs repenting for having buried his daughter alive before his conversion.

26. *Kisukumi*—a wart or growth in the sexual organs which brings ill fortune on spouse or children. The woman whose husband or children keep dying has been a pathetic butt of fear and hate in folklore and thought back as far as ancient times. Often it is supposed that a jealously possessive demon wants her for himself. This is at the basis of the Tobit story. The story of Tamar (Gen. 38) looks like an adaptation of such a story. The vaginal-bean explanation given here is somewhat unique, unless there is an analogy among the Azande in the witchcraft stuff found in the intestines. "Old wise women," *wazee wanawake waganga*—literally "old women doctors" or "women elders who are practitioners."

27. This sort of "everyone is worn out and not as in the days of yore" attitude is common and ancient in many cultures throughout the world. Starting intercourse too young or masturbation are the favorite explanations. This account at least witnesses to the use of abortion in traditional societies (cf. V 87).

28. Professor Edward Alpers writes: "This probably refers to Kingalu mwana Shaha, the most powerful of the Luguru chiefs and leading rain-caller in the nineteenth century. He had hundreds of wives. He was visited by Holy Ghost missionaries in 1870. As his name indicates, his father was a *shaha* and he was born on the coast by Bagamoyo (thus indicating the intimacy of the coast-hinterland link). He lived at Kinole in the Uluguru Mountains."

3. Children's Games

1. *Geli* is broadly similar to tipcat. Velten, ad loc., notes that the cat is 20 centimeters in length.

As the saying goes, children's stories, songs, and games have been brought out of the nursery and into the study. The artistic, technological, and psychological well-being of a people depend in part on the recreational opportunities given its children. The history of games often gives clues to the history of contact between peoples, but obviously games can be invented spontaneously. For instance, this game in East Africa may be related to the Indian *guli dandah*, which in turn can be discerned in Gandharan carvings in the Swat Valley dating back to the third or fourth centuries. It may have reached Europe as a result of Hellenistic and Macedonian contacts.

2. In India and Indonesia the competition between kites consists of dipping their strings in adhesive and glass powder and then trying to cut the strings on the other kites by adroitly paying out or bringing in one's own line over exactly the same place on the other's string. When this cut the other line in the Himalayas, we cried, *Wo gaya patang* ("There goes a kite"), and the person who seized the kite as it landed, repeating the proper formulas, was the new owner. In the windy season at Bangkok one sees the smaller, more agile "female" kites trying to outmaneuver the heavier, blundering "males."

3. *Kuru* is in Swahili songs the call of the turtledove for its mate. There are various layers of meaning in these children's songs, and adults must be prepared to accept failure of understanding.

4. The first words of this song (*watoto mnara*) may be translated "children of Mr. Tower." After the manner of children's insults, it may be saying a Mr. Tower made love to the mother, and the singer is going to tell father (*pater*) who *genitor* was.

5. A hen is the symbol of a good wife.

6. *Watu wa makonde* is taken to refer, not to the Makonde people, but to *makonde*, "vegetable plots." [These are strictly lands that are cleared for annual

crops and then abandoned, as opposed to *mashamba*, privately owned, permanent plantations of fruit trees and long-term crops.—J. de V. A.]

7. *Chiriku*, used onomatopoeically. It is also the name of a finch, *Crithagra butyrocea*.

8. Another bawdy song referring to an old man's impotence.

9. "Watermelons and cucumbers": in a number of folklores these appear as analogues of uterus and penis. The Swat Pathan proverb says: For begetting, a woman; for love, a boy; for sheer delight, a watermelon. Velten explains these lines, however, to the effect that the twelve indicates days and nights. The man took a second wife and spoke much of her, but then he returned to the first.

10. The children sit with their legs stretched out, holding their feet with their hands.

11. The kanzu is the long shirtlike garment that reaches below the knees.

12. *Konya* can be broadly rendered "bosom friends." This forming of a pact between boys by such devices as the intertwining of little fingers, use of formulas, and ratification by a third was exactly the ritual used by Anglo-Indian boys at a British-type boarding school at Simla in the thirties. An adult analogue may be found in the blood-brotherhood ceremony described by Mtoro elsewhere.

13. The children put one fist on top of another, and the one with the fist on top at the end of the song wins. The same game with the contenders grasping a staff is also known worldwide.

14. Gongoni and Mnyanjani are parts of Bagamoyo town.

15. It is impossible to convey tongue twisters in translation, so they are left in Swahili. Possible meanings are:

(a) Have you, my brother, a female chicken at your house?
(b) Yesterday I ate pineapples.
   That is not how I got diarrhea. (Or: That is not what I said.)
(c) Let them be killed.
   Those who kill you are killed.
(d) How many is eight and eight? (Or: I say, how many is eight?)

4. School

1. "The Teacher"—as pointed out in chap. 1, this translates *mwalimu*, which indicates in the *Desturi* the teacher in the Qur'an school, who may also fulfill certain parsonlike roles in the mosque and community. The home, the mosque community, and the Qur'an school can help to make the untutored child into a well-mannered Muslim gentleman. The boys themselves have little good to say of the school at the time. Some alumni will speak of them with horror and disdain, many with respect and affection. Some of those who have gone far into Western education will point out mistakes of educational psychology in the Qur'an school and the production of cultural schizophrenia

by the juxtaposition of Qur'an school and modern Western secular education, the latter of which is increasingly compulsory in African countries. At the same time, however, these informants can be nostalgic for the values, the religion, and the discipline imparted. See the Bibliography.

2. *Ufito* or *ubati*—these originally referred to the cane or switch used to chastise the pupils and hence came to be applied to the customary fee paid when a new scholar joined.

3. The "Angel of Death," *Israili*, appears frequently in stories and poetry.

4. The Arabic words are a selection of passages from the last suras of the Qur'an, calling for help from and refuge in Allah and for protection from devils and so forth (including, we hope, teachers). Together they exercise a pupil in the shape of most letters of the alphabet, in initial, medial, and final positions.

5. This is learned, like much else, by heart in Arabic, a direct method not unsuited to the kind of ability small boys possess.

6. "School fees," *ada*—customary gifts.

7. The passages mentioned are taken from suras 112, 98, and 85. *Ya sini* is 36. *Juzuu ya 'ama* indicates the last, or thirtieth, division of the Qur'an, which starts at *An Nabaa*, sura 78.

8. There is a certain alliterative and assonative interplay but no etymological connection between the words *adabu* ("behavior, manners") and *azabu* ("punishment"). Frequently as a stranger wanders through a village the small boys will stare or shout, and one will hear an older person reminding them, "Adabu, adabu."

9. "Confuser," Swahili *wasiwasi*, can also be translated "confusion."

10. Though more is said elsewhere (e.g., V 81) about girls' initiations and entry into womanhood, wifeship, and motherhood, the information is not as full as it is for boys. Ear piercing is mentioned. The so-called female circumcision of Muslim women, which entails "an incision severe or slight in the upper sexual parts" and sometimes includes clitoridectomy, is not practiced among the Swahili. See the Bibliography. *Kigori* is a maiden before menstruation. Anon. DSM notes that it is significantly not a Swahili word but rather Zaramo or Kwere.

11. We may compare the "perfect" woman and her duties as defined in a poem by a Swahili poetess, "Utendi wa Mwana Kupona," included in J. W. T. Allen's *Tendi* (Nairobi, London, Ibadan, 1971). (Cf. the biblical Book of Proverbs, chap. 31.)

12. Kungwi (tutrix)—see n. 6 in chap. 1. Utunda: A string of beads around the loins which a respectable woman will never be without. It has many uses: a sacramental reminder of the modesty, dignity, and holiness of woman; a belt to which sanitary napkins can be attached; a means of wearing decorations as an aid in coquetry. [It may be that the European chastity belt developed as an overstated embodiment of the first.] African men who have consorted with Western women will remark on the feeling of repulsion and scandal they have upon realizing that these persons do not wear the utunda.

13. *Elimu*—literally "knowledge," from the Arabic root *clm*; specifically the study of Islamic law.

14. As in many of the passages dealing with Islamic matters, the Swahili here is heavily Arabicized: *subalkhairi—subh al-khēr*—"good morning."

15. *Min Hajj*—Dr. Jan Knappert (in a letter of March 3, 1978) points out that "the fuller title is *Min Hāj at-Tālibīn*, of *An-Nawawi*, a well-known textbook of Shafeitic law, translated by L. W. C. Van den Berg under the title *Guide des Zélés Croyants*, 3 vols., French and Arabic, Batavia, 1882."

16. The whole of this section is strongly reminiscent of the Anglican country parish or the Jewish tradition in Eastern Europe where the Hasid movement was flourishing. The well-born girl takes her dowry and sets up a small business, running it ever pregnant and at the same time serving God in the community (especially among the women and girls), while the still penniless mwalimu or reverend or rabbi goes on with his ministry, studies, and prayer. Beyond this two-become-one state, it is thought, there can be no higher form of human life.

5. Of the Qur'an Teacher

1. There is no priesthood or monkery in Islam, but there is a clergy. Because Mtoro writes with such evident sympathy and inner appreciation of both the Qur'an school and its teachers, it comes as no surprise to learn from Bwana Idi that he was a favorite pupil and promising teacher.

2. The string has 100 beads, 99 for the beautiful names and 1 for the essential name: Allah. The Christians copied the rosary from the Muslims, who got it from the Buddhists, who may have gotten it from the followers of Lord Shiva. The decimal system based on the cipher seems to have followed parts of the same route.

3. This is a most important piece of detail about the Islamization of black Africa. Nothing is said of circumcision; although in many unlearned circles that is taken to be important, it is actually in some schools of Muslim law only *sunnat* ("customary"), not *fard* ("obligatory"). Also, in these parts of Africa, traditional circumcision is usual (as it is becoming among the Nacirema), so that the adult decision to Islamize is rendered easier.

4. The *shahada* is the great Muslim declaration of faith. In a very real sense this direct and single-hearted declaration constitutes the center of being a Muslim. "And not his son" is a peculiar addition to the shahada and reminds us that Swahili Islam has stood in the front of the firing line, in the face of the modern militant "Christian" onslaught, since the days of Vasco da Gama. In addition, some superficially Christianized converts came over to Islam, and their repudiation of doctrines of sonship must be made clear to them.

5. This shows an admirable understanding of the faith/works dichotomy with which theologians both Muslim and Christian have struggled. For Mtoro, faith is a matter of the heart. Orthopraxy and the law come immediately afterward and arise out of faith.

6. *Qibla*—the niche in the wall of the mosque which indicates the direction of Mecca, which is locally north. [In Arabic the niche is usually referred to as *mihrab*, and *qibla* refers only to the direction of Mecca, but in Swahili the word *qibla* is used for both, and also, often, for "north."—J. de V. A.] Because of the importance of siting mosques correctly, astronomy and geography are important parts of elimu.

7. "There is no compulsion"—this is the echo of a well-known *hadith*. The writer may have had partly in mind the then-current belief among officials and missionaries that many had become Muslim because the sultan and ruling powers were Muslim. Actually, in tropical Africa more became Muslim under the European colonial powers.

8. "To slaughter meat"—meat is unlawful to eat unless one slaughters it by cutting the throat and letting the blood drain, in the orthodox manner, using the name of God. Correct slaughtering has taken on great prominence in East African Islam. The revolt of the Muslim pages against Kabaka Mutesa had this as one of its causes. Muslims later assumed a monopoly of butchering in Uganda.

9. *Watoto kusomesha, taabu kubwa, pato lake dogo*—"teaching children is hard work for little reward." This could be made the terse motto of any leading teachers' college from Columbia to Canton.

6. Manners

1. Children's manners—*adabu*—again illustrates the intertwining of Muslim and African customs. The Swahili gentleman is indeed a person of exquisite manners, of whom the Victorian explorers could truthfully remark (as indeed was their highest praise of Jesus Christ), "He was a gentleman."

2. When a small boy near Saint Thomas's Mount, Madras, passing under a mango tree around noon happens to yawn, his mother will hurriedly cover his mouth because of fly-about spirits that can leap into a person. Sneezing carries worldwide ill-health connotations, as we can see by the traditional responses it inspires, from "Ring-a-ring o'roses, atishoo" to " 'Sundheit" and "Coughs and sneezes spread diseases." Belching is much deprecated in Western manners but elsewhere comes into its own as a delight to the belcher and an expression of appreciation of the host's hospitality.

3. The greeting *shikamuu* (literally "I hold your feet") and the answer *marahaba* ("be at ease") are the normal greetings between junior and senior. *Mwinyi*—"Sir"; *mwinyi wangu sayyidi*—"the sayyid my son"; *mwana wangu sayyidi*—the sayyid my daughter." The Arabic *sayyid* means "lord, nobleman" and here may refer to the sultan of Zanzibar or just mean "sir." In Swahili *mwinyi* means "lord, proprietor" and here may refer to the sultan of Zanzibar or just mean "sir."

4. It is amazing to find just how much human good manners vary from place to place. We should recognize, however, the difference between man-

ners (from the heart) and etiquette (from the book): if your manners are good, you will be forgiven breaches of etiquette; if your manners are bad, you can meticulously obey every rule and still fail to be "accepted." The late Roland Allen used to recall this conversation from his days in China at the turn of the century:

ROLAND ALLEN: Who among the Europeans has the best manners?

CHINESE TUTOR: Bishop Scott.

ROLAND ALLEN: But we all know that the bishop knows nothing of Chinese customs.

CHINESE TUTOR: You asked about manners.

5. "Under the tree"—it is not so much that the woman's tutrix taught her while sitting under a tree as that *myomboni* is a technical term for initiation. *Kumbini* can be used in the same way, literally "in the camp."

6. "Featherbrained"—literally "a heart of maize stalk," light and valueless.

7. A good society provides mechanisms for the reconciliations, with dignity and without loss of face, of parents and children. To be adult in any society means being independent from the parents, and proving one's adulthood (to oneself and to others) may even involve the humiliation of the elders. Most parents can also do with a reminder that their "little boy" is now a man. To belittle one's parents, however, is to belittle oneself; besides, it annoys the ancestors, who may send illness and death. Therefore the state must not be allowed to endure, and it must be covered and atoned, at-oned.

Meyer Fortes's *Oedipus and Job in West Africa* (London, 1956) contains a deeply sensitive passage about the West African father who, having been insulted by his son, will not come near the ancestral shrines lest the shades should realize his deep hurt and visit harm upon his son. Compare also something of the thought on the father-son relationship in "The Piper at the Gates of Dawn" in Kenneth Grahame's *Wind in the Willows*.

In Ghana a younger person will leave a calabash of beer by the offended elder's door. If the elder drinks it, he has signaled reconciliation.

7. Of Swahili Greetings

1. If these greetings seem long-winded and complicated, we must bear in mind that Kabaka Mutesa, whom some Ganda historians call their Peter the Great, introduced them into Buganda in order to modernize and streamline the customary greetings. They are certainly not lacking in sophistication, and the variable elements add a drop of wry. Now the meaning is often difficult to recover, and we have depended on Velten's interpretation. For notes on *mwinyi* ("sir") and *mwinyi wangu sayyidi*, see our note on V 55 above (n. 3, chap. 6).

2. As explained below in the chapter on the subject (chap. 22, V 222 ff.), the *jumbe* is a person with some royal authority and attributes, so "chief" is a reasonable, though not perfect, translation. The waziri holds an official

status, while the shaha inherits his status from his ancestors. [These ranks are unique to Shirazi settlements and not known in usual Swahili ones. The jumbe, in Malindi and points north, was the town council, and the *mwenye mkuu* in Zanzibar was the pre-Omani sultan. *Sheha* is probably a better spelling of this word, which is the equivalent of *sheikh* or *shee* further north: *shaha* is a colonial rendering designed to support the view that the Shirazis must have been Persian, whereas they may well have originated in Africa.— J. de V. A.]

3. As in all Muslim countries, a senior woman has great honor, especially among gentlemen.

4. These two greetings are given in Arabic transliterated as *sabalkheri* and *'llah bil kheri*. Similarly, "praise be to God" translates *al hamdu lillahi*.

5. "Go and be hungry"—a jocular way of saying, "Stay with us and be ever well fed."

6. "Go and eat with the blind"—meaning, "May the people you meet be gullible."

7. *Hongera* too means "congratulations" and is in effect synonymous with the word—*pongezi*—so translated.

8. "Magician"—*mchawi*, "sorcerer."

8. Putting the Child through the Initiation Camp

1. Since boys unfortunately lack anything dramatic like a menarche to indicate that they are leaving the amorphous androgyny of childhood, many peoples make use of the symbolic wounding of circumcision. The Jews for excellent religious reasons took a puberty rite back into childhood; elements of the American medical profession have done the same but throw up smoke screens about hygenics. For Muslims it is a matter of ritual purity: hence the consecration of the sex organs is deeply meaningful in a man's life and greatly assists him in walking righteously before God and in respecting his own manhood and the womanhood of those about him. In African traditional custom there is so much of the subtle and the unspoken that the full wonders of these matters have only recently come to be somewhat more clearly understood by outsiders.

The Swahili rite described here appears to be somewhat truncated, especially when compared with the more elaborate Yao-Makonde rites on the Rondo Plateau in southwest Tanzania or the Gisu rites on Mount Elgon in Uganda. It looks as if they were already on their way out, and circumcision practice among the Swahili has come to be not dissimilar from that in America. In the rites and ceremonies described here, we find layer upon layer of meaning and the running together of traditions deriving from the different groups that history brought together. For more details, see the specialist works cited in the Bibliography.

2. Normally circumcision came after Qur'an school. The initiation camp was a great school of good manners and general self-discipline. The "likenesses," made out of straw, leaves, clay, and wood, with the accompanying proverbs and songs, together with the physical rigors, were effective visual aids in education. The old was left behind, the new imprinted.

3. Mtoro relates the word *nyago* to the likenesses, the frightening images, connected with the dance. In etymology the word can be connected with the regular plural of *unyago*, "initiation ceremony," which itself can be related to *nyago*, "loins, genitals, lap." For Sacleux (*Dictionnaire Swahili-Français*, s.v.) and Stigand (*Land of Zinj* [London, 1913], p. 155) *unyago* had come to signify an obscene dance to instruct the young. Scholars are still in the process of uncovering deeper meanings and tracing its migration into Swahili country from the south and southwest.

4. *Tibu*—"medicine, perfume," sandalwood dust made into a paste with powdered cloves, rose water, and *dalia*, a saffron-colored powder. The description of the ceremony, the words uttered, and their underlying theology are a masterpiece, for they keep well within Islam while being loyal to the spirit of traditional African ancestor veneration. In the Indian subcontinent, where the superseded Hindu ceremonies are still practiced by a Muslim's neighbors, it is less easy to be sure that one is not being un-Islamic.

5. "Beer" (*pombe*) is very much a part of many African religious celebrations, aside from being a source of nourishment and vitamins. It is a tribute to the seriousness of African Muslims that so many of them have eliminated such drinks from their lives.

6. *Ngariba* or *mwinzi*—the circumciser or master of ceremonies. Originally the words meant "stranger, foreigner, hunter." He is assisted by the *shuwali*, who stays on to help the kungwi, the tutrix.

7. *Kumbi*—the name used for the initiation camp. *Ukumbi* means "courtyard, enclosed place." Probably the association with *mkumbi*, the bush *Ochna albo-serrata*, which has many healing and magical uses, is secondary. In various places the flowering of a certain bush will indicate the time for the opening of an initiation "class year."

8. The boys are called "maidens" by analogy with the girls' initiation. Some translators would prefer "novices." Their tender of wounds and mentor is called kungwi, as is the girls' tutrix.

9. *Kiranja*—the beginner. By this state of Swahili culture, circumcision is no longer a test of manhood. Little boys can scream and run away. Where it is a test of manhood, as, for instance, among the Gisu, to be first is an honor, and one's cowardice can preclude his getting a bride.

10. "Kerosene"—literally "European oil." Perhaps Mtoro means *spiritus fortior*, or surgical spirits.

11. In Velten's translation, this is given as "When I think of the hot oil that will be applied as the last medicine, I tremble with fear [*Angst*]." The translation given here takes up the symbolism of whiteness in the coconut paste, in toddy (a palm wine), and in ejaculation.

12. "Whitewash," *mzimu udongo mweupe.* To be daubed with (literally) "white spirit powder" is to guard one when in weak condition from spirit influences and also to warn passersby of the *numen.* In addition, the initiates are temporarily dead, white being the color of ghosts.

13. *Mramba* (*mlamba* in standard Swahili)—a small black bird that cries before sunrise (*Dicrurus fugax*). Its song can be interpreted as *Kule kule kume-kucha,* "There, there, the sun is rising."

14. "House of the ancestral spirit," *nyumba ya zimwi.* J. W. T. Allen translates it as "in the devil's house," perhaps an Islamization. His notes at this point also suggest "ghoul" as a translation and state that some ghouls are about the size of a rat.

15. "Magistrate," *hakim*—appointed by the sultan of Zanzibar and subordinate to the *liwali,* the sultan's chief representative in a given area.

16. "All good behavior"—*jamii ya adabu,* literally "the whole of good manners." Indeed, the kumbi generally succeeded in satisfying most parents where the Western universities have not. Perhaps the intensity (to put it mildly) of the initiation experience drives the lessons home more readily than examinations and grades.

17. Hours spent thinking out exegeses for these songs yield fascinating results. His notes indicate that Velten had the advantage of consulting Mtoro, who, however, seems to have hidden the obvious bawdy meanings from his Victorian colleague in some places in his explanations (not in his text). "Dove," *pugu,* the same as *pugi* in Gikuyu and standard Swahili, *Chalcopeleia afra,* can here signify "girl." "Trap," *mgono,* can also mean "(place for) sexual intercourse, (place to) sleep, cage." "Beast," *nyama,* can mean "penis," snake-bite, circumcision, or defloration. Forests and wells need no exegesis. "Wealth," *mali,* may mean the cattle of the bridal guarantee and may also be a euphemism for *mani,* "semen."

18. *Shundi,* also called *tipitipi* or *dudunizi*—a coucal that sings in the evening.

19. *Mkumbi*—perhaps a place name, but in this context it refers to the bush connected with initiation.

Kwarara—Velten takes it to be a wild fruit eaten in times of famine. This use is not now known. Probably it is a variant of *karara* (see V 190) and means to buy a coconut tree that will be in bearing later on.

20. "A hole"—presumably the camp.

21. *Shemnungwi, kakaguu*—the names of these fish now seem to be obsolete. Velten's explanation is "Father, give me money to buy a slave girl. If we do not agree, I will sell her and marry a wife. If we do not agree, I will give her a divorce."

22. This song signifies the refusal of one man in courtship, the success of another, and the consummation of his love.

23. "Stump," "sickle"—clitoris and penis.

24. Velten interprets this as signifying four stars surrounded by twelve others, the Pleiades.

25. Velten interprets this as follows: The tree is a king who died. His offspring sprang up. There is no doubt of their legitimacy.

26. A slave is not allowed to wear shoes (see V 258). One who wants to give himself airs will wear them and strut and resemble in arrogance Rashidi, an Arab famous for his cruelty to slaves.

27. The lads are now a new family—"Initiator, we are yours"—and each neophyte is a brother to the others, with the initiator who acts on behalf of the ancestors being the senior.

28. "Horns and pipes"—this is J. W. T. Allens's regular translation of *siwa na zumari*. See J. de V. Allen's appendix on musical instruments.

29. The time has come for the initiate, the pilgrim into the "over there," to be reintegrated. A totally new beginning is made, former clothes are thrown away, the new men are shaved and bathed. They are shut into an *ukingo*, a canopy that keeps out evil and keeps in the numen.

30. *Mwegea*—the liver-sausage tree, *Kigelia pinnata*. This delightful story, full of laughter, indicates a way of reassuring a young man.

9. The Customs of Girls

1. The mystery of the onset of menstruation is appropriately marked in many traditional civilizations. It is difficult for a contemporary westerner to appreciate the awe, wonder, and hence holiness associated with menstrual blood. Perhaps the best account one can get in the West would be from a modern, highly educated, orthodox Jewish woman; certainly women anthropologists have also helped free us somewhat from our inverted Victorianism. Something of the joy, mystery, and bewilderment of attaining womanhood comes through in this account. See the Bibliography.

2. *Kigori, mwari, kungwi*—Mtoro defines the terms. See also notes to V 45 (chap. 4, nn. 10–12).

3. "Diet," *mwiko* or *miiko* in the plural and collective sense. Certain foods are avoidances for certain men or women. A child can inherit these from both parents, and a pregnant woman may have to observe her child's avoidances as well as her own. The "Polynesian" word *tabu*, which can be found in various forms in use from Papua New Guinea to Easter Island, should not be indiscriminately used of Africa, though explorers' and missionaries' use of it has put it into international English.

4. "Carry a doll"—we may compare the Fante and Ashanti art form.

5. The utunda is the string of beads a girl always wears around the loins. See note on V 46 (chap. 4, n. 12).

6. Tibu, dalia—sandalwood paste and a saffron-colored ointment.

Maua maulidi—literally, "flowers of the festival." A Swahili woman subtly and tastefully uses her scent stone to blend and give off olfactory signals that those around her can unconsciously pick up or to disguise and gently overlay others.

7. *Kaniki*—indigo-dyed calico.

8. *Muyombo*—the bark cloth tree (*Brachystegia*). Some under Freudian influence considered its significance phallic. More probably it is also to be associated with the kindred tree of life symbolism.

9. *Pombe*—beer. We were specifically told that it is not brewed at the boys' initiations. Islam in Africa often penetrates men's societies much more thoroughly and more quickly than it does women's.

Togwa—unfermented beer.

10. The kungwi, or tutrix, can start her teaching through dance, singing, riddles, and the like. A girl is given an oral *Kamasutra* concerning how to behave sexually and what to expect, and the range of teaching continues on to cover the whole of deportment and manners.

11. The basic meaning is obvious enough. The bucket that grasps with its mouth, the spear that pulses, the grinding of buttocks, and the other images certainly need no explanation at this level. There are, however, deeper meanings in addition to these.

12. The verse is impossible to unravel. Perhaps the woman is saying that the month has become round and she wants to sleep, or that the month has turned around and there is no period.

13. *Zoka kulu la mlali la pingapinga*—Dr. Edward A. Alpers in regard to the mbenda dance and the great snake of Mlali writes: "There are also Luguru links, referring to the domination of the Mlali matriclan over the famous Kolero cult which has Maji Maji connections." If *mlali* is related to *kulala*, "to sleep," a possible translation is "the great snake of the sleeper."

14. Kohl, or antimony, is used as eye makeup. Not only does it protect the eyes from certain diseases, it drives away bad spirits. Kohl made from ersatz material can be dangerous. The reintegration of the girls, now women, follows much the same procedure as that for the boys. It is obvious, however, that since the girls (unlike the boys) are initiated nearer maturity, their reintegration truly marks their arrival as adults and is part of a natural sequence that is followed by marriage. Thus one might tentatively conclude that the women's ceremony is the more meaningful original, while the men's is the derivative analogue. One wishes one could invert Mtoro's order and meet the women's rites first.

15. The subject of the girls'/women's reintegration into society leads naturally to traditional societies' guard over the womb and the resultant emphasis on virginity. (It should be noted here that the German *entjungfern* captures *kumbikiri* better than "deflower" does. Traditional societies are very practical about it all: they believe that the male is quickly aroused, will promise the earth, and can easily be "disarmed," while a woman takes longer to arouse, but in the end may give in to the temptation to want full intercourse rather than anything short of that (such as the various other ways indicated to them in initiation camp). Even so, if she does not become pregnant, there are ways to simulate virginity on the wedding night and thereby to satisfy all concerned. If she becomes pregnant, the matter can be adjusted by marriage. As a

last resort, there is abortion, which is certainly no modern device.

Beyond the merely practical side, religion would add the idea of a woman's "purity"; however, even in Christianity the purity required was primarily in the mind and only thence in the body. A comparison of Church of England marriage registers with baptismal records in literal-minded Victorian times quickly indicates the high number of pregnant brides.

When sexual intercourse and procreation are no longer inextricably interwoven, when jealousy and exclusiveness are looked upon as bad, and when it is accepted that a woman's sexual nature is fully as deserving of fulfillment as a man's, virginity in a physical sense as a concept of importance may fade away. The effects this has on male-female relationships, marriage, and religion are not easy to assay.

Much of the matter of guarding womenfolk may go back to the man who, when faced with the heavy price of parenthood, wants some guarantee that the child is not another man's. As the Ashanti proverb says, Everyone knows who the mother is. The man who cherishes a woman and her children for the pure joy of it is still somewhat of a rarity, and the matter remains enshrouded with hypocrisy and unnecessary agony to the innocent. One supposes that Hardy's interminable *Tess* is trying to tell us just that.

16. A slave is presumably blamed for assisting or not preventing the intrigue.

17. "Legitimate," "legitimizing," *halali*, *ninahalalisha*, that is, in regularity with the sacred law.

10. Of Amulets

1. Human beings have made use of amulets for thousands of years. Thanks partly to the mindless quips and jibes of Victorian missionaries, however, "modern and advanced" Muslims deprecate amulets and the attendant sciences, looking on them as part of the old Middle Eastern pseudoscience and superstition, which Islam is meant to shed as people understand it more fully. On the other hand, these sciences have their fascination and their kinship with modern empirical natural science. One must hear what the *Dammapada* says, that the cosmos is mind shaped: If amulets have positive effect for certain minds, it is unempirical to deny their power.

2. *Usira* is the ash of the burned skin of a reptile or animal used as an amulet to protect a person against that reptile or animal. The "doctor" is the *mganga*. Unfortunately, we are not told the name of the basic root. The apotropaic and healing symbolism of gourd, cucumber, oil, honey, ash of snake's skin, and black and white combine to make this a powerful device. Note the magic power of the number seven in the next paragraph.

3. Again we find African traditional material combined with that of Islamic origin, with the mganga (traditional doctor) and the mwalimu (Qur'an teacher) standing side by side. On the town/country dichotomy, see the Bibliography.

4. Ya sini—sura 36; 112:1—"Say, 'God is one' "; 113:1—"Say, 'I fly for refuge to the Lord of the daybreak' "; 114:1—"I fly for refuge to the Lord of men"; *Ayat al Kursi*, the throne verse, 2:256.

5. Suras 36; 20; 3. Other suras in frequent use for amulets are 1, 6, 18, 44, 55, 67, and 78. The five special verses of protection are 2:256 (the verse of the throne); 12:64; 13:12; 15:17; and 37:7. The last two suras, 113 and 114, are also called the "two protectors."

6. *Johari 'lqurani*—"jewels of the Qur'an"; Andhuruni—"spare me"; *Seifu 'llahu 'lqate'i*—"the piercing sword of God."

7. Mtoro's theology is, as usual, careful and correct. A person wearing an amulet has in his heart the feeling that nothing can harm him, but against *qudra ya mungu* this protection naturally is powerless.

8. *Rakaa*—the cycle of movements and words that make up the unit of Islamic prayer.

9. "Book of the People of Badr," *ahli Badiri*, refers to the Qur'anic passages concerned with the Battle of Badr, in which by the power of prayer the Prophet overcame an enemy that vastly outnumbered his own army.

10. The amulet does not lose its power when stolen.

11. Sura 112. First from right to left, top to bottom. Then turn on side, start at second from new top, and read right to left to new bottom. Complete with the top outer part of present position, that is, bottom to top of original outer right—*Qul huwa 'llahu ahadu 'llahu 's-samadu | Lam yelid wa lam yūlad wa lam yakun lahu ahadu | Kufuwan*.

11. Of Marriage

1. As befits the most important Swahili rite of passage, the section on marriage is the fullest and most complete in the *Desturi*. Although it portrays specifically the *harusi kuu*, the "great wedding," which everyone hopes to have once (though divorce and remarriage are the commoner lot), it has much to tell us about the complicated institution of marriage, whose infinite variety— throughout the world as well as throughout history—nothing can stale. As our minds range from the multiple divorce system prevalent in the United States, which seems to some an abrogation of the institution, to Hindu pundits who worry that some of their more strictly arranged and monogamous unions so kill choice that they amount to nothing more than child betrothals uniting extended families, we can learn much from Mtoro. It is noteworthy, too, that his account is a brilliant piece of figure skating, for he omits or does not elaborate on matters that would cause Islamic doctors or European Victorians to cast scorn on the Swahili. The confinement of the bride before marriage, for instance, is not mentioned, and the bawdy implications of the songs are left to well up in the reader's own mind.

In the marriage of Muslims the basic idea is one of contract, in which there must be the consent of both parties (the bride's is through her guardian, often her father, grandfather, paternal uncle, or elder brother). The contract concerns their reciprocal duties and includes the *mahr*, the suitable dowry to be given. Though the *qadi* or the imam and the Islamic religion play important roles, the marriage is not actually held in the mosque. (At Kibuli Mosque in Kampala, brides in white dresses rented from Goan tailors used to appear in a room adjoining the mosque in order to be photographed, but this was by analogy with the practices of their Christian sisters.) Such a contract can, obviously, be terminated by legal means. On the other side of African Traditional Religion, marriage is regarded as a coming together of two groups, between whom the potential of the one basic human power, the woman's childbearing capacity, is being transferred. There must be a compensation and guarantee that the transaction will be honored, hence the "bride-price," or, more correctly, the "marriage surety." There must be agreement after full consultation of the members of the group and a symbolic exchange of gifts. Again, the coming together can end in a separation, after due process; and, again, the wedding is attended with rejoicing.

This chapter records a classical bringing together of the two wedding ceremonies, together with their attendant rites, which merge and harmonize into one. The Muslim heart of the matter takes place at the mwalimu's *baraza* ("solid stone bench under a porch," place for public meetings, hence office). Witnesses are called, the *mahari* ("bridal guarantee") is declared, the fatiha recited, a wedding *hotuba* ("sermon") delivered. The man consents to the contract, the woman's representative speaks for her. There is a prayer for general blessing and especially for children. The customary (traditional African) ceremony is in the uxorilocal bridal bower, the president being the kungwi, the person who sponsored her into womanhood. There is a rite of entry, and the husband must pay a forfeit to the kungwi before he can come in. The kungwi gives him his wife. He offers gifts for taking her hand, for her revealing herself to him, for her "uncovering her lap." He gives her a ring, a bangle, or a chain. He goes out of her room and partakes of the wedding cup and sends her rice and meat. There is a communion meal. The songs are of a more African than Islamic flavor. Then the couple goes to bed, and the kungwi ensures there is evidence of virginity (be it actual or simulated).

2. "The messenger," *msenga*—the go-between.

3. *Uweleko*—refers to the band of cloth like those used for carrying an infant on one's back; it is a gift from the bridegroom to his mother-in-law to commemorate her carrying. *Kondavi*—the bandage around the womb of a woman in childbirth.

4. "Tambourine"—a type of drum admitted as licit by certain types of Muslim law (see n. 6 below). The Islamic influence throughout this part of the proceedings is marked. Scent and "chews," but no beer, are distributed. The ngoma, the African drum in its mrungura form (see n. 5), is mentioned only once (V 98), and then it is beaten by a servant to announce a message. The songs too are nearly all in Arabic.

5. *Mrungura*—a long drum around six inches in diameter and thirty inches high, standing on a wide base.

6. "tambourine . . . *diriji*"—*tari la njia*, the tambourine for playing on the way; a portable hand drum. The word *diriji* by itself indicates another tambourine, a larger and less easily moved drum. In the perennial discussion in East Africa as to whether Islam really permits ngoma (drumming and dancing), a kind of compromise can be reached by the use of tambourines large and small, for there is a tradition that the Prophet was once welcomed with these. (We may compare the "cymbals and dances" of the Bible.) Mtoro's songs and dances often, though not always, reveal their Arab or African provenance, Islamicity, or traditionality by the language and instruments used.

7. The precentor "lines out" the words (as black American congregations of the old days used to phrase it), and the people repeat them. The second and third songs are in Swahili, the fourth, fifth, and sixth in Arabic.

8. "Water lilies" indicate, according to Velten's footnote, "a place of peace and joy." The reference is clearly to the future of happiness which the bridegroom promises the mwana, or child, lady.

9. "Wasiwasi"—the whisperer who lurks behind (sura 112), becoming here the Confuser, or Confusion, a devil's youngest son who ignores his mother's warnings about schoolboys (see V 45). As in Milton's work, the devils easily steal the limelight from the rather lifeless angels, who are programmed to do God's will and are reputed by some to be eunuchs.

"Iblis" is the proud spirit who, being created out of fire, refused to do obeisance to Adam, made of clay.

10. "Ahmad"—Muhammad's heavenly name; "precursor" because he was God's first creature.

11. "This dance"—not *ngoma*, the general African traditional Swahili word for a dance or drumming, but *tari*, a "tambourine."

12. *Abjad* is a system of divining with numbers based on the numerical value given to letters of the Arabic alphabet; it goes back to pre-Islamic times. Among Yoruba Muslims, the *ifa* oracle, which is not unlike the I Ching, may be consulted.

13. It is the board, not the piece of ebony, that has the numbers on it. The numbers are the alternative values of the letters, alif = 1, be = 2, jim = 3, etc. Mtoro appears not quite to know the system, for m = 40, h = 8, d = 4, and he misspells *Fatuma*.

14. Literally, "she is a pest and then becomes normal." The second, and perhaps the third, are the only really tolerable houses in which a married couple can find themselves. The advice of this poem on matrimony seems to coincide with that of Mr. Punch: "Don't." In a very similar poem (Ms. no. 406, Dar-es-Salaam Institute of Swahili), the second house is also the good one.

15. *Bao*—a game with a board in which there are holes, sometimes sixteen, sometimes thirty-six. Seeds or stones are used as counters.

16. As is usual with many wedding songs, these are suggestive and even outrightly sexual in nature. Velten in his notes on the Swahili text points out

the exact nature of the mast that the consul (the bridegroom) will erect, but takes it that the bride is sleepy and wants to go to bed. The cotton-ginning ceremony is yet another reminder how time-consuming being a good Swahili must have been.

17. *Fungate*—the original Bantu root for "seven" was related to this word; hence it could come to mean a week. More details of the fungate are given at V 125. Cf. V 116. Old Dr. Danquah of Ghana used to say Ghana gave the Jews and Europeans the week. It certainly looks as if the Bantu had it before Islamic contact.

18. "I am ready"—*labeka*, the old Arabic liturgical response that, for instance, the pilgrim says during the *hajj*. "I do"—*naam*.

19. In this benediction there is again a magnificent and compatible mixture of Islam and African Traditional Religion. The words *heri, sudi na baraka*, ("good luck, happiness, and blessing") are Arabic, while *mapendano* ("mutual love") is pure Swahili. Swahili is in some ways as well off as New Testament Greek in words for love and in this regard is richer than English.

20. "Look as in a glass"—i.e., watch your husband discreetly. These songs are not easy to attribute to specific situations. They are as exquisite and enigmatic as miniature paintings from the hills of Himachal Pradesh.

21. "He digs weeds," etc., are taken by Velten to be the bride's reply to the question "Where is your husband?" The next song portrays a girl without a husband as a captain without a sailor, searching everywhere to recruit a man. A woman should not be like a net receiving all fishes!

22. His dress is that of the coastal gentleman: kanzu—the long shirt with sleeves; *joho*—a black cloak with loose sleeves. [There are photographs of well-dressed Swahili ladies and gentlemen in Charles Eliot, *The East African Protectorate* (London, 1905), pp. 14, 44.—J. de V. A.]

23. *kono*—related to *mkono*, the arm or hand, the "hand price"; *kipakasa*—"the price for touching"; *fichuo*—"the price for unveiling."

24. In this verse the bride balks at the heavy, coarse work of pounding maize, but the man insists. Calico is a cheap cloth, so she means, "I care nothing for your love if you think you can get me cheaply. If you really love me, buy a slave to help me pound the maize."

25. This verse may be self-contained and may be the message of a young man to his love.

26. This was the lament of the maiden for her unfaithful lover, who has left her with child.

27. This verse may be the song of a man, jealous of his lovely wife, to his slave woman Mwana Kombo, telling her to remain in the house and keep busy drawing water. That lady replies that there is plenty of water in the well—it is not like a water hole or spring, where you have to wait. The reference is to a proverb: The frog guards the well, and yet people fetch water. The frog is the image of the cuckolded husband. The last sentence is a well-known proverb: Watching a beautiful woman lest she take lovers is futile.

28. The song of a woman to another, who has accused her of not repelling the latter's husband's advances.

29. The complaint of a woman that her husband has strayed. A magic pouch normally contains "medicine" for happiness, and a husband, according to this verse, is medicine. The woman is singing to another woman with whom her husband committed adultery; the latter replies in the last line, "Don't be jealous."

30. A woman who fears that her husband loves another speaks thus to him: she would rather die than share him with another woman.

31. A woman whose lover has deserted her hears that his next relationship is in difficulties. Knowing him as well as she does, she could explain why, so she is singing to the other woman, "Leave him to me." In all these songs there are layers upon layers of alternative meanings.

32. A wife learns that her husband is restless, because he wants to take a second woman. In the house of this other woman there is not so much as a mat. He will be like the frog that has to guard the well in which he lives, but since anyone can draw the water, the frog, thinking itself to be the owner, is in reality cuckolded. Drawing other men's well water is symbolic of adultery.

33. This stanza perhaps refers to the reminders a widowed person has of a good spouse who died before his or her time, or to those of a lover when the beloved is absent.

34. Cassava roots are pounded and mixed with water form a dough (manioc) from which stiff porridge is cooked. It is often poisonous until properly cooked: a symbol for the unmarried woman. "Rats" are adulterers. "Wells" and "cisterns" and "ponds" are female symbols.

35. This is a prayer in the best African tradition, in which both men and women join, perhaps antiphonally. The name of God used throughout is Mungu, and the petitions are for very definite empirical benefits. At the same time we see the fine Islamic philosophy that a jealous character is his or her own god and therefore has no other.

36. This washing of the bridegroom's feet is carried out by the woman who initiated the bride into womanhood. On behalf of the bride, it symbolizes his welcome into partaking of the benefits of that initiation, and it involves cleansing and protecting him so that he may so partake. The interpretation of this rite in the following song as washing with water from the well of Zamzam at Mecca, where Hagar obtained water for Ishmael, illustrates how easily African rites can be genuinely Islamized.

37. "Two by two"—i.e., the rupees, two rupees making a riale, a Maria Theresa dollar.

Upate is a brass dish, used as a cymbal by the *masogora*, "helpers."

38. As a counterpart to the demand for a woman's virginity, traditional societies have an at times brutal insistence that the man soon demonstrate his potency. Unlike the case with the woman, however, the man's lack is not easily disguised. Presumably, bridegrooms in those days, if they failed initi-

ally, were much better able to perform later, despite pointed questions from the families concerned and coarse taunts from various young men, than many young men today, who seem to be more easily put off and need help rather than ridicule.

Watani—"joking relations." Fuller notes on them will be found when their activities at funerals are discussed (V 214–215, 220).

39. The wedding canopy, prominent also in the Jewish wedding ceremony, symbolizes the royal canopy, the togetherness into which bride and groom are placed, the warding off of that which is outside. The Swahili word used is *ukingo*, and it also occurs in the description of how the cloths that have washed a corpse are carried behind a covering of this kind. Probably all these canopies are meant to ward off the radiation effects of the numinous, which is so powerfully present, and the envy and evil such things attract.

40. An immediately virilocal marriage is by no means the rule in Africa. [Matrilocalism is normal among most Swahilis, and virilocalism, as far as I can discern, only among the Shirazi subgroup; but this is debatable.— J. de V. A.]

41. A woman's obedience and seclusion is insisted on by traditionalists of Islamic background not only in East Africa but in northern Nigeria, Pakistan, Uttar Pradesh and Bradford in Yorkshire. It is seldom universally attained: for one thing, it demands servants and a way of life generally available only to the upper economic classes, for in nonurban areas one of a woman's chief values is her ability to work in the field, and such labor is not secluded. [Most Swahilis were, in a sense and in their own eyes, urban. It is true that lower-class women were generally not veiled. From about 1880 until (in places like Lamu) about 1960, however, the seclusion of upper-class Swahili women in small towns was as rigid as anywhere in history.—J. de V. A.]

42. The lore of the love potion is, of course, well known in many literatures. In this case the "potion" (*dawa ya pendo* literally means "medicine" or "medication of love") takes the form either of roots put in food or else of cuts rubbed with a special substance. The "groin" that has the secret cuts is the woman's mons veneris.

43. Qur'an 4:3 permits a man to marry two, three, or four women, provided he can act equitably toward all of them. A number of written accounts of life in a polygynous household give the impression that it was at least as happy as any "average" Western monogynous family. On the other hand, every single one of the many individuals personally asked by this writer who grew up in such households in Africa or Asia has spoken of the misery and humiliation of the womenfolk. Winifred Allen, who knows very many polygynous Swahili households, disagrees totally. She says the *sharīʿa* governing this situation was well known and carefully obeyed. Modern apologists point out that no man can be equitable to four women, and anyone with a sense of humor can see that the Qur'an is pointing to monogyny. Most people assume without question that polyandry is "bad," but it may answer many a problem.

44. Khitima—a Qur'an reading for the soul of the deceased.

Dhu'l hijja—the twelfth month of the Islamic calendar, "the Lord of the pilgrimage." The Swahili word is *mfunguo tatu*, which means the third month.

45. The principle of the *levir* and the rights and duties of the husband's male relative (*ndugu*) are enunciated in the Bible, where the stories of Tamar (Gen. 38:6 ff.) and Ruth depend upon them. It is hard to be sure of a sui generis levirate among the Swahili, though it may be significant that the technical term (*mwingilizi*, literally "the one who enters") for the husband is not Semitic in root.

46. A *sharifu* is one of the descendants of the Prophet through his grandson Hasan. A *sayyidi* (mentioned elsewhere) is a descendant through the other grandson, Husain.

12. Of Dances for Enjoyment

1. "Dances"—*ngoma* means both "drum" and "dance" in most Bantu languages, and to many Africans the two are synonymous. For most people the beating of drums combined with dancing has soul-stirring effects; for some, drums and dancing are associated with sexual intercourse. To some, drums are inappropriate when women only are dancing, and in fact women who themselves play drums are sometimes assumed to have Lesbian associations. Stricter Muslims look on drumming and dancing askance and seek to eliminate these activities over the course of time. This was the policy of certain Hadhrami Sunni sharifs who in the latter half of the nineteenth century gained considerable influence under the Busaidi sultans. Others seek to encourage more licit forms, like boys dancing to tari, or tambourines, which were apparently used in the presence of the Prophet. Modernity and changes of fashion also took a heavy toll of most of the dances mentioned. (See the Bibliography and the appendix on music and dance.)

2. *Jumbe* may be translated "chief" and *ujumbe* "chieftaincy." In the Bagamoyo context it signified a member of one of the old "royal" families who partook of certain corporate sacral functions going back to ancient times and also exercised some political power. The title has to be distinguished from *mwinyi*, which often signifies "possessor" or "master" (as a title) or is perhaps the remnant of an older form of government. In German East Africa the term *jumbe* came to include such posts as *mwangi*, *mtemi*, *mwami*, and *mkulungwa*.

3. Something may be discerned in this ngoma kuu (great dance) of the elements of Bagamoyo society. A slave may not dance, though a woman slave attendant may circle with a chief. If a slave plays, he does so with bare head and feet. The freemen (the proud *waungwana*) are prominent, the shaha and waziri who have inherited or attained special status have their place, then come the jumbes.

4. This dance appears to have been danced by factions who sang antiphonally, litanywise (in this case the Mtondoo people and the Sitirihali folk).

They seem to have consisted of two general lines or shallow crescents of people facing one another, each line dancing back and forth or sending out "champions" who confronted the other side. Here we see how closely some dances approximate ritual battles. See the Bibliography.

5. On the instruments used, see Appendix III.

6. "Unyanyembe"—the country of the Wanyamwezi, capital Tabora (Kaze) or Urambo, at the junction of the routes to Lake Victoria and Lake Tanganyika. Swahili traders reached it fairly early in their travels and used it as a base for their expeditions into the Congo and Buganda.

7. We see here stated on an elemental level the basic human need for factionalism and competition, a need that has generated such diverse events as the rivalry between "houses" artificially set up by the masters in Arnold's English public-school system, the family plague that beset the late medieval Italian cities so starkly portrayed in *Romeo and Juliet*, and the civil war that destroyed European hegemony in 1914–1918. To sing, dance, and potlatch out hostility seem more enjoyable ways to ruin. Among the Enga of Highland New Guinea, for example, this type of quasi-warfare takes the form of the "pig exchange," though in some years actual warfare reemerges.

Pishi of rice—about four pints or six pounds.

8. Fungate—a part of the wedding celebrations, mentioned above. There is a hint here of a pre-Islamic seven-day week. Gongoni is a quarter of Bagamoyo.

9. *Kolekole* and *kowana*—fish, known for stupidity or other such qualities, used here as names for the opposite group.

10. "Like you"—this English translation is ambiguous; the meaning is closer to "similar to." This is apparently the song of a woman being divorced by her husband.

11. "And they become friends" (Swahili *rafiqi*)—we may compare Ibn Battuta's description of the friends West African women kept in his day (*Ibn Battuta in Black Africa*, ed. and trans. Hamdun and King [London, 1975], pp. 388–390).

12 [Dances remarkably similar to the kiumbizi are reported from West Africa, Trinidad, and other places.—J. de V. A.] The *bondogea* is a special drumbeat.

13. In this dance the women of Swahili society appear in their appropriate functions and ranks—maiden, initiate, initiator-tutrix, and married woman. There are both African and Arab dances in which very old women played an essential role, but these are not mentioned here.

14. In this verse we may suppose a young woman begs her lover not to rush ahead to sexual intercourse, because all may be ruined by such haste. [This is only one possible interpretation, however. It depreciates these songs to suppose that any of them have less than four or five possible meanings.— J. de V. A.]

15. "Learning" is *elimu*, the Islamic higher studies referred to in chap. 4.

16. The kigori is the girl who has not yet been recognized as having had her

first menstrual period. Once she is so recognized, she begins the education of initiation and becomes a mwari (see chap. 9). A girl's first ovum may become fertilized if she is having regular sexual intercourse, but beyond this the song speaks of the feelings of any young woman, no matter the calendar age, who finds herself pregnant before she feels ready for children.

17. Velten takes this to be the lament of a man who has been committing adultery and hears from his wife that she has done the same. Innumerable folk songs from England and the United States contain this common theme of the (usually) woman's sorrow that her lover has coldly packed his bags.

18. Mkwaja is a place between Pangani and Sadani.

19. Velten says this refers to a man from Sadani who, because of his bad mouth, was murdered by another.

20. The song of a mwari who did not please her tutrix.

21. There seems to be some historical reference here, difficult now to recapture, but see the *Utenzi wa vita vya wadachi kutamalaki mrima* [On the German conquest of the coast] by Hemedi bin Abdallah el Buhriy (Dar-es-Salaam, 1960).

22. "What will you do with two"—wives, one at Mwavi and one at Shangani.

23. Velten takes this to be the lament of a maiden. The Swahili keep a small oil light burning as they sleep, and Nasoro had once slept by her and taken the opportunity to commit theft.

24. Velten remarks that Swahili girls carry everything, however small, on their heads, so their age mates have plenty of opportunity to flip anything so carried off to the ground.

25. In the sepoy dance we have a piece of material for which we can give a definite *terminus ante quem*, for we know that Indian soldiers, even Baluchis in the sultan's service, did not come to the coast much before the middle of the nineteenth century. The dance may be related to the Gujerati stick dance (*danda natch*).

26. The Nubians were Muslim mercenaries recruited by people like Gordon, Emin Pasha, and Lugard to serve colonial expansion. The imperial power was able to use the Indian sepoys as a counterbalance when the Nubians went beyond bounds.

27. Lloyd William Matthews was a British naval officer, born in 1850, who helped to train the Zanzibar army from 1878 onward. By the time he died in 1901, he had served five sultans and served them well. Professor T. O. Ranger writes: "His loyal service, his decorations and general glitter, his representation of power, his military activities along the coast; all make him an archetypal figure for admiration." See the Bibliography.

28. *Kakatua*—if the name of this bird is of Indian background, it is a kind of hoopoe. The Swahili term itself suggests a bird that pounds its victims on rocks or breaks them with its beak. The word may simply be a version of "cockatoo."

29. *Kitambi buraa*—a flowing sheet. *Kaya za dismali*—a head-covering veil,

about half a yard long. Note the transvestism that is a feature of this dance.

30. We met the great snake of Mlali above in the women's initiation song, signifying a phallus (V 85). On Gobore, see the discussion of modern dances at V 142).

31. *Kisekeseke*—a bird with an onomatopoeic name which we have failed to identify any more than Sacleux, who notes only *nom d'un oiseau*. [It may be a pied wagtail.—J. de V. A.]

32. This procedure is still followed in Tanzania today. We have met the waziri, (prime minister), the executive officer of such associations, before. The *mkuu*—literally "the great," a recognized leader.

33. [The Maniema came from eastern Congo (Zaïre), mostly as slaves or ivory porters, sufficiently early in the nineteenth century for them to form part of the core group (*wa-Swahili haswa*) of such nineteenth-century towns as Ujiji and Dar-es-Salaam. Evidently, they were not "core" at Bayamoyo.— J. de V. A.]

34. "Lubangula"—perhaps this refers to the great southern African leader.

13. Of Spirits

1. The word translated "spirits" is *pepo*. *Spirits* is hardly a perfect term but is the best we have, for *compulsion-neurosis* or *hysteria* and the like are even worse. Attendance at seances and observation of the manifestations of such spirits lead one to think that they are things (denizens?) of the mind which are released or brought into being by certain factors; they are objective in a sense, controllable—or excitable—by people or factors outside one's own mind. For a guide to the extensive reading matter in this area, see the Bibliography.

2. "Hold polytheistic beliefs in male and female spirits"—the Swahili is *wameshiriki pepo*. The awesome and dreadful root *sh-r-k* is used, which indicates the ultimate sin, in Muslim eyes, of associating a person or thing with God. Mtoro clearly indicates his views here, and at the end he reiterates that he personally considers the pepo business poppycock.

3. "A spirit in need of reduction"—Swahili *kupunga pepo*. It would be easy for us to make the translation of this chapter more immediately intelligible but much less accurate by varying the English translations of these two words according to the context, for they have no real equivalent in European languages. They should be treated as technical terms, however, and always translated by the same words, even when this leads to somewhat strained English.

Those who believe in pepo clearly envisage them as in some sense sentient beings with whom it is possible to converse, but no distinction can be drawn between them and diseases or the cause of diseases, nor can distinction be drawn between the pepo and the patient. Therefore, any pepo may, like a fever, move from the limbs to the head, and it is usually wrong to describe a pepo as "entering" a person or being "driven out." When Mtoro speaks of putting money on the head of the pepo, we are tempted to translate this as on the head of the patient; but to do so obscures the fact that the pepo and the patient are one. At the end the pepo has not been "driven out": the pepo goes home in good health; but the person is different. He or she is now *mteja*, which has been translated "initiate." The pepo has *not* been removed. Regarding the verb *kupunga*, to translate it as "exorcise" seems quite incorrect, because it can be used equally of the pepo and the patient; but it is not easy to find a single English word to fit all contexts. The word "reduce" has been used: it may be understood simultaneously in its normal and its medical sense, and it is applicable to a pepo considered as a spirit, a disease, or a condition, as well as to the sufferer. The patient is reduced, not to his or her original condition, which can never be restored, but to a satisfactory condition in which he or she can resume everyday life (as mteja). (It is to be noted that Mtoro usually, but not invariably, makes the tacit assumption that the patient is a woman.)

The remark that pepo come where there is trouble between husband and wife is significant. The cult is a means by which the underdog or person who feels slighted can get redress; we may compare similar cults among the Hausa, the *zar* cult in Ethiopia, and some aspects of the *jok* cult in Acholi. There may be some connection between the appearance of such cults and the recent lessening in women's fullness of life—for instance, in places where a more strict legalistic interpretation of Islam has overtaken an African traditional system, in the United States, where American women were "fluffed" after being removed from the jobs they held during World War II.

4. The raising of the pepo to the head, to which there are frequent references, has to be understood in a double sense. Insofar as the pepo has a local habitation, it means that the pepo is located in the head. Insofar as the pepo is incorporeal, it means that the symptoms rise to the head.

5. The word "patient" in this paragraph is a translation of *mteja*, which could well be translated "initiate." The color symbolism of white, red, and black, the painting, the change of clothes are all indicative of initiation (see the Bibliography regarding color symbolism). In the next paragraph we may note how closely the pepo and the patient are identified, for it is literally the pepo's face that is painted.

6. The word translated "patient" here is *mwele*, one normally used of a sick person. The next word translated "doctor" is *fundi*, which indicates an expert, a craftsman. This may be a master of ceremonies, not the officiating mganga. The conversation is reminiscent of the rigmarole one has to go through to talk down a drug "high" or try to understand someone whose brain has been addled by LSD.

7. It is impressive how objectively Mtoro has described the pepo cult. Only in such phrases as "gives a demonic name" (*jina la kijini*) does he reveal his own deeply Islamized thinking. (At the end, however, he feels free to state his own opinion: for him it is balderdash.)

8. The drinking of blood is as repellent to a Swahili Muslim as it is to a Jew.

In a cult like this, the very doing of something totally obnoxious is part of the remaking, the new birth, of the person concerned.

9. *Dungumaro*—this pepo is described below at V 155.

10. The reader will recall that Mtoro had left East Africa and was working in Germany.

14. Of Spirit Dances

1. "Kinyamkera," or sometimes *Chamkera*, is more commonly used of the "dust devil." The verb-*kera* means to annoy, and Anon. DSM points out that it is considered quite a minor devil, adding that the dust devil is thought to be a little devil that picks up scraps of sweet things. For that reason children are not allowed to eat such things while standing up.

"A pagan spirit," *kishenzi*—pagan almost in the original derogatory sense of "rustic." The differentiation of spirits is reminiscent of 1 Corinthians and Acts. Some German Christians said of their behavior with regard to the Nazi phenomenon, "We did not discern the spirits." For remarks on the extensive literature available on spirit phenomena, the reader is again requested to consult the Bibliography.

2. The top of the ear is taken between finger and thumb, and the spirit *in the head* is addressed. After the fumigation and the identification of the pepo, there is a pause while resources are collected to make the reduction possible.

3. "female initiates"—*wateja wake wanawake*. *Mteja* as noted above is sometimes to be translated "patient," but the scene is one of initiation and here "initiate" is better. At V 151 the song "You, my girl" uses the word *mwari*, which is employed of "maiden" initiates in puberty ceremonies.

4. For the types of drum mentioned see Appendix III. Anon. DSM notes that the dogori is a Zaramo drum.

5. These songs, like many throughout the book, are under Zaramo influence, as Velten's notes indicate. "Kinyamhunga" is the Zaramo by-form of the name of this pepo. ("Sengwa," below, is another by-form.) The implication is that it is this pepo and none other that has come upon the person.

6. "Kilima"—Anon. DSM gives the order of precedence as Shamng'ombe, Kirima, Ngwindi, Qitimiri, Nyari, Msandai, Mlangamo, Jinibara, Subihani, Mori. Bwana Idi and others at Bagamoyo report that Kilima and Shamng'ombe have been ousted by two other pepo, Bwana Mkubwa and Ngwindi. Their reduction is similar to that of Kilima, but in the case of Bwana Mkubwa it is very expensive and may cost 200 shillings. On the naming day the senior mteja wears a sword and joho. At Bagamoyo, one can still hear the tap, tap, tap of pepo dances at night and attend seances.

7. This method of treatment is reminiscent of the use of wide-coverage antibiotics when Western doctors are mystified.

8. Mark 3:27, paralleled in Matthew, chap. 12, and Luke, chap. 11: "The

strong man armed keeps his house till there comes a stronger than he." The climax in naming is akin to Jesus' question to Legion, Mark 5:9.

9. Despite his repugnance toward blood drinking, Mtoro refrains from any snide remarks, except perhaps in his aside that a turban with two peaks has two horns to indicate that it is a devil's turban. In most cases the pepo's origin corresponds with the instruments, food, and vocabulary used. Some dances seem nearer Islam: Arab swords are used, Allah is invoked, blood drinking is omitted, and tambourines, not drums, are used. Unfortunately for the absolute consistency of this thesis, the Qitimiri dance from Arabia, with all its Islamicity, is danced with drums and involves blood drinking. It would appear as if Islam and African Traditional Religion were not in watertight compartments. For someone who had had only one abortive brush with pepo, Mtoro's knowledge is remarkably elaborate. Perhaps he is editing other people's material.

10. "Catgut rhythm," *utumba wa paka*—as Velten suggests, the sound of the Swahili imitates the rhythm: "The stomach of *the* cat." The spirit is Dungumaro and is addressed as "Lolo" and *tate*, "father."

11. "Water lilies"—we saw in the wedding dances that these flowers signify peace and quiet.

12. In this song *Lolo* is spelled *Lelo* in the original Swahili. The exegesis of this verse is peculiarly difficult. Lines 1, 2, 5, and 6 are presumably addressed by the new initiate (who is in a sense the pepo) to the pepo, with the older initiates joining in. Lines 3, 4, and 7 are the words of all the initiates, in which the new one joins. "Simbamwene" is a title also used, for instance, by the Shambala, Doe, and, as Dr. Edward Alpers points out, by the Zigua rulers of Morogoro town.

13. Though not many of them were Muslims at the end of the nineteenth century, the Galla from the Swahili point of view are an Islamized people. The songs include many Arabic words and Islamic expressions, and the accompaniment is on *matari* hand drums permissible by the ruling of some scholars. The words "if you are a doctor" are addressed to the pepo, a request for it to signify by the piece of paraphernalia its human "seat" or "habitation"; it is to pick up something to show where its interests lie. The mganga often carries medicines and charms in a horn. A horn can also be used as a repository of power which can seek out and identify thieves or harm enemies. Once at a seance of Baganda in Kampala, the spirit of the lake indicated its lordly presence when the medium picked up a paddle and "rowed" around the hut. When another *lubaale* came upon her, she festooned herself with the creeper favorite to it.

14. "Kisiki" and "Manoru" are bynames for this pepo. This is perhaps the song of women who desire their own offspring so they do not have to work for others. Rice can be a symbol for semen.

15. "Allah" here translates the exclamation *Hala*! This may indeed repre-

sent the name of God, but it may be just an ecstatic exclamation. "Mtelehi" is another name for the pepo being invoked.

16. "Majuma" is a common name for a woman.

17. This type of divining is reminiscent of the procedures of *Ramli*, a west Asian divining system with figures drawn in the sand.

18. "Melons and gherkins" are taken by Velten to represent intrigues and hostile images, because of their intertwining growth habits.

19. "Toast,"—*mkate wa bisi*—this has been translated "millet bread," but since this gentleman from Europe is eating biscuits and eggs, "toast" is not too farfetched. There is further information about spirits in chap. 18 (V 187).

15. Women's Work

1. Although one wishes that Mtoro had given us more material on women, when all his scraps are collected they give us a general summary of a Swahili woman's life and work. As with most traditional portraits, it can be summed up with the biblical Prov. 31:10: "The price of a good woman who can find? Her worth is above that of rubies." The modern Western woman resents what she sees as a mixture of idealization on the one hand and valuation purely by her usefulness to the male on the other. Judging by such works as Mwana Kupona's "On the Wifely Duty," edited and translated by J. W. T. Allen in *Tendi* (London, 1971), it is possible that some such descriptions were probably originated by women. Perhaps one of the major differences between modern woman and her traditional counterpart is that the former does not spend most of her time being pregnant and fetching water and fuel. See the Bibliography for the extensive literature.

2. "Cakes," *lado*—the word is from Hindustani. "Pesa" below is also of Indian provenance, the coinage used being the rupee, which used to divide up in India into 16 annas or 64 paisa or 192 pies. See Appendix II, "Weights and Measures."

3. *Kibaba*—approximately a pint. "Togwa" is an unfermented beer. "Toddy," *tembo*—palm wine. "Strong and sweet," *kali na tamu*—as Devonians say of cider: "rough or sweet." See also Amos Tutuola, *The Palm Wine Drinkard* (London, 1952).

Kinanda—[a big-bellied lute of great antiquity, of Swahili origin. The udi is of Persian or Arab origin. —J. de V.A.]

4. "Maua" or "Flowers"—the name of the woman who sells the drink.

5. "Sorcerer"—*mchawi*.

6. *Wanalewa kama chozi*—literally "as drunk as sunbirds." This may be an expression like "as tight as a tick," for sunbirds do squawk and flop about; however, the word *chozi* may be derived from *-choka* and mean no more than "drunk and incapable." Perhaps sunbirds seem to tap the base of flowers for nectar as tappers cut palms for toddy.

7. The possibilities of variegated patterns with Afro hair are endless. In

Yorubaland diagrams offering forty-eight suitably named styles may be seen. [The Pokomo traditional styles are especially noteworthy.—J. de V. A.]

Mardufu, related to *rudufu* and *maradufu*, is from the Arabic root *radafa*, which has to do with doubling. *Za kufundika*, related to the root *funda*, "knot."

8. "Sitahamili" means "I cannot hear it." This is repeated at V 185 among work songs. It has to be borne in mind that the face-to-face position is the norm only among such peoples as northern Europeans and United States Americans. (Cf. Malinowski and the Trobrianders on missionaries.)

9. Velten takes this to mean that good men are hard to get and the woman singing has lost the man of her delight.

10. The Prophet strongly advocated the use of a piece of wood for cleaning the teeth. A twig from the mswaki bush or from the *neem* or similar tree, chewed and used for cleaning teeth and massaging gums, is considered by some to be superior to the toothbrush.

11. "Cosmetics"—*uzuri wa wanawake*—literally "womanly beauty."

12. *Hal Badiri*—also rendered *Ali Badiri*, a reading from a book of magic verses. At the Battle of Badr the power of the Prophet's invocation against his pagan enemies destroyed them. The power of the recitation will discover and attack a thief.

13. *Ukindu*—the split leaves of the wild date, *Phoenix reclinata*.

14. *Ukili*—the woven strips made from the *mkindu* which, being joined together, form a mat.

15. *Mdaa*—a plant, *Euclea multiflora*.

16. "Mkumbi yellow"—a kind of yellow color. The mkumbi (*Ochna alboserrata*) is the bush connected with initiation (cf. V 69).

17. *Pima*—four *dhiraa* (cubit lengths of about eighteen inches).

18. *Kanga*—in the context of mat patterns that look like bird markings, this indicates speckling similar to that of the guinea fowl.

19. *Gongo*—a small black bird with red and yellow markings.

20. *Jamvi*—a heavier, larger undermatting on top of which mats (*mikeka*—the type described above) are placed. [It is made of doum or *hyphaene* palms.—J. de V. A.]

16. Men's Work

1. *Mishikaki*—meat roasted (dried and smoked) and skewered on a stick.

2. *Ngalawa*—outrigger canoe.

3. Bwana Idi explains that they knew where the deeps surround a reef. They anchor on the reef but throw their lines into the deep water.

4. These are two kinds of little fish.

5. *Nyenga*—a young ray later called *taa*.

6. "Give me two cloths, else I will not joy you in bed."

7. Boat building can be almost a religious task, sometimes calling for

temporary celibacy. By the beach at Bagamoyo one may still see boats being
built in the old way.

8. Velten takes *ngombe*, translated "cow," to refer to the sail. In Arabic
bakara, "cow," can be used of a type of dhow.

9. The songs may originally have referred to particular incidents or people:
Mother Yaya may have kept a wayside stall. Magwangwaa may have been an
overseer who served insufficiently cooked cassava. The *suria* ("concubine")
and the biting slave girl are not remembered beyond this.

10. We met this song before (V 171).

11. This is very similar to "The Song of the Guest" given at V 268–269.
"The *first* visit" may contain a little irony, for even a distinguished visitor who
has outstayed his or her welcome is eventually given a hoe.

17. Concerning Cultivation

1. "Hunger makes a sincere prayer." The opening of a new field in the
wilderness is a sacral event, hunger (*njaa*) is ever near, and the power of *mwitu*
(the "bush") to give or deny is absolute.

2. We met this bush twice above, at V 69 and V 175. The mixing of a
yellow bark with the seed brings baraka. This blessing, besides its psychological and parapsychological effects, may indeed be a way of assisting fertiliza-
tion through interaction with bacteria or the warding off of harmful insects.

3. "Kuikui"—the king of the birds.

4. "Jamvi"—a thick, coarse mat.

5. "Alms"—*sadaka kuwapa maskini*—the Islamic care for the poor (cf.
Deuteronomy).

6. They inherit pepo as mali. Being the chair of a spirit has something of
the hereditary in it as well as something of the voluntary. One can enter into
one's property or, like Mtoro (V 148), refuse it.

7. Cassava—*muhogo*—the crop especially for njaa, hunger, famine, or
when (as here between rains and hence between crops) food runs short. The
Swahili can transform this "need" crop, however, through culinary magic.

8. By a sort of sympathetic magic they decree how tall the tree shall be.
The connection of phases of the moon and planting is not mere fancy; it is
found in wide varieties of traditions. The Swahili also developed "breeding"
of better coconuts and mangoes by selection.

9. *Kidaka*—the small coconut as yet without juice.

10. [Swahili feel as strongly about the coconut as Arabs do about camels.
Sheikh Ahmed Sheikh Nabhany, a Kenyan poet cited in the Preface and
author of "Tears for Allen" in Appendix IV, has written a poem, *Mashairi*,
listing sixty-eight different uses of the coconut. Its title is "Umbuji wa mnazi
wa Kiwandeo".—J. de V. A.]

11. The most popular tree for tembo is the *mvumo*, but the methods can be
applied to other palms. "The top"—*kilele*. Anon. DSM rightly points out that

if you cut the kilele you kill the tree. The incision is made in the upper part at the base of the flower stem.

12. [In general in this chapter it looks as if Mtoro and his informants knew little about farming; or the situation at Bagamoyo was indeed different from that of Mombasa and the north; or again, topics such as land tenure were politically too hot to handle, and he purposely ducked them. He does not bring out the all-important distinction between *shamba* and *konde* (see chap. 3, n. 6), nor does he discuss the key question of which tasks were performed individually and which communally or cooperatively. He does, however, give the lie to the myth that all agriculture was performed by slave labor.— J. de V. A.]

13. The price in the Utete area, southward from Dar-es-Salaam, is still the same.

14. "As he sways about"—both in his occupation up a tree and in his drunkenness.

18. Of Dissolving Marriage

1. The whole procedure for divorce (*talaka*) has to this point been Islamic. Now, however, the kungwi, the woman's tutrix in traditional African initiation, who gave her in marriage (V 109), washes her free of it.

2. The remainder of this chapter (V 194–197) has not been included in this edition. It is a summary of the law of Islam on the subject of divorce, and better, clearer, and more accurate summaries are available both in English and in Swahili. See the Bibliography.

19. Of Diseases and Their Cure

1. To assess Mtoro's section on disease at its true worth, we must remember that until little over a century and a half ago, Muslim-Arab medicine was in many ways at least as useful as European. Thus early in the last century a French gentleman at Lucknow got more help for his stones from a hakim than he did from a Western practitioner. Mtoro's material is based on experience, tradition, some Arab medicine and the "I got wet and caught a cold" etiology. To look for a good traditional African theory of spirit causes of disease, wholeness, well-being, and health is too much, but there is a great deal of sound practice and common sense here. In Swahililand and places like it, where it has been possible to test on this writer's own person some of the maladies and traditional African cures he mentions, in a number of cases the diagnosis and treatment proved excellent. Where Mtoro seems to depend on a general Indian Ocean tradition, however, the treatment is severe and ineffective. (For severity and useless infliction of pain, one may recall the "treatments" undergone by Saint Francis or George Washington.) It should also be noted that present-day medicine is not without similar attempts at cure. For

books on these themes, see the Bibliography. The Makerere Medical School had devoted much attention to the lasting values in traditional medicine, and it is likely that much light will be thrown on the subject by writers there, in Korle Bu (Accra), Lagos, Ibadan, and other such places.

"Cold fever," presumably rigor, a rising fever, may be the common cold, and the remedies are traditional, rather like the European's recommendation of hot drinks and putting the feet in a mustard bath. Wrapping up until you sweat is another old remedy. If the fever is malarial, the relief is only temporary.

The description of "hot fever," steady high fever—for example, typhoid—is good and applies, of course, to any such fever, not necessarily that caused when the body is exposed to heat. The treatment, the application of water all over, is sensible: as it evaporates, it will cool the patient. If the malady is sunstroke, this treatment coupled with lots of rest and liquids may assist natural recovery. Before the advent of modern medicine, however, if the fever was caused by typhoid, termination by death often overtook treatment.

2. *Ahtam fashadh*: a catena of the names of spirits (according to Bwana Idi and Velten). The treatment of smallpox: It is recommended that the pocks be treated with cloth containing hot sand. This, one supposes, sterilizes them so that they do not become secondarily infected, which is sensible. They heal then with less scarring. The rest of the treatment of smallpox is rather superstitious. The point about smallpox beginning with pains in the joints is very sound. This is often true.

3. *Buba* (usually used for "yaws")—yaws is confused with syphilis. It says here that yaws attacks chiefly the nose. There are two kinds of yaws of the nose: *gangosa*, with loss of tissue and bone destruction, and *goundou*, which causes thickening of the bones of the nose. He mentions lesions in the armpits and around the anus, which is where confusion with syphilis comes in. He is probably thinking of the condylomas of secondary syphilis, which do resemble the lesions of secondary yaws to some extent. Blue vitriol is not very effective, but in those days nobody had any very effective cure for the disease.

4. Leprosy obviously was known to be infectious, and in those days there was no cure. He says that at first pustules appear. This is not true unless there is secondary infection. The loss of the fingers and toes may be due to the so-called trophic sores where the leprosy has affected the nerves, causing loss of sensation, so that injuries followed by sepsis occur without causing pain; or it may be due to absorption of bone, with shortening rather than loss of the fingers and toes, the nails being left on the stumps.

5. *Upele* (usually translated "scabies")—he seems to confuse scabies with eczema. We take it he means eczema. He says that there are two varieties, scaly, which is probably eczema, and pimply, which may be true scabies. It would not be surprising to see popular urticaria (reaction to insect bites) and fungus infections included in these categories. They, too, are itchy, pimply, scaly, and common. Modern health workers in the tropics will tend to label

many such things as scabies and treat for eczema, and then, at the clinic, they will be found to be a fungus infection.

6. *Maradhi ya mti*, "scrofula," here is tuberculosis of the skin. He says that its particular disfigurement is to destroy the nose. This is, of course, true of lupus vulgaris, the common form of cutaneous tuberculosis, and it can be associated with the disease elsewhere, such as tuberculosis of the spine with the hunchback.

7. Hydrocele is congenital, not hereditary. It is true that some men get it later in life; but it has nothing to do with having too many lady friends. None of us have ever heard any person's testicles creak or croak, and this seems to be a bit of imagination or else the patient's self-consciousness. There is no medical treatment for this condition. The fluid has to be let out either by tapping or by an operation to remove the membrane that secretes it.

8. The "congenital" form present at birth goes away by itself in a year anyway, so this treatment is likely to appear very successful.

9. Syphilis and gonorrhea are recognized as venereal. The treatment is not very effective. It is recognized here that syphilis is, generally speaking, a more serious disease than gonorrhea. There is some confusion. He mentions bleeding gonorrhea, which is bilharzia. True gonorrhea is referred to quite often as *kisonono cha usaha* and bilharzia as *kisonono cha damu* or, better, *kichocho*.

10. This applies more to gonorrhea than to syphilis.

11. *Maradhi ya pumu na kifua kikuu*—Velten, clearly by a slip, gives *pumu* as *Schwindsucht* and *kifua kikuu* as "asthma"; but *kifua kikuu* is well known as consumption.

The description of consumption, pulmonary tuberculosis, is very, very good. It is recognized that the disease is communicable and very often fatal, because even as late as 1940, in Tanganyika, once pulmonary tuberculosis was diagnosed, there was little likelihood of the patient surviving for more than a couple of years or so.

Pumu is often used for "asthma"; but the symptoms given do not fit this condition. Certainly asthma is normally worse, not in the rains, but rather in the dry season; nor is diarrhea or diabetes consistent with asthma. The use of the words *pumu*, *pumzi*, and *pumzika* make it clear that the reference is to a respiratory disease or group of diseases; but we cannot be certain of the exact meaning of the phrases "his breathing" (*pumzi*) is *juu kwa juu* or that "he breathes (*hupumzika*) like a cat." The breathing of a cat has many forms— quick, gasping, purring, spitting, and so forth. The description may be a reference to some psychosomatic condition or gastroenteritis or to tracheitis complicating some dehydrating disease, such as typhoid or diabetes.

12. *Kiunza*—the board that closes the niche in the side of the grave.

13. The description of whitlows is very interesting. Poulticing with shark oil may have a fair amount of sense in it, particularly as for a long time vitamin A was commonly used for skin lesions in Africa, and shark oil does contain a lot of vitamin A. The use of *tungufa*, "sodom apple" (*Solanum bojeri*), for this is

noteworthy. It is recommended sometimes for warts, but not for septic conditions.

14. *Baridi yabisi* (dry cold) is the established term for "rheumatism." The description of rheumatism is fascinating. It is not necessarily a clear diagnostic category in Western medicine. He is perhaps thinking of rheumatic heart disease, and it is interesting that they should associate the heart disease with rheumatic symptoms; but of course it is wrong to say that the patient recovers from that in about a month. He or she may recover from the acute attack in that time; but usually it goes on for a very long period indeed. Since he does not mention limb pains, though, he may be referring to a wide range of psychosomatic illnesses.

15. *Baridi ya rutuba* (wet cold) is usually translated "dropsy." Here it apparently means hepatitis as well as dropsy, though cirrhosis of the liver is a possibility. Regarding the reference to the face of the patient going yellow and his being forbidden to eat fat meat or butter, they obviously recognized that these foods were bad for patients with jaundice. True dropsy, where you have salt retention in the body, is an indication for reducing the salt in the diet, and that is recognized here. Mtoro's statement that salt will contribute to swelling is a fine chemical observation. The avoidance of sitting still with dropsy is consistent with current awareness of the hazard of deep vein thrombosis in dropsy and the preventative benefit of avoiding immobilization.

16. *Tambaa*, the root, means "to creep." *Tambazi*—according to the *Standard Swahili-English Dictionary*, this means an abscess of some sort; but it is not clear what kind of abscess it is that starts in the belly and then bursts on the surface. Dr. White used to think of tambazi as a sort of cellulitis, rather than an abcess (which was rare in African in those days), or, what is perhaps more likely, as a liver abscess associated with amebiasis—hence the value of charcoal in the dysentery of amebiasis or any other dysenteric condition. The description, however, is insufficient to allow us to be sure of what tambazi here really is.

17. "Charcoal," *mkaa*—perhaps just plain charcoal or charcoal made from the bark of an Indian tree sold by Indians.

18. Some think the name *tende* or *matende* might be due to the resemblance of the knots of enlarged glands that patients get in the early stages to bunches of dates (tende); but this only adds to Mtoro's etymologies.

19. *Safura* ("jaundice")—here it says that at first the patient has swellings all over. This is of course dropsy. Dr. White has seen a few, not many, patients with infectious hepatitis who have started off with generalized edema. It is interesting that this had been noticed by the Swahili. They do not turn yellow because the limbs are full of pus, but because of bile pigment in the bloodstream. This pigment is derived from the coloring matter of the blood, hemoglobin, and jaundice is a debilitating disease. It is quite sensible to give iron in some form, and obviously they had noticed the value of syrup; as we know today, sugar does protect the liver from infection to some extent. If, however, the ailment is not infectious hepatitis but active hepatitis super-

imposed on chronic liver disease with dropsy, iron therapy has no established value here.

20. *Jongo*—usually translated "gout," but this description does not fit gout. Dr. White thinks this is a description of some kind of cramp. The rubbing in of castor oil is a useful form of massage. We do not know why something heavy is put on the back or the chest; but it is of interest that the Arabs, in the treatment of what we now know under the name of slipped disc (not very good terminology), recommended standing on the patient's back to relieve low back pains, so something heavy on the back would be considered useful for the muscular spasms of lumbago associated with disc lesion.

21. Herpes—to grind copper coins and to apply the water to the sores is a form of mild antiseptic. It probably did no harm and may have done some good. Herpes zoster (shingles) does affect the area supplied by certain nerves, and so does leprosy. It may be that there is confusion here between herpes and the early stages of leprosy; but the two diseases are of course quite distinct, and one does not turn into the other. *Choa* can also mean "fungus."

22. Prickly heat—The treatment is sensible, to cool the skin. Obese people whose ancestors came from cooler climes suffer especially. Mtoro gives the only type of effective treatment available even now.

23. Fits—there are superstition and confusion here. Fits may be due to fevers; they may be due to epilepsy; they may be due to specific diseases, like meningitis or even rabies.

24. The description of a wart as a pimple with a hard top is a very nice one. It can of course be cut off with a razor. The subsequent part of the treatment is rather dubious.

25. A squint can only be cured operatively, and they would not have had any operative treatment.

26. *Mwingajini*—*Cassia occidentalis*. *Mkablishemsi* etymologically suggests some kind of sunflower, a well-known medicinal plant. "The treatment is applied first to the good eye and then to the other"—this is very good counsel indeed, because a conjunctivitis can be transferred from one eye to the other, and if the fingers (or something containing the medicine) touch the bad eye first and then are applied to the good eye, they can transfer the infection. It is a good principle to treat both eyes, because of the likelihood of the patient rubbing the eye and transferring the infection to the other.

27. Deafness, of course, is not always caused by an insect entering the ear; but the treatment for this horribly unpleasant condition is sensible.

28. That there is no cure for dumbness may very well be true in the majority of cases. People often seek a cure for a short frenum to the tongue in babies, fearing it will prevent them speaking. Many healers cut the tongue, but usually it will grow and not cause any speech difficulty.

29. Madness—the Swahili treatment was no more sensible or effective than some contemporary Western practice.

30. "Droppings"—literally "saliva." Cf. V 212.

31. The chigoe flea.

20. Of Burial

1. This part of the treatment of burial is straightforwardly Islamic, though traditional features peep through here and there (see the Bibliography). It is sad that so few dirges are given. Perhaps the Islamic reformers had made their influence felt here most, or perhaps Mtoro is being deliberately guarded.

2. "Nor are slaves"—[as an indication of "belonging," to have a family burial plot was second only to having a central stone-built house or a mosque associated with your name.—J. de V. A.]

3. "Jamvi"—a piece of plaited matting made from coconut fronds. The watani are what are termed "joking relations." This is adequate enough when a man is allowed obscene jokes with someone else's womenfolk, but hardly describes the special relationship of these people who have certain rights and duties in connection with death. (We saw also how they mocked an impotent bridegroom, V 115. Their presence at funerals and their fees are mentioned at V 215 and 220, and their fee in blood brotherhood at V 252.)

4. "Threefold protection"—at the doorstep they lift the bier (janeza) up and down three times. This is vaguely interpreted as apotropaic of spirits and probably goes back to very ancient ideas of spirits who crouch at thresholds (cf. Gen. 4:7). It is a worldwide belief found to this day, for instance, in Bangkok.

5. The pot of water may in some sense represent the soul? The text can be taken to imply that the bier was placed inside the mosque area and then taken to the burial and that the bereaved spouse is at the burial. [In the past most mosques had a women's section. Then perhaps in the eighteenth, but probably in the nineteenth, century, in some places (e.g., Lamu) they had their own separate mosques. By 1900 it would be very unusual for women and men to enter the same mosque. Today the position is changing slightly, but on the whole women do not attend mosques but pray at home.—J. de V. A.]

6. Mashambizo means "washing," for the cloths partake of the numen of death.

7. "Canopy," ukingo—at V 117 we read that the bride went to her husband's house in a canopy. We may compare the archuated lintel or canopy arch over royalty in Byzantine iconography and the tabernacle in Christian eucharistic art.

8. "Pea leaves"—the female pudenda.

9. "Alms"—sadaka. Hitima from Arabic khitima—recitation of portions of the Qur'an. "Party," karamu—an act of generosity consisting of providing food for all and sundry, especially the poor.

10. "Sorcerers," wanga—the exact difference between sorcery and witchcraft in Swahili is as imprecise as it is in nontechnical English. A little later the text uses mchawi (more strictly "sorcerer") as a synonym of mwanga.

11. The case of Mother of Abraham (in former times a woman was addressed as "daughter of———" until she became "mother of———"; only very close friends used personal names, and then rarely) upsets standard

theories in that she was young, married, and the mother of a child. A witch, according to the textbooks, is usually a frustrated marginal or fringe person. Bwana Mtoro takes it that in the end she had *maradi ya wazimu*, an illness connected with the shades.

12. "Condolence," *tanzia*. For the nasalization we may compare *tumbako*, *jampan*, "tobacco," "Japan."

13. "Truly we belong to God, and truly we return to him. This is the way of the world and of the hereafter."

14. "Jumbe"—a chief. See chap. 7, n. 2 (V 122) and the next chapter. On the musical instruments mentioned, see Appendix III.

15. Anon. DSM says that the custom of removing clothes at funerals is peculiar to the shomvi (chiefly persons) and is not universal.

16. "To play cards and the great drum"—this zeugma is in the original text.

17. Not to be seen publicly eating is a feature of old African kingship found as far westward as Lake Chad. A sharifu is a descendant of Hasan, the Prophet's eldest grandson.

18. "Pebbles"—normally small bits of hard coral.

21. *Of the* Jumbe

1. The jumbeate is a fascinating institution: it had commercial as well as religious features. Many details remain a mystery. In some ways this chapter is sadly incomplete and abbreviated, but the *Desturi* was not meant to be long or exhaustive.

2. "Mkomatembo"—a personage who figures in the local lore and genealogies of Bagamoyo in the 1880s. His name seems to be connected with some feat as a killer of elephants. [It may mean "beer of the doum palm." —J. de V. A.] Makame of Shani was jumbe of Winde and Ukasimu of Shanga. The kishina and the mwanamama are dances with drumming.

3. Dr. Knappert points out this is a proverb referring to the wisdom of keeping secrets, a vital quality in a chief. He needs the discretion as well as the caution of a man dealing with his wife's mother, the patience and perseverance of a shrimp fisher.

4. "Common folk," "commoners"—Swahili *vijana*, "the youth, the people bearing arms," as compared with the children and the old.

5. "To purchase or to rent"—[as *konde* or *shamba*, see chap. 17, n. 12.— J. de V. A.]

6. *Ubani*—literally "incense," here "tip."

7. Field inquiry on the spot leads one to think the salt was sea salt deposited as the brackish soil dried out.

8. It is difficult to tell what this ceremony was, as Mtoro's language is carefully guarded. Clearly it was some propitiation of ancestor spirits.

296

NOTES

22. Of Taxes and Tolls

1. "The sayyid" is the sultan of Zanzibar, who claimed descent from
Husain, the Prophet's grandson.
Farasila—about thirty five pounds avoirdupois, or 16 kilograms.
2. The European and American "explorers" (who were following mainly
in the tracks of "Arabs," who were largely Swahili) as little understood *bongo*
as the poor Africans were to understand the hut tax introduced by the colonial
powers (in the following paragraph).
3. "Kitambi"—pieces of cloth.
4. Bwana Mtoro's apologia for the colonial government no doubt exposes
him to the accusation of being a "lesser running dog of the hated imperialists."
It is, however, one of the few testimonies left by these unfortunate middlemen
who believed in the virtues of progress and development. (Even Matthew the
tax collector had little praise for his own kind in his gospel.)

23. Swahili Journeys

1. The Swahili were great travelers, though before the nineteenth century
they did not go inland. This may have been owing in part to the relative lack of
usable firearms in the pre-Omani period. Again, the cheap Manchester and
American cotton cloth and Indian goods were probably not available in
sufficient quantity to make the journeys worthwhile—J. de V. A.]. They
were also great colonizers and missionaries too, introducing rice and tomatoes
and founding Ugandan and Zaïrean Islam.
2. The omens given are unexpected in places. For instance, it is not in
many traditional societies that meeting a woman is considered auspicious,
even one with goods in her hands. In the matter of omens and superstitions, it
is perhaps salutary to recall that in the West, there is usually no row 13 in a
great jet and that tall buildings often have no floor 13.
3. It is said that Gauguin, having taken to himself a Tahitian *vahenge* of no
great age, went fishing. He caught a certain fish, and his fellow fishermen told
the painter that this meant his lady was lying with another man. On returning
home, for a joke, he accused her. She confessed.
4. *Matanohi*—"bittern," further north known as *mumbi*.
5. *Shorwe*—east-coast black-capped bulbul, a fruit eater.
6. Indians of various kinds flit in and out of Bwana Mtoro's pages. Once
again he is precise in his use of terms and seems to know which of the Indians
were Muslim (Khoja Ismaili, Ithna^{c}asheri, Bohra) and which Hindu. Gujer-
atis had been on the East African coast for centuries. From at least Sayyid
Said's day onward they provided the capital and loans that enabled the
Swahili to undertake their amazing inland expeditions up to the great lakes
and beyond. In due time they outfitted the European and American adventur-
ers as well and assisted with the commissariat for railway and empire builders,
the "pacifiers," the expeditionary forces of World War I, and the settlement of
the Highlands. They have been little understood and loved by either African

or European. *Mukki* is probably *Mukhi*, a term of official honor in an Indian *jamaat*.

7. *Kareati, buraa*, etc.—various types of cotton cloths, mostly originally from Indian looms, but mill-made materials from Lancashire and New England were competing and taking over as European domination grew.

8. "Your shades are alive"—*vivuli vizima*. A somewhat un-Islamic sentiment, but the ancestors are to be "placated" on return with sadaka and a Qur'an reading.

9. *Kome*—a staff carrying a flag and some charms.

"Nyamwezi"—a conglomeration of African peoples around Tabora-Kazeh loosely given this blanket title, who provided porters and were themselves engaged in trade from the coast to the river Congo and beyond.

10. "Nyanyembe"—Unyanyembe is marked by atlas makers as due south of Lake Victoria on the caravan route between Ujiji on Lake Tanganyika and Bagamoyo.

11. "Kitambi"—length of cloth five to six dhiraa (cubits of eighteen inches) long.

12. "Dear merchant"—*Jenab Tajiri. Jenab* is a recognized honorific among Islamized Indians.

13. "Mpwapwa"—a stage on the great caravan route across Tanganyika from the sea to the great lakes. It lost importance once the railway was built.

14. "Maniema"—a region of the Lualaba-Lomami area where the Swahili and Arabs purchased ivory and slaves.

15. "Nguu—these are presumably the Nguu hills north of Morogoro.

"Uhehe"—in south central Tanzania in the bend of the upper Rufiji. Mtoro is indicating that they no longer went on the far expeditions.

16. "Rods," "sticks"—these are six-foot-long poles lashed to a load. The porter can use them to balance the load on his head or to rest it with the ends of the poles on the ground.

17. *Ngara*—the ornamental headdress worn on special occasions.

18. Mtoro does not fully understand the customs of the Nyamwezi but records them faithfully. A man who every year or two has to leave his womenfolk to travel for six to twelve months develops a ritual. Just before he leaves, to make the parting possible, he creates a kind of symbolic altercation so that he can get away without breaking down. At a moment of weakness he covers himself, hiding from the spirits who are powerful and can do harm. An offering is also made to the spirits of the way.

19. Appropriately, the songs are in a Swahili that contains a Kinyamwezi admixture. The Nyamwezi as men in the middle sing songs that insult both the coasters and the inlanders.

24. Of Blood Brotherhood among the Swahili

1. The making of blood brotherhood is a fairly widespread custom in various parts of Africa. Its symbolism is pretty obvious. An animal's blood is

poured out, its flesh is separated up, a vital organ such as the liver is shared between the prospective "brothers"—after a blood-causing incision has been made in each of them and the blood put on the meat. At the end Bwana Mtoro gives a Muslim alternative to the ceremony, for blood eating even in symbolic form is abhorrent to a person of Muslim background.

2. "Watani"—the so-called joking relations.

25. Of Slavery

1. Bwana Mtoro's account of slavery is of great importance because it is by an African who had firsthand experience (we saw above how his slave saved his life while they were out collecting taxes for the Germans). Slavery was basic to many of the old African societies, as indeed it had been throughout the world. The Qur'an and the *sunnah* accept slavery but make it plain that Allah has no more love of it than he has of divorce and that Allah, of all good acts, loves most to see persons given their freedom. African traditional slavery and Islamic slavery could easily be reconciled and the slave given the rights Islam guarantees him or her. Basically, Christianity denies that in the spirit there can be such a thing as either slavery or divorce: starry-eyed idealism can be accompanied by a most horrible reality, however, as is demonstrated by the old transatlantic slave trade and the present divorce industry. [In the Swahili case we have to bear in mind that there was no prison system (apart from the stocks referred to below) and no capital punishment. It is also true that slavery as practiced by the Swahili themselves (as opposed to the slave trade) was of a relatively humane and assimilative type. This does not mean that it did not have unpleasant aspects, and these probably increased as Arabs deeply involved in the trade came to dominate the coast during the nineteenth century—J. de V. A.] The final comment on the late Arab-dominated East African slave trade and the racism that followed it was the genocide of the Arab in Zanzibar at the Revolution of 1964. An old Asian, outside the Bait-ul-Ajaib at Zanzibar's capital, remarked in 1976, "The streets literally ran with the blood of the children of the slave owners." For the wickedness of American slavery (both Northern and Southern) one blames not Christianity but the Americans; for the amelioration of slavery in West Asia one praises not Arabs or Persians but Islam.

2. Mtoro correctly distinguishes two types of mzalia, those who were still slaves (first through sixth generations) and those who were free (the seventh generation), but his representation is extremely condensed.

3. "Customs," *desturi za watu*—literally "customs of human beings."
"Raw slaves"—*mjinga*.

4. We may compare the various Delhi and Zanzibar sultans who were the sons of slave women or concubines. There is oral tradition in Buganda that a certain great Kabaka was the son of a slave woman, whom his father sold to the coast people. Others say this is mere calumny.

5. *Pepeta*—grains of rice, seed rice, hence a special preparation of green rice, used as a quasi-sacramental gift—for instance, to mark a very special friendship.

Msima—a spike of young sorghum, here indicating a small proportion as a kind of tip.

6. "Kanzu"—a long shirt. Velten notes that Msengesi was an Arab of Zanzibar noted as a pederast.

7. "Silver dollar," *riale ya Shami*—Syrian riale, properly the Maria Theresa dollar, though Zanzibar and German East Africa had such coins.

8. "Kanga"—the piece of cloth worn by a free woman when not in public. She wears one around her from ankle to breast, another over her shoulders or head. Their gay and lively colors contrast both with the black street overall worn by respectable Muslim women in public and the greater nakedness of a slave woman. The *kaya* is the headcloth worn by a free woman, not a slave. [The *buibui*, or black veil, was imported from Shihr under the influence of Hadhrami sharifs only about 1910. Before that only Hadhrami women wore it, and in Lamu it was still not worn by a majority of women, according to Frau Ruth Dammann, as late as 1936.—J. de V. A.]

9. "Free birth is matrilineal" is more African than Islamic.

10. Ya sini—sura 36. The power of the Qur'an reinforces the sympathetic magic of the knotting.

26. Of Generosity

1. Of *ukarimu*, "generosity, hospitality": Here we have another example of how Islam can seek out and reinforce the finest in African traditions. [The extremely important role of hospitality in Swahili society may be traced to historical causes, namely chronic lack of manpower in most Swahili settlements, and the key cultural (as opposed to economic) role of trade in that society.—J. de V. A.]

2. Anyone who has wandered from country to country without secure citizenship must envy the stranger and pilgrim sojourning in Swahili lands.

3. This manner of cooking is a sign of particular favor and affection.

4. "Kibaba"—about a pint, here used as a measure of food.

5. "On the fourth day, the hoe"—quoted as a proverb by Dr. Julius Nyerere. Even an honored guest must work eventually. See V 186 for a combination of this song with the following one, wherein the guest is welcomed on the first visit, or until "his return home"—a none-too-subtle hint.

6. To hide in this way is as sinful as being a miser or a usurer.

27. Of Vows

1. "The wind"—*upepo*. See chap. 13, n. 1. "Sharifu"—a descendent of the Prophet who himself possessed power.

2. "Vows"—*naziri.* The vows mentioned here are typically Islamic (cf. V 21, n. 23).

3. "Hal Badiri"—sura 3: Egyptian 119f., Indian 123, mentions the Battle of Badr by name, but it is referred to by implication in other places, for instance in 8:5–19, 42–48. A catena from the Qur'an, recited with intention to assist the righteous and discomfort the sinners, could be used to discover stolen or strayed property.

28. Of Oaths and Ordeals

1. The English word *ordeal*, if not used as a cliché, brings to mind pain and suffering. The German *Gottesurteil* is nearer the original meaning. It is a means of letting the truth be known.

2. "Magician" is here used to translate *mwanga. Mganga,* which has consistently been translated "doctor," is once translated "magician" because the sense so demands it here. The Swahili has been inserted a few times to enable the purist to keep track.

3. Sura 17: Egyptian 83, Indian 81—"And say: 'Truth has arrived, and falsehood has disappeared,' for, verily, falsehood must disappear." The African doctor (mganga) is happy to make use of the Qur'an to reinforce his oracle. Among the Yoruba, touching iron is also used in this kind of way.

4. The Qur'an teacher (mwalimu) is again found functioning side by side with the mganga.

5. Ya sini—sura 36. We may suppose that someone who knew he or she was guilty would out of fear have a dry mouth to begin with, whereas a person sure of his or her innocence would normally have a damp mouth.

6. *Sanga*—a very large needle. The more cruel and dangerous ordeals seem to come from inland.

7. "Lady Makuka"—a woman who died in the distant past in Bagamoyo. Dungumaro and Punda are pepo.

8. Rustics and women use these oaths but *wanaume,* "men," swear by Allah.

29. Examples of Swahili Beliefs about God's Creation

1. The author's (one suspects from the style that this chapter is not by Bwana Mtoro) "scientific," modernistic superciliousness in this chapter is, happily, an isolated instance. Presumably it is only those who can be dated as "modern" who insist on treating their great-grandparents' myths as if they were their ancestors' science. For the basic traditional Islamic teachings see s.v. *khusuf,* "eclipses," and related words in the standard works of reference mentioned in the Bibliography. [The Qur'an mentions that a darkening of the sun and/or moon will precede the end of the world, hence the nervousness and prayer when such a thing occurs.—J. de V. A.]

2. If "beanstalk" here symbolizes the path of the rising moon, the meaning is that they had hardly seen the moon.

3. *Ulimwengu, ule mawingu*—the Swahili are passionate etymologizers. Taking *ulimwengu* another way gives us *ulimwe*, "cultivated land," from *kulima*, "to cultivate." *Nguu* means "hill." That the earth is supported on the horns of a cow is common "Muslim world" mythology.

4. We are, after all, at sea on the same ocean that Sindbad sailed. The *Desturi* does not give us much inkling of the great myths and legends of his people or of their epics and poetry. In fairness, however, this is not to be expected from a book concerned with customs.

5. The chapter heading in German is finer—*Donner und Blitzen*. For the "use" of lightning mentioned, no explanation has been found. In the distant background there may be some idea of metal derived from meteorites. Anon. DSM says that this metal is derived from the captains of Arab ships (*bedeni*). *Suwesi*, iron and steel of excellent quality, is connected with Suez or possibly the Swiss.

6. This belief about shooting stars is also to be found in many parts of "the Muslim world."

7. African theologians like J. S. Mbiti insist that the ancestors were venerated, not worshiped. Here we may take it that the ancestors are revered and approached, but a careful addendum has been made to indicate that it is their prayer to God which assists with the blessing of rain. The ox is slaughtered at the graves with a fatiha and Islamic ritual. Islam and African Traditional Religion have meshed excellently here. Stories of African kingdoms that accepted Islam when a Muslim's prayer brought rain abound in West Africa.

8. We may compare the red heifer and its ashes in the Pentateuch, Deuteronomy, chap. 21, and Numbers, chap. 19. [The ox-killing ceremony is tremendously important in Swahili culture. It may well be pre-Islamic. In Mombasa, Zanzibar, and other towns it is associated with the beginning of the old Swahili (not Islamic) New Year. Elsewhere it has been adapted to serve other functions. Dr. El-Zein thinks the Lamu wa-ungwana use it to snub the sharifs; I do not agree with him. Swahili poetry is also full of less-than-clear references to young bulls, which presumably hide some folk symbolism. Mtoro is here arguably playing down its non-Islamic aspects, as indeed, until a few years ago, did everyone else—J. de V. A.] Dr. Knappert points out the ox also functioned in a similar way in ancient Arabia; see *Encyclopedia of Islam* 4 (Leiden, 1974):270.

9. Ya sini—sura 36. For the standard Islamic teaching on prayer for rain, see the *Encyclopedia of Islam* and T. P. Hughes, *Dictionary of Islam* (London, 1895) s.v. *salat 'l-Istisga* and commentaries on sura 7:55−57. *Burdai*, also spelled *burudai*—prayers for cooling, refreshing (compare Tertullian's use of the root -*refrig*), hence forgiveness, reconciliation, and accompanying benefits.

30. Of High Days

1. As one would expect from their history, the Swahili have a complicated calendar system. There is a year connected with rain and heat, with the winds and seasons for sailing, with some former Shia[c] Islamic and Persian influences that are being hotly discussed, with the Islamic general calendar, and with the European. The Swahili New Year celebration has some of the characteristics of the old Iranian *Nauroz*, but one must be beware of trying to link them too closely.

2. This song is sung by a school group of serenaders, who are asking for alms that will be passed on (it is hoped) to the teacher. The second half of the song is a challenge to another group.

3. Akida Abdallah was a corrupt petty official about whom nothing further is known.

4. Magubeda was a man who loved this kind of fish.

5. Here Mtoro gives the hours by Swahili rekoning. This meal is from 9 to 10 P.M. *Futari* is from the Arabic *iftār*, "breaking fast." The observances for Ramadhan and the Feasts (*[c]idain*), which are great events on the coast, are standardly Islamic with the exception of the dances. Mtoro does not give any detail on the second great festival, *Idd-ul-Haj*.

6. *Bembe*—the coaxing delicacies sent to somebody one loves or wishes to honor. [Nowadays in Kenya it means any little snack eaten in any evening during Ramadhan, although it is true there is a special celebration on the twenty-seventh.—J. de V. A.]

7. "Penalty," *kafara*—from the Semitic root for at-one-ment by "covering." "Kibaba"—about a pint.

31. Double Meanings

1. Apart from this first example, this collection of proverbs is not very inspired. This is a pity, since we are dealing with a continent where the word is power and life, and exquisite riches are enshrined in proverbs. The reader may be able to augment this Spartan serving by consuming something from the collections mentioned in the Bibliography.

2. Compare the Ashanti proverb (sometimes adapted to beards): When your neighbor's thatch is afire, keep a bucket handy to douse your own.

3. Compare the Ashanti gold weight showing the puff adder, who cannot fly, catching the sunbird.

32. Our Restraints in the Past

1. "Sorcerer"—*mchawi*. "Charged with casting a spell"—the verb root *roga* is used throughout this paragraph.

2. Death by burning is looked upon in Islam as a very cruel and unusual punishment.

3. The Liwali was an official appointed by the sultan of Zanzibar. "Gandalo" is the Swahili expression, *mqatale* the Arabic. The pima is about six feet.

4. "Officer," *Jemadar*—a rank retained by the British Indian Army. His troops were Baluchis from the Makran coast of Pakistan. A street in Bagamoyo is still named after them—or, rather, after their descendants who settled there.

33. Of the Law of Stealing

1. This is an important chronological notice and witnesses to the antiquity of the *shariᶜa* in the Swahili lands.

2. "Custom," *mila*, is contrasted with law (shariᶜa) above, which is pretty strictly Islamic. The writer fails, however, to mention the all-important matter of witnesses.

34. Of Assault and Homicide

1. *Pazi*, "magistrate"—we can gather from the gloss below, *pazi, ndio hakim*, and the internal evidence that he was a leader or elder with some armed men who could act for him. Bwana Idi says he was a clan head. Early German documents indicate he was the paramount chief of the Zaramo population.

2. As severe as Islamic law sometimes seems to be, everything is done by due process, and it is sometimes milder than the traditional law, or mila (cf. ᶜurfi law in Arabia), which, like the oldest part of the Pentateuch, is often a *lex talionis*. Earlier this century both Westerners and many Muslims looked askance at Muslim law. Kemal Ataturk summarily swept it aside as the enemy of "modernization." Today in Saudi Arabia and Pakistan, as well as in other places, people are reasserting it, pointing to the vandalism, looting, rape, crowded prisons, and choked courts of the Western world.

35. The Customary Law of Debt

1. "An Indian or a Hindu," *mhindi au banyani*—the phrase indicates that Mwalimu Baraka bin Shomari was able to differentiate between Indians in general and *banians*. Mtoro's Indian merchants appear to have been Muslim *khojas* rather than banians.

Appendix I. The Swahili World of Mtoro bin Mwinyi Bakari

1. For Velten's description of Mtoro and his other collaborators as "pure Swahili persons," while Bwana Idi Marijani of Bagamoyo described him as a Zaramo, see Preface, pp. ix–xi and nn. 6 and 7.

2. For some of the more recent contributions to this debate, see W. Arens,

"The Waswahili: The Social History of an Ethnic Group," *Africa* 45.4 (1975); C. Eastman, "Who Are the Waswahili?" *Africa* 41.3 (1971); and "Ethnicity and the Social Scientist," *African Studies Review*, vol. 18, no. 1 (1975); F. F. Madoshi, "The Meaning of the Word *Mswahili*," *Kiswahili*, vol. 41, no. 1 (1971); and Ibrahim Noor Shariff, "Waswahili and their Language: Some Misconceptions," *Kiswahili*, vol. 43, no. 2 (1973).

3. See J. de V. Allen, "Town and Country in Swahili Culture," in *Symposium Leo Frobenius*, (Cologne and Yaounde, 1974).

4. For the organization and importance of agriculture in the typical Swahili economy, see M. Ylvisaker, *Lamu in the 19th Century: Land, Trade, and Politics* (Boston, 1979), and J. de V. Allen, "Swahili Culture and the Nature of East Coast Settlement," *International Journal of African Historical Studies* (in press).

5. See F. Cooper, *Plantation Slavery on the East Coast of Africa*, (New Haven, 1977).

6. I call them Shirazi-Swahilis to distinguish them from the elusive category of people who appeared from time to time in British colonial census reports as "Swahili-Shirazis," which seems to have meant those very few Swahilis who could not be subsumed as "Arabs" or members of any other tribe. For previous studies of the Shirazis, see A. H. J. Prins, *Swahili-speaking Peoples of Zanzibar and the East African Coast*, 2d ed. (London, 1967), especially pp. 13–14 and 94–97; G. L. T. Wijeyewardene, "Some Aspects of Village Solidarity among Ki-Swahili Speaking Communities of Kenya and Tanganyika" (Ph.D. diss. Cambridge University, 1961); W. F. McKay, "A Pre-colonial History of the Southern Kenya Coast" (Ph.D. diss. Boston University, 1975); and A. P. Bailey (née Caplan), "Land Tenure: Its Sociological Implications with Special Reference to the Swahili-speaking Peoples of the East African Coast" (M.A. thesis, London School of Oriental and African Studies, 1965), as well as the earlier works cited elsewhere.

7. See W. Ingrams, *Zanzibar, Its History and Its People* (London, 1931), p. 129, citing Burton. F. B. Pearce, *Zanzibar, The Island Metropolis of Eastern Africa* (London, 1920), which is replete with Social Darwinist arguments for a Persian "Shirazi" culture in East Africa. See especially pp. 250–252, 351–352, and 414.

8. J. S. Kirkman in J. Strandes, *The Portuguese Period in East Africa*, ed. J. S. Kirkman (Nairobi, 1968), pp. 309–310.

9. See H. N. Chittick, "The 'Shirazi' colonisation of East Africa," *Journal of African History*, vol. 6, no. 3 (1965) for the classic statement of this theory.

10. This view is to some extent confirmed by the large number of oral sources that go on to equate Shiraz with *Arabuni* ("Arab lands") and even, in some cases, Mecca. For a good discussion of the whole question, see McKay, "Southern Kenya Coast," especially pp. 25–30 and 42.

11. See G. L. T. Wijeyewardene, "Administration and Politics in Two Swahili Communities" (Paper delivered at the East African Institute of Social Research Conference, January 1959).

12. A. C. Hollis, "Notes on the History of the wa-Vumba, East Africa," *Journal of the Royal Anthropological Institute* 30 (1900); but see also H. E. Lambert, "The Taking of Tumbe Town" *Bulletin of the East African Interregional Swahili Committee* 23 (1953); 36—46.

13. Ingrams, *Zanzibar*, p. 129, who, however, notes that in Pemba only some of the leading families have Shirazi myths, in Zanzibar fewer still.

14. McKay, "Southern Kenya Coast," p. 34.

15. McKay, "Southern Kenya Coast," pp. 57—60. The post-1630 Diwanis belonged to the Ba-Alawi lineage of sharifs, which could trace its descent back to Inat in Hadhramawt, but their ancestors had probably lived for some generations in Pate or Kau-Ozi before coming to Vumba.

16. For recent discussions, see McKay, "Southern Kenya Coast," pp. 47—52; T. J. Hinnebusch, "The Shungwaya Hypothesis: A Linguistic Reappraisal," in *East Africa Culture History*, ed. J. T. Gallagher (Syracuse, 1976); and T. T. Spear, "Traditional Myths and Linguistic Analysis: Singwaya Revisited," *History in Africa* 4 (1977), and *The Kaya Complex* (Nairobi, 1978), pp. 35—38.

17. A. C. Hollis, "History of the wa-Vumba'; A. H. J. Prins, *Swahili-speaking Peoples*, pp. 95—96.

18. H. E. Lambert, *Studies in Swahili Dialects V: Chi-Chifundi*, East African Swahili Committee (Kampala, 1958) is the classic study of the Chi-Chifundi, or Shirazi, dialect. W. H. Whiteley, in his study of the neighboring Ki-Mtangata dialect, *Studies in Swahili Dialects I: Ki-Mtangata*, East African Swahili Committee (Kampala, 1956), p. 4, gives evidence of the volatile nature of Swahili dialects. Evidence for classifying Ki-Vumba as a southern dialect (which would mean that most of the leading wa-Vumba must have adopted it after their arrival from the Kau-Ozi region in the north) is to be found in H. E. Lambert's *Studies in Swahili Dialects II: Ki-Vumba*, East African Swahili Committee (Kampala, 1957).

19. *Shaha* is usually so spelled by Western scholars because they have convinced themselves it is connected with the Persian term *shah*. *Sheha*, a Shirazi-Swahili dialect version of the Arabic word *sheikh* (of which the Bajuni dialect version, for instance, is *shee*) seems to me much more likely.

20. These and other titles are discussed by A. H. J. Prins, *Swahili-speaking Peoples*, p. 96.

21. The passage in the *Pate Chronicle* which states that the existence of jumbes in the southern Swahili world is evidence that it was once ruled by Pate, since these were all originally agents of the Pate *yumbe*, or council, can, I think, safely be dismissed as a typical piece of Pate chauvinism. It is curious and perhaps significant, though, that the term *Diwan*, which in Persia means a council (or one of the public buildings associated with it), should also be applied in Vumba (and later among the Shirazi-Swahili confederations) to mean the ruler's person. Prins's suggestion that the two terms in fact mean something like "jumbe/Dewan in council," i.e., acting with his title-holding

supporters, is unsupported elsewhere and does not seem altogether plausible.

22. For a discussion of the mwinyimkuu of Zanzibar, see Ingrams, *Zanzibar*, pp. 147–153.

23. Though they existed, the wa-ungwana, for the concept of u-ungwana, is mentioned in the following places in the text: V 24, V 86, V 94, V 122–123, V 184, V 222, and V 231. What may well be a valuable text, from the point of view of enabling us to unravel the complex political institutions of the region in an earlier age, is the proclamation of the installation of a new jumbe set out in V 222. This suggests that the wa-ungwana may have been associated only with certain settlements or locations.

24. See J. de V. Allen, "The Swahili House: Cultural and Ritual Concepts Underlying Its Plan and Structure," in J. de V. Allen and T. H. Wilson (eds.) *Swahili Houses and Tombs of the Coast of Kenya*, Art and Archaeology Research Papers (London, 1979).

25. The ruins of numerous stone mosques and tombs remain. See the appendix in McKay, "Southern Kenya Coast." The only evidence that there were ever stone houses in the region is the passage from Hollis cited above, n. 12. The absence of the ruins of stone houses does not mean, however, that they could not have existed, for it is permissible to use the stone from ruined houses for other purposes—to strengthen mud and thatch houses, for instance, or, burned down and converted into lime, for walls or other types of buildings—whereas ruined mosques and tombs are traditionally not recycled, except perhaps for other mosques.

26. The only ancient settlement outside the Shirazi heartland whose description makes it sound as if it might have had a Shirazi-Swahili type of government is Mogadishu, as described by Ibn Battuta in the mid-fourteenth century. See G. S. P. Freeman-Grenville, *East African Coast: Select Documents*, 2d ed. (Oxford, 1966), pp. 27–31. A possible distinction between the Shirazi-Swahilis and those of the Lamu Archipelago is that the former laid more emphasis, among regalia instruments, upon drums, while the latter seem to have treated the side-blown horns, or siwas, as much more important.

27. As McKay pertinently observes: "People do not usually migrate and found towns, although this is invariably the way it is remembered in oral traditions" ("Southern Kenya Coast," p. 42).

28. There appear to have been at least eight or nine pre-1630 stone-built settlements between Tanga and Bagamoyo (see H. N. Chittick, *Annual Report of the Antiquities Department, Tanganyika Government* [Dar-es-Salaam, 1958]). Unless we assume that some or all of these were of Shirazi-Swahili foundation in the centuries *before* the wa-Vumba established themselves in Vumba, thereby causing a Shirazi-Swahili dispersion, we must accept that they had been founded by some other Swahili subgroup but were so decayed by the seventeenth century that the incoming Shirazi-Swahilis were able to take over their government with little trouble.

29. Freeman-Grenville, *East African Coast*, pp. 238–240. See also

S. Feierman, *The Shambaa Kingdom, A History* (Madison, Wis., 1974), pp. 127–129, 133.

30. See chaps. 21–23 of the *Desturi*, especially V 227–228. Many of the items of which the jumbes managed to appropriate at least a share for themselves are the same as those upon which the Portuguese in earlier centuries had claimed a monopoly. See Freeman-Grenville, *East African Coast*, pp. 178–179, 184.

31. McKay, "Southern Kenya Coast," pp. iii, 66–68, 109–113, and passim.

32. Rainmaking is discussed at V 283–284, and divining is mentioned in a number of places. By the time Mtoro wrote, however, the curing of illnesses, the granting of protection against supernatural forces, and divining were largely the work of the mwalimu, that is, the religious teacher learned in Islamic books (who might well be a newcomer—see V 48–51—and an Arab or at least arabizer), whereas it is probable that in earlier centuries these functions had been more the province of the political leaders, the jumbes and their officers.

33. Hollis, "Notes on the wa-Vumba"; T. Ainsworth Dickson, "The Regalia of the wa-Vumba," *Man* 20 (1921).

34. The following sections of the *Desturi* touch on the magical and other means by which the Swahilis managed to monopolize the caravan trade: V 89–91; V 236–252.

35. For Ujiji and its culture, see S. Hino's three fascinating studies in *Kyoto University African Studies* 2 (1968): 51–154, and the companion study in the same journal, vol. 5 (1971), pp 1–30.

36. See J. de V. Allen, "Swahili Culture Reconsidered: Some Historical Implications of the Material Culture of the Northern Kenya Coast in the 18th and 19th Centuries," *Azania* 9 (1974).

37. Allen, "Swahili Culture Reconsidered," especially pp. 133–135. Sacleux's dictionary, based largely on research carried out in the 1890s in Zanzibar, gives the term *usta-arabu* (see under *S*), but describes it as *inusité*, that is, "little used" or perhaps "archaic." It may have had a limited use in earlier times (though I know of no example of it in the pre-1900 literature), but Krapf's dictionary, published in the 1880s and based largely on his experiences in the 1850s, does not mention it.

38. J. S. Trimingham, *Islam in East Africa* (Oxford, 1964), p. 22.

39. This date is somewhat arbitrary, but I would argue that the earliest Omani immigrants to acquire political power—e.g., the Nabahani dynasty of Pate—were, or soon became, completely acculturated. One or two groups, like the Mazrui of Mombasa and perhaps the earliest Omani governors of Zanzibar, likewise survived only by becoming at least partly acculturated. From about 1780, however, the attitude of the Omani newcomers changed, and they began to seize power at all costs and without any immediate concessions to their new subjects. No doubt the growth of the demand for

slaves, which enabled them to equip themselves with numerous firearms, was not unconnected with this new attitude.

40. Trimingham, *Islam in East Africa*, p. 73.

41. In Strandes, *Portuguese Period*, p. 313. Cp. Prins, *Swahili-speaking Peoples*, p. 11. For a controversial personal account of British colonial discrimination against non-"Arab" Swahilis, see Hyder Kindy, *Life and Politics in Mombasa* (Nairobi, 1972).

42. This simplistic pattern requires some refinement. It seems clear, for instance, that arabizing went ahead rapidly in Lamu, in the northern Swahili world, very shortly after the Omanis won a political foothold there in the 1812–1821 period. On the other hand, it is certainly true that—no doubt because of the relatively slight impact of British colonialism on the Lamu district—quite a number of people there had no doubts about their Swahili identity right up to the time of independence, despite Kirkman's assertions to the contrary. It was mostly the upper classes, in fact the wa-ungwana, who indulged in arabizing. Abdulhamid El-Zein, *The Sacred Meadows* (Chicago, 1974), even suggests that the "big" families of Lamu adopted their Arab family names only about this time.

43. See Alice Werner's entry under "Zanzibar" in *Encyclopaedia of Religion and Ethics* 12 (1919). Cp. Prins. *Swahili-speaking Peoples*, pp. 11–12, nn. 1, 4.

44. Ingrams, *Zanzibar*, p. 130. This is only one instance where this phenomenon is recorded.

45. See, for instance, V 15, V 64–65, V 121, V 147, V 210, V 254–255, V 303. Of all these references, only that in V 147 (where his Arab friend is mentioned only in passing, but where Mtoro himself obeys his mwalimu and defies an unorthodox Swahili custom regarding spirit reduction) does not imply at least a faint criticism of the Arabs.

46. The man responsible for the publication of Tippu Tip's autobiography was Professor Heinrich Brode. It seems not impossible that we have here one of those instances of foreign (in this instance, German colonial) scholars taking sides in an African cultural dispute. Brode may well have had sympathy with the arabizers; Velten almost certainly felt himself to be on the side of the antiarabizers.

47. Brode's first edition of this work was published in *Mitteilungen des Seminars für Orientalische Sprachen* (1902–1903) and was later expanded into the English biography by Brode which appeared as *Tippoo Tip* (London, 1907). The most recent edition, which is bilingual, is *Maisha ya Hamed Muhammed el Murjebi yaani Tippu Tip kwa maneno yake Mwenyewe*, ed. by W. H. Whiteley and published by the East African Literature Bureau (Nairobi, 1959; reprint eds. 1966, 1970, 1971).

48. See, for example, H. M. Stanley's description quoted in L. Farrant, *Tippu Tip and the East African Slave Trade* (London, 1975), p. ix and a number of other references in the same work.

49. Whiteley, *Maisha*, p. 17[n]. It is an easy step from this to the confusion, embarrassingly common among Europeans writing on nineteenth-century

Swahili society, of *freeman* with *freedman* (the latter implying slave origins); and Farrant, *Tippu Tip*, is only the latest of a series of writers to use the terms more or less indiscriminately. There is, of course, a world of difference between them, and no Swahili could seriously regard a freeman (*mu-ungwana*) as identical to a freedman (*mu-hadimu* is probably the nearest equivalent).

50. Whiteley, *Maisha*, pp. 140–141.

51. See n. 6 above. The trend has, of course, reversed itself to some extent, especially in Tanzania, since independence. Prins, *Swahili-speaking Peoples*, p. 12, n. 7a. One area where the term *Swahili* retained its flattering overtones throughout the colonial period was in the Tanganyikan interior, especially in towns like Ujiji, where colonialism had relatively little impact.

52. See E. Rzewuski, "*Asili ya Bangwana*—Origine des Bangwana," *Africana Bulletin* 21 (1974). *Bangwana* is the same word as *wa-ungwana* or *wangwana* in the Kisangani (Kingwana) dialect.

53. See the references cited in n. 2.

54. See, however, A. P. Caplan's "Boys' Circumcision and Girls' Puberty Rites among the Swahili of Mafia Island, Tanzania," *Africa* vol. 46, no. 1 (1976).

55. See, e.g., G.S.P. Freeman-Grenville's account in "The Coast, 1498–1840" in *The History of East Africa*, ed. R. Oliver and G. Mathew (Oxford, 1963), vol. 1, p. 168.

Appendix III. Ngoma: *Music and Dance*

1. There is nowadays, however, at least one imported drum, the *sambuku*, a small standing drum played with both the fingers and the palm of the hand and having a special skin pad. This is used for *tarabu* performances and is probably from India.

2. See J. de V. Allen, "A Note on the Nomenclature of Swahili Side-Blown Horns" in *African Musicology* 1 (in press).

3. W. H. Ingrams, *Zanzibar, Its History and Its People* (London 1931, repr. 1967). The relevant chapter on this subject is chap. 37, pp. 399–411, but most of the following chapter also concerns music and songs. See also A. H. J. Prins, *Swahili-speaking Peoples of Zanzibar and the East African Coast*, 2d ed. (London, 1967), pp. 112–113.

4. There is a considerable literature on this topic. A good summary is A. M. Jones, "The Influence of Indonesia: The Musicological Evidence Reconsidered," *Azania* 4 (1969): 131–145.

5. There is a dance called the manganja. As is often the case, there is a dispute as to whether it derives from the interior, specifically from the Maniema peoples of eastern Zaïre (so Ingrams, p. 407, where the dance is called Maniema or Kumba) or whether it comes from Kilwa (Sacleux).

6. A. C. Hollis, "Notes on the History of the *wa-Vumba*, East Africa," *Journal of the Royal Anthropological Institute* 30 (1900): 275–296: Ainsworth

Dickson, "The Regalia of the wa-Vumba," *Man* 20 (March 1921): 33–36.

7. For the problem of tambourines in Islam, see chap. 11, n. 8.

8. Transverse horns are reported from prehistoric Ireland and from South America, but not from any part of the world from which they could conceivably have spread by diffusion to the African continent. On the continent itself, however, they are widespread, from the east to the extreme west coast.

9. J. de V. Allen, "The *Siwas* of Pate and Lamu: Two Antique Side-Blown Horns from the Swahili Coast," *Art and Archaeology Research Papers* 9 (1976): 38–47; Hamo Sassoon, *The Siwas of Lamu, Two Historic Trumpets in Brass and Ivory* (Nairobi, 1975).

10. See Sassoon, *The Siwas of Lamu.*

11. C. H. Stigand, *Land of Zinj* (London, 1913; reprint ed., Cass, 1966), pp. 52–54; G. S. P. Freeman-Grenville, *The French at Kilwa Island* (Oxford, 1965), p. 37, quoting A. P. Lienhardt, *Oriental Art*, vol. 9, no. 2 (1963): 106, n. 2. For the many functions of Swahili regalias generally and siwas in particular, see J. de V. Allen, *Swahili Regalias* (Nairobi: Kenya Historical Association, forthcoming).

12. The gunda, too, is sometimes a drum in the hinterland of Mombasa and on the northern coast of Tanzania.

13. But Krapf associates the baragumu with war and general emergency.

14. Mtoro gives the proverb as written above. It appears elsewhere as *Mbiu ya mgambo akilia ina jambo*, but oddly enough, although *haina* is the negative form of *ina*, the meaning is hardly changed, since *jambo* may mean "news" or perhaps "slightly bad news" but certainly not very serious news. Thus *ina jambo* means "there is something up," while *haina jambo* means "there is nothing much up."

15. Cow horns are also associated with women in Mtoro's kigoma (V 126–127). Generally speaking, Swahili women play different musical instruments from Swahili men. See J. de V. Allen, "Musical Instruments of the Swahili Coast," in *Musikgeschichte in Bildern: Ostafrika* [History of music in pictures: *East Africa*] (Leipzig, forthcoming).

16. The equation of *anafil* with *nafir* I owe to Sassoon, *The siwas of Lamu*, cited above in n. 9. It is, of course, conceivable that the Portuguese described small side-blown horns as nafirs, i.e., anafils. Such inexactitude would hardly be their exclusive prerogative. Allen's translation of the *Desturi* refers to zumari throughout as either "pipe" or "flute," and Sassoon himself, in his subtitle, followed Vasco da Gama in describing the siwas as "trumpets."

17. Alan Boyd, "Musical Instruments of Lamu," *Kenya Past and Present* 9 (1978):2–7.

18. By Prof. E. Dammann, who has in his possession a kinanda belonging to the late Mohamed Kijumwa, the famous Lamu poet and wood carver. It is also described by Skene in "Arab and Swahili Dances and Ceremonies," *Journal of the Royal Anthropological Institute* 47 (1917):413–434, on p. 416. He mentions that it usually has seven strings, six of which formerly were made of

sheep gut "but are now made of twisted silk" and the seventh, the base string, made of copper wire. Ingrams, in *Zanzibar*, illustrates a "native mandolin (Arab *ood*)" opposite p. 416 which, it must be admitted, does not altogether fit the description of an instrument resembling a European lute.

19. G. S. P. Freeman-Grenville, *East African Coast: Select Documents* 2d ed. (Oxford, 1966), p. 54. For other references, see Allen, *Swahili Regalias*.

20. It is to be hoped that we shall know a good deal more on this topic after the completion of two doctoral dissertations that are now in preparation, one by Carol Campbell of the University of Washington, Seattle, and one by Alan Boyd for the University of Indiana, Bloomington. Meanwhile almost the only studies of Swahili music by professional musicologists are two that concern the recitation of Swahili tendi (short epic poems), one by Beverley L. Parker, "*Tendi* Metre as Sung in Five Performances," in the introduction to *Tendi*, ed. J. W. T. Allen (London, 1971), pp. 29–41, and the other by A. M. Jones, "Swahili Epic Poetry: A Musical Study," *African Music*, vol. 5, no. 4 (1975/6): 105–129.

21. For this controversy, see especially Lienhardt's introduction to *The Medicine Man—Swifa ya Nguvumali by Hasani bin Ismail* (Oxford, 1968), and M. Strobel, "From *Lelemama* to Lobbying: Women's Associations in Mombasa, Kenya," in *Hadith 5: History and Social Change in East Africa*, ed. B. A. Ogot (Nairobi, 1976), pp. 207–235.

22. For full reference, see n. 18 above.

23. For full reference, see n. 3 above.

24. Eva Wiesauer, "Swahili and Bajun Traditional Dances," *Bulletin of the International Committee on Urgent Anthropological and Ethnological Research* 16 (1974):19–21.

25. See chap. 14, n. 6.

26. Prins, *Swahili-speaking Peoples*, p. 96.

Appendix IV. In Memoriam

1. This section is based on an address presented at Merrill College, University of California, Santa Cruz, on May 16, 1979. One of Allen's idiosyncrasies was to spell his own name *Iohn*. In this section that spelling has been retained.

2. J. W. T. Allen remained active in scholarship until the day of his death, despite increasing ill health. Other work by him, prepared for publication by his friends, may be expected to appear during the coming years.

Bibliography

Works of General Interest

Students of the Swahili language and culture are fortunate in having available two nineteenth-century dictionaries, both of them major works of scholarship. Ludwig Krapf's *Swahili Dictionary* (London, 1882; reprint ed., Gregg, 1964) not only brings the reader into the presence of a great man working in and around Mombasa in a pioneer situation, but enables us to date the use and meaning of words in the mid-nineteenth century. It is also uniquely valuable in that Krapf's search for converts led him to spend much of his time among the poorer and more marginal Swahili groups. He was interested in religious matters—though not particularly so in Islam—and includes many proverbs and an occasional poem, which are a great delight. The other dictionary, *Dictionnaire Swahili-Français*, 2 vols. (Paris, 1939, 1941), is the work of Charles Sacleux, a Holy Ghost father who did most of his research in and from Bagamoyo at the end of the nineteenth century. It is far and away the best Swahili dictionary ever written, amazingly comprehensive and admirably erudite. It, too, contains innumerable tidbits for the delectation of the careful reader. Unfortunately, Sacleux's transliteration of the Arabic script in which Swahili used to be written is very different from any modern system.

For handy reference, the *Standard Swahili-English Dictionary* (Oxford, 1939; republished many times since), though it has defects, is useful. It subsumes much of the heritage of study of the Universities' Mission to Central Africa, as well as that of the Territorial Education Departments, the London School of Oriental and African Studies, and the Inter-Territorial Language Committee of the East African Dependencies.

These dictionaries can be used by the nonexpert in conjunction with our Index, where the Swahili is given for technical terms and concepts.

313

General bibliographies are, unfortunately, less satisfactory. Marcel van Spaandonck's *Practical and Systematic Swahili Bibliography* (Leiden, 1965), is mainly linguistic though not without value for other disciplines. Alberto Mioni, "La bibliographie de la langue swahili," *Cahiers d'Etudes Africaines* 27 (1967):485–532, is of more use to students of history and religion. The most recent is Richard Wilding's *Swahili Culture: A Bibliography of the History and Peoples of the Swahili Speaking World* (Nairobi, 1976). While undoubtedly of use to scholars, it is patchy and so poorly laid out as to be very difficult to use. It also appears to be blissfully unaware of previous bibliographical work. Finally, it includes nothing published after 1974, a fact that is worth noting, for the volume of publications on Swahili topics swells annually.

Valuable short bibliographies are published at the end of a number of scholarly works that are mentioned elsewhere, notably A. H. J. Prins's *The Swahili-speaking Peoples of Zanzibar and the East African Coast (Arabs, Shirazi, Swahili)*, published in the International Africa Institute's Ethnographic Survey Series (which is the place every Africanistics student has to start), 2d ed. (London, 1967). See also C. S. Nicholls's *The Swahili Coast: Politics, Diplomacy, and Trade on the East African Littoral, 1798–1856* (London, 1971) and A. P. Caplan's *Choice and Constraint in a Swahili Society* (Oxford, 1975). B. G. Martin's bibliography in *Muslim Brotherhoods in 19th Century Africa* (Cambridge, 1976) adds some sources on Islam in Arabic and Turkish as well as other material on his topic. Also of value are the bibliographies published in *Tanganyika Notes and Records*, later *Tanzania Notes and Records*, especially in the late 1960s and 1970s, when Brian Langlands was compiling that section. There are also a number of journals from which bibliographic and other information can be extracted, such as *Swahili* and its predecessors, written mostly by and for linguists; *Africa*, with an anthropological emphasis, and *Azania*, published by the British Institute in Eastern Africa and specializing mainly in archaeology and precolonial history; and *The Journal of African History* and, more recently, *The International Journal of African Historical Studies* and *History in Africa*, all of which include some classic articles relevant to the subject. The most complete bibliography of Swahili literature is J. W. T. Allen's *The Swahili and Arabic Manuscripts in the Library of the University at Dar-es-Salaam* (Leiden, 1970).

Among general studies, two must be pointed out as covering between them almost all the themes covered in the *Desturi*, although often less fully and sometimes rather more controversially. Of the first twenty chapters of the *Desturi*, only the subjects of chapters 3, 7, and 19 are not at least touched upon by either Prins in his *Swahili-speaking People*, already cited above, or by J. Spencer Trimingham in *Islam in East Africa* (Oxford, 1964). The former work, attempting to pioneer the sociology and to some extent the history of the entire Swahili world, is heavy going but contains an enormous repository of facts and useful bits of information which compensate for its lack of an overall shape. Trimingham's book, one of a series on Islam in Africa which is absolutely basic reading for anyone interested in the subject, has been severely criticized, especially for its handling of the topic of Muslim societies in the interior of East Africa, but remains in the view of many the most satisfactory short account of Swahili society and institutions. If one were to read only two books as a background to the *Desturi*, this would undoubtedly be one of them. The other, perhaps rather surprisingly, is T. O. Ranger's *Dance and Society in Eastern Africa* (Berkeley, Los Angeles, and London, 1975). This is one of those admirable books that tells us an enormous amount about the background of its subject—that is, about "society"—even if it does not actually deal with anything that could be described as choreography. Although it by no means confines itself to the Swahili coast, it does explain Swahili society from about the beginning of the present century, as a whole and at all levels, in a way that helps us make sense of much of what Mtoro has to say about the end of the last.

Other general studies can be divided into the early ones, mostly written before 1920, and those written since 1950. In English, at least, there are remarkably few written in between, although in German some excellent articles came from the pen of Ernst Dammann from the 1920s onward—it is hoped that there are still more to come. Of the early British scholars, we can do worse than to start with the relevant chapters of C. H. Stigand's *Land of Zinj* (London, 1913; reprint ed., Cass, 1966), dated though some parts of it are, for he was an observant and accurate reporter. His work compares favorably with two studies by colonial administrators: F. B. Pearce's *Zanzibar, The Metropolis of East Africa* (London, 1920; reprint ed., Cass, 1967), and W. H. Ingrams's *Zanzibar, Its History and People* (London, 1931; reprint ed., 1967), almost the only significant book covering the area in the 1920–1950 period. (Of particular interest in the latter is the account of the material culture, belief systems, songs, and dances of what he calls the "native tribes" of Zanzibar. His discussion of Swahili medicine is almost the only one in existence apart from Mtoro's and includes a section on spirit possession.) Attention should also be drawn to the works of Bishop Steere, W. E. Taylor, W. Hichens, and Alice Werner, especially Werner's entry under "Zanzibar and the Swahili People" in the *Encyclopaedia of Religion and Ethics*, (Edinburgh, 1919), 12:845–849. In German the foremost scholars were Justus Strandes, whose work was translated as *The Portuguese Period in East Africa*, ed. J. S. Kirkman (Nairobi, 1961), and F. Stuhlman, whose *Handwerk und Industrie in Ostafrika* was published at Hamburg in 1910. Nor should we forget the other works of Velten, notably his *Prosa und Poesie der Suaheli* (Berlin, 1907).

Academic study of the East African coast took an upward turn in 1948 with the appointment of James Kirkman to excavate the ruins of Gedi near Malindi. He has published steadily ever since, and although many nowadays would disagree with his conclusions, his facts are impeccably set out for all to study in his various archaeological reports of Gedi and other sites (including Fort Jesus in Mombasa), while his *Men and Monuments of the East African Coast* (London, 1964) is as witty and readable a book as one could ever hope for on an academic theme. Apart from Kirkman's work, in the last two decades archaeology has been covered largely by the publications of the British Institute in Eastern Africa. The heaviest of these, in every sense, is the two-volume report entitled *Kilwa, An Islamic Trading City on the East African Coast*, by the director, H. N. Chittick (Nairobi, 1974). Also from the British Institute is P. S. Garlake's *Early Islamic Architecture of the East African Coast* (Nairobi and London, 1966). Both authors suffer from the disadvantage, when interpreting the history of the region, of believing that the Swahilis as a community do not exist. A more realistic view is taken by G. S. P. Freeman-Grenville, whose chapter in *The [Oxford] History of East Africa*, ed. R. Oliver and G. Mathew (Oxford, 1963), 1:129–168, probably remains the most balanced account, although contributions by Chittick and by F. J. Berg to *Zamani, A Survey of East African History*, ed. B. A. Ogot, 2d ed. (Nairobi, 1974), pp. 98–11 and 115–134, respectively, add some new material. (Regarding the pre-Portuguese period, mention should also be made of Gervase Mathew's own chapter in the 1963 Oxford history just mentioned, edited by Oliver and himself, pp. 94–127, which broke a good deal of new ground, some of which has since remained untrodden.) Freeman-Grenville also compiled a most useful collection of documents, *The East African Coast: Select Documents from the First to the Earlier 19th Century* (Oxford, 1962; reprint ed., 1966), which includes translations of Arabic, Chinese, Portuguese, and French as well as Swahili material. (It contains, among other things, the *Swahili Chronicle of Bagamoyo*, originally collected by Velten.)

Turning to the work of sociologists and anthropologists, in addition to *Swahili-Speaking Peoples* Prins has published two studies of Lamu on the northern Swahili coast, *Sailing from Lamu* (Assen, 1965) and *Didemic Lamu* (Gröningen, 1971). Although important for an understanding of Swahili society as a whole, they are not especially relevant as background reading for the *Desturi*, since Lamu was and is a Swahili settlement of a very different type from Bagamoyo. (Much of *Sailing from Lamu* is, however, relevant to the sections in chapter 16 dealing with fishing and boat building.) John Middleton and Jane Campbell's *Zanzibar, Its Society and Its Politics* (Oxford, 1965) is disappointingly brief. A. P. Caplan's *Choice and Constraint in a Swahili Society*, already mentioned, is a modern account of a village on Mafia Island, which is much nearer, socially as well as geographically, to Mtoro's Bagamoyo but is still significantly different. It contains, however, much that is important for an understanding of the Swahili world as a whole. Two recent studies of Lamu which have relevance to the Swahili world as a whole are Marguerite Ylvisaker's *Lamu in the Nineteenth Century: Land, Trade, and Politics* (Boston, 1979) and Abdulhamid El-Zein's *The Sacred Meadows: A Structural Analysis of Religious Symbolism in an East African Town* (Evanston, 1974). The former is a valuable contribution to our understanding of Swahili life in the last century and especially of the role of agriculture in most Swahili settlements, although the land-tenure system there described was significantly different from the one around Bagamoyo in Mtoro's time—and agriculture was less important, and the caravan business more so, in Bagamoyo in the 1890s than in most settlements of a similar size. El-Zein's book has been hailed as epoch making in terms of its handling of problems facing social anthropologists, but it is regarded as controversial by most other scholars with any personal knowledge of Lamu. While it can hardly be ignored, it should be treated with caution.

Two attempts to interpret Swahili society and culture through Swahili poetry are P. Lienhardt's edition of Hasani bin Ismail's *Swifa ya Nguvumali—The Medicine Man* (Oxford, 1968) and Seyyid Abdalla bin Ali and J. de V. Allen, *Al-Inkishafi—Catechism of a Soul* (Nairobi, 1977); the former is particularly relevant to the *Desturi* because it focuses on conflicts between Islam and African Traditional Religion on the Tanzanian coast. Dr. Jan Knappert has published numerous books and articles on Swahili literature and culture. Of these, *Traditional Swahili Poetry* (Leiden, 1967), *Swahili Islamic Poetry*, 3 vols. (Leiden, 1971), *Myths and Legends of the Swahili* (Nairobi, 1970), and *An Anthology of Swahili Love Poetry* (Berkeley, Los Angeles, and London, 1972) may particularly be mentioned. Dr. Knappert's work on Swahili songs may be consulted in his volume *A Choice of Flowers* (London, 1972; see especially the glossary), "Swahili Proverb Songs," *Afrika and Übersee* 59 (1976):163–172, and his *Four Centuries of Swahili Verse* (London, 1979). His *Survey of Swahili Songs* is forthcoming from Heinemann of London.

First-rate scholars working within the strictly Islamic tradition have never been lacking in Swahili society, any more than have scholars of literature, collecting traditional poetry and writing their own. The twentieth-century educational system, however, drove a wedge between such people, who did not feel at home except when writing in Swahili (and were consequently much neglected in the West and have for the most part been ignored by non-Swahili publishers), and a smaller group of scholars who were also Anglophone (or perhaps we should say Europhone), of whom Mtoro was in a sense the precursor, found their ways into Western and new African universities and gained access to an audience outside the Swahili world as well as within it. The student who learns sufficient Swahili to be equally at home in either intellectual milieu will be richly rewarded. Even a few hours a week over a period of two years spent with Dorothy V. Perrott's *Teach Yourself Swahili* (London, 1951), yields rewards beyond one's deserts. A number of sets of tapes are available, including those produced by Linguaphone and the Monterey Defense Language Institute. One can obtain some glimpse of the achievement of the Swahili by studying editions of their poetry by scholars from outside who deeply respected the local people and tried to serve by helping to collect and preserve their literature while presenting parts of it to foreign readers. A study of Swahili achievement in poetry and reflection on the science of prosody can begin with the material collected by J. W. T. Allen in *Tendi* (London, 1971). In Swahili prose there is available a fine example almost contemporary with the *Desturi*, the autobiography of Tippu Tib, *Maisha ya Hamed bin Muhammed el-Murjebi, yaani Tippu Tib, kwa maneno yake mwenyewe*, as dictated to a German, H. Brode, first published in a German journal in 1902–1903 and republished with an English translation by W. H.

Whiteley through the East African Literature Bureau in 1959, with several reprints since. Of particular interest is Tippu Tib's insistence that he was an Arab, in contrast to Mtoro's emphasis on Swahili identity and culture. A brief overall view of the development of the language as a whole will be found in Wilfred Whiteley's *Swahili: The Rise of a National Language* (London, 1969).

Besides their prowess as experts in the law (mentioned toward the end of this Bibliography), local Swahili scholars excelled in exegesis of the Qur'an and in theology. Something of their achievement can be grasped from Dr. Bradley Martin's works cited. If possible, works like Sheikh Saleh Al-Farsy's *Tarehe ya Imam Shafi na Wanavyuoni Wakubwa wa Mashariki ya Afrika* (Zanzibar, 1945) should be consulted.

Modern scholars who are themselves Swahili and can use English as well as anyone in the world include, notably, Professor Ali Mazrui, whose works remind us that Swahili civilization is of more than African importance. Said Hamdun's running prose translation contained in *Ibn Battuta in Black Africa* (in collaboration with Noel King, London, 1975) shows a superb mastery of Arabic and English. Professor Mohamed Abdulaziz's *Muyaka: Nineteenth Century Swahili Popular Poetry* (Nairobi, 1979) is of importance, especially as a precursor. Works that will, we hope, arouse much healthy controversy are Abdallah Khalid's *The Liberation of Swahili from European Appropriation*, Vol. I, *A Handbook for African Nation-building* (Nairobi, 1977). (Volume II is said to be entitled *True Swahili, a Grammar of an African People's Literary Language*. It had not appeared at the time of writing.)

Turning to the specific field of Islam, we must first note the bibliographical material originally collected by C. H. Becker under the title *Materialen zur Kenntnis des Islam in Deutsch Ostafrika* in *Der Islam* 2 (1911):1–48, translated and republished by B. G. Martin as "Materials for the Understanding of Islam in German East Africa," *Tanzania Notes and Records* 68 (1968):31–62. Also available is A. H. Nimitz's "Islam in Tanzania: An Annotated Bibliography," *Tanzania Notes and Records* 72 (1973):51–74. The bibliography in B. G. Martin's *Muslim Brotherhoods in 19th Century Africa* has already been mentioned, and along with this book, attention should be drawn to several articles by the same author, especially "Notes on Some Members of the Learned Classes of Zanzibar and East Africa in the 19th Century," *African Historical Studies* vol. 4, no. 3 (1971): 524–545, and "Arab Migrations to East Africa in Medieval Times," *International Journal of African Historical Studies*, vol. 7, no. 3 (1974): 367–390. Referring to East African Islam in a still earlier period are several articles by R. Pouwels, notably "Tenth Century Settlement of the East African Coast: The Case for Qarmatian/Ismaili Connections," *Azania* 9 (1974):65–74, and two important articles by J. Schacht, "An Unknown Type of Minbar and Its Historical Significance," *Ars Orientalis* 2 (1952): 149–173, and "Further Notes on the Staircase Minaret," *Ars Orientalis* 4 (1961):137–141. There is also Schacht's more general "Notes on Islam in East Africa" in *Studia Islamica* (Paris, 1964–1965), 23:91–136, based on two visits to the region. Trimingham's *Islam in East Africa* has already been mentioned.

For all its faults it remains valuable, not least because its author, with a wide experience of studying Islam in Africa and the Middle East behind him, has a sharp nose for what he politely calls "the Arab racial myth, combined with the strong Arabism of Hadhrami influence" (p. 22). It can be supplemented by reference to the bibliography in Noel King's *Christian and Muslim in Africa* (New York, 1971). Another useful work is J. Knappert's "Swahili Religious Terms" in *Journal of Religion in Africa*, vol. 3, no. 1, (1970):67–80.

For investigating the relationship between *Desturi*'s Islam and the Islam of the European textbooks, the reader who has little or no Arabic should begin by looking up a key word in Thomas Patrick Hughes, *A Dictionary of Islam* (London, 1885). This magnum opus was compiled in Peshawar by an Anglican missionary over a couple of decades in the last century, and it is a classic of its kind, although parts of it are badly dated—the India of its day saw a good deal of mud flinging among Christians, Ahmadiyya Muslims, Arya Samaj, and so forth. Tribute from the Muslim side was paid when Muhammad Ashraf of Lahore reissued it in 1965, omitting "the more tendentious passages." It was also reissued by the Oriental Reprint Company at Delhi in 1976. Its greatest value to the student is that its headings are in English, so that if he or she has no knowledge of Arabic, Hughes may be used to find out what word to look up in the full-sized *Encyclopaedia of Islam*, the headings of which are in transliterated Arabic although the text is in English. If access to this larger work is not possible, the *Shorter Encyclopaedia of Islam*, ed. H. A. R. Gibb and J. H. Kramers (Leiden and London, 1961), is invaluable. This collects the articles relating to religion and law in the first edition of the *Encyclopaedia of Islam*. The authors are nearly all Europeans writing in a critical, analytical way of how things ought to be according to the textbooks. Some of them have seen field work in central areas such as colonial Egypt or Syria. Reading these articles one begins to understand the Muslim scholars who look upon such scholarship as the academic side of imperialism; with this proviso, however, they are a useful guide to orthodox and classical usage. The two-page "Register of Subjects" under English headings is especially valuable to the student who is unfamiliar with Arabic.

With the same caveat about colonialism in mind, it is useful to read some books from the last century which provide parallels to *Desturi*, C. Snouck Hurgronje's *The Achehnese* (Leiden, 1906), is a classic, though anyone who reads it should try to visit the cemetery at Acheh in Sumatra and meditate on the "native" and Dutch dead killed in the colonial war that is its background. E. Lane's *Manners and Customs of the Modern Egyptians*, (London, 1836; frequent reprints, including 1971) and C. A. Herklots's *Islam in India*, (London, 1832), are a great delight, despite the creeping British imperialism that forms their backdrops.

In the study of the Holy Qur'an European Islamists use Gustav Fluegel's *Textus Arabicus* (Leipzig, 1883; reprint ed., Gregg, 1965) as a basic source for textus receptus and numeration. With it goes Fluegel's *Concordantiae Corani Arabicae* (1842, 1965). The Royal Egyptian (Cairo, in many editions) is a better text; and for student purposes A. Yusuf Ali, *The Holy Qur'an: Text, Translation, and Commentary*, published by Muhammad Ashraf, 2 vols. (Lahore, 1934; frequently reprinted), is valuable because of its clear Arabic text, literal translation, and copious subject index. A. J. Arberry, *The Koran Interpreted* (London, 1955), is holding its place as a first-rate translation, and W. Montgomery Watt's *Companion to the Qur'an* (London, 1967) is based upon it. For the reader of Swahili there is the Ahmaddiya translation, in excellent Swahili, which goes back to the late Sheikh Amri Abedi, who studied at Rabwah in Pakistan before he rose high in Dr. Nyerere's cabinet. The commentary is marked by the normal virulent tendentiousness of such groups toward people who do not accept their Messiah. Then there is Sheikh Abdalla Saleh al-Farsy's magnificent *Qurani Takatifu* (Nairobi, 1969, 1974), which is available in East Africa at a nominal price thanks to the generosity of Kuwait and other Arab Muslim countries.

The African Traditional Religion and various belief systems that provide the other dimension to the background of the *Desturi* have been described by some of the greatest anthropologists in history, a few of whom were also arguably among the finest minds of our century. More recently African theologians have taken up the topic. Probably the place to start is with Evans-Pritchard's *Nuer Religion*, followed by John Mbiti's *African Religion and Philosophy* (London and New York, 1969). Dr. Mbiti is a Kenyan, Kamba is his first language, Swahili the second, then come German and English. A basic working bibliography on the various main topics of African Traditional Religion will be found in it and in Noel Q. King's *Religions in Africa* (New York, 1970).

Additional Bibliography for Selected Topics

WHO ARE THE SWAHILI?

A start may be made in Prins and Caplan, cited above. A. I. Salim's *Swahili-speaking Peoples of Kenya's Coast, 1895–1965* (Nairobi, 1973), while dealing mainly with political developments in the present century, has a useful chapter entitled "The Conflict of Cultures, 1900–1940," pp. 139–168. S. Feierman's *The Shambaa Kingdom: A History*, (Madison, Wis., 1974) focuses on the interior rather than on the coast, has valuable insights, and can be read in conjunction with Abdallah bin Hemedi 'l Ajjemy's, *The Kilindi*, ed. J. W. T. Allen et al. (Dar-es-Salaam, 1963). J. de V. Allen's "Swahili Culture Reconsidered: Some Historical Implications of the Material Culture of the Northern Kenya Coast in the Eighteenth and Nineteenth Centuries," *Azania* 9 (1974):105–138, and "Town and Country in Swahili Culture," a chapter in *Symposium Leo Frobenius* (Cologne and Yaounde, 1974), pp. 298–316, attempt to bring ethnographic and sociological evidence to bear on the problem of Swahili identity. Readers may follow the copious discussion that has taken place in journals during the last few years by starting with Carol M. Eastman's "Who Are the Waswahili," *Africa*, vol. 41, no. 3 (1971): 228–236, and continuing on to Marc Swartz, "Religious Courts, Community, and Ethnicity among the Swahili in Mombasa," *Africa*, vol. 49, no. 1 (1979): 29–41. See also the notes to Appendix I in this volume. On the **town of Bagamoyo**, which has a tourist and Ph.D. industry of its own, see especially Walter T. Brown; "A Pre-colonial History of Bagamoyo" (Ph.D. diss., Boston University, 1971), and August H. Nimitz, Jr., *The Role of the Muslim Sufi Orders in Political Change* (Ph.D. diss., Indiana University, 1973; the university copy has apparently been taken, but university microfilms will supply). *A Survey of Bagamoyo Township* by the Department of Architecture, University of Lund (1968 and 1969), is a most useful resource. The "tribes" mentioned may be followed up in the general ethnographic works mentioned, but the Zaramo have a special importance at Bagamoyo. Lloyd W. Swantz's "The Zaramo of Tanzania" (M.A. thesis, Syracuse University, 1956) has been distributed since 1965 by the Nordic Tanzania Project.

ON CHAPTER 1

The **mganga**, the traditional practitioner: See C. K. Omari, "The *Mganga*, a specialist of His Own Kind," *Psychopathologie Africaine*, vol. 8, no. 2 (1972): 217–231; Peter Lienhardt, *Swifa ya Ngurumali—The Medicine Man* (Oxford, 1968); and Michael Gelfand, *Witchdoctor* (London, 1964), as well as the works mentioned under the pepo cult. On the kungwi, or tutrix, see the section on women's initiations below.

ON CHAPTER 2

The **birth of a child**: On the maulidi, see Jan Knappert; *Swahili Islamic Poetry*, (Leiden, 1971) 2:41, 46, 48, ff. Also a good part of vol. 3 (Leiden, 1971).

On **riding to paradise**: Jan Knappert, *Traditional Swahili Poetry*, chap. 5. Generally on the use of Arabic in various charms, rituals, and invocations such as the frequently mentioned Hal Badiri, see Jan Knappert's "The Function of Arabic in the Islamic Ritual of the East African Coast," *Actes du Ve Congrès des Islamisants et des Arabisants* (Brussels, 1971). On the **outdooring** and other such ceremonies discussed throughout the *Desturi*, Spencer Trimingham's *Islam in East Africa* and Noel King's *Religions of Africa* give basic bibliographies. On **color symbolism**—as, indeed, on most exegeses of rites of passage—one must go back to Victor W. Turner's works, beginning with *The Forest of Symbols* (Ithaca, 1967), *Drums of Affliction* (Oxford, 1968), and *The Ritual Process* (London, 1969). *The Eranos Jahrbuch* for 1972 had a lot on color symbolism; see especially the chapter by Dominique Zahan. On **low fertility** along the coast, see R. E. S. Tanner and D. F, Roberts, "A Demographic Study in Northeast Tanganyika," *Population Studies* 13 (1959—1960):61—80.

ON CHAPTER 4

The **meeting of traditional with Islamic education** at primary and middle level: Abdu Kasozi has published a number of documents available in mimeographed form from Makerere University, Kampala; see also L. K. Fox, *East African Childhood* (London, 1967), and compare an excellent autobiographical novel by Camara Laye, *Ambiguous Adventure* (London and New York, 1968).

ON CHAPTER 8

Boys' initiations: Apart from the basic books mentioned and the Victor Turner classics cited, see A. P. Caplan's "Boys' Circumcision and Girls' Puberty Rites among the Swahili of Mafia Island," *Africa*, vol. 46, no. 1 (1976): 21—33, for newer bibliography. Hans Cory's "Jando" in the *Journal of the Royal Anthropological Institute* 77 (1947):159—168, and 78 (1948):81—95, and *African Figurines* (London, 1956) are relevant to the *Desturi*. A number of unpublished figurines are to be found in the Cory Collection at Dar-es-Salaam Museum.

ON CHAPTER 9

The **customs of girls**: A full and excellent treatment and bibliography is to be found in Margaret Strobel's *Muslim Women in Mombasa, 1890—1975* (New Haven and London, 1979); (see too A. P. Caplan's article, cited above. A classic in the field is Audrey Richards's *Chisungu* (London, 1956). Marja-Liisa Swantz, "Religious and Magical Rites of Bantu Women in Tanzania," mimeographed (Dar-es-Salaam, 1966), is, unfortunately, hard to come by, but a good part of it is in her *Ritual and Symbol in Transitional Zaramo Society* (Uppsala, 1970). To put the chapter in its larger context, see, for instance, Nancy J. Hafkin and Edna G. Bray (eds.), *Women in Africa* (Stanford, 1976), and Judith Brown, "A Cross-cultural Study of Female Initiation Rites," *American Anthropologist* 65 (1963): 837—853, which has been extensively followed up, as has Denise Paulme (ed.), *Women of Tropical Africa* (Berkeley and Los Angeles, 1960). Books bearing on the topic which have been given a mixed reception include Mary Daly's *Gyn-ecology* (Boston, 1978), Janice De Laney's *The Curse: A Cultural History of Menstruation* (New York, 1976), and Paula Weideyer's *Menstruation and Menopause* (New York, 1975).

ON CHAPTER 10

Charms and amulets: A good place to go for a bibliography is A. H. J. Prins, "Islamic Maritime Magic," in *Word and Religion, Kalima na Dini*, the

Ernst Dammann *Festschrift* (Stuttgart, 1969), pp. 294–304. See also H. S. Schuster, "Magische Quadrate in islamischen Bereich," *Der Islam* 49 (1972): 1–84. On **johari 'lQurani**, a translation of Al-Ghazali's *Kitāb Jawāhir al-Qur'an* by M. A. Quasem appeared in London in 1977.

ON CHAPTER 11

On **marriage**: The appearance of Margaret Strobel's book makes it unnecessary to go into detail, but to her bibliography one should add Françoise Le Guennec-Coppens, "Les ceremonies du mariage chez les femmes 'Swahili' de l'ile de Lamu," which will soon be published as a booklet by the Lamu Society at Nairobi, and Gill Shepherd, "Two Marriage Forms in the Comoro Islands: An Investigation," *Africa*, vol. 47, no. 4 (1977):344–359. The following give the wider context: Meyer Fortes (ed.), *Marriage in Tribal Societies* (Cambridge, 1962); Isaac Schapera, *Married Life in an African Tribe* (Evanston, 1966); Jack Goody and S. J. Tambiah, *Bridewealth and Dowry* (Cambridge, 1973). Henri Junod's *Life of a South African Tribe*, 2 vols. (London, 1927), has a valuable account of the Levirate marriage (it remains on this and many other subjects a classic). There is much material in Swahili—see Sheikh Saleh Abdulla al-Farsy, *Ada za barusi katika Unguja* (Dar-es-Salaam, 1955), Hamed bin Saleh el-Busaidy, *Ndoa na talaka* (Dar-es-Salaam, 1962) and sections of Al-Amin ibn Ali Mazrui, *Uwongozi* (Mombasa, n.d.; reprint ed., 1955), and his *Ndoa na Talaka katika Sharia* (Mombasa, 1936; reprint ed.).

ON CHAPTER 12

On **General Sir Lloyd Matthews**, see R. N. Lyne, *An Apostle of Empire* (London, 1936).

On **Swahili moieties and factions**, see A. H. J. Prins, *Didemic Lamu* (Grö-ningen, 1971); M. Strobel on **lelemama** in B. A. Ogot (ed.), *Hadith*, Vol. V; T. O. Ranger's *Dance and Society in Eastern Africa* (Berkeley, Los Angeles, and London, 1974); and Peter Lienhardt's edition of Hasani bin Ismail's *Swifa ya Ngvumali—The Medicine Man*, (Oxford, 1968).

ON CHAPTERS 12–14

Spirit possession and its dances: R. Skene, "Arab and Swahili Dances and Ceremonies," *Journal of the Royal Anthropological Institute* 47 (1917):413–434; H. Koritschoner, "Ngoma ya Shaitani, an East African Native Treatment for Psychical Disorders," *Journal of the Royal Anthropological Institute* 66 (1936): 209–219. John Beattie and John Middleton's *Spirit Mediumship and Society in Africa* (London, 1969) may be supplemented by reference to I. I. Zaretsky and C. Shambaugh, *Spirit Possession and Mediumship in Africa and Afro-America: An Annotated Bibliography* (London, n.d.) Farouk Tharia Topan has unfortunately not published his distinguished 1971 London thesis, "Oral Literature in a Ritual Setting: The Role of Spirit Songs in a Spirit-Mediumship Cult," which is a full-scale exegesis of the rites using the Victor Turner paradigms.

ON CHAPTER 16

Sailing and boat building: See A. H. J. Prins, *Sailing from Lamu* (Assen, 1965), and G.F. Hourani, *Arab Seafaring in the Indian Ocean* (Princeton, 1951).

ON CHAPTER 19

Of diseases and their cure: A detailed bibliography is available in K. David Patterson, *Infectious Diseases in Twentieth Century Africa*, (Waltham, Mass., 1979). See also Z. A. Ademuwagun et al. (eds.), *African Therapeutic Systems and Health*, and Steven Feierman, *Health and Society in Africa*, a working bibliography. Both are published by the African Studies Association (Waltham, Mass., 1980). By way of comparison, one may refer to Charles Leslie's *Asian Medical Systems* (Berkeley, 1976). Some standbys originally produced at Mulago, Makerere University's teaching hospital, include Hubert Trowell, *Diagnosis and Treatment of Disease in the Tropics*, revised by John R. Billinghurst, 4th ed. (London, 1968), A. G. Shaper, M. S. R. Hutt, and J. Kibukamusoke, *Medicine in a Tropical Environment* (London, 1971), as well as Dr. Maurice King's various works leading on from his editing of *Medical Care in Developing Countries* (London, 1966).

The topic bibliography in King's *Religions of Africa* also provides a good beginning for reading on African medicine and healing. Something of the debate on the value of non-Western traditional medicine will be glimpsed in such works as Erwin H. Ackernecht's *Medicine and Ethnology* (Baltimore, 1971) and Virgil J. Vogel, *American Indian Medicine* (Norman, 1970). J. O. Kokwaro's *Medicinal Plants in East Africa* (Nairobi, 1976) gives a glimpse of the new work being done in East Africa.

ON CHAPTERS 20 AND 28

For information on **witchcraft and sorcery** and also on **ordeals and oracles**, one may start with John Middleton (ed.), *Magic, Witchcraft, and Curing* (New York, 1967); Mary Douglas (ed.), *Witchcraft Confessions and Accusations* (London, 1970); and Max G. Marwick, *Sorcery in Its Social Setting* (Manchester, 1965). Lucy Mair's *Witchcraft* (London, 1969) and Geoffrey Parrinder's *Witchcraft, European and African*, (London, 1958) remain rich in insight. The classics are E. E. Evans-Pritchard's *Witchcraft, Oracles, and Magic among the Azande* (Oxford, 1937), and Clyde Kluckhohn's *Navaho Witchcraft* (Cambridge, Mass., 1944).

On **burial**: Trimingham is again most helpful. If possible, one should read

Sheikh Abdulla Saleh al-Farsy's *Mambo ana yofanyiwa maiti na hukumu za eda* (Zanzibar, 1956).

ON CHAPTER 21

On the **jumbe**: It is interesting to compare the evolution of royal power in Abdallah bin Hemedi 'lAjjemy's *Habari za wakilindi* (Dar-es-Salaam, 1962), trans. J. W. T. Allen (Boston, 1963) and in Ghana under Dr. Nkrumah's; see Noel King, "Kingship as Communication and Accommodation," in F. F. Bruce (ed.) *Promise and Fulfillment* (Edinburgh, 1964).

ON CHAPTER 23

Swahili journies: An excellent lead-in is E. A. Alpers, "The Coast and the Development of the Caravan Trade," in I. N. Kimambo and A. J. Temu (eds.), *A History of Tanzania* (London, 1969), pp. 34–56. As part of their trading and exploring, the Swahili were great colonizers and missionaries. They founded Islam in Uganda and Zaïre. On the former, see Abdu Kasozi, Arye Oded, and Noel King, *Islam and the Confluence of Religion in Uganda*, (Tallahassee, 1971); on the latter, the *Maisha ya Tippu Tip*, the Swahili conquistador of the eastern Congo, ed. and trans. W. H. Whiteley, *Journal of the East African Swahili Committee* 1958 and 1959 supplement, East African Literature Bureau (Nairobi, 1966, 1970, 1971). The most recent book concerning the literature about him is probably F. Bontinck, *L'autobiographie de Hamed ben Mohammed el-Murjebi Tippo Tip* (Brussels, 1975).

For the geographical background here and throughout, see *Tanganyika [Tanzania] Atlas*, 3d and later eds. (Dar-es-Salaam, 1956 and later), and L. Berry, *Tanzania in Maps* (London and New York, 1971). The British colonial Ordinance Survey, here as in India, did a great job, if only to allow officials to know where the people and wealth were to be found. Their maps remain a basic study to anyone desiring to learn about a former British possession.

ON CHAPTER 25

Slavery: Capt. R. S. Rattray's *Ashanti* (London, 1923) gives a classical account of African domestic slavery. For East Africa, see Abdulaziz Y. Lodi, *The Institution of Slavery in Zanzibar and Pemba*, Scandinavian Institute of African Studies, report no. 10 (1973), E. A. Alpers, *The East African Slave Trade* (Nairobi, 1967), and *Ivory and Slaves in East Central Africa* (Berkeley, Los Angeles, and London, 1975), as well as R. W. Beachey, *The Slave Trade of Eastern Africa* (London, 1976). F. Cooper's *Plantation Slavery on the East Coast of Africa* (New Haven, 1977) and his article "The Problems of Slavery in African Studies," *Journal of African History* 20 (1979):103–125, give a full survey of the spate of literature and do much to put the study on an equal footing of high academic systematization as its West African or American counterparts.

ON CHAPTER 29

Swahili beliefs about creation: Jan Knappert's *Malay Myths and Legends* (Singapore, forthcoming) details the Islamic, "Indian thalassocracy," or local origins of most of the beliefs mentioned and cites relevant literature.

ON CHAPTER 30

Swahili high days and holy days: Sir John Gray's "Nairuzi or Siku ya Mwaka," *Tanganyika Notes and Records* 38 (1955):1−22, remains basic, but the British colonial tendency to see Persian or other "higher civilization" influence everywhere has to be carefully watched. On possible **early Shia connections** with East Africa, see the appendix by S. A. A. Rizvi in Hamdun and King's *Ibn Battuta in Black Africa* (London, 1975) and R. L. Pouwels in *Azania* 9 (1974):65−74.

ON CHAPTER 31

Saws, proverbs, and wise sayings: There are many fine old collections in this area, like W. E. Taylor's *African Aphorisms* (London, 1891); C. Velten's *Prosa und Poesie der Wasuaheli* (Berlin, 1907); and later Ernst Dammann's *Sprichworter aus Lamu, Westermann Festschrift* (Berlin, 1955), pp. 174−180, to which full references will be found in Jan Knappert's "On Swahili Proverbs," *African Language Studies* 16 (1975):117−146. Collections by Sheikh Abdalla Saleh al-Farsi and others have been published in East Africa. For M. E. Mnyampala's fine collection, see *Swahili*, vol. 33, no. 1 (1962−1963).

ON CHAPTERS 32−48

The application of Islamic and traditional law is a perennial topic of thought and discussion for the Swahili of the coast. There is no doubt that it has done much to mold and hold the people. Since this subject falls outside the scope of Mtoro's work, we have largely excluded it, apart from one or two excerpts that illustrate its fascinating character. Anyone wishing to pursue the study further should do so in Velten's original edition and translation and in such Swahili-language works as Sheikh al-Farsy's *Ndoa na Talaka* (Zanzibar, 1965) and Sheikh Ali Hemedi El-Buhry's *Mirathi* (trans. P. E. Mitchell) and *Nikahi* (trans. J. W. T. Allen). See also Arthur Phillips and Henry F. Morris, *Marriage Laws in Africa* (London, 1971), for general bibliography. Jan Knappert's *Islamic Law in East Africa* (forthcoming) will no doubt augment the material to be found in the standard works cited early in this Bibliography.

Of course nothing can take the place of a field visit. Tanzania welcomes tourists under certain conditions set for the good of the guest and of the host country. In some places—like the stretch from the international airport to Kilimanjaro, or around Dar-es-Salaam and Kunduchi Beach—the usual first-class pampering facilities are available to those who can pay for them. For the most part, one has to share the conditions and hardships that local people accept as part of life and Tanzania's chosen role at home and abroad. Graduate students and researchers have to obtain permission and abide loyally by certain rules. The old colonial archives at Dar-es-Salaam, Nairobi, and Entebbe have much still to tell us. Zanzibar and Potsdam present their own problems of access. M. H. Nassor's *Guide to the Microfilms of Regional and District Books* (Dar-es-Salaam, 1973) and the Marburg list of 1973 of the German Records at the National Archives of Tanzania and at various places in Germany provide tantalizing fare.

It is always rewarding to browse in the local newspapers, in periodicals like the *African Ecclesiastical Review*, published at Eldoret, and in the prolific pamphlet and ephemeral literature in which "ex-patriates" who have given their lives to Tanzanian service are allowed to play an honorable part. Nor, finally, should we forget the family of the vernacular *Habari na Desturi za. . .* [Information about the customs of such-and-such a people . . .] literature in which quite often part-time and amateur antiquarians have worked to set down what they believe should be recorded, often in the teeth of considerable difficulties. Of this remarkable genre, Mtoro's work is in a real sense the progenitor and model.

Index

Abdallah, Akida, 302 n. 3
Abjad, numerical divining system, 67, 275 nn. 12, 13
Abortion, 59, 272 n. 15
Abubakar Sheikh, Amina, 251
Abubakar Sheikh, Khadija, 251
Abubakar Sheikh, Kupona, 251
Adabu, 263 n. 8. *See also* Manners
Adultery, 277 nn. 28–32, 34, 281 n. 17; omens, 158; slavery as punishment for, 169; suspicion, 38, 276 n. 26. *See also* Compensation
African Literature Bureau, 248
African themes, 249
African Traditional Religion, 212, 227, 228, 249, 274 n. 1; bibliographies and studies, 319, 320; and Islamic conflict and convergence, 272 n. 3, 285 n. 9, 301 n. 7, 317, 322
Afterbirth, disposal of, 258 n. 2
Age, affecting greetings and traditions, 41–42
Agriculture. *See* Cultivation; Men's work; Slaves, labor; Women, working
Ahmad, 275 n. 10
Ahtam fashadh, 133, 290 n. 2. *See also* Spirits
Akida, 216, 245. *See also* Dance
Akika, 12
Albinos, 17, 19
Allen, Iohn Willoughby Tarleton, 247–250
Allen, J. de V., xii, 233

Allen, J. W. T.: scholarship, 252–254; *Twamililia Allen*, 251
Alms and almsgiving, 128, 178, 288 n. 5, 294 n. 9, 308 n. 2
Aloes, 80, 117
Alum, 118
American Revolution, 247
Amir and amiri, 150, 216
Amulets, 6, 15, 33, 60–62, 79, 160, 189, 272 n. 1, 273 nn. 7, 10; studies of, 322–323
Ancestors, 189, 204, 225, 266 n. 7, 301 n. 7. *See also* Circumcision; Reduction
Ancestral spirits, 296 n. 8, 297 n. 8
Angels, 6
araaita, 3
Arab: customs, 225; greetings, 43; identity claimed by Swahilis, 224; influence of, 201, 221, 222, 224, 225, 227, 229, 230, 308 n. 42; music, 240–241; role in slavery, 169–170; Tippu Tip, 225. *See also* Arab racial myth; African Traditional Religion, Islamic conflict; Islam; Muslim religion; Swahili, identity
Arabic transliteration, 255 n. 5
Arab racial myth, 222. *See also* Racism
Architecture. *See* Stone-built settlements; Stone house; Stone mosques and tombs.
Aristocrats, 220. *See also* Elite; Rank and title; Ungwana; individual titles
Asthma, 136, 291 n. 11

329

Trimmingham, J. S., 222
Tuberculosis, 291 n. 6
Tuesday, 10
Tumbatū, 221
Tumeuya, 43
Turban: devil's, 285 n. 9; for jumbe, 149;
  marriage agreement, 64
Tutu. *See* Drums (types)
Twamlilia Allen, 251–258
Typhoid, 290 n. 1

Ubani, 151, 295 n. 6
Ubati. *See* Ufito
Uchawi, 182. *See also* Sorcery
Udi, 286 n. 3
Ufito, 27, 263 n. 2
Uganda, 248
Uhehe, 297 n. 15
Ukarimu, 299 n. 1. *See also* Generosity;
  Hospitality
Ukili, 287 n. 14
Ukindu fronds, 118, 287 n. 13. *See also*
  Matting
Ukingo. *See* Canopy
Umbilical cord, 7
Ungwana (also u-ungwana, wa-ungwana),
  216, 220–223 passim, 225, 226, 229,
  306 n. 23; privileges of, 212, 216;
  seniority, 223; trade function, 218
Units of measure, 232
Unlucky day, 10
Unyago. *See* Dances
Unyanyembe, 280 n. 6
Upatu, 236, 237 n. 37
Upele, 135, 290 n. 5
Upepo, 299, n. 1
Urban superiority, 218
Urine, to prevent blindness, 134
Urticaria, 290 n. 5
Ushombwe water, 106
Usira, 272
Utamaduni, 222
Utunda, 31, 55, 260 n. 21, 263 n. 12, 270
  n. 5
Uwekelo, 64, 274 n. 3

Vaginal bean. *See* Kisukumi
Values, 212, 228, 243
Vasco da Gama, 240, 264 n. 4
Velten, Carl, viii, xii
Venereal disease, 291 nn. 9, 10. *See also*
  Syphilis; Gonorrhea
Vijana, commoners, 295 n. 4

Vikuku, 237. *See also* Musical instruments
Vinegar, 137
Vinyago, 242
Virgin, bride-price, 64
Virginity, 277 n. 38; loss of, 58–59;
  proof of, 76; significance of, 271–272
  n. 15
Visitor, 180
Vows, 181, 260 n. 23
Vumba (also wa-vumba), 215–216, 306
  n. 28
Vumi. *See* Drums (types)

Wallahi, 185. *See also* Mungu
Wanga, 294 n. 10. *See also* Sorcerer
Wangwana, 225
Wanyamwezi, 280 n. 6
Wari, 56
Warts, 139, 233 n. 24
Washing, of feet, 75, 277 n. 36
Wasiwasi, 263, n. 9, 275 n. 9
Watani, 77, 143, 146, 168, 278 n. 38, 294
  n. 3, 298 n. 2
Water lilies, 275 n. 8, 285 n. 11
Waziri, 41, 148, 150, 216, 266—267 n. 2
Weapons, 204–205
Wedding. *See* Marriage
Weights and measures, 114, 231–232,
  286 n. 3
Wells, 154, 277 n. 34
White, sign of death, 269 n. 12
Whiteness, in initiation, 268 n. 11
Whitlows, 134, 291 n. 13
Widows, 79–80
Wiesauer, 242, 243
Winding sheet, 142, 143
Witchcraft. *See* Sorcery
Women: dances of, 243; dress of, 299
  n. 8; honored, 267 n. 3; humiliation
  of, 278; in seclusion, 278 n. 41; status
  of, 243, 280 n. 13; studies about, 322;
  victims of pepo, 283 n. 3; wise, 260
  n. 26; working, 114–119, 121, 276
  n. 24, 286 n. 1. *See also* Behavior;
  Childbirth; Dances; Girls, customs;
  Kungwi; Marriage; Menstruation;
  Pregnancy
Word play. *See* Double meanings
World. *See* Creation beliefs
Worms, remedy, 14

Xylophone, 236

Ya sini, 183, 263 n. 7, 273 n. 4, 300 n. 5; in amulets and charms, 61, 62, 176, 199 n. 10; to bring rain, 190, 301 n. 9; for building house, 33
Yao, 1
Yawning, 36, 265 n. 2
Yaws, 134−135, 290 n. 3
Yellow, 287 n. 16
Yellow bark, 288 n. 2

Zaire slave export, 282 n. 33
Zanzibar, 225, 228
Zanzibar Museum, 235, 237
Zanzibar-Pemba region, 235
Zanzibar Revolution of 1964, 224
Zaramo, 1, 170, 227, 235
Zeugma, 295 n. 16
Zigua, 1
Zumari, 241
Zungu spirits, 246

DATE DUE

11-17-90			
MAR 2 5 1998			
DEC 0 9 1998			
GAYLORD			PRINTED IN U.S.A.

UGANDA

LAKE VICTORIA

KENYA-TAN

MUSOMA

RUANDA

BURUNDI

Sukuma

CONGO

LAKE TANGANYIKA

•UJIJI

URAMBO•   •TABORA

Nyamwezi

Hehe

SHIRAZI HEARTLAND
▤ ORIGINAL
▦ EXTENDED

LAKE NYASA

Ngo
• SON

0   50   100

30° E

N. RHODESIA-NYASALAND